KU-378-121

ELIZABETH'S RIVAL

The Tumultuous Tale of Lettice Knollys,
Countess of Leicester

NICOLA TALLIS

Michael O'Mara Books Limited

This paperback edition first published in 2018

First published in Great Britain in 2017 by
Michael O'Mara Books Limited
9 Lion Yard
Tremadoc Road
London SW4 7NQ

A CIP catalogue record for this book is available from the British Library.

Papers used by Michael O'Mara Books Limited are natural, recyclable products
made from wood grown in sustainable forests. The manufacturing processes
conform to the environmental regulations of the country of origin.

ISBN: 978-1-78243-924-0 in paperback print format
ISBN: 978-1-78243-751-2 in e-book format

1 2 3 4 5 6 7 8 9 10

www.mombooks.com

Cover design by Claire Cater
Typeset by Ed Pickford

Front cover images (from left to right): © Woburn Abbey Bedforshire, UK /
Bridgeman Images; © Reproduced by Permission of the Marquess of Bath, Longleat
House, Warminster, Wiltshire, Great Britain; © National Portrait Gallery

Text from the Kenilworth Game Book reproduced by kind permission of
Viscount De L'Isle from his private collection.

Printed and bound by CPI Group (UK) Ltd, Croydon, CR0 4YY

For Sylvia,

the very best of mothers.

CONTENTS

List of Illustrations.. ix

Genealogical Tables....................................... xi

Dramatis Personae xiv

Timeline xxii

Author's Note...xxiv

Introduction... xxv

Prologue xxxi

1 Hiding Royal Blood 1

2 Darling to the Maiden Queen......................... 19

3 Captive to the Charms of Lettice Knollys 38

4 The Goodliest Male Personage in England 57

5 Flirting with the Viscountess 78

6 Death with his Dart hath us Bereft..................... 91

7 Faithful, Faultless, Yet Someway Unfortunate,

    Yet Must Suffer 107

8 His Paramour, or his Wife............................ 119

9 Great Enmity 137

10 Up and Down the Country........................... 153

11 A Marriage in Secret 165

12 One Queen in England 173

13 A She-Wolf 186

14 My Sorrowful Wife.................................... 200

15 Our Mistress's Extreme Rage 214

16 A Continual Fever 228

17 My Best Friend..................................... 246

18 Disgraced Persons 265

19 Some Wonted Unkind Words........................ 277

20 The Arch-Traitor Essex 293

21 Mildly Like a Lamb 311

22 The Wars with Thunder, and the Court with Stars....... 324

Epilogue 334

Appendix 1: Epitaph to Lettice, Countess of Leicester......... 337

Appendix 2: Following in Lettice's Footsteps – Places to Visit... 339

Notes and References.................................. 341

Bibliography... 379

Acknowledgements 389

Index... 391

LIST OF ILLUSTRATIONS

Lettice Knollys, Countess of Leicester, George Gower, *c.* 1585 (© Reproduced by Permission of the Marquess of Bath, Longleat House, Warminster, Wiltshire, Great Britain).

Elizabeth I when Princess, at the age of about thirteen, Guillaume Scrots, *c.* 1546 (Royal Collection Trust © Her Majesty Queen Elizabeth II, 2015 / Bridgeman Images).

Robert Dudley, Earl of Leicester, Unknown Artist, *c.* 1575 (© National Portrait Gallery, London).

Sir Francis Knollys, Unknown Artist, 1586 (© Greys Court, Henley-on-Thames, Oxfordshire, UK / National Trust Photographic Library / John Hammond / Bridgeman Images).

Lady Katherine Knollys, Steven van der Meulan, 1562 (© Yale Center for British Art, Paul Mellon Collection, USA / Bridgeman Images).

Greys Court, Oxfordshire (© Nicola Tallis).

Walter Devereux, first Earl of Essex, Unknown Artist, 1572 (© National Portrait Gallery, London).

Penelope and Dorothy Devereux, Unknown Artist, *c.* 1581 (© Reproduced by Permission of the Marquess of Bath, Longleat House, Warminster, Wiltshire, Great Britain').

Elizabeth Knollys, George Gower, 1577 (© Montacute House, Somerset, UK / The Phelips Collection / National Trust Photographic Library / Derrick E. Witty / Bridgeman Images).

Kenilworth Castle, Warwickshire (© Nicola Tallis).

Leicester House (© SOTK2011 / Alamy Stock Photo).

Bear and ragged staff, St Mary's Church, Warwick (© Nicola Tallis).

Tomb of 'the Noble Imp', St Mary's Church, Warwick (© Nicola Tallis).

Miniature of a lady thought to be Lettice Knollys, Unknown Artist, seventeenth century (© Private Collection / Bridgeman Images)

Lettice Knollys effigy in St Nicholas's Church, Rotherfield Greys (© Nicola Tallis).

Elizabeth I, George Gower, c. 1588 (© Woburn Abbey Bedforshire, UK / Bridgeman Images).

Robert Devereux, second Earl of Essex, after Marcus Gheeraerts the Younger, early seventeenth century, based on a work of c. 1596 (© National Portrait Gallery, London).

William Cecil, Lord Burghley, Unknown Artist, seventeenth century (Private Collection; Photo © Philip Mould Ltd, London / Bridgeman Images).

Tomb of Lettice Knollys and Robert Dudley, Earl of Leicester, St Mary's Church, Warwick (© Nicola Tallis).

THE KNOLLYS FAMILY

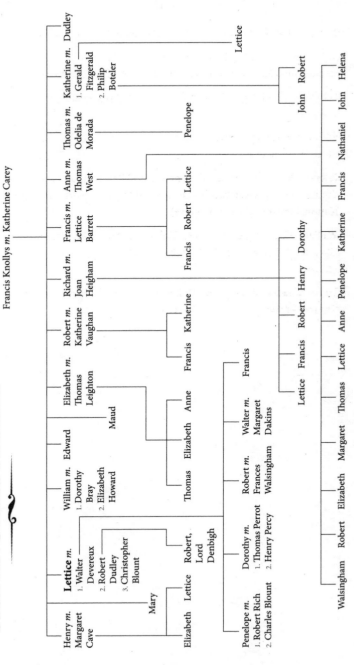

THE DEVEREUX FAMILY

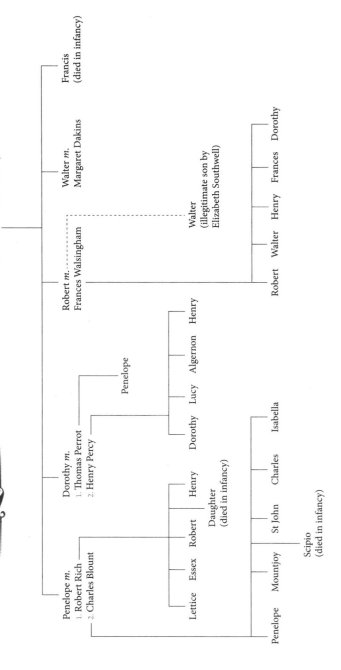

Walter Devereux *m.* **Lettice Knollys**

Penelope *m.*
1. Robert Rich
2. Charles Blount

Dorothy *m.*
1. Thomas Perrot
2. Henry Percy

Robert *m.*
Frances Walsingham

Walter *m.*
Margaret Dakins

Francis
(died in infancy)

Lettice Essex Robert Henry

Daughter
(died in infancy)

Penelope

Dorothy Lucy Algernon Henry

Penelope Mountjoy St John Charles Isabella

Scipio
(died in infancy)

Robert Walter Henry Frances Dorothy

Walter
(illegitimate son by
Elizabeth Southwell)

THE TUDOR & STUART FAMILY

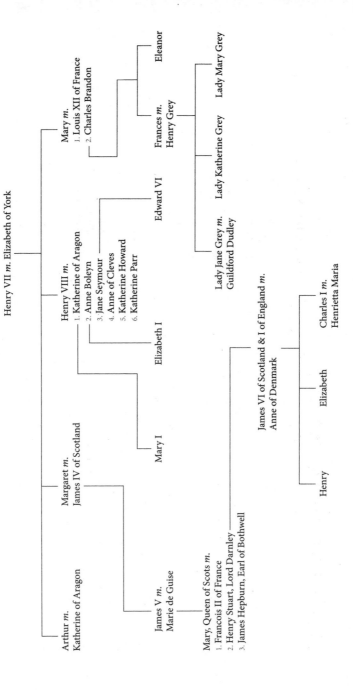

Henry VII *m.* Elizabeth of York

Arthur *m.*
Katherine of Aragon

Margaret *m.*
James IV of Scotland

Henry VIII *m.*
1. Katherine of Aragon
2. Anne Boleyn
3. Jane Seymour
4. Anne of Cleves
5. Katherine Howard
6. Katherine Parr

Mary *m.*
1. Louis XII of France
2. Charles Brandon

James V *m.*
Marie de Guise

Mary I

Elizabeth I

Edward VI

Eleanor

Frances *m.*
Henry Grey

Mary, Queen of Scots *m.*
1. Francois II of France
2. Henry Stuart, Lord Darnley
3. James Hepburn, Earl of Bothwell

Lady Jane Grey *m.*
Guildford Dudley

Lady Katherine Grey

Lady Mary Grey

James VI of Scotland & I of England *m.*
Anne of Denmark

Henry

Elizabeth

Charles I *m.*
Henrietta Maria

Elizabeth's Rival: The Tumultuous Tale of Lettice Knollys, Countess of Leicester contains a whole host of complex and interesting characters, some of who played a larger role in Lettice's life than others. Below is a short biographical list of some of the people who feature in her story.

Blount, Charles (1563–1606)

The lover and later second husband of Lettice's daughter Penelope, Charles Blount was popular at court and with the Queen. Together, he and Penelope would have six children, five of whom survived infancy. The couple were secretly married on 26 December 1605, a marriage that outraged James I. Sadly, however, Charles did not live long to enjoy his marriage, dying on 3 April 1606.

Blount, Christopher (1555/56–1601)

Lettice's third husband came from a Catholic family and may have worked as a double agent for the Queen's spymaster, Sir Francis Walsingham. He was the Earl of Leicester's Master of Horse, bringing him into regular contact with Lettice. The couple were married in July 1589 – a marriage which to all appearances was happy. Blount was a loyal supporter of Lettice's son Robert, and in turn seems to have won his trust. As such, he became embroiled in the Essex Rebellion in 1601, and was executed for his role on 18 March.

Cecil, William (1520–1598)

Cecil, later ennobled as Lord Burghley, was a figure Lettice knew for her whole life. A friend of her father's, Cecil was also Queen Elizabeth's chief advisor. Lettice wrote to Cecil on a number of occasions, frequently seeking both his advice and intercession on a variety of issues. Chief among these was Cecil's help with resolving her financial circumstances.

Devereux, Dorothy (1564?–1619)

Dorothy was the younger of Lettice's two daughters. In 1583, she secretly wed Thomas Perrot, a marriage that earned Queen Elizabeth's outrage and Dorothy's subsequent banishment from court. Following Perrot's death in 1589, the same year Dorothy remarried Henry Percy, ninth Earl of Northumberland. Despite a period of separation, the couple reconciled and had four children. Dorothy spent much of her time living at Syon House, and it was there that she died in 1619.

Devereux, Penelope (1563–1607)

Lettice's first-born child, Penelope, was born at Chartley. She grew to become one of the most celebrated beauties of the Elizabethan era, and as such was the muse for Sir Philip Sidney's *Stella*. She was also a favourite of the Queen's. Penelope was close to her family, including her mother, and was particularly fond of her brother, Robert, Earl of Essex. Penelope married Lord Robert Rich in 1581, but it was a notoriously unhappy marriage. Nevertheless, the couple had five children, of which four survived. She soon became embroiled in a passionate affair with Charles Blount, but remained married to Lord Rich. The couple eventually divorced in 1605, and Penelope and Charles were married later that year. Charles died in 1606 and Penelope died on 7 July 1607.

Devereux, Robert (1565–1601)

Lettice's eldest son was her pride and joy. Following the death of his father, Robert became a ward of Lord Burghley, and was sent to Cambridge to complete his education. He rose to become Queen Elizabeth's favourite, but his haughty and arrogant behaviour ultimately led to his downfall. Having led an unsuccessful Irish campaign in 1599, Robert returned home to explain his conduct to the Queen. His behaviour resulted in his arrest, and following a rebellion to topple the Queen's government, Robert was executed for treason in 1601.

Devereux, Walter (1539–1576)

Lettice almost certainly met her first husband at court, and although the date of their marriage is uncertain it had definitely been concluded by early 1562. Together they had five children, four of whom survived infancy. In 1572, Walter was created first Earl of Essex, and the following year he left England on a campaign to colonize Ulster. It achieved nothing, and was a waste of both time and valuable resources. He returned to England briefly in 1575 in order to beg the Queen to continue funding the campaign, and was back in Ireland the following year. He had barely arrived when he fell sick, dying of dysentery on 22 September 1576.

Devereux, Walter (1569–1591)

The younger of Lettice's two surviving sons from her first marriage. Upon the death of his father, young Walter became the ward of the Earl of Huntingdon. As such, he spent much of his time in Huntingdon's household in York, where he met his future wife, Margaret Dakins. Walter accompanied his elder brother to France in 1591, and was fatally shot during a skirmish at Rouen.

Dudley, Ambrose (c. 1530–1590)

The elder brother of Robert Dudley, Earl of Leicester, Ambrose became Lettice's brother-in-law. He was married three times, but unfortunately produced no surviving children. He was close to his younger brother, and his tomb can be seen alongside that of Robert and Lettice in the Beauchamp Chapel of St Mary's Church, Warwick.

Dudley, Robert (c. 1532–1588)

The son of John Dudley, Duke of Northumberland, Robert rose to become the favourite and suitor of Elizabeth I. He married Lettice in a ceremony at Wanstead on 21 September 1578, a marriage that earned the Queen's enmity. Robert was forgiven, and was swiftly restored to the Queen's favour. At the end of 1585, he led an expedition to the Netherlands, but failed to achieve military glory. He died on 4 September 1588 at Cornbury Park.

Elizabeth I (1533–1603)

Elizabeth was the kinswoman of Lettice's mother, who may have been her half-sister. She became Queen of England in 1558, and was fond of her Knollys relatives. She promoted them to important positions in her household, and showed them great favour. When she discovered that Lettice had married her favourite Robert Dudley, however, it led to Lettice's permanent banishment. Elizabeth ruled England for forty-five years, dying childless in 1603. As such, she was the last reigning monarch of the Tudor dynasty.

Knollys, Anne (1555–1633)

Lettice's younger sister was married to Thomas West, second Baron De La Warr on 19 November 1571. Together the couple had six sons and eight daughters, including one named after her aunt, Lettice. The state of Delaware, meanwhile, was named after Anne's son, Thomas West, Baron De La Warr, who became the first English governor of Virginia in 1609. In around 1618 another of Anne's sons, John, travelled to Virginia, where he served as the Governor. Like her mother and other members of her family, Anne faithfully served in Queen Elizabeth's household for many years. A likeness of her, painted by Robert Peake, still survives.

Knollys, Edward (1546–*c.* 1575)

Very few details of the life of Lettice's younger brother are known. He sat in Parliament for Oxford in 1571 and 1572, and is not known to have married.

Knollys, Elizabeth (1549–*c*. 1605)

Lettice's younger sister was a favourite with the Queen, who she served loyally for many years. She is listed as a recipient in the New Year's gift rolls on many consecutive years. In 1578, she married Thomas Leighton, a marriage that was met with the approval of the Queen. Together the couple had a son and two daughters. Elizabeth bore a striking resemblance to Lettice, and like her sister, had her portrait painted by George Gower. She died in around 1605.

Knollys, Francis (*c*. 1512–1596)

Lettice's father was otherwise known as 'The Elder' in order to distinguish him from his son and namesake. He married Katherine Carey, a true love match that produced sixteen children. He was well favoured by Elizabeth I, and sat in Parliament for many years. He was a staunch Puritan with strict morals, but he was also a caring father. Francis died in 1596, and was buried in St Nicholas's Church, Rotherfield Greys.

Knollys, Francis (1553–1648)

'The Younger' Francis was Lettice's brother. He served as an MP for Oxford, Berkshire and Reading, and later joined Sir Francis Drake on his expedition to the Caribbean. Francis was also a member of Robert Dudley's household, and accompanied him to the Netherlands where he was knighted. He married Lettice Barrett, his sister's maid, and together the couple had three sons and six daughters. He was buried in St Laurence's Church, Reading.

Knollys, Henry (before 1521–1583)

The younger brother of Sir Francis Knollys, Henry was Lettice's uncle. He was close to his elder brother, and in March 1546 he was made a Sewer of the Chamber. Like his brother, Henry also sat in Parliament regularly. He worked on several diplomatic missions, and was also employed by the

Queen to examine Catholic prisoners in the Tower. He never married, and died in 1583.

Knollys, Henry (1541–1582)

Lettice's elder brother lived an action-filled life. He was a favourite of the Queen's, having been created an Esquire of the Body, and like his father also sat in Parliament. In 1578, he joined Sir Humphrey Gilbert's quest to set up a new colony in America. However, he showed a greater interest in privateering. He married Margaret Cave, the daughter of Sir Ambrose Cave and Margaret Willington. It was a good match, for Margaret was 'rich and an only child'. The couple had two daughters, and their magnificent tomb effigy, flanked by the effigies of their daughters, can still be seen in St Nicholas's Church, Stanford-upon-Avon. The youngest, Lettice, married William Paget.

Knollys, Katherine (1524–1569)

Lettice's mother was the daughter of Mary Boleyn, almost certainly by her royal lover Henry VIII. Little is known of Katherine's early life, but she met Francis Knollys at court in 1539 and the couple were married the following year. Together they would have sixteen children, of which Lettice was the third. Katherine devotedly served Elizabeth I until her death on 15 January 1569. She was buried in Westminster Abbey.

Knollys, Katherine (1559–1632)

The youngest of Lettice's sisters was born the same year as Elizabeth I's accession. Lettice and Katherine were close, and Katherine may have spent some time living with her sister following the death of their mother. Katherine married Gerald Fitzgerald, Lord Offalay, by who she had a daughter, Lettice. Following his death, she remarried Philip Boteler, and the couple had four sons. Towards the end of her life, Katherine was living with Lettice, in whose household inventory her chamber is listed.

Knollys, Lettice (1543–1634)

Lettice was the third child of Francis Knollys and Katherine Carey. She was married first to Walter Devereux, by who she had four surviving children. Lettice was in great favour with her kinswoman Elizabeth I, but her clandestine marriage to Robert Dudley in 1578 earned her the Queen's enmity. Despite attempts to reconcile with Elizabeth, the two remained estranged. Following Dudley's death, Lettice married Sir Christopher Blount, his Master of Horse. It was a happy marriage, but Blount was executed for complicity in the rebellion of Lettice's son in 1601. The rest of her life was spent in peaceful obscurity.

Knollys, Richard (1548–1596)

Lettice's brother Richard was one of the witnesses at her wedding to Robert Dudley. He was an MP for Wallingford, and married Joan Heigham.

Knollys, Robert (1550–1619)

Affectionately known by the Queen as Robin, Robert was another of Lettice's brothers. He was an MP for Reading and Breconshire, and Keeper of Syon House from 1584–87. Robert was also a part of the entourage of his nephew, Robert Devereux, but avoided implication in the 1601 rebellion. He frequently participated in tournaments, and died in 1619.

Knollys, Thomas (1558–*c.* 1596)

A portrait of Lettice's brother Thomas once hung in Leicester House. He became Governor of Ostend in 1586, and married Odelia de Morada. She was the daughter of the Marquess of Bergen, and together the couple had a daughter, Penelope. Thomas died in late 1596.

Knollys, William (1544–1632)

Lettice's brother was a favourite at court, and served under Robert Dudley in the Netherlands. He also became an MP, and was appointed Lord

Lieutenant of Berkshire. At the time of his father's death, William was his eldest surviving son, so inherited most of Sir Francis's estate. He was held hostage by his nephew during his 1601 rebellion, and later testified against him. William was married twice, but fell in love with one of the Queen's ladies, Mary Fitton, who was also the Earl of Pembroke's mistress.

Leighton, Thomas (*c.* 1530–1610)

Thomas was the husband of Lettice's sister, Elizabeth. He was knighted in May 1579, and was a close associate of Robert Dudley, Earl of Leicester. Leighton had vast military experience, and was appointed Governor of Guernsey. He did not have as much influence under James I, and died in Guernsey in 1610. He was laid to rest there, in the church of St Peter Port.

Percy, Henry (1564–1632)

The second husband of Lettice's daughter Dorothy, Henry Percy was the ninth Earl of Northumberland. Nicknamed the 'Wizard Earl' because of his scientific interests, Percy was arrested in 1605 for alleged conspiracy in the Gunpowder Plot. He was fined and condemned to imprisonment at the King's pleasure. He was released in 1621, and spent much of the remainder of his life in peaceful retirement and obscurity. He died on 5 November 1632 at Petworth, where he was laid to rest beside his wife.

Rich, Robert (1559?–1619)

Robert Rich, third Baron Rich, became the first husband of Lettice's daughter, Penelope Devereux. He was an unpleasant character who was unhappily married, but for many years tolerated his wife's adultery. Following his divorce from Penelope, Rich later remarried, taking as his second bride Frances, daughter of Sir Christopher Wray. She was a widow, and they were married in 1616. Two years later Rich was created Earl of Warwick, but he did not live to enjoy his new title for long. He died on 24 March 1619, and was buried at Felsted with his second wife.

TIMELINE

7 September 1533	Future Elizabeth I is born
26 April 1540	Francis Knollys marries Katherine Carey
6 November 1543	Lettice Knollys is born
28 January 1547	Henry VIII dies at the Palace of Whitehall
September 1547	Francis Knollys is knighted
6 July 1553	Edward VI dies at Greenwich Palace
12 February 1554	Lady Jane Grey and Guildford Dudley are executed
4 February 1555	First Protestant burning of Mary I's reign takes place
10 June 1557	Francis and Katherine Knollys are in Frankfurt
17 November 1558	Mary I dies and Elizabeth I succeeds
1560?–1562?	Lettice marries Walter Devereux
January 1563	Penelope Devereux is born
17 September 1564?	Dorothy Devereux is born
10 November 1565	Robert Devereux is born
15 January 1569	Katherine Knollys dies
31 October 1569	Walter Devereux 'the younger' is born
4 May 1572	Walter Devereux is created Earl of Essex
Summer 1573	Walter sails for Ireland
Summer 1574	Lettice travels to Buxton
July 1575	The Princely Pleasures at Kenilworth are staged
22 September 1576	Walter Devereux dies in Dublin
21 September 1578	Lettice marries the Earl of Leicester at Wanstead
July 1579	Elizabeth I is informed of Lettice's secret marriage
6 June 1581	'The Noble Imp' is born at Leicester House
19 July 1584	'The Noble Imp' dies at Wanstead

10 December 1585	Leicester lands at Flushing in the Netherlands
22 September 1586	Battle of Zutphen is fought
8 February 1587	Mary, Queen of Scots, is executed
July–August 1588	The English fleet engages with the Spanish Armada
4 September 1588	Leicester dies at Cornbury Park
July 1589	Lettice marries Sir Christopher Blount
8 September 1591	Lettice's son Walter is killed in Rouen
19 July 1596	Sir Francis Knollys dies
8 February 1601	The Essex Rebellion takes place in London
25 February 1601	Robert Devereux is executed
18 March 1601	Sir Christopher Blount is executed
24 March 1603	Elizabeth I dies at Richmond Palace
10 February 1604	Lettice files a case in the Star Chamber against Robin Sheffield
10 May 1605	Star Chamber delivers a verdict in Lettice's favour
7 July 1607	Penelope Devereux dies
August 1619	Dorothy Devereux dies
27 March 1625	James I dies, succeeded by Charles I
25 December 1634	Lettice Knollys dies

AUTHOR'S NOTE

I ALWAYS TAKE great pleasure in transcribing sixteenth-century material. It helps me to feel fully immersed in the period about which I'm writing. I have, however, modernized all of the spelling and punctuation from contemporary books and documents, in order to create a clearer narrative.

All monetary values have been presented with the contemporary amount, followed by the modern-day equivalent in parentheses. All conversions were done according to the National Archives Currency Convertor (www.nationalarchives.gov.uk/currency), and are approximate values. Please also be aware that they may be subject to change.

Finally, for clarity, all dates have been calculated using the modern-day Gregorian calendar, under which the year turns on 1 January.

INTRODUCTION

OF THE MANY intriguing women who are scattered throughout the Tudor period, all with their own unique tale to tell, why Lettice Knollys? The simple answer is 'why not?' She was a striking and spirited Early Modern woman, whose long life interplayed with the great dramas of the age, and her full story has been overlooked for too long. Though there have been short pieces about her, and she has featured in books about her kinswoman Elizabeth I, and her second husband, Robert Dudley, Lettice has never been the subject of a full-scale biography. Yet hers was a life that was as turbulent and intriguing as it was long. It is its length that makes it all the more remarkable, for she lived to the extraordinary age of ninety-one – a staggering rarity in an age when the average life span was around forty.

In his *Romance of the Peerage*, the Victorian writer George L. Craik stated that 'the very name of Lettice Knollys will probably be new', but he duly acknowledged that 'she was one of Queen Elizabeth's relations'.[1] She was nearer, in fact, than many people realized, but Lettice's claim to fame and right to a dedicated biography goes much further than that.

For many years Lettice was close to her kinswoman Elizabeth I, but she spent the larger part of the Queen's reign living in disgrace. The reason for this was that she became the Queen's rival, and it was a circumstance that Elizabeth would never forgive. Lettice was not, however, a political rival in the same way as Mary, Queen of Scots, or Lady Katherine Grey, who, like Lettice, were also Elizabeth's kinswomen; indeed, the rivalry between Lettice and Elizabeth was of a far more personal nature, unmuddied by politics, and one that was completely unique. It struck to the very heart of Elizabeth and wounded her deeply. For a woman so powerful, who could mete out the most severe punishments on her political enemies, the fact that she could not destroy Lettice must have been all the more bitter.

Over the centuries Lettice's reputation has become blackened, thanks largely to material that was written and published during her own lifetime. In 1584, a scandalous anonymous tract known as *Leicester's Commonwealth* appeared in England. Its full title was *The Copy of a Letter Written by a Master of Art of Cambridge*, and the piece, which was aimed at Lettice's husband the Earl of Leicester, was incredibly hostile – not least because the authors had an axe to grind. Written by Catholics who were pleading for religious toleration – and whose beliefs were completely at odds with Leicester's own Protestant views – it is hardly surprising that they viewed him with such animosity.

Both Leicester and the Queen tried desperately to suppress its circulation, but with little effect, and in any case, the damage had been done. The authors were clearly well informed on gossip that was circulating at the time, and as such were able to put their own spin on it. The work had a profound effect on shaping later writers' views on the Earl, and his reputation. Walter Scott's famous 1821 novel, *Kenilworth*, paints him as an ambitious individual who is desperate to win the Queen's favour – to such an extent that his steward arranges the murder of Leicester's first wife, Amy Robsart. In turn, *Leicester's Commonwealth* was also derogatory about Lettice, and it is this that has contributed to her image as both an overtly sexual seductress and, more shockingly, a murderess. Most of the claims made by the authors of the *Commonwealth* can be discredited, but this did not stop others from jumping to similar conclusions. The chronicler William Camden, for example, drew much of the material for his *Historie of the Most Renowned and Victorious Princess Elizabeth*, better known as the *Annales*, from *Leicester's Commonwealth*, and he too presented a negative view of Lettice, one that has had great influence and endurance through the centuries. It was at the suggestion of the Queen's advisor, Lord Burghley, in 1597 that Camden began to think of compiling a history of Elizabeth's reign, but he did not start writing it until 1607 – four years after the Queen's death. Though he gleaned some of the information for his narrative from people who were close to the Queen and her courtiers, Camden's work was intended to highlight Elizabeth's achievements. It was consequently highly critical of anything and anyone at odds with this. The trend of casting Lettice in a bad light has largely continued to the present day. Robert Lacey, the biographer of Lettice's son the Earl of Essex, related that she was 'Wilful and impetuous, she insisted always on having her own way, dominating her son Robert in his youth and then dogging his footsteps at Court.'[2] This image has also been highlighted in popular culture. In the 1971 *Elizabeth R* television series, in which Angela Thorne adopted the role of Lettice, she is portrayed as a highly spirited woman who, following her fall from grace, was eager to antagonize Elizabeth I, played by Glenda Jackson. She is outspoken, haughty, arrogant and unrepentant. Although at various points in her life Lettice did display some of these traits, it is by no means the whole story.

What makes Lettice all the more remarkable is her longevity: her life spanned the reigns of seven monarchs (including Lady Jane Grey), and two dynasties; she was born during the kingship of Henry VIII and witnessed the Tudor monarchy in all its glory, before its ultimate demise following the death of Elizabeth I in 1603. In its place the Scottish Stuart dynasty established itself firmly on the English throne, uniting the kingdoms of England and Scotland for the first time. Lettice lived through all of this and more, for hers was a period during which the country underwent significant change, ravaged by war, political upheaval and religious turmoil. Many of these changes and the events they brought with them impacted upon Lettice and her family, who also faced their own challenges. Although Lettice herself was not always actively involved in, or a witness to, all of the tumultuous happenings, those closest to her often were. Husbands, children, kin; Lettice's family were always at the very centre of events, watching and participating as the plots, politics and wars of the era unfolded. As such, Lettice experienced the theatre of her day in a very different way; her life offers us an extraordinarily personal lens through which to view the turbulent world of the sixteenth and seventeenth centuries. Her story is not just one of melodrama, but rather a tapestry of episodes and intrigue that wove its way through the centuries and the lives of her family. Ultimately, it was only Lettice who survived them all.

A friend suggested the subject of this book to me, but I did accidentally stumble across it some time before. In September 2015, I was visiting the magnificent St Mary's Church in Warwick in order to check a source for my first book. While I was there, I stopped to take a look at the double tomb Lettice shares with her second husband, Robert Dudley, Earl of Leicester. It struck me that I'd never read a biography of Lettice, and that I didn't actually know much about her. At that time I delved no further, but when I came back to it a couple of months later I was astonished to find that there was no full-scale biography of her. Even more interestingly, what had been written about her primarily painted her in a less than favourable light. I was intrigued to know how much of this – if any – was justified, and to learn more about why Lettice earned Elizabeth's loathing.

Additionally, having spent years researching and writing about Lady Jane Grey and her family for my first book, *Crown of Blood: The Deadly Inheritance of Lady Jane Grey*, in many ways this felt like the next part of the story for some of those who were involved. Jane's husband, Guildford Dudley, was the younger brother of Robert, Lettice's second husband, and he too had played a role in the tragedy of the Tudor queen: unlike his brother, however, Robert would survive the disaster that engulfed his family. In some respects this narrative picks up the threads from that fatal moment, and continues to weave them together to form the next intriguing part of the tale. Lettice, who had never met the ill-fated queen and was only nine years old at the time of Jane's execution, could never have known that she would in time have become Jane's sister-in-law.

As is always the case when working with the past, there are frustrating gaps in the sources. For example, aside from her date of birth, virtually nothing of Lettice's early life is known. Despite this, I was pleasantly surprised by the quantity and quality of surviving material relating to Lettice's life: here were all of the ingredients that were needed to piece together a compelling narrative. The Dudley and Devereux Papers, preserved at Longleat House, are a crucial source. They provide us with an assortment of details that relate to Lettice's own life, and those of her husbands and family. They were once in Lettice's custody, kept at her Staffordshire residence of Drayton Bassett. At her death the papers passed first to her grandson, the third Earl of Essex, and at his death in 1646 to his sister, Lettice's granddaughter, the Duchess of Somerset. When she died she left all of the family papers to her grandson, Thomas Thynne, who also purchased Drayton Bassett at his grandmother's request. When Thynne inherited Longleat House in 1682, he brought all of the family papers with him and they have been at Longleat ever since.

A number of Lettice's own letters also survive, largely dating from the later years of her life, and primarily addressed to her eldest son, the Earl of Essex. These provide fascinating insights into her character and the relationships she shared with her children, on whom she evidently doted. Letters to her friend Lord Burghley also survive, revealing the way in which Lettice approached her business affairs, and demonstrating a stubborn streak in her character that she passed on to her children. What is sadly missing are her letters to her husbands – only one letter, addressed to her third husband, Sir Christopher Blount, survives, and this is short. This means that we have to look elsewhere for clues about the relationships she shared with them. According to *The Complete Peerage*, Lettice is also 'the little western flower' on whom 'the bolt of Cupid fell' in William Shakespeare's *A Midsummer Night's Dream*.[3] Lettice's son, the Earl of Essex, is likely to have been an early patron of Shakespeare, and it has also been suggested that his story and that of his mother were the inspiration behind *Hamlet*.[4]

Lettice left behind a whole host of descendants, and few people realize that she is the ancestor of Queen Elizabeth II through her mother.[5] Similarly, it is from the descendants of Lettice's younger sister Elizabeth and her husband Sir Thomas Leighton that the Duke and Duchess of Cambridge are commonly descended. Her unusually advanced age at the time of her death meant that she outlived many of her contemporaries, and was thus the last of the great Elizabethans. There is, though, something even more intriguing about her, something which was never openly acknowledged during her own lifetime: it is highly likely that she was also Henry VIII's illegitimate granddaughter. If this is indeed true, then although Henry's direct legitimate descendants became extinct following the death of Elizabeth I in 1603, the line of his illegitimate ones lives on to this day.

Until now Lettice's story has always been on the fringes of history, and few have recognized her significance on the dramatic stage of sixteenth-century England. The time has finally come for Lettice to reclaim the spotlight that she once held during her lifetime and for us to see the world of the Tudors through her eyes.

PROLOGUE

AT SEVEN O'CLOCK in the morning on 21 September 1578, a wedding ceremony was conducted within the privacy of a country house in Wanstead. The groom was Robert Dudley, Earl of Leicester, favourite and one-time suitor to Queen Elizabeth – but the monarch was not the bride. Dressed in a 'loose gown', in a possible indication of pregnancy, the woman who exchanged marital vows with the Earl was the Queen's kinswoman, the widowed thirty-four-year-old Lettice Knollys, then Countess of Essex. With Lettice described by the Spanish ambassador as 'one of the best-looking ladies of the court' and resembling as she did Elizabeth in looks, it was little wonder that she had enthralled Leicester.

Plans for the couple's marriage had been underway for some time, and prior to the wedding at Wanstead another ceremony had almost certainly been performed elsewhere. But there was a cloud hanging over the newlyweds' bliss: the wedding was a closely guarded secret, and Leicester was determined that it ought to remain that way for as long as possible. The reason? Queen Elizabeth had not given the royal consent necessary for such a marriage, and neither was she likely to. Though she would not marry him herself, since the death of Leicester's first wife in 1560 Elizabeth had been fiercely jealous of any woman who showed an interest in her favourite. They had been close to one another since childhood – so close, in fact, that it was widely believed that the Queen would marry him, and Leicester had cherished hopes that his suit would come to fruition.

But despite Leicester's determination, just months after the clandestine ceremony at Wanstead, the secret was out. Elizabeth was incandescent with rage, and Lettice was permanently banished from court. The Queen never forgave her cousin for her perceived betrayal, and Lettice was to suffer the consequences of Elizabeth's fury for the rest of her life. Though her wedding was the catalyst, it was by no means the only episode for which Lettice would earn the Queen's enmity. As time went by, more scenes in the jealous feud between the two women began to unfold. Lettice's secret marriage signified a dramatic turning point in her relationship with Elizabeth, and the Queen's attitude towards her would never be the same again. Lettice's long life would see her contend with great scandals, treasonous plots and deep tragedy – all of which Elizabeth was heavily involved in. Though separated by jealousy, the lives of the two women would remain closely entangled – whether they liked it or not. The morning of 21 September 1578 was only the beginning.

CHAPTER 1

Hiding Royal Blood

I N THE HEART of the Chiltern Hills in the Oxfordshire countryside lies the picturesque village of Rotherfield Greys. At the centre of the village is the idyllic restored Norman church of St Nicholas, which houses the magnificent double tomb of Sir Francis Knollys and his wife, Katherine Carey.[1] Commissioned by the couple's second son William, Earl of Banbury, in 1605 as a memorial to his parents, surrounding the tomb are the kneeling effigies, or 'weepers', of the Knollys's children. One in particular, depicted at the head of her sisters and dressed in a red robe with a rich coronet indicative of her status, is striking: the third Knollys child, Lettice.[2] Her resplendent effigy does not convey any of the turbulence and drama that consumed her life, or her reputation as one of the most notorious women of the Elizabethan era. Hers was a life that was full of ambition, danger and tragedy, and it was at Rotherfield Greys that it all began.

Greys Court, her parents' manor house in Rotherfield Greys, was the setting for the birth of Lettice Knollys on 'the Tuesday present after all Hallows Day', 6 November 1543.[3] A birth date given with such precision is unusual for this period, and is solely thanks to the Latin dictionary produced in Venice, and still in its original calf binding, that was once owned by Lettice's father, Sir Francis Knollys.[4] Sir Francis not only used the dictionary to document Lettice's date of birth in his own hand, but also proudly recorded the date of his marriage to Lettice's mother in 1540. He also noted the births and times of day in date order of thirteen of Lettice's siblings.[5] Almost exactly a year after their marriage and prior to the arrival of Lettice, her mother had given birth to her first child, Henry (or Harry), 'the Tuesday before Easter Day [12 April] 1541'.[6] Henry was named after the King, Henry VIII, while the choice of name following the birth of a daughter in October 1542, Mary, was in honour of her maternal grandmother. Lettice's unusual choice of Christian name was a compliment to her paternal grandmother and was a shortened form of Laetitia, the Latin word for happiness.[7] It was a fitting name for a girl born into such a close and loving family that cared deeply for its members. Her parents were devoted both to one another and to their children, and raising their family would be their greatest priority.

SIR FRANCIS KNOLLYS had been born in around 1512, probably at Rookes Manor in Hampshire, and was the eldest son of Robert Knollys and his wife, Lettice Peniston.[8] The Knollys family had a history of royal service to the Tudor family, and Robert Knollys had been a henchman to the first Tudor king, Henry VII. He was later appointed to wait on the King's eldest son, Prince Arthur, for which he received £5 (£2,400) per year as reward.[9] Following Arthur's untimely death in 1502, Robert reverted to serving the King, assuming the role of Gentleman Usher of the Chamber. Robert continued to faithfully serve his successor, the handsome and athletic Henry VIII who succeeded in April 1509, and was well favoured for his loyal service. In around 1510 Robert was married to Lettice Peniston, the daughter of Sir Thomas Peniston and Alice Bulstrode.[10] The Penistons were a family of Buckinghamshire descent, settling in Hawridge, and it may have been that the match was arranged through Robert's contacts at court. On 9 July 1514, the King jointly granted the couple the manor of Rotherfield Greys, and they were fortunate in so much that the annual rent the property commanded was a single red rose, payable at midsummer.[11] Thus began the Knollys family's residency and association with the Oxfordshire manor of Greys Court.

Robert and Lettice had four children, of which Francis was the eldest. His birth was followed by those of Henry, Mary and Jane, although all of their birth dates are unrecorded.[12] Henry never married, and Francis remained on close terms with his brother into adulthood. Nothing, however, is known of his relationships with his sisters.[13] Few details of Francis's early life and education are known; according to tradition he attended Magdalen College, Oxford, but there is no contemporary evidence to support this.[14] The abilities and interests that he displayed later in life suggest that he was well educated, and it may well be that he did attend one of the notable colleges. Francis may also have spent some time during his early years at court, for when his father died in 1521 the hand of Henry VIII's royal patronage was extended to his heir.[15] Francis's mother remarried, taking as her second husband Sir Robert Lee, who hailed from her native Buckinghamshire.[16] Lee was a Knight of the Body to Henry VIII, thereby providing Francis with another close link to the royal court. Similarly, in 1527 when Henry VIII began annulment proceedings in order to end his marriage to Katherine of Aragon, splitting from the Catholic Church in Rome and establishing the Church of England with himself at its head, Francis was supportive of the King's bold move. His primary motivation was religion, for Francis became well known for his Protestant beliefs. He was also steadfastly loyal to the Crown, and would remain active in its service for the rest of his life. From 1534 he began to sit in Parliament, another occupation that he treated with the utmost seriousness, and in which he would continue for the next six decades.

Francis's portraits, painted in later life, show a serious-looking man with a beard that had turned grey, and a long face and nose. The best surviving likeness of him, which now hangs at his former home, Greys Court, was painted in 1586 by an unknown English artist, and depicts him in his later role of Lord Treasurer of the Household.

In 1539, Francis was evidently well regarded by the King, for in that same year he was appointed one of fifty Gentlemen Pensioners, or Troop of Gentlemen as they were originally called: a ceremonial mounted guard who acted as an escort to protect the King. This was a great honour, and he would remain among its numbers until 1544. It was in November 1539 that, at court, Francis met and fell in love with his future wife, Katherine Carey. Katherine had only recently arrived, having been appointed to serve the King's bride-to-be, Anne of Cleves, who was currently embarking on her journey to England. Anne was not to the King's liking, though, and he was supposedly repelled by her personal qualities. Nevertheless, in January 1540 he and Anne were married; it was to be a marriage that lasted just six months before being annulled. Elsewhere, however, the twenty-eight-year-old Francis's courtship with Katherine was of short duration, for as Francis's Latin dictionary reveals, just five months after Katherine's arrival at court, on 26 April 1540, he and the sixteen-year-old Katherine were married. No details of the wedding survive, but as Katherine was part of Anne of Cleves' household it seems likely that the marriage was conducted in London where the court was in residence. The marriage was particularly advantageous for Francis, for in Katherine's veins almost certainly flowed the royal blood of the Tudors, a fact of which he, and many others, were likely aware.

On the surface Katherine Carey purported to be the daughter of William Carey and his wife, Mary Boleyn. Though the Carey family had been well-respected courtiers hailing from Wiltshire, it was the Boleyns who were in possession of the more prestigious links. Katherine's mother, Mary, was the eldest daughter of Sir Thomas Boleyn and Lady Elizabeth Howard, the daughter of the second Duke of Norfolk.[17] The Boleyns were a family of Norfolk origin, but at the start of the sixteenth century they had settled at Hever Castle in Kent. Sir Thomas Boleyn was in high favour with Henry VIII, and was particularly valued for his diplomatic service abroad. It was through Sir Thomas's auspices that in 1514 his young daughter Mary had been fortunate enough to secure a placement in the entourage of the King's younger sister, eighteen-year-old Mary, who was travelling to the French court in order to marry the French King, Louis XII. At fifty-two Louis was in poor health, and he died on New Year's

Day 1515, bringing his marriage to an abrupt end after just three months. Though her mistress returned home in May – once again a married woman after conducting a clandestine marriage with the Duke of Suffolk – Mary Boleyn remained in France. Here she embarked on a very brief affair with the new French King, François I, lending support to Robert Lacey's claim that 'It was not for nothing, whispered her [Lettice's] many detractors, that her grandmother had been the lascivious Mary Boleyn.'[18] Lacey, the biographer of Lettice's son the Earl of Essex, was not the only writer to seize upon this, using Mary's royal affairs as a way of extrapolating her personality and making her appear sexually promiscuous. Royal affairs aside, however, there is no evidence that this was so. In 1519, Mary's father summoned her home to England, and when she returned she found a place in the household of Henry VIII's wife, Katherine of Aragon. Before long her father's thoughts turned to arranging her marriage. He settled on the rising courtier William Carey, who was well favoured by the King, and on 4 February 1520 Mary and William were married in the Chapel Royal at Greenwich Palace.[19] It was a sumptuous wedding, which the King himself honoured with his attendance.

However, Mary did not settle into matrimonial harmony for evermore. At some time, almost certainly after her marriage to William Carey, Mary caught the King's eye and the two began an affair.[20] Mary was not the first of Henry VIII's mistresses. For the most part, though, the King conducted his extramarital affairs discreetly, and as such his liaison with Mary was shrouded in such secrecy that there is no evidence to prove precisely when it started, its duration, or when it ended. Grants made by the King to William Carey indicate that it may have begun around February 1522 and ended in 1524, but the affair may never have come to light had it not been for the events which followed.[21] What is more, the affair would have the most profound consequences.

In 1523, Mary Boleyn fell pregnant at exactly the same time as her affair with Henry VIII is likely to have been in full swing. The following year she gave birth to a daughter, and the King was almost certainly her father. In an ironic twist given the nature of their adulterous relationship, the baby was named after Henry's Queen, Katherine of Aragon; baby Katherine was born in around March or April 1524. By this time, Mary's affair with the King may have come to an end – perhaps because of her pregnancy. As the King's mistress, Mary had never attracted any attention, and no reference was made to her daughter's paternity. For this reason Katherine was easily passed off as being William Carey's daughter. The King certainly never acknowledged Katherine Carey as his, and her sex rendered him unlikely to do so. Although those involved almost certainly knew the truth of the matter, Katherine was never acknowledged as anything more than Elizabeth's cousin.

Henry did have one – or possibly two – other illegitimate children. However, he only ever acknowledged a son, Henry Fitzroy, who was the result of an affair with Bessie Blount, and was later created Duke of Richmond. Fitzroy was so beloved by his father that, despite Henry already having a legitimate heir in his daughter Mary, for a time many people believed that in the absence of a legitimate male heir Henry would allow Fitzroy to succeed him. Fitzroy's untimely death in 1536 put an end to all such rumours.[22]

Mary Boleyn's circumstances were very different from those of Bessie Blount. Unlike Bessie, Mary was a married woman at the time of her affair, and there were her husband's feelings to consider.[23] If the King were to acknowledge Katherine, then it would have been a source of public humiliation for William Carey, who would have been ridiculed as a cuckold. Likewise, Katherine's sex rendered her of no political use to the King, and it was therefore far better for everyone involved if the matter remained under wraps. As such, Katherine took William Carey's name and was raised as his child.

Mary remained William Carey's wife, and two years after the birth of her daughter she gave birth to another child. On 4 March 1526, a son, named Henry after the King, joined her daughter in the nursery. By this time Mary's affair with the King was certainly over, and unlike

Katherine, baby Henry was probably the child of William Carey.[24] How much William knew of his wife's affair or of Katherine's paternity is unknown. If he was aware of what was going on then, in public at least, he turned a blind eye, as would have been expected of him. The grants of lands made to him during this time may have been made as a grateful acknowledgement of his compliance. In return, the affair was conducted with such discretion that little is known of the circumstances, and at the time few of his contemporaries are likely to have had any knowledge of it. In any case, William's feelings did not grow to be a concern, for on 22 June 1528 he died of plague.

Mary's affair may never have come to light had it not been for a strange twist in circumstance. The King had lost all interest in Mary, but in 1526 his roving eye had fallen on her sister, Anne. Within a short space of time Henry was madly in love with her, his passion heightened by the fact that Anne proved herself to be remarkably different to her elder sister.

Mary Boleyn was not a demanding mistress, and by comparison with her sister she appears to have been unambitious. She had complied with the King's wishes, and following the end of their relationship she had slipped discreetly into the background. Anne had seen the way in which the King had used her sister before tiring of her, and was determined not to go the same way. She therefore refused to become Henry's mistress in the physical sense, instead holding out for more. The King was not used to being denied, and Anne's tactics had the desired effect. So inflamed by desire was he that Henry determined to seek an annulment from his first wife, Katherine of Aragon, and marry Anne instead. The case became the talk of Europe: England was torn apart, as both Katherine and the Pope in Rome refused to comply with the King's wishes.

The annulment proceedings dragged on for many years, causing endless stress for those involved. Katherine of Aragon refused to acknowledge that she was anything other than the King's true wife, and their daughter Mary proved to be equally obstinate. It was during this time, however, that the King made his only ever reference to his affair with Mary Boleyn. The conversation that took place between Sir George Throckmorton, a gentleman at court, the King and his chief minister, Thomas Cromwell, only came to light in 1537. Throckmorton, who was opposed to the King's separation from Katherine, related that he had 'told your Grace I feared if ye did marry Queen Anne your conscience would be more troubled at length, for it is thought ye have meddled both with the mother and the sister. And his Grace said "Never with the mother." And my lord Privy Seal [Cromwell] standing by said "Nor never with the sister either, and therefore put that out of your mind."'[25] Despite Cromwell's hasty intervention, the King's reaction made it clear that he had indulged in an affair with Mary Boleyn. What was more, Throckmorton was already aware of it. This suggests that there were others at court who also knew of the liaison, and there is further intriguing evidence to support this.

In the 1580s Sir Philip Sidney, the nephew of Robert Dudley, Earl of Leicester, and brilliant young courtier and poet, composed *Astrophil and Stella*. A sequence of 108 sonnets and 11 songs, the poem is about a lover, Astrophil, and his beloved, Stella. It has long been known that Sidney's muse for Stella was Katherine Carey's granddaughter and Lettice's eldest daughter, Penelope Rich, whom the poet describes as 'the richest gem of love and life'.[26] Sidney plays on Penelope's surname, 'Rich' throughout, but the poem is also littered with references to royalty that seem to confirm Penelope's royal heritage. For example:

> *Rich in the treasure of deserv'd renown,*
> *Rich in the riches of a royal heart,*
> *Rich in those gifts which give th'eternal crown.*[27]

Perhaps more significantly, at another point Sidney writes:

> *Another humbler wit to shepherd's pipe retires,*
> *Yet hiding royal blood full oft in rural vein.*[28]

Such blatant references seem to indicate that it was well known in court circles, and almost certainly within her own family, that Katherine Carey was really the King's daughter. If true, it meant that Katherine's daughter Lettice was Henry VIII's granddaughter. Although Lettice and her family would never have dared to speak openly about it, her royal heritage provides an interesting and valid grounding for her pride in her family, and her self-assured nature. Lettice grew into a young woman who was both confident and spirited, and it is plausible that this partly stemmed from her knowledge of her royal lineage. She could not declare it, but Lettice was a Tudor, and one who would come to display many of the dynasty's famed character traits.

IN JANUARY 1533, the Archbishop of Canterbury, Thomas Cranmer, married Henry and Anne Boleyn in secret. Henry's marriage to Katherine of Aragon was declared null and void, and their daughter Mary illegitimate. Both mother and daughter had been banished from court and were forbidden from meeting with one another, much to their distress. With the Pope refusing to conform to the King's demands, that same year the Church of England was officially established, signalling Henry's permanent split from the Catholic Church in Rome. Instead, the King established himself as Head of the Church of England, a move that caused a great divide among his subjects. At the time of their marriage Anne Boleyn was already pregnant, and the King was confident that the child she carried was a prince. He was to be bitterly disappointed, however, for on 7 September, between three and four in the afternoon, Queen Anne gave birth to 'a fair lady', named Elizabeth after the King's mother.[29] The Imperial ambassador, Eustace Chapuys, informed his master the Emperor Charles V that Elizabeth's birth had led to the 'great reproach of the physicians, astrologers, sorcerers, and sorceresses, who affirmed that it would be a male child'.[30] Nevertheless, the infant was healthy, and greatly resembled her father with flame-red hair. In time this child, Elizabeth, who was almost certainly a half-sister of Katherine

Carey and thus an aunt to Lettice and her siblings, would find that her life became intimately entwined with Lettice's own.

⁂

ELSEWHERE, THE YEAR after Princess Elizabeth's birth, Mary Boleyn secretly remarried. It was a love match, and her second husband was William Stafford, a man of far inferior social status hailing from a minor gentry family.[31] As Mary herself acknowledged, 'For well I might a had a greater man of birth and a higher, but I ensure you I could never a had one that should a loved me so well nor a more honest man.'[32] When her marriage came to light, she explained to the King's chief minister Thomas Cromwell that 'love overcame reason', despite the fact that she knew that her clandestine marriage 'displeases the King and Queen'.[33] So outraged was Anne Boleyn at her sister's remarriage to a man beneath her that she banished Mary from court. Mary was unrepentant and in a stinging slight to her sister, she insisted that 'I had rather beg my bread with him than to be the greatest Queen christened.'[34] She and Stafford retired into a life of obscurity, and eventually may have travelled to Calais, where Stafford was a member of the garrison. If this was so, then they probably returned to England with Anne of Cleves at the end of 1539, for in January 1540 Stafford was appointed a Gentleman Pensioner in the King's household alongside Francis Knollys.[35]

⁂

FOLLOWING THE DEATH of William Carey, the wardship of Katherine's brother Henry was granted to their aunt, Queen Anne, but nothing is known of Katherine's whereabouts. She could have remained with her mother, and may even have travelled with Mary and her new stepfather to Calais. Alternatively, and possibly more likely, is that Katherine was sent to join the household of the Princess Elizabeth, which had been established at the nursery palace of Hatfield, just outside London.[36] This may have been done at the instigation of the King, or of Anne Boleyn, both of whom could have deemed it appropriate to place the two girls together.

It is evident that Katherine and Elizabeth spent time together during their youths, for by the 1550s the two had formed a strong bond. Following Katherine's death in 1569, the contemporary poet Thomas Newton composed an epitaph to her memory.[37] One section in particular bears witness not only to the close relationship that Katherine and Elizabeth shared, but perhaps also offers further confirmation that Katherine's true paternity was known in contemporary circles:

> *Among the Troupes of Ladies all,*
> *and Dames of noble race,*
> *She counted was, (and was indeed)*
> *in Lady Fortunes grace.*
> *In favour with our noble Queen,*
> *above the common sort,*
> *With whom she was in credit great,*
> *and bare a comely port.*[38]

Katherine's whereabouts during this time may be a matter of speculation, but those of her brother, Henry, are easier to ascertain. Following his mother's remarriage, Henry was sent to the abbey at Syon. It was while he was here that, in 1535, the vicar of Isleworth, John Hale, scathingly referred to young Henry as being the King's bastard. According to Hale, he had been introduced to 'young Master Carey', whom he had been told 'was our sovereign lord the King's son by our sovereign lady the Queen's sister, whom the Queen's grace might not suffer to be in the court'.[39] This is the only contemporary reference to Henry Carey being the son of the King, and it is a claim that was almost certainly incorrect.

⎯⎯⎯⎯⎯⎯

ANNE BOLEYN'S SUPREMACY was of short duration, and after several failed pregnancies following Elizabeth's birth, including the miscarriage of a male foetus on the day of Katherine of Aragon's funeral, the King had

had enough.[40] He still had no legitimate male heir to succeed him, and he was not prepared to give Anne any more chances. Her fall was swift, and on 2 May 1536 she was arrested and taken to the Tower of London. Thirteen days later she was charged with adultery with five men and incest with her own brother, George. The charges were almost certainly falsified and engineered through the connivance of Thomas Cromwell, but they were enough to condemn Anne, her brother, and those accused with them. On 17 May, all of the condemned men were executed on Tower Hill, and two days later, on 19 May, Anne herself met her end; an expert French swordsman, within the confines of the Tower of London, removed her head with one swift stroke. Despite four pregnancies, her marriage to Henry VIII had produced just one living child, Elizabeth. That two-and-a-half-year-old little girl was now motherless.

Following the executions of Anne and George, Mary was the only Boleyn sibling to survive the disaster of 1536. She had long since retreated into obscurity and thus had played no role in the events leading to Anne's fall. The rest of the Boleyn family shared in Anne's disgrace, and were no longer the dominant party at court. The Seymours took their place, and eleven days after Anne's execution Henry VIII married Jane, who had once served both of his previous wives. The effects of Anne's fall also extended to her daughter. Her parents' marriage was proclaimed null and void, resulting in the disinheriting of the young Elizabeth, who was deprived of her title of princess: from now on she was to be known simply as the Lady Elizabeth.

The next occasion on which Katherine Carey's name appears is in November 1539. Two years earlier, on 12 October 1537, the King's third wife Jane Seymour had produced the King's desired legitimate male heir, Prince Edward, 'conceived in lawful matrimony'.[41] The news of the safe deliverance of the 'goodly prince' was greeted with 'triumphing cheer' and *Te Deum* was sung in many of the churches in London in celebration.[42] The festivities were, however, tinged with tragedy when Queen Jane fell ill. On 24 October she died from an infection sustained during childbirth. Henry VIII was distraught at the death of his wife, and it was some time before he was able to consider marrying again. By November 1539, though, he was preparing for his fourth marriage. The match with the German Anne of Cleves was based on politics rather than personal passion. Although Anne was travelling to England with her own entourage, at court the King began appointing a household of English ladies to serve her. It had been more than two years since the death of Queen Jane, and competition for places was high. Among the ladies who had been appointed to serve the new Queen Anne was Katherine Carey.[43] Such an appointment was a great honour for the fifteen-year-old Katherine, and on the surface appears to be rather surprising. Following the fall of Katherine's aunt, Anne Boleyn, the family had been living under a dark cloud and had lost all of their influence with the King. Thus, in 1539, just three years after Anne's execution, there appeared to be no reason for the King to promote the dead queen's niece. Katherine's appointment is therefore strongly suggestive of the King's concern for her welfare, and could be taken as an indication that he was aware that she was his daughter. It is true that another of Katherine's relatives, Katherine Howard, later the King's fifth wife, was also chosen to serve Anne of Cleves, but her uncle, the Duke of Norfolk, had been responsible for securing her appointment.

Katherine may have come to court directly from the household of the Lady Elizabeth, who was now six years old. She had, though, barely arrived when she became acquainted with Francis Knollys. As a Gentleman Pensioner, Francis was also known to Katherine's stepfather, William Stafford, and they had all three been a part of the welcoming party charged with greeting Anne of Cleves upon her arrival in England. When Francis and Katherine married in April 1540, their marriage proved to be a very happy one. This was a rarity in an age in which marriages were based on politics and social advantage rather than personal happiness, and the couple's love endured until the end of their lives. There is no indication that Sir Francis indulged in extramarital affairs – also unusual in an era in which men frequently took mistresses. He clearly doted on Katherine, and addressed many of his letters to her as his 'loving wife'.[44]

Soon after their marriage the newlyweds took up residence at Rotherfield Greys, which was secured for them by the King and Act of Parliament. Almost immediately after their wedding, Katherine fell pregnant, and over the course of her marriage she would prove to be a fertile bride. Lettice's family was a large one, but there has been confusion over the number of children the Knollyses produced. According to Katherine's memorial plaque in Westminster Abbey, she and her husband had a total of sixteen children, eight boys and eight girls, of whom at least twelve survived infancy. However, on the couple's double tomb effigy in Rotherfield Church, only fifteen are shown, seven sons and seven daughters, and an infant lying beside Katherine. To add further confusion to the matter, in Sir Francis's Latin dictionary he lists fourteen children: eight sons and six daughters. The last to be recorded was a son, Dudley, who was born and died in 1562, and who is almost certainly the infant depicted lying next to Katherine on the tomb effigy in Rotherfield Church. It is probable that Katherine's memorial plaque in Westminster Abbey, stating that she had sixteen children, is correct. One of the unnamed daughters may have died at birth, or perhaps even been stillborn. Infant mortality was high in the sixteenth century, and it was not unusual for a family to have experienced the loss of at least one child. An entry in the gift rolls of Elizabeth I lends support to this. It reveals that on 18 May 1563, the year after Dudley's birth, the Queen gave 'three gilt bowls with a cover bought of the goldsmith's' as a gift for 'the christening of Sir Francis Knollys, his daughter'.[45] It was this daughter that was the youngest of the Knollys brood, and the Queen's gift indicates that she had probably been asked to stand as godmother to the child. Unfortunately, no further details of the little girl, including her name, are known. She probably died soon after she was christened.

Lettice's birth was followed by those of seven younger brothers and six sisters: William (1545), Edward (1546), Maud (1548), Elizabeth (1549), Robert (1550), Richard (1552), Francis (1553), Anne (1555), who may have been named after her great-aunt Anne Boleyn, Thomas (1558), Katherine (1559) and Dudley (1562). Dudley, who died just a month after his birth, was named in honour of Robert Dudley, a man who would later become an integral part of Lettice's story.[46] In between the births of these children, one of the unnamed daughters was presumably also born.[47] Little is known of the lives of Mary, Maud and Edward. Edward was certainly alive in September 1568, by which time he would have been just shy of his twenty-second birthday, for at that time Francis Knollys wrote to William Cecil that 'I have six sons living, besides my eldest.'[48] He is also portrayed on his parents' tomb as an adult sporting a beard in the same manner as his brothers. It may have been the case that he had no desire for public life, or that he suffered from some ailment which prevented him from doing so. This can, though, only ever be a matter of speculation. As for Mary and Maud, by 1561 one of them was serving in the household of Katherine Willoughby, Duchess of Suffolk. It is unclear which sister was placed there, but the Duchess was a friend of the Knollyses, which explains the appointment.[49] It is possible that whichever of them did not join the Duchess of Suffolk's household died early, or like their brother Edward, possibly refrained from public life or was unable to participate.

Such frequent childbearing doubtless impacted upon Katherine Knollys's health. Indeed, so common was pregnancy for her that her only surviving portrait depicts her showing off an impressive belly. Now in the Mellon Collection at the Yale Center for British Art in New Haven, Connecticut, USA, the portrait is dated 1562, the same year as Dudley's birth. For some time the identity of the sitter was debated, but there is good evidence to suggest that it is Katherine. Completed by the Flemish artist Steven van der Meulan, the pregnant sitter, who bears a strong facial resemblance to Henry VIII, wears an identical pendant to that which can be seen adorning Katherine's effigy in Rotherfield Church.[50] Fashioned from pearls and diamonds in a circular setting around a central stone, the pendant lends credibility to the identification of the portrait as Katherine. Her gold girdle ends in a large oval tablet, which has always been believed to represent Mars, armed with a spear and a shield, who personifies a Greek proverb meaning 'Be prepared' – a fitting message given Katherine's condition and the perils of childbirth.[51] On closer inspection the jewel provides even further evidence to confirm Katherine as the sitter: it is, in fact, a gentleman adorned in the uniform of the Gentleman Pensioners, a clear indication of the first office to which Katherine's husband had been appointed by the King. It was this post that had been the first sign of Henry's favour to Francis, and was therefore hugely significant. A small dog stands next to her: a symbol of marital fidelity that was unusually accurate in this case. The final evidence to support the identification of Katherine Knollys comes in the fact that the portrait was in the possession of her descendants until 1974, when it was sold, along with other Knollys family portraits, at Sotheby's. The inscription *Aetatis suae 38 Ao Dom 1562* on the portrait reveals that Katherine was in her thirty-eighth year at the time that it was painted, which may have been in the final weeks before she gave birth.[52] There are no other known portraits of Katherine with which to compare it, but the effigy on her tomb also bears a strong resemblance to the sitter. These sorts of pregnancy portraits are unusual for this period, and the reason behind its commissioning is a mystery. Katherine was in the service of Elizabeth I in 1562, whose likeness was also taken by the artist, and it is possible that she had become familiar with the artist through her royal mistress. It is also possible that, this being a later pregnancy, Katherine's family desired to have a likeness taken of her in the event that she should die in childbirth. Whatever the circumstances, though Katherine survived her pregnancy, her child did not.

JUST FOUR MONTHS prior to Lettice's birth, on 19 July, her maternal grandmother Mary Boleyn died at Rochford Hall, the Essex home that she had inherited just four days previously.[53] Meanwhile, following the death of her second husband in 1539, Lettice's paternal grandmother Lettice Peniston had remarried for a third time, taking as her husband Sir Thomas

Tresham. The marriage is unlikely to have met with Francis's approval, for the Treshams were a family renowned for their steadfast devotion to Catholicism – completely at odds with Francis's Protestant beliefs.[54] It may have been this marriage that caused a family rift between Francis and his mother, for when she died in 1558 she cut both of her sons from her first marriage out of her will. Neither does she appear to have shown any interest in her Knollys grandchildren. Instead she left her remaining possessions to the children she had produced with her second husband.[55]

Lettice's immediate family were a close-knit unit; although her father was a more serious, sombre character who always spoke of his children more formally than he did of his wife in his letters, it is clear that he shared a good relationship with them. He also cared deeply about their welfare, and worked hard in order to ensure that they were well provided for. When money was a worry to him he would later write of his sons that

> *I fear that their youthful stout hearts will not abide misery: and yet if God took me away tomorrow, I should not leave four nobles yearly revenue: and should be sorry to think they should adventure the gallows for lack of living! But if my courtly countenance were taken away, I would leave them such an example of a contented poor life, that they should better contain themselves to live within their compass.*[56]

In an age in which family networking and kinship meant a great deal, Francis's concern for his family was crucial, and in years to come the support of her family would be vital to Lettice. Their sheer numbers ensured that there was always someone that she could turn to, and they often worked with one another's interests in mind. She grew up to be close to her parents and most of her siblings, many of whose portraits later hung in her homes. In her youth, though, the time that she spent with her parents may have been sporadic. Francis was often at court, while during the 1540s Katherine appears to have resided primarily in the countryside, though this would later change. Katherine had a reputation for wisdom;

Thomas Newton later wrote that she had 'A head so straight and beautified, with wit and counsel sound', and she was a steady influence on her children.[57] Lettice was therefore fortunate to have two shrewd parents, who provided an excellent moral example to their children.

The place of Lettice's birth and the setting for the majority of her childhood was the charming Greys Court; the beautiful manor house set in the Oxfordshire countryside, a little over forty miles from London that was her parent's main residence. There had been a building on the site of Greys since Domesday, and the house is now 'a patchwork of many layers and materials'.[58] Owned by the De Grey family throughout the medieval period, after a brief period of ownership by the Lovell family, the estate had been granted to Lettice's grandparents in 1514.[59] As the traveller John Leland asserted in 1542, 'It may not yet be forgotten in Henley that it used to belong to Lord Lovell, and that as a result of his attainder it was granted to Knollys.'[60] By the time that Lettice's parents settled at Greys, it comprised a fourteenth-century manor house and tower, with Tudor embellishments. Leland described it thus: 'As you enter the manor house you see on your right hand three or four very old stone towers, a clear indication that it was at one time a castle. It has a very large courtyard paved with brick and surrounded with timber buildings; but this is of a later period.'[61] As the century progressed, Lettice's father undertook a programme of lavish rebuilding at Greys in the hope of a royal visit – his wish was granted when Elizabeth I later visited for a day, before moving elsewhere to stay.[62] Throughout her life, Lettice paid frequent visits to her childhood home, and sought refuge there on more than one occasion in the comforting presence of her family.

Greys Court offered Lettice and her family a comfortable home that provided easy access to London, yet was far enough away from the intrigues of the royal court. It would not be long, however, before the events taking place elsewhere in the realm impacted upon this peaceful domestic existence, and separated Lettice's family.

CHAPTER 2

Darling to the Maiden Queen

O N 28 JANUARY 1547, when Lettice was three years old, the great Henry VIII, who had torn his country apart by means of his split from the Catholic Church, died at the age of fifty-five. Katherine Knollys's probable father was a distant figure to her and her family, and his death cannot therefore have been mourned with anything more than what was customary following the death of a monarch. Henry was succeeded by his nine-year-old son, Edward VI – the longed-for male heir whose birth had cost Jane Seymour her life. Shortly before his death, Henry had appointed a Regency Council to rule during Edward's youth, and when the old King died Edward's maternal uncle Edward Seymour immediately proclaimed himself head of this. Within a short time he was both Duke of Somerset and Lord Protector, and as such the most powerful man in England.

The Knollys family looked set not only to continue to enjoy royal favour during Edward's reign, but also to rise higher. For Francis this was necessary, for the demands of a growing family were placing an increasing strain on his finances. He had served as Prince Edward's Master of the Horse, a prestigious position and a sign of great favour, but there was more to come. On 20 February, the young King was crowned in Westminster Abbey, and the following day a celebratory joust took place. Francis was one of six gentlemen who participated, alongside Richard Devereux, whose son would later become intimately acquainted with Lettice.[1] Francis Knollys and his wife were devoted to the Reformed faith (the term Protestant was not adopted in England until the 1550s), and were raising their family to adhere to the same. Likewise, the young King was fanatical about his faith, and throughout his reign Edward would take radical steps to ensure that the religious reform started by his father was continued in an ever more zealous manner. Francis Knollys was eager to ensure that Lettice and her siblings were raised as Protestants, but he was by far the most zealous. It was not long before he began mixing in Protestant circles, and among his friends were William Cecil, 'an exceeding wise man, and as good as many', who was in the service of the King's uncle, the Lord Protector.[2] Together with other religious enthusiasts, Francis began attending religious meetings at Cecil's London house, where the group would discuss the meaning of the sacrament of the altar.[3]

During the reign of Henry VIII, Francis had continued to sit in Parliament, and he and his brother Henry were among those who sat in the first Parliament of Edward's reign. He had also embarked on a military career, most notably serving with the King at the siege of Boulogne in 1544. This looked set to continue under Edward VI; in 1547 the Lord Protector opted to continue the 'Rough Wooing' begun by Henry VIII – an attempt to forcibly arrange the marriage of King Edward with the four-year-old Mary, Queen of Scots – and Francis was among those who accompanied him and the English army as they made their way towards Scotland to battle the Scots into submission.[4] When the two armies met near Musselburgh and engaged in battle on 10 September, it resulted in a crushing defeat for the Scots. Francis distinguished himself at the Battle of Pinkie Cleugh, and by way of reward the Lord Protector knighted him on the battlefield. His military prowess was in no doubt, and would later be inherited by several of his sons.

As Edward VI's reign progressed, so too did Francis's career. In his home county of Oxfordshire he was particularly well renowned, and in 1547 he became a Justice of the Peace. He was also given other posts in the county, including the constableship of Wallingford Castle in 1551, not far from Greys, and the stewardship of nearby Ewelme.[5] Such posts would have kept Francis busy in Oxfordshire, but he also continued to attend court. In January 1552, he participated in two tilts, one with his brother

Henry, and continued to ingratiate himself with the young King. His brother did likewise, and the previous summer he had been sent to France to treat for a marriage between the young King and Henri II's daughter, Elisabeth.[6] The plans came to nothing, but it was not the last time Henry would be used for diplomatic missions.[7]

While her father was making a name for himself at court and in the local neighbourhood, Lettice and her siblings were being raised at home. Little is known of her early life, but it seems probable that it was her mother who oversaw the education of Lettice and her brothers and sisters. There is no record of Lady Knollys visiting court during Edward VI's reign, and with no queen there, there was very little place for her. That is not to say that she did not pay the occasional visit, but during these years she was frequently pregnant, producing four children in Edward's six-year reign alone. It is therefore likely that Lettice's mother was able to devote these years to raising her family, and overseeing the smooth running of her household at Greys Court.

When it came to educating the Knollys children, it is possible that the Magdalen College scholar Julius Palmer, who was later burned at the stake at Newbury in 1556 as a Protestant heretic, tutored Lettice. The martyrologist John Foxe noted that Palmer, who had 'a very prompt and ready memory', was 'a teacher of children in the house of Sir Francis Knollys', but does not stipulate which children.[8] Four of Lettice's brothers later attended Eton College, the prestigious boy's school founded by Henry VI in 1440, and went on to Magdalen College, Oxford, but there was no such parallel available for girls.[9] Judging by Lettice's numerous surviving letters, she received an education befitting of her rank. She had an elegant hand, and was not afraid of committing her thoughts to paper, expressing herself clearly, confidently and authoritatively. It is likely that she was also given some grounding in languages, an essential skill for a courtier – her eldest daughter would later be celebrated for her understanding of Spanish.[10] In addition, she and her sisters were taught all of the practical skills that were essential for women in order to manage their own households when they married. Lettice later put these to good use, ordering the smooth running of her household when her first two husbands were absent from England. She seems to have been a skilled needlewoman, and a later inventory of her belongings reveals that she owned a large quantity of sewing materials.[11] The girls would also have been taught manners and etiquette, and are likely to have received instruction in dancing and music. Her mother may have been particularly fond of music, for adorning the effigy of the double tomb of Lettice's parents in the church at Rotherfield Greys, several instruments are depicted next to Lady Knollys. And Lettice later found a similar enthusiast in her second husband, who owned various instruments and made regular payments to musicians during the course of their marriage.[12] Later in life Lettice also hunted, an outdoor pursuit that she was fond of and to which she would have been introduced during her childhood, in addition to the popular sport of hawking.

The spiritual welfare of his children was of the utmost importance to Sir Francis Knollys, and all of his children were raised in the Protestant faith. He was particularly concerned that his daughters ought to be brought up in godliness, and in relation to this he would later write that 'experience teaches what "foul crimes" youthful women fall into for lack of orderly maintenance. My will is good, they cannot lack as long as I have it, but there is no more "to be had of a cat but the skin".'[13] Francis's strict morals played a central role in the childhoods of Lettice and her siblings, and he was well known for his serious behaviour. In later years a humorous tale was related, whereby Francis

had his lodging at court, where some of the Ladies and Maids of Honour used to frisk and hey about in the next room, to his extreme disquiet a nights, though he had often warned them of it; at last he gets one to bolt their own back door, when they were all in one night at their revels, strips off [to] his shirt, and so with a pair of spectacles on his nose, and Aretine in his hand, comes marching in at a postern door of his own chamber, reading very gravely, full upon the faces of them. Now let the reader judge what a sad spectacle and pitiful fright these poor creatures endured.[14]

Such a story is perhaps indicative of the kind of reaction Lettice and her siblings would have received if they had misbehaved at home! Similarly, Francis was a man who liked routine. Each New Year he gave the Queen a purse of sovereigns, the only change being the purse in which they were presented; in 1562 'a purse of blue silk and gold knit', and the following year 'a purse of red silk and silver'.[15]

At home at Greys Court, Lettice would not have lacked for company. By 1552 there were nine Knollys children including Lettice, who would have turned nine in November. Four of her siblings were under the age of five, the youngest being Richard who was born in May 1552, and the eldest being eleven-year-old Henry. With so many youngsters, Greys Court must have been a hub of youthful energy, with little place for peace and quiet, and no shortage of playmates. As Mary and Lettice were the two eldest daughters, they would have been expected to help out with their younger siblings, and so Lettice would have received an early introduction to the skills of motherhood. She was surrounded by an abundance of brothers and sisters, whose care would have occupied much of her time. It was through them that she is likely to have developed her love of children, for motherhood would be something in which she excelled.

⁓

WHILE LETTICE AND her siblings were raised in the Oxfordshire countryside, elsewhere in England the young King Edward had been devoting his attentions to the development of Protestantism within his realm. In January 1549, the Act of Uniformity was passed in Parliament, confirming the use of Protestant rites in all churches across the country. The Act also prescribed the Book of Common Prayer, written in English by Archbishop Thomas Cranmer, as the sole religious text in churches, and all of the Popish imagery associated with Catholicism was removed.

Matters had also taken a turn in the political arena, and following a *coup d'état* in 1549 the Lord Protector had been ousted from power. Despite a brief period of rehabilitation, on 22 January 1552 he was executed for felony. John Dudley, who was created Duke of Northumberland in 1551, assumed his place. Northumberland had quickly taken up the reins of power in England, and was fully supportive of the King's religious policies. However, when the fifteen-year-old Edward fell ill at the beginning of 1553, it soon became clear that he was not going to live long enough to ensure that his religious reforms were securely in place. To the alarm of the King and his most fervent religious supporters, as young Edward was childless the next in line to the throne was his half-sister, Mary, the only surviving child of Henry VIII's marriage to Katherine of Aragon. By extreme contrast to Edward, Mary was a devoted Catholic. She had also spent the entirety of Edward's reign refusing to conform to his religious policies, much to his fury. She had defiantly ordered the Catholic Mass to be celebrated in her chapel, and there was no doubt that if she succeeded Edward she would attempt to return England to the folds of the Church of Rome. Although Elizabeth, the younger of Edward's half-sisters, was a Protestant, it was impossible for the King to rule out one half-sister without also disinheriting the other. Thus it was that, with the support of the Duke of Northumberland, Edward drew up a document, 'My Devise for the Succession', whereby he attempted to overturn the provisions set out in his late father's will. Edward's Devise passed over both of his half-sisters on the grounds of their illegitimacy, enforced by law during the reign of Henry VIII following the annulment of his marriages to their mothers. Instead, Edward named his Protestant cousin Lady Jane Grey, whom Henry VIII had nominated in the event of all three of his children dying childless, his heir. Edward's health declined so rapidly that there was no time for the Devise to be passed through Parliament. Therefore, in order to ensure that the terms of the Devise were upheld, Edward demanded the signatures and allegiance of his councillors. Despite his religious convictions, Sir Francis Knollys may have been glad that he was not a member of the King's Council, and was therefore not required to sign. Nevertheless he would have heard of the trepidation of many of those who did, feeling wary and fearful about what was to follow.

On 6 July, Edward VI died a painful death, probably of a pulmonary infection, at Greenwich Palace. Over the course of the next thirteen days, a bitter power struggle ensued. In accordance with the dying King's wishes and in an attempt to retain his own power, the Duke of Northumberland had Lady Jane Grey, now his daughter-in-law following her marriage to his son Guildford in May, proclaimed Queen.[16] But nobody had counted on the popularity or fighting spirit of Edward's Catholic half-sister, Mary. Having rallied huge support, on 19 July all allegiances to Lady Jane Grey were forgotten and she was deposed in favour of Mary. Contemporary chroniclers in London reported that as she was proclaimed Queen Mary I, there were 'bonfires in every street', while the bells were 'ringing in every parish church', so great was the elation of the citizens.[17] On 22 August, Northumberland was executed, and Lady Jane Grey and her husband were imprisoned in the Tower.[18]

Francis Knollys did not involve himself in the coup to place Lady Jane Grey on the throne, but he was alarmed when, as Edward VI had feared, Mary made it clear that she was indeed intent on reverting England to the Catholic faith. Having won her kingdom without shedding a single drop of blood, she immediately took steps to restore the Catholic faith. A month after her accession, however, she issued a proclamation declaring that she would not force any of her subjects to embrace Catholicism. Though many of them accepted this and had good cause to hope that their lives would not be unduly affected, for others the re-establishment of Catholicism in the realm signalled disaster: the Knollys family were foremost among them.

During the first Parliament of her reign in October, one of Mary's first steps was to have the legislation that had once declared her illegitimate revoked – there was to be no doubt in anybody's mind that she was a true and legitimate heir of Henry VIII. She also began to reverse all of the religious changes that had been put in place by her half-brother. Within months, the Book of Common Prayer that had become an integral part of Edward VI's church had been outlawed, and the Catholic Mass had been reintroduced. Mary met with little resistance from the majority of her subjects, and those who did resist found themselves speedily imprisoned; Archbishop Cranmer, and Bishops Latimer and Ridley being chief among them.[19] The Queen's plans to return England to the folds of Rome were furthered when, in January 1554, negotiations for her marriage to the Catholic Philip of Spain, the son of her cousin the Holy Roman Emperor Charles V, were concluded. On 23 July, Philip arrived in Winchester, 'accompanied with noblemen as well of England as of his own country, with trumpets blowing and bells ringing'.[20] Mary and the court had journeyed to meet him, and on 25 July, two days after his arrival, Mary and Philip were 'honourably married with great solemnity' in a magnificent ceremony at Winchester Cathedral.[21] Thirty-eight-year-old Mary felt 'a violent love for him', but for the twenty-seven-year-old Philip the marriage was merely a matter of policy.[22] Mary now had a foreign Catholic consort, and England, it seemed, was set on following a very different path from the one prescribed by Edward VI.

The idea of a Catholic England repulsed Francis Knollys; he was incredibly principled, particularly about his staunch Protestant views. The Imperial ambassador would later describe him as being 'a terrible Protestant', and his faith was an issue on which he was not prepared to compromise.[23] It was with this in mind that, in the same year as Mary's accession, Francis left England. Taking his eldest son Henry with him, he travelled to Geneva, probably setting sail from Dover on 16 September.[24] It must have been difficult for him to leave his family behind at this time, for only the previous month his wife had given birth to another son, Francis, born on 14 August. His business, though, was of the utmost importance, and time was very much of the essence. It was the belief of historian Christina Garrett, writing in 1938, that Francis was sent abroad as an envoy to meet with John Calvin in Geneva, and his disciple Pierre Viret at Lausanne, on behalf of William Cecil.[25] Garrett argues that Francis was tasked with obtaining Calvin's permission for a colony of English Protestant immigrants to settle in Geneva, and this theory does sound credible.[26] It would have been an arduous journey, particularly for the twelve-year-old Henry, but before 20 November father and son had reached Geneva. On that day, Calvin wrote a letter of introduction to his follower, Viret, on behalf of two English gentlemen who had recently been his guests. The men are likely to have been Francis and Henry, and young Henry in particular made an impression on Calvin. While he believed that 'the father of the young man, is a person of good birth, and was wealthy in his own country', Calvin reserved his greatest compliments for Lettice's brother.[27] Henry, he wrote, 'merits higher praise for piety and holy zeal; for, under the reign of King Edward, seeing that the Church suffered from want of pastors, he undertook voluntarily the labours of that office'.[28] Impressive behaviour for a twelve-year-old.

It was probably with some positive assurance from Calvin that Francis and his son were able to return home to England. They had certainly arrived by the autumn of 1554, for at this time Lettice's mother fell pregnant once more. For a short time life resumed its normal course in the Knollys household.[29] However, as Mary's reign progressed, her toleration for English Protestants began to dissolve. Her fervour to rid her realm of heretics was heightened by the encouragement of several of her ministers, notably Cardinal Reginald Pole and Bishop Edmund Bonner, who were almost as fanatical as she was. Mary was also supported by Parliament, who reintroduced all of the old heresy laws. This enabled Protestants to be tried for heresy, and executed if they were found guilty. On 4 February 1555, the first Protestant burning of Mary's reign took place, and others swiftly followed.[30] During Mary's five-year reign 'divers burned in Smithfield for heresy' and elsewhere in the realm, including Edward VI's former Archbishop of Canterbury, Thomas Cranmer, who was 'disgraded of all his orders and dignities' and burned at Oxford on 21 March 1556.[31] The historian William Camden, who would later write the first history of Elizabeth I's reign, wrote that Mary's 'days have been ill spoken of, by reason of the barbarous cruelty of the Bishops, who with a most sad spectacle, in all places polluted England by burning Protestants alive'.[32] It was becoming clear that nobody was safe, as the burnings affected all levels of society. As known Protestants, the persecution placed Sir Francis Knollys and his family in serious danger.

In order to avoid persecution, many English Protestants were fleeing England for Europe, seeking refuge in Protestant-dominated cities such as Frankfurt, Geneva, Zurich and Strasbourg. Katherine Willoughby, Duchess of Suffolk, was among those of the nobility who had abandoned her home country, eventually finding sanctuary in Poland, while Katherine Knollys's stepfather, William Stafford, also fled. Stafford and his second wife Dorothy Stafford, who he had married in 1552, reached Geneva in March 1554 with their children.[33] He may have crossed paths with Francis and Henry, but what is certain is that he would never see his stepdaughter Katherine or his home country again; still in Geneva, Stafford died on 5 May 1556. To make matters worse, the Knollyses would have been alarmed to discover that during the first examination of Julius Palmer, the man formerly employed as a tutor to their children, Francis's name had been mentioned. When Palmer was brought before the Mayor of Reading accused of heresy, Foxe alleged that one of the 'greatest proofs against him' was that 'certain servants of Sir Francis Knollys and others, resorting to his lectures, had fallen out among themselves, and were like to have committed murder; and therefore he was a sower of sedition, and a procurer of unlawful assemblies'.[34]

Although Francis himself had been accused of nothing, the fact that his name had been raised was troubling. With friends and family leaving England and under question, the net around Protestants and the Knollys's circle was tightening. It was not long before Lettice's family had resolved to abandon their home.

Following his meeting with Calvin in Geneva, Francis felt confident of receiving a safe haven in Europe, and consequently decided to leave England with his family. By the summer of 1555, he and Katherine had added another child to their brood, a daughter, Anne, who was born on 19 July. As parents to eleven children, given the logistical difficulties of sixteenth-century travel it was inconceivable for the whole family to desert England in order to flee into self-imposed exile. Travelling by both land and sea was fraught with many dangers; the journey could take weeks. At some point, therefore, a decision was made for the family temporarily to separate, and it cannot have been an easy one. The first one to leave was Francis; it is unclear precisely when he left England, or if he took any of his children with him, but he had probably gone on ahead in order to secure a proper home for his family, who would follow him shortly. His brother Henry also left, and may have travelled with him. The first occasion on which his name is mentioned is in the winter of 1556, by which time he had reached Basle in Switzerland. It is possible that he met William Stafford's widow Dorothy and her children while he was there, for following the death of her husband earlier that year it was to Basle that Dorothy had relocated with her young family.

No matter how short a period of time they perceived their separation to be, it was a heart-wrenching decision for Francis to leave behind his home, his beloved wife and his children. Back in England, meanwhile, Lettice's mother was making preparations to join her husband. It was simply not possible for Katherine Knollys to take her eleven children abroad with her, but the prospect of leaving some of them behind was also difficult to contemplate. She had no choice, and by 10 June 1557 she and her husband, together with five of their children and a maid, were in the German city of Frankfurt.[35] Whether Katherine journeyed to Basle first to meet Francis is unclear, but she had been reunited with him before June, for their son Thomas was born at the beginning of 1558, on 'ye Wednesday before Candlemas Day'. Their separation does, however, explain why there was almost a three-year gap in between the births of their daughter Anne in July 1555 and Thomas. Once in Frankfurt the family settled in a house owned by John Weller, a burgher of the city, and there they remained for more than a year, free from the threat of persecution but separated from half of their children.[36] As Camden later related, though it was self-imposed, Francis 'for the truth of the Gospel had been banished into Germany'.[37]

The identities of the five children who joined their parents in exile abroad are unknown, but it is unlikely that Lettice was one of them.[38] More probable is that Katherine Knollys took the youngest of her children with her while places for the remaining six children, including Lettice, were presumably found with people whom the Knollyses trusted. In an age that was rocked by religious turbulence, Lettice's parents were hopeful that either their remaining children would eventually be able to join them or that the family would be able to return home at some point in the future.

If Lettice did not accompany her parents, where was she? In November 1556 she turned thirteen, and it is possible that, having almost certainly remained in England, she joined the household of her twenty-three-year-old cousin, the Lady Elizabeth, at Hatfield. The epitaph on Lettice's tomb in St Mary's Church, Warwick, states that 'in her youth [she] had been, Darling to the maiden Queen', and it may be that a place was found for her with Elizabeth, and possibly for her fourteen-year-old sister Mary, too. If this was the case, then her placement there was probably a favour for Lettice's mother. It was, though, by no means a safe option, for Elizabeth too faced danger during Mary's reign.

UNLIKE LETTICE, HER kinswoman Elizabeth had enjoyed none of the parental stability that the Knollys were able to offer their children; nor had her family life been as happy. Elizabeth was just short of her third birthday when her mother, Anne Boleyn, had been executed. Like her half-sister Mary before her, she had been declared illegitimate by her father, excluded from her place in the line of succession, and banished from her father's presence. The rest of Elizabeth's childhood had been spent cast under a cloud, enjoying brief periods of rehabilitation before losing her father's favour once more. There is no doubt that all of this had an intense effect on the young girl, and shaped her attitudes and behaviour as she grew. By the time that she was eight years old, she had witnessed the death, annulment and execution of three more of her father's brides: Jane Seymour, Anne of Cleves and Katherine Howard. This had shown her that matrimony was by no means a stable course, and was fraught with insecurity. It was not until Henry VIII married the twice-widowed Katherine Parr on 12 July

1543 that life began to take a more stable course for Elizabeth.[39] Katherine took a great interest in all three of her royal stepchildren, and chose to supervise the education of both Prince Edward and Elizabeth personally. Under Katherine's watchful eye, Elizabeth flourished.

After her father's death, Elizabeth remained in Katherine's care, primarily at her palace of Chelsea, and continued with her lessons. However, in May 1548 the revelation of a dangerous flirtation with Katherine's fourth husband, Edward VI's younger maternal uncle Sir Thomas Seymour, led to her banishment from the Queen Dowager's household. It was an experience that would tarnish Elizabeth's reputation, but it taught her a valuable lesson about her dealings with men.

In appearance, Elizabeth had inherited many of the Tudor characteristics, including flame-red hair like her father. The Venetian ambassador reported that 'her face is comely rather than handsome', she was tall and slim, 'with a good skin, although swarthy' which she had inherited from her mother.[40] She also had fine eyes and 'above all a beautiful hand of which she makes a display'.[41] She was one of the most intelligent young women in the kingdom, and had been privileged enough to be taught by some of the finest minds in the country, including William Grindal and the accomplished scholar Roger Ascham.[42] Under Ascham's tutelage Elizabeth excelled, and her brilliant mind impressed many of her contemporaries, including her tutors. Ascham later enthusiastically praised 'my illustrious mistress, the Lady Elizabeth', who 'shines like a star'.[43] John Foxe also wrote about her in complimentary terms, relating that she did 'rather excel in all manner of virtue and knowledge of learning'.[44] She was particularly skilled at languages, and wrote and spoke several fluently. These included Latin, French, Spanish, Italian and Greek, and she continued to do the exercises in translations that she had started as a child for the rest of her life. One of the most notable surviving examples of her work was the translation of Marguerite d'Angouleme's verse *The Mirror or Glass of the Sinful Soul*, which Elizabeth translated from French to English as a New Year's gift for Katherine Parr in 1544.[45] William Camden would later praise her talents, including her *modest gratuity, excellent wit, royal mind, happy memory, and indefatigable study of learning, insomuch before she was seventeen years of age, she understood well the Latin, French and Italian tongues, and was indifferently well seen in the Greek. Neither did she neglect music, so far forth as might beseem a Princess, being able to sing and play on the lute prettily and sweetly.*[46]

Like Lettice, Elizabeth had also been raised as a Protestant and she shared similar views to her half-brother Edward, to whom she was close. The two were only four years apart in age and also had their academic interests in common. The same could not be said of her half-sister, Mary. Their father had separated from Mary's mother, Katherine of Aragon, in order to marry Elizabeth's, and the wound ran deep. The emotional impact that her parents' annulment case had had on Mary had been overwhelming. It had caused a huge rift between father and daughter, as Mary refused to obey her father's demands that she acknowledge her mother's marriage to have been invalid. Further resentment had been caused when Anne Boleyn had ordered Mary to join the household of her baby half-sister at Hatfield. Despite the unhappy circumstances in which she found herself, and to her own surprise, Mary had grown fond of Elizabeth. There was a seventeen-year age gap between the half-sisters, and consequently Mary had in many ways assumed the role of mother to Elizabeth, playing with her and showering her with gifts.

Following the death, though, of Henry VIII, the relationship between the two half-sisters had become more strained. Mary had been shocked by Katherine Parr's speedy remarriage to Thomas Seymour, and she disapproved of Elizabeth's decision to join Katherine's household.[47] Besides that, their religious differences were starting to become more apparent. When Edward VI died, during the brief days of Lady Jane Grey's queenship Elizabeth laid low at Hatfield, waiting to see how events unfolded. When Mary successfully toppled Jane, Elizabeth was determined to share in her glory. She wrote Mary a congratulatory note, and set out for the capital in order to greet her. On 3 August, Elizabeth was by Mary's side as she entered London in triumph, but despite this outward display of loyalty, beneath the surface tension simmered. Nevertheless, she participated in the celebrations for Mary's coronation, travelling through London on 30 September with her former stepmother Anne of Cleves in a 'rich chariot covered with cloth of silver' behind the Queen.[48]

Elizabeth was a well-known Protestant, but in spite of this she appeared outwardly to conform with Mary's religious policies. In December 1553, the Imperial ambassador had informed the Emperor Charles V that when Elizabeth left court for her own estates, she had written to ask the Queen 'for ornaments for her chapel: copes, chasubles, chalices, crosses, patens and other similar objects. The Queen had ordered all these things to be sent to her, as it was for God's service and Elizabeth wished to bear witness to the religion she had declared she meant to follow.'[49] Mary and her advisors were yet suspicious of Elizabeth's true motives, and with good reason.

In January 1554, the Wyatt Rebellion came to light, and for Elizabeth, matters were about to become a whole lot worse. The plot, led by a Kentish gentleman named Sir Thomas Wyatt, was an attempt to protest against the Queen's intended Spanish marriage to Prince Philip, but there was also a more sinister twist. Another of the rebels' primary objectives was to remove the Catholic Queen Mary and replace her with her Protestant half-sister Elizabeth. The rebellion was crushed, but it would have fateful consequences for many. Since her arrest in July 1553, Lady Jane Grey had languished in the Tower of London; on 13 November she had been condemned for treason, but no further move had been made against her. She had no knowledge, involvement or place in the Wyatt Rebellion, but her father did. The Duke of Suffolk's involvement, as a key conspirator, sealed his daughter's fate, and that of his son-in-law. On the morning of 12 February 1554, Jane and Guildford Dudley were executed, and eleven days later Suffolk followed them to the block.[50]

Following the discovery of Wyatt's treason it was not long before the Queen's officers came knocking at Elizabeth's door, as she had known they would. On 9 February they had arrived at Ashridge, the palatial Hertfordshire residence which had been left to Elizabeth by her father, and in which she had passed many of her turbulent adolescent years. They informed her that she must accompany them to the safety of London, where they could be sure to monitor her activities. It was not the first time she had been summoned, for just weeks earlier, at the outset of rebellion, the Queen had personally written to her half-sister, inviting her to court for her own safety. But Elizabeth was determined to resist all attempts to cage her, and eager to see how events played out she had declared that she was too ill to travel the twenty miles to the capital. Preoccupied with the suppression of the rebellion, the Queen's Council had let her be. Once the danger had passed, though, and the traitor Wyatt had been incarcerated in the Tower, Elizabeth had to be brought to heel.

Summoned to London for questioning, Elizabeth repudiated everything. If the Council wanted a confession from her, other tactics would be required. For this reason the decision was taken to send Elizabeth to the Tower, in the hope of extracting an admission of her guilt. It was Palm Sunday, 18 March, when Elizabeth was 'had to the Tower from Westminster by water privily'.[51] The rain poured ceaselessly as she boarded a barge that conveyed her to the mighty fortress, and as she landed at the Tower wharf, she took the opportunity to declare her innocence: 'Here landeth as true a subject, being prisoner, as ever landed at these stairs; and before thee, O God! I speak it, having no other friends but thee alone.'[52] Always her father's daughter, Elizabeth knew how to maximize the Tudor propaganda system, and played it for all it was worth. It was a moving speech, but one which did nothing to alter her situation.

In a further distressing twist, Elizabeth was led through the Tower precincts to the Royal Apartments, close to where the scaffold that had recently severed Lady Jane Grey's head still stood. Whether by chance or design, she was taken to the exact same rooms that her mother had once occupied in the days leading up to her execution less than two decades earlier.[53] Despite her perilous circumstances, Elizabeth would confess to nothing. She was clever, and while plans for the Wyatt Rebellion had been laid, she had been careful to ensure that there was nothing that could directly incriminate her – much to the Council's frustration. There was no doubt that she had been kept informed of the progress of the rebellion, for Wyatt himself had admitted as much under interrogation, but no evidence could be found that she had indeed approved of, or participated in, the plans. She had been mindful, and had given only non-committal oral replies to Wyatt's messages.

Under pressure Elizabeth kept her composure, yet still the Queen and Council were determined to break her down. Convinced of her half-sister's guilt, Queen Mary had remarked to the Imperial ambassador, Simon Renard, that 'Elizabeth's character was just what she had always believed it to be', and the Council began to turn up the pressure on the unfortunate girl.[54] No evidence against her was forthcoming; Thomas Wyatt declared Elizabeth to be blameless as he stood on the scaffold on 11 April, and ultimately Mary was left with no choice: on 19 May, the anniversary of her mother's execution, Elizabeth was removed from the Tower and 'went through London Bridge in her barge' to Richmond Palace, but her imprisonment was not at an end.[55] The following day she began the journey to the crumbling royal palace at Woodstock, 'there to remain at the Queen's pleasure'.[56] Once there, Elizabeth was forced to endure almost another year of house imprisonment under the supervision of Sir Henry Bedingfield, a Catholic gentleman who was utterly loyal to Queen Mary.[57] It was not until the spring of 1555 that she was summoned to attend on the Queen at Hampton Court. By that time Mary believed herself to be pregnant and had retired from the noise and dirt of London for her confinement. She had high hopes of producing a son – a Catholic prince to succeed her – but alas, to Mary's sorrow the pregnancy was a phantom one.

That autumn Elizabeth was allowed to withdraw to Hatfield, and there she remained for the majority of the remainder of Mary's reign. She had survived the ordeal of imprisonment, and had emerged from the Tower unscathed, but Elizabeth would never forget these experiences. Now a free woman, Elizabeth lived quietly on her estates, but she still managed to earn the Queen's enmity. In 1557, the Venetian ambassador claimed that Mary bore Elizabeth an 'evil disposition', and this is no exaggeration.[58] Though Elizabeth may technically have been at her liberty, the Queen still distrusted her, and on that account had installed 'many spies and guards in the neighbourhood who keep strict watch on all persons passing to and fro'.[59]

IT IS UNCERTAIN how much contact Elizabeth had with Katherine Knollys during their childhoods, but it is clear that it was enough for them to become close. As they grew, they likely also communicated by visits or letters, and it is probable that Elizabeth was also the namesake and godmother of Lettice's younger sister, born in 1549.[60] If Katherine had entrusted her daughter Lettice, and possibly Mary too, to Elizabeth's care as she prepared to join her husband abroad, then it was almost certainly during this time that the foundations of the relationship between Elizabeth and Lettice were laid. Cemented by their kinship and shared love for Lettice's mother, the two youngsters formed a warm and close friendship.

Elizabeth was devastated when she learned that Katherine was preparing to leave England. She was, though, determined to reassure her kinswoman and friend that their separation would only be of short duration. It was with this in mind that Elizabeth wrote Katherine a letter:

Relieve your sorrow for your far journey with joy of your short return, and think this pilgrimage rather a proof of your friends, than a leaving of your country. The length of time, and distance of place, separates not the love of friends, nor deprives not the show of goodwill. An old saying, when bale is lowest boot is nearest: when your need shall be most you shall find my friendship greatest. Let others promise, and I will do, in words not more, in deeds as much. My power but small, my love as great as them whose gifts may tell their friendship's tale, let will supply all other want, and oft sending take the lieu of often sights. Your messengers shall not return empty, nor yet your desires unaccomplished. Lethe's flood hath here no course, good memory hath greatest stream. And, to conclude, a word that hardly I can say, I am driven by need to write, farewell, it is which in the sense one way I wish, the other way I grieve.

Your loving cousin and ready friend,

Cor Rotto [broken heart].[61]

There could be no clearer demonstration of Elizabeth's friendship than this, and it is one of the most affectionate surviving letters she ever wrote. If Lettice and Mary were taken into Elizabeth's service at this time, then they would have been treated with the same warmth that Elizabeth displayed to their mother. What is more, their presence may have helped to ease the void that Katherine was about to leave in Elizabeth's life.

———⟡———

ELIZABETH WAS NO longer Mary's prisoner, but the rift between the two half-sisters was never healed. Despite her phantom pregnancy, Mary remained hopeful of producing an heir. Tragically for Mary, in 1557 a further suspected pregnancy ended in the same manner: no baby and bitter disappointment.[62] Elizabeth, meanwhile, lay low, watching and waiting. Camden related, probably quite accurately, that 'all mens minds and eyes were bent towards her, as towards the sun rising'.[63] And though a cloud still loomed ominously over her head, unbeknown to her and her supporters that cloud was about to be lifted. It would have life-changing consequences not only for Elizabeth and England, but for Lettice and her family, too.

CHAPTER 3

Captive to the Charms of Lettice Knollys

I N THE EARLY hours of the morning of 17 November 1558, everyone at St James's Palace waited with bated breath. Queen Mary, who had long been weakened by illness, had lain sick for weeks, and those who attended her knew that her end was imminent. Finally, at six o'clock in the morning, the Queen died, her five-year reign now over. Mary and her half-sister Elizabeth had never been reconciled, and to the end Mary had cherished hopes of producing an heir to succeed her. For some time, though, she had known that 'the eyes and hearts of the nation already fixed on this lady as successor to the Crown'.[1] Eventually, she had no choice but to accept harsh reality – motherhood had evaded her – and, with considerable reluctance, on 6 November she acknowledged Elizabeth as her heir, to the great joy of the people. Lettice's kinswoman, the twenty-five-year-old Elizabeth, now became Queen Elizabeth I of England. According to her admirer Camden, who always spoke favourably of her, she was 'of beauty very fair and worthy of a Crown'.[2] On the day of her accession it was reported that 'the bells in all the churches in London rung in token of joy; and at night bonfires were made, and tables set out in the streets, where was plentiful eating and drinking, and making merry'.[3]

Elizabeth had always been popular, and though her half-sister had once been equally so, by the time of her death the warmth of feeling towards Mary had faded. She had become unpopular as a result of the religious persecution she had imposed upon her people, and for involving her realm in her husband Philip's foreign wars. This had also resulted in the loss of Calais in 1557, England's last remaining possession in France, which came as a devastating blow to the English. It was little wonder, then, that her subjects greeted Elizabeth's succession with genuine heartfelt enthusiasm. Indeed, for the entirety of her reign Accession Day would be enthusiastically celebrated each year.[4] At the time of Mary's death, Elizabeth was twenty miles north of London at the old nursery palace of Hatfield. She had been aware that the Queen's death was approaching, not only from the reports she had received, but also because for some days prior to Mary's death courtiers had begun to gravitate to Hatfield, eager to ingratiate themselves with the woman that they knew would soon be their queen. The Venetian ambassador had noted that 'Many persons of the kingdom flocked to the house of my lady Elizabeth, the crowd constantly increasing with great frequency.'[5] It is possible that Lettice was there to witness this flurry of activity at the formerly peaceful residence. If she were by Elizabeth's side at this time, Lettice would have seen how quickly people abandoned a dying monarch in order to ally themselves with the new one – it was something that was not lost on Elizabeth, and that would affect her later behaviour.

When the news of Mary's death was brought to her, Elizabeth declared to those around her, 'My Lords, the law of nature moveth me to sorrow for my sister: The burden that is fallen upon me maketh me amazed.'[6] She would later claim that she had wept tears of grief for Mary, but nobody else was there to see them. Six days after Mary's death, on 23 November, Elizabeth left Hatfield behind as she journeyed to London, 'attended with a thousand or more, of Lords, Knights, Gentlemen, Ladies and Gentlewomen'.[7] She was going to take possession of her kingdom.

Immediately upon her accession Elizabeth treated the responsibilities of monarchy with the utmost seriousness. As Camden explained, by 'experience and adversity' Elizabeth 'had gathered wisdom above her age', and she had begun the business of ruling before she had even left Hatfield.[8] While she was there she immediately began the critical task of appointing her Council. Lettice's father Sir Francis Knollys was still in exile abroad, but foremost among those appointed was his friend William Cecil, at whose house Francis had once attended religious meetings. Cecil was made Elizabeth's Principal Secretary on the same day as her accession, and for the rest of his life would remain at the forefront of affairs during the Queen's reign. Though she did not always take his advice, Elizabeth trusted his opinions and admired his intelligence, so much so that she gave him a fond nickname: Spirit. As time went on, Cecil would also come to be well acquainted with Lettice's affairs, too.

IN 1557 THE Venetian ambassador had described London as 'the metropolis of the kingdom, and truly royal, being with reason regarded as one of the principal cities of Europe'.[9] It had 'handsome streets and buildings', and 'is most opulent' thanks to its trade links with the rest of Europe.[10] Nevertheless, the country that Elizabeth had inherited was a weak one. Elizabeth was determined to change this, and throughout the course of her reign England would steadily evolve into one of the most powerful nations in Europe. By the time of her death it had become a vastly different country from the one that her sister had ruled, her stable rule helping to make it both peaceful and strong.

Elizabeth had always been popular, and her succession was greeted not only with sincere exuberance by her subjects, but also with relief: with Mary died the religious persecution of Protestants that she had imposed so fervently. Thanks to the martyrologist John Foxe and his famous *Acts and Monuments*, which charted the burnings throughout the course of Mary's reign, Elizabeth's predecessor would be remembered by posterity as Bloody Mary.[11] Almost three hundred people were burned, with London witnessing more burnings than any other diocese. Initially, Elizabeth would take a very different course; though she was a Protestant queen she was prepared to tolerate Catholics in her realm. Regardless, in April 1559 the Acts of Supremacy and Uniformity were passed in

Parliament, confirming Protestantism as the official form of worship in England. As her reign progressed and events transpired beyond her control, so too did her religious tolerance begin to fade. Although Elizabeth never burned any Catholics, she did hang, draw and quarter more than two hundred, thereby bringing her close to level with Mary; many were also imprisoned.[12] At the time of her succession, though, this was all in the future, and for the moment Elizabeth was able to indulge in the adoration of her subjects. Lettice and her family were among those who celebrated Elizabeth's succession, and with good reason. Not only did their close ties of kinship with the new queen mean that they were well placed to receive her favour, but the end of the religious persecution and the establishment of a Protestant queen meant that her parents and siblings were now able to return home from their self-imposed exile.

They wasted no time in doing so, and probably left Frankfurt in December.[13] They were not alone, and among those who began returning to England were the Duchess of Suffolk and Dorothy Stafford, the second wife of Katherine Knollys's stepfather, with whom the family remained on good terms.[14] By 14 January 1559, and after several years apart, Lettice's parents and the five children they had taken with them were back on English soil, reunited with Lettice and her siblings.[15] By now there was a new addition, Thomas, who was almost a year old. What was more, shortly after their return home Katherine Knollys would have learned that she was once again pregnant. Lettice would not have been the only one who was overjoyed at being reunited with her family; Elizabeth, now Queen of England, had not forgotten the meaningful words she had once written to Lettice's mother. She was elated by Katherine's return, and from now on she was determined that Katherine would leave her side only in extraordinary circumstances.

The succession of Elizabeth I signalled the start of the most prestigious period of the Knollys family's career. Their close kinship and the warm relationship they shared with the Queen ensured that they were always going to be given privileged positions at her court, and they were not to be disappointed. Elizabeth was fond of her maternal Boleyn relatives, and for the entirety of her reign members of that side of her family would remain close to her. There were plenty of them to be had. The successful breeding record of the females in Lettice's family ensured that the next generation was always close at hand, ready to fill any vacant posts that might arise. By contrast to members of Elizabeth's paternal family, chiefly the sisters of Lady Jane Grey, Katherine and Mary, for whom Elizabeth's dislike was evident, she did not view her mother's relatives as a threat. This was because, unlike the Greys, they did not have a claim to the throne, and they in turn rewarded her trust with loyal service. In the same month as the Queen's accession Lettice's uncle, Henry Carey, was nominated for a knighthood and on 13 January 1559 the Queen created him Baron Hunsdon.[16] The Queen had always been, and always would be, fond of Hunsdon, whom she referred to as 'my Harry', often signing herself 'Your loving kinswoman' in her letters to him.[17] The following day Lettice's father, newly returned from exile, was made the twentieth member of the Queen's Privy Council, and was also appointed Vice-Chamberlain of the Queen's Household.[18] This role required him to support the Chamberlain, Lord Howard of Effingham, another of the Queen's relatives, who was responsible for the smooth running of the Royal Household.[19] These were both privileged positions that demonstrated the Queen's faith in Sir Francis and his abilities, and were roles that he took seriously. The real sign of favour, though, was saved for Lettice's mother: Katherine Knollys was appointed one of four ladies of the Queen's bedchamber.[20] She was also given another important job: that of caring for the Queen's pet parrot and monkey. Her position was not quite the most prestigious post in the Queen's household, for the role of Chief Lady of the Bedchamber was reserved for Kate Ashley, Elizabeth's former governess who had been by Elizabeth's side since the earliest days of her childhood.[21] However, upon Kate's death in 1565, Katherine would step up to take her place. By this time Elizabeth had grown even more attached to Katherine; New Year was the main gift-giving event at the Tudor court, and that year Lady Knollys presented the Queen with 'a pair of sleeves and a partlet of white lawn [a type of material] netted'.[22] In return, she received 'a tablet of gold set with five diamonds two rubies and a pearl pendant' – a clear sign of Elizabeth's love for her kinswoman, made all the more significant given that she was the only one of the Queen's ladies to receive such a gift; everyone else was given gilt pots or gilt covers.[23]

In addition to Katherine, other members of the Knollys family took positions in the Queen's household: Katherine Knollys's sister-in-law Anne Morgan also became one of the Queen's ladies, and on 3 January fifteen-year-old Lettice was made a 'gentlewoman of our privy chamber'.[24] She was followed by her nine-year-old sister Elizabeth twelve days later.[25] Lettice's first official 'job' earned her an annual salary of around £33 (£5,600), a very respectable sum for a girl of her youth.[26] Such places in the Queen's household were highly sought after; only the most entitled of ladies were fortunate enough to receive them, and they always came from good families. There is no mention of Lettice's elder sister Mary among the appointments, and the reason for her exclusion remains a mystery.[27] Lettice's place served to highlight her favour with the Queen – and was perhaps more highly regarded than her sister Mary.

The structure of the Queen's ladies hierarchy was a confusing one: as Chief Lady of the Bedchamber, Kate Ashley held the highest post. Beneath her were the four ladies of the bedchamber, followed by twelve ladies, gentlewomen and maids of the privy chamber, and six maids of honour. These more junior members of the Queen's household all came under the supervision of the mother of the maids, whose responsibility it was to keep them in check. Lettice's appointment to such a highly sought-after position ensured that she came into daily contact with the Queen, and helped to attend to all of her needs. These included washing her, dressing her, arranging her hair and jewels, and serving her food. Elizabeth was never alone, and, this being so, her ladies were also expected to be companionable by playing cards, dancing, talking, and reading to her when she requested it.[28] For Lettice to be performing such tasks, the

Queen must have been fond of her, and she in turn would have considered it an honour to be so close to Elizabeth.

Lettice and her fellow ladies were all expected to dress finely, but in such a way as not to outdo the Queen. Elizabeth was extraordinarily fond of clothes, and her ladies' role was to 'emphasise her peerless beauty and magnificence'.[29] In consequence, they were only ever permitted to wear black or white.

Lettice's position in the Queen's household also meant that she remained close to her mother. Besides Lettice and her sister Elizabeth, two of her uncle Henry Carey's daughters, Lettice's cousins Katherine and Philadelphia Carey, were also made maids of honour. Hence a close-knit family unit surrounded the Queen. One modern historian calculated that throughout the course of Elizabeth's reign, there were 103 members of the Carey family alive, many of whom were at court.[30] This placed the Knollys family in an exceedingly strong position, and one in which the women were of paramount importance. Decorum ensured that the Queen's sex meant that her female attendants were able to obtain closer and more regular access to her than any of her male courtiers. Lettice and her fellow ladies were among the few who were admitted to the Queen's bedchamber – the only space in which, although she was never alone, Elizabeth was granted relative privacy, away from the ever-watchful eyes of her court. This put the Queen's ladies in a powerful position, for their very proximity to the monarch meant that they were perfectly placed to promote the interests of themselves and their families. They were also well placed to ask their royal mistress for favours if the need arose. Indeed, anyone who sought the Queen's favour knew that one of the best ways to obtain it was to enlist the support of one of her ladies, and as such they were the recipients of frequent gifts. Though 'A few days after the Queen's accession she made a speech to the women who were in her service commanding them never to speak to her on business affairs', this did not prevent her from talking to them about such things.[31] Consequently, Lettice and her colleagues would have come to hear many things that others would have longed to. Her very position meant that she was both an integral part of the court, and more crucially, a member of Elizabeth's inner sanctum. She was one of the few that saw the Queen's private, as well as her public, persona.

All of the Queen's ladies dined at the monarch's expense at a table in the Great Chamber that was reserved especially for their use, and they were at the very centre of court life. They were, however, forced to share living quarters, which were often cramped and uncomfortable. Lettice and her family became well acquainted with other noble families, and the court was the perfect place to make new alliances. Blanche Parry, for example, one of the Queen's closest ladies and the keeper of her jewels, became close to both Francis and Katherine Knollys, and later the friendship was cemented by marriage when Blanche's niece, Katherine Vaughan, was married to Lettice's younger brother, Robert.[32] Lettice, too, was fond of Blanche, and would be the recipient of a fine diamond when the latter died in 1590.[33] Friendships aside, the court was never a peaceful, relaxed place to live, for the rivalry between various parties as they vied for the Queen's favour was constant.

As Lettice was Katherine Knollys's daughter, the Queen was naturally inclined to look favourably upon her, and the two shared a great deal in common. Not only did they resemble one another in looks – like Elizabeth, Lettice had the flame-red hair of the Tudors – but they also had a similar temperament. As time would reveal, both could be arrogant and stubborn, but at this point in their lives such traits do not appear to have caused a problem. The description on Lettice's epitaph of her being Elizabeth's 'Darling' suggests that the two shared a good relationship. In a further sign of her favour, in 1564 Lettice was among other women of the court to whom the Queen would make a gift of black velvet to be made into a gown, and there would have been other gifts of a similar nature that have gone unrecorded.[34]

The Queen's favour was an honour, but it came at a high price. Elizabeth was a jealous and demanding mistress who expected to be the foremost priority to those who served her. As such, she did not like the idea of her ladies marrying, and frequently lectured them on the subject. Determined to preserve her own single state, her feelings on matrimony in turn came to impact upon her household. Her godson, Sir John Harington, later related that 'She did oft ask the ladies around her chamber, if they loved to think of marriage? And the wise ones did conceal well their liking thereto; as knowing the Queen's judgement in this matter.'[35] Little wonder, then, that many of her ladies were often too afraid to tell her if they wanted to do so. When, in 1563 for example, the Queen learned of the betrothal of her Chamberlain, Lord Howard, to Lettice's cousin Katherine Carey, she was initially so outraged that she banished them both from court.[36] They were later forgiven, but it was a lesson that would surely have stuck with Lettice: one wonders how many of the Queen's lectures on marriage she was exposed to while in her service. Elizabeth did, though, give her ladies permission to marry if she believed the match to be advantageous to them.

Many ladies also indulged in sex before marriage, often resulting in pregnancy. There are many examples of this throughout the course of Elizabeth's reign, and it was inevitable that the Queen would discover the truth. The result was always the same: Elizabeth was left seething and the guilty couple would be banished from court, and sometimes imprisoned. Very rarely did Elizabeth forgive such importunities, and those who committed them had to be prepared to face the consequences. When a married member of the Queen's ladies became pregnant, she let it be known that it was an inconvenience to her to allow them to be released from her service. She always expected them to return to court immediately after they had given birth, and Katherine Knollys was no exception. It is certainly possible that this may explain the gaps between the births of Katherine's daughter and namesake, born on 21 October 1559, and Dudley in 1562. The Queen hated to be parted from her, and although Katherine presumably left court in order to give birth to Katherine, Dudley and the unnamed daughter in 1563, it was not long before she was back. By this time, she and her husband had been granted the lease of Syon House in Middlesex – the former abbey in which Katherine's brother had spent part of his childhood.[37] Syon was closer to court than Greys, and it seems that the Knollyses chose to install their younger children here while they fulfilled their royal duties. Although this ensured that they were nearer, it did not make the separation any easier.

Elizabeth's constant demand for Katherine's presence put a huge strain on the Knollys's family life, and meant that Katherine did not have the time she craved – and had once enjoyed – to devote to her family. Although Lettice and her sister Elizabeth saw their mother on a daily basis as part of the course of their everyday duties to the Queen, the same could not be said for the rest of the Knollys family. It was this that later caused Lettice's father to lament to his wife that 'happy were we, if we were disgraced, I from my trust and you from your love, that we might retire us by just occasion to lead a country poor life abased from our courtly countenance: whereunto I thank God I am ready to prepare myself for my part if you shall like thereof'.[38]

Fond of Katherine though she may have been, this did not prevent Elizabeth from lashing out at her during one of her frequent temper tantrums. Sir Francis later reminded his wife that 'for the outward love that her Majesty bears you, she makes you often weep for unkindness to the great danger of your health'.[39] Lettice would have likely witnessed these displays, and may also have been a victim of Elizabeth's tongue. Neither was it just Lettice's mother who was burdened by the Queen's demands. Her father was also kept exceedingly busy, and was regularly sent both abroad and across the country on royal business. Though he claimed that 'I am proud to live in the court', Francis also later told his wife that 'I can humble myself without shame to abase my countenance as low as my living, and to imprint in my children an example thereof to keep them from the gallows and all worldly shames.'[40]

IT WAS FOLLOWING the advice of the renowned astrologer John Dee that, on 15 January 1559, Elizabeth was 'with great solemnity crowned' in a ceremony of the utmost splendour in Westminster Abbey, 'most renowned for the Inauguration of the Kings of England'.[41] All of the peers of the realm were there to witness it, including the Queen's family, who revelled in her glory. The day prior to the coronation, the Queen had processed through the city with 'Royal Pomp' in order to be seen by her people, who cheered rapturously as she passed.[42] The citizens had spared no expense in preparing a whole host of lavish entertainments for the delight of their monarch, in order to 'express their love and joy' for her.[43] Elizabeth had the common touch in the same way that her father had done, and took the time to gracefully acknowledge their appreciation. For coronation day the Knollys family were present in full force, and Lettice, her sister Elizabeth and their cousin Katherine Carey were among the ladies who were granted coronation livery. For Lettice this consisted of beautiful crimson satin and gold tinsel, which complemented her red hair perfectly.[44] Lettice was among the procession accompanying Elizabeth that included 'a notable train of goodly and beautiful ladies, richly appointed'.[45] Foxe, who was a great admirer of Elizabeth's, noted that as she entered the city, the Queen was greeted by the people's 'prayers, wishes, welcomings, cries, tender words, and all other signs'.[46] As Elizabeth journeyed from Westminster Hall to the Abbey she walked along a rich blue carpet. No sooner had the Queen stepped on a piece than eager souvenir seekers began tearing it apart, causing the Duchess of Norfolk, who was walking behind her, to keep tripping in the holes. Elizabeth's popularity was at its peak, and Lettice was there to witness it.

QUEEN ELIZABETH WAS unmarried, and the most eligible bride in Europe. Even before her succession, suitors had vied for her hand, but now she was Queen of England in her own right and an infinitely more attractive prospect. However, not everyone was impressed with her, and in October 1559 the Imperial ambassador, Bishop de Quadra, sniffed that she was 'a spirited and obstinate woman'.[47] Immediately after she became Queen the matter of Elizabeth's marriage intensified, and offers for her hand began to appear. It was not only assumed but also expected that Elizabeth would take a husband. The concept of female rule in England was still a new one – despite the brief queenship of Lady Jane Grey, the only real precedent for a queen regnant had been set by Elizabeth's half-sister, Mary, and even she had had the support of her husband, Philip of Spain. At twenty-five years old at the time of her succession, Elizabeth was still young enough to produce a male heir to succeed her, and in the eyes of her male councillors there was no time to be wasted. Although she was young, the fragility of life meant that the succession was a constant worry, and bearing an heir was of paramount importance. She was barely able to adjust to her new-found status before her advisors began to pile on the pressure. It was an issue that would be raised time and again throughout the course of her reign, as Elizabeth herself proved to be more than reluctant. Numerous candidates were suggested, including the former husband of her half-sister, Philip, who would later become one of Elizabeth's most dangerous enemies. Philip's nephews, the Archdukes Ferdinand and Charles, were also put forward, as was Prince Eric of Sweden.[48] Elizabeth refused, though, to commit herself. Her behaviour was extraordinary, and few of her councillors truly believed that she intended to remain single. Moreover, it was not just her male advisors, but also her female attendants who attempted to persuade her to the contrary. Kate Ashley was particularly eager to see her royal mistress joined in matrimony. But Elizabeth had already learned some important lessons about royal marriage during her childhood, chiefly that it was laden with danger and uncertainty. These experiences had left her with scars that would never fade. Her reasons for wishing to remain single were more than just personal, though. In the sixteenth century, wives – even those of royal standing – were still expected to be subservient to their husbands, an idea that on a political level Elizabeth abhorred. The example of her half-sister Mary, who, although a queen regnant, had shared much of the burden of government with her husband, loomed before her; Elizabeth was of stronger character than Mary, and was determined not to share her power in the same way. She was resolved on being the sole mistress of her realm.

In the first Parliament of her reign in February 1559, at which Sir Francis Knollys was present, the Commons had drafted a petition in which they begged the Queen to marry. They were anxious for her to do so as soon as possible in order that she might produce an heir to safeguard the succession. Elizabeth, however, had other ideas. She made her feelings on the matter of her marriage very clear, and, in Camden's words, she addressed those present thus: 'to satisfy you, I have already joined myself in marriage to an husband, namely, the Kingdom of England. And behold the pledge of this my wedlock and marriage with my kingdom.'[49] At that she took her coronation ring from her finger in an indication that this was indeed her marriage ring. Everyone was astonished, and more so when she added, 'And, in the end, this shall be for me sufficient, that a marble stone shall declare that a queen, having reigned such a time, lived and died a virgin.'[50] It was a claim that few believed, and the matter of the Queen's marriage continued to be a hot topic of conversation. While the Queen remained unmarried the question of her heir and who would succeed her would be one that led to both speculation and strife: Elizabeth refused to name anyone. It was widely believed that her cousin Lady Katherine Grey, sister of the executed Jane, would be named as her heir, and Katherine also seems to have harboured hopes in this quarter. In March, the Spanish ambassador Count de Feria recalled a conversation he had had with Katherine:

lady Katherine, who is a friend of mine and speaks confidentially to me, told me that the Queen does not wish her to succeed, in case of her (the Queen's) death without heirs. She is dissatisfied and offended at this, and at the Queen's only making her one of the ladies of the presence, whereas she was in the privy-chamber of the late Queen, who showed her much favour. The present Queen probably bears her no goodwill.[51]

Given the fate of her elder sister, Katherine's behaviour was unwise. It is little wonder, therefore, that Elizabeth disliked her. Even so, her refusal to name an heir placed Elizabeth under great pressure to marry and produce a child of her own. Moreover, despite her hardened declaration to Parliament of her intention to remain married to her country, as the course of her reign progressed Elizabeth's attitude to marriage wavered on more than one occasion as potential suitors presented themselves.

Following the coronation, as Elizabeth tried to find her feet and adjust to life as Queen of England, so too did Lettice begin to settle into life at the royal court. Elizabeth was a popular queen, who was at the very centre of court life. She not only needed, but also expected to be admired and revered by all of those around her – particularly the men, with whom she would frequently flirt. In spite of her desire to remain single, Elizabeth enjoyed the company of men and had a naturally flirtatious nature. This never, though, went beyond the bounds of decorum, and was all conducted according to the practice of courtly love. The Queen was the unobtainable mistress who all men admired and adored, paying court to her even though they knew that to do so would prove fruitless. Elizabeth happily played along, and while she graciously accepted the compliments of her male courtiers, that was as far as it went. It was a display that Lettice would have witnessed on many occasions.

Devotion to the Queen was compulsory, and her courtiers were constantly showering her with gifts and compliments in an attempt to win her favour. In November 1559, a year after her accession, the Venetian ambassador had been told that Elizabeth 'lives a life of magnificence and festivity such as can hardly be imagined, and occupies a great portion of her time with balls, banquets, hunting, and similar amusements with the utmost possible display'.[52] The Queen was particularly fond of dancing, and Lettice was expected to participate in much of this merriment. She was probably among those who took part in 'a double mummery [a form of entertainment involving music and dancing]', whereby 'one set of mummers rifled the Queen's ladies, and the other set, with wooden swords and bucklers, recovered the spoil'.[53] Lettice would also have been exposed to the flirtatious atmosphere of the court, and there were plenty of young men from whom she could receive courtly compliments. Despite such attentions, a woman's virtue was still her most prized possession – the Queen had a strong sense of morality, and neither Lettice nor her watchful father would have allowed any flirtations to develop any further. Similarly, flirtatious behaviour had to be conducted subtly and away from the Queen's eye: it was very much Elizabeth who was the star of the show, and she never let any of those at court forget it.

THE QUEEN TOOK great care of her appearance – she was particularly fond of fine clothes and jewels, and also liked perfume. Throughout the course of her reign the size of the royal wardrobe dramatically increased, as did the number of jewels entering the royal collection. Like Elizabeth, Lettice was striking in looks. She sat for her portrait as many as seven times throughout the course of her life, and some of her likenesses survive, the best of which now hangs in Longleat House. What is remarkable is Lettice's resemblance to the Queen. Her portrait shows an attractive woman with the same red-gold hair inherited by Elizabeth. She has a slim frame with long hands, like Elizabeth's, delicate features, dark eyes and a high forehead. Even allowing for some artistic licence, by most standards Lettice was very attractive. At fifteen, moreover, long before this portrait was painted, she was growing into a beautiful young woman. At court her manners would have become more refined, and her tastes more sophisticated; her charm and her personality were developing. She was also approaching marriageable age, and it was little wonder that, like the Queen, she drew admiration from many of those who saw her. Although neither of Lettice's elder siblings, Henry and Mary, were yet married, it is probable that their parents had begun to give some thought to her prospects. Lettice's post in the Queen's household meant that she was well placed to make a good marriage – with her royal mistress's permission – and it was not long before she had caught the eye of a suitor.

WALTER DEVEREUX, VISCOUNT Hereford, was the eldest son of Sir Richard Devereux and his wife, Dorothy, the daughter of George Hastings, Earl of Huntingdon.[54] His portrait shows a handsome man with a brown beard, dressed in armour with his hand proudly placed on his helmet in a demonstration of his military prowess. According to Walter's biographer, Walter Bourchier Devereux, who was writing in 1852, the house from which Walter was descended 'was of high rank in Normandy'.[55] Bourchier Devereux was a descendant of Walter's, and compiled biographies of Walter and several of his direct descendants having consulted a number of primary sources – some of which were contained in private archives. He also collated a large number of letters written by Walter and his heir, which were printed in his first and second volumes of *Lives and Letters of the Devereux Earls of Essex*. The papers show how the Devereux ancestors, part of the Evereux family, had accompanied William the Conqueror on his mission to England in 1066. They had settled in Herefordshire, but as time wore on, the family gradually began to edge their way into Wales.

Walter's grandfather and namesake had been in great favour with both Henry VIII and Edward VI, proving himself to be a man of exceptional ability in both a military and a political capacity.[56] On 2 February 1550, the young King rewarded Walter's grandfather for his loyalty by creating him Viscount Hereford. His appointment was also a grateful acknowledgement of his dutiful support in the coup to topple the King's uncle, the Lord Protector, from power. His involvement in a later coup – that to make Lady Jane Grey queen – sadly landed him in the Tower. On 27 August 1553, he was granted 'the commodity of the garden and gallery', and was later released, retiring to his manor house of Chartley in Staffordshire and leaving public life behind him.[57] His son, Richard, was also well favoured by Edward VI, and was made a Knight of the Bath at the young King's coronation on 20 February 1547.[58] The previous year Richard had acquired the lordship, manor and park of Lamphey in Pembrokeshire in an exchange with the Bishop of St David's, and it was a wise investment. The fourteenth-century Lamphey Palace would become an important Devereux manor, and the family began to firmly establish themselves in Wales.

On 16 September 1539, three years after Richard's marriage to Dorothy Hastings, the couple's eldest son was born at Carmarthen Castle in Wales.[59] He was named Walter after his grandfather, and according to *The Complete Peerage* he was christened at Carmarthen in the church of St Peter's two days after his birth.[60] Carmarthen was a mighty fortress of Norman origin that formed the administrative centre for South Wales. It had been significantly rebuilt in the thirteenth and fifteenth centuries, and was an important stronghold. It was at Carmarthen that, in 1456, Edmund Tudor, father of the first Tudor king Henry VII, died.[61] By the time of Walter's birth, Carmarthen was still very much a medieval castle set in one of the oldest towns in Wales: there could have been no greater contrast to the picturesque country house of Greys Court in which Lettice had been born. Walter was one of four surviving children.[62] Carmarthen, however, was not suitable for raising children, and the Devereux siblings seem to have spent much of their childhoods at Lamphey, in the rolling countryside of Pembrokeshire. It was here that Walter's widowed mother continued to live following the death of his father, Sir Richard Devereux, in 1548, and here that she would remain until her own death in 1566. Richard had died during the lifetime of his father – Walter's grandfather and namesake. Thus, when the older Walter died on 17 September 1558, he was succeeded by his grandson who had turned nineteen the previous day.[63] Walter the elder was laid to rest in Stowe church in Chartley, Staffordshire, where the tomb he shares with both of his wives still survives.[64] With his death, the young Walter succeeded to the titles of Viscount Hereford, Lord Ferrers of Chartley, Bourchier and Louvaine. Until he reached the age of twenty-one he was still a minor, and was therefore unable to assume responsibility for his finances and estates.

Camden described Walter as 'A very excellent man' in whom 'honesty of manners strived with nobility of birth', and at nineteen he was in his prime.[65] As a young man with a bright future, the glitz and glamour of the court in London was a far more alluring prospect than a life in distant Wales. Following the accession of Elizabeth I, in the same manner as many other young men, Walter began to spend much of his time at the new Queen's court. He spent lavishly on clothes during this period; his tailor's bill reveals that between October 1559 and May 1561 over £150 (£25,500) was laid out on finery, ensuring that he had all of the fashionable garments that were essential in order to make a good impression.[66]

It was while he was at court that Walter first encountered Lettice Knollys, who was growing into a woman possessed of charm and character. The court was full of beautiful and eligible young ladies, but Lettice clearly stood out. The two may have begun by exchanging nothing more than polite pleasantries, but Bourchier Devereux describes how Walter 'soon became captive to the charms of Lettice Knollys, a fair maiden of the court, celebrated for her beauty and spirit'.[67] We have no information about the couple's courtship; we do not know when it started or how it was conducted, but what is clear is that Walter fell in love with Lettice, and she in turn fell in love with him.[68]

In September 1560, Walter reached his majority, and as a result was able to come into his full inheritance; in material terms this meant that he was granted an annuity of £200 (£34,000). Now in a position where he was able to support a wife financially, Walter set his sights firmly on Lettice, just shy of her seventeenth birthday. They were both young, and were both from families who were keen advocates of Protestantism. It was a good match on both sides; Walter's old and noble lineage combined with the favour Lettice's family held with the Queen meant that they were well suited. In many respects they also shared similar personality traits, both Walter and Lettice would later become known for their fiery tempers.

The Queen made no secret of the fact that she preferred her ladies to remain single, so the subject of Lettice's marriage must have been approached tentatively. It was presumably a match that met with the approval of Lettice's parents, and it may have been one of them who broached the matter with the Queen. In this case, though, there is no suggestion that the marriage of Lettice and Walter was met with anything other than her approval – there is certainly no evidence that she voiced any objections, so, presumably, she viewed it as significantly advantageous for Lettice. Consequently, plans for the couple's wedding were able to proceed.

No details of Lettice and Walter's wedding survive, and even the date is unknown. Various possibilities have been suggested, from late 1560, after Walter attained his majority, to the first few months of 1562 at the very latest.[69] A date in 1561 seems to be plausible, given that that same year Lettice's salary ceased, indicating that she had left the Queen's service. The wedding is likely to have taken place in London, and it is certainly possible that, given her familial relationship to the Queen and her presence in the Royal Household, the Queen may have attended the wedding.[70]

Lettice was the first of her siblings to marry, and, to all appearances, her marriage was based at least as much on personal feelings as on policy. What is certain is that Lettice had made a very respectable match. More than that, at sixteen years old she was also Viscountess Hereford. Her looks, charm and family connections had secured her a husband, but Walter Devereux had not been the only one who had noticed her. Indeed, while at court there was another man with whom Lettice became acquainted – one who would transform the course of her life: his name was Robert Dudley.

CHAPTER 4

The Goodliest Male Personage in England

THE CHARISMATIC AND attractive Robert Dudley, described by a contemporary as 'the goodliest male personage in England', was Queen Elizabeth's favourite.[1] What was more, everyone at court, as well as the rest of the country and abroad, knew it too. In the sixteenth century, the idea of a favourite was by no means new. In a world in which rules of etiquette and deference dictated the way in which people behaved towards their sovereign, monarchs encouraged different forms of relationships. Favourites were those individuals closest to the monarch, who entertained them, were loyal to them, and perhaps offered the most intimate personal connection outside of their family. They also attracted gossip and jealousy. Of all of Elizabeth's favourites, it is Dudley who has gained the most fame and notoriety, and Dudley who came the closest to wooing the 'Virgin Queen'.

Born on 24 June, probably in 1532, Robert was the son of John Dudley, Duke of Northumberland, and Jane Guildford.[2] The Dudley family had first come to prominence through the machinations of Robert's grandfather, Edmund. Edmund had been an able financial administrator to Henry VII, and throughout the course of his royal service he had amassed great wealth for himself. He was vastly unpopular, and at the onset of Henry VIII's reign he was imprisoned and executed on a charge of treason on 17 August 1510. Edmund's son John, Robert's father, was highly ambitious, and was determined to claw back the Dudley family honour. Henry VIII did not hold a grudge, and John's influence steadily increased throughout the King's reign. He distinguished himself as a soldier, and was knighted by the Duke of Suffolk at the age of nineteen during the French expedition of 1523. John's star continued to rise under Henry VIII, and in 1544 he joined the King's invasion force for the siege of Boulogne. Three years later, he was also among the ranks of the Lord Protector when he headed the invasion of Scotland in 1547.

Having achieved glory in a military capacity, John turned his attentions to the political arena. Forgetting any former loyalty he once had to the Lord Protector, John instigated his overthrow in 1549, and established himself firmly in his place. It was under the young King that John rose to the height of his influence, and he was created Duke of Northumberland in 1551: he was now the most powerful man in the kingdom.

John had married Jane Guildford, the daughter of his former guardian Sir Henry Guildford, in whose house he had been raised. It was a genuine love match, and together the couple would have thirteen children. The third of five surviving sons, Robert may have been born in London, perhaps in the fourteenth-century Ely Place in Holborn (once the home of the bishops of Ely) that was his father's main residence in the capital.[3] Though he was interested in learning, John Dudley was a soldier rather than a scholar, and it was his wife who garnered a reputation as a great intellect. However, both she and John perceived the importance of knowledge, and had determined to ensure that all of their children were well educated. The family were a close one, and would remain so for the entirety of their lives.

As well as Ely Place, John Dudley also owned estates in the southeast, particularly in Kent, but as time went on, his power base began to shift increasingly to the Midlands. Dudley Castle, situated in between Birmingham and Wolverhampton, was his main stronghold, but in 1547 he had also been granted the former royal fortress of Warwick Castle.[4] Warwick was described by the Tudor traveller John Leland as 'magnificent and strong', and would have been well known to Robert, who took a great interest in the town.[5] John Dudley's tactic of building up his base in the Midlands would be a pattern that was later followed by Robert and his elder brother, Ambrose.

Robert's education would stand him in good stead, and for the rest of his life he would be celebrated for his scholarly interests – in 1564 he was even appointed Chancellor of Oxford University. He was good at languages and understood both Latin and Italian, and probably also French. He also enjoyed maths and science, and had a lifelong interest in navigation; he and his brother Ambrose would later be the main backers for one of Sir Martin Frobisher's expeditions to locate the Northwest Passage, and Robert also supported and took a great interest in the career of the privateer Sir Francis Drake.[6] The great John Dee, the same astrologer who had suggested the date of Queen Elizabeth's coronation, may have influenced his interest in this area. Dee had spent some time acting as tutor to Robert's eldest brother, John, and so it is reasonable to suppose that he also had some contact with Robert. The seventeenth-century antiquary Anthony Wood would later claim that nobody knew Robert better than Dee.[7]

In years to come, Robert would be regarded as an important and influential patron of many scholars and artists. Throughout his life more than a hundred books would be dedicated to him – more than to any other courtier.[8] Notably, the chroniclers John Stow and Richard Grafton would both dedicate their work to him. He was a great collector who was fond of art, amassing a huge collection of paintings by the time of his death. He also commissioned numerous portraits of himself, and sat for various artists at least twenty times.[9] Many of these likenesses still survive, bearing testament to Robert's prepossessing appearance – his portrait appears more in contemporary collections than that of anyone else, with the exception of Elizabeth I.[10] He was dark in looks, earning him the nickname 'The Gypsy' from his enemy the Earl of Sussex, and he was undeniably handsome.[11] At a little under six feet he was tall by contemporary standards, with a slender and athletic build.

Even Camden, who was hostile to him, described him as being 'a man of a flourishing age, and comely feature of body and limbs'.[12] He had a long nose and grew a beard in accordance with the latest trends, and was always dressed in the latest fashions. An inventory of his wardrobe taken just months before he died reveals that he owned numerous costly garments, including cloaks, nightgowns and doublets. His surviving accounts, meanwhile, reveal regular payments for items of clothing such as gloves from Spain.[13]

Robert also enjoyed more energetic pursuits, for he was remarkably athletic and a keen sportsman. He was interested in dogs, and made regular payments to his spaniel keepers for their upkeep; on one occasion compensation had to be made to the owner of 'a hen which the spaniel killed'.[14] He was also an expert horseman and a talented jouster, and would regularly take part in tournaments. Edward VI once recorded in his journal that Robert and seventeen others, including his brother Ambrose and a 'Mr Knollys', who may have been Lettice's father or uncle, Henry, 'ran six courses each at tilt against the challengers and accomplished their course right well'.[15]

Robert was also a committed Protestant. In the years to come he would demonstrate his enthusiasm for his faith on many occasions, earning him a reputation as a religious radical. Like Sir Francis Knollys, his beliefs were considered to be Puritanical, and his accounts show that he paid preachers to preach for him on many occasions. This did not, however, prevent him from employing Catholics in his household. The Blounts, a noble and traditionally Catholic family, were just one example, and one of its members would later come to be closely linked with Lettice's story.

On 4 June 1550, Robert had married Amy Robsart, the daughter of a Norfolk landowner, Sir John Robsart. The two had probably met the previous year, when Robert had accompanied his father into Norfolk in order to suppress Kett's Rebellion, an armed protest against land enclosure.[16] It was a love match, and although a more advantageous match could most certainly have been made for Robert, his parents were indulgent and, already having a brilliant marriage lined up for their eldest surviving son, John, gave their consent. Their second son, Ambrose, was already married, to Anne Whorwood, the daughter of Sir William Whorwood of Staffordshire.[17] The Dudleys were also aware that, as Amy was her father's heir, Robert would eventually inherit substantial lands in Norfolk, and for that reason may have deemed the marriage a wise investment for their son's future. Significantly, though, after Amy's death Cecil would observe that 'carnal marriages begin in joy and end in weeping'.[18]

The day before Robert and Amy's wedding, Robert's eldest brother John was married to Anne Seymour, the eldest daughter of the toppled Lord Protector.[19] It was a lavish ceremony at Richmond Palace (sometimes referred to as the Palace of Sheen), and was attended by the King.[20] The following day Robert and Amy were also married at Richmond Palace, and the King made a note in his journal of the gruesome entertainment that was provided after the wedding ceremony: 'certain gentlemen tried to see who could be the first to take away a goose's head which was hanged alive on two crossed posts'.[21] Robert's father was unfortunately unable to attend, for he had fallen ill. In spite of that, he must have been pleased to know that the marital prospects of two of his sons were now settled. Little is known of Robert and Amy's life together – there is no evidence to suggest that they were anything other than happy – but the time that they were able to spend with one another was limited. Robert's frequent absences at court meant that they were often separated, and as the events of 1553 began to spiral out of control, that looked unlikely to change.

It was with Northumberland's connivance that, when Edward VI fell fatally ill in 1553, he drew up his famous will 'My Devise for the Succession'. This was to have serious consequences for the Dudley family, including Robert. On 25 May, Robert's younger brother, Guildford, was married to Lady Jane Grey, binding the two families together. Jane's bridegroom may have been Robert, had he himself not been already married by this time. When the King died and Northumberland began making moves to establish his daughter-in-law, Lady Jane Grey, as queen, he was embarking on a dangerous plot in which Robert and his brothers were to become hopelessly entangled. The Dudleys were a close-knit family who always stuck together, and there was no question of Robert doing anything other than supporting his sister-in-law's claim. With this in mind, his father had entrusted him with an important task, and on 7 July he had been sent at the head of a force to apprehend the Lady Mary. Mary had fled to East Anglia, and it was there that Robert journeyed, determined to achieve his mission. He made it to East Anglia, but did not succeed in capturing Mary. He was still there when Mary was proclaimed Queen on 19 July, a situation that spelled disaster for the Dudleys.[22]

Robert's father and three of his four brothers, John, Ambrose and Harry, were captured in Cambridge, where they had travelled in order to support Robert's mission. They were returned to London and imprisonment in the Tower, where Jane and Guildford were already incarcerated. Robert, meanwhile, was apprehended in King's Lynn, and taken to join his father and his brothers in the Tower, arriving on 26 July. These were dark days for the Dudleys, for they had all committed treason, and the penalty for treason was death. Uncertainty loomed over Robert, but it seemed that only his father would suffer for his crimes. While Northumberland was executed, Robert and his brothers remained imprisoned.

Thus far, Queen Mary had been merciful towards Lady Jane Grey and the Dudley brothers, but she did concede that justice needed to appear to have been done. On 13 November, Robert's brothers Ambrose, Guildford, Harry and his sister-in-law, Jane, were forced to stand trial at London's Guildhall.[23] They were all found guilty of treason, and condemned to death. Robert, meanwhile, remained in the Tower, his trial delayed. The reason for this was that, unlike his father and his brothers, Robert had been sent to East Anglia immediately upon the death of Edward VI. Therefore the majority of his treason had been committed outside of London. Because of this it was believed that he fell under jurisdiction outside of London, and as such, further preparations were required before he could be tried in the capital.

On 18 December, Rowland Lea, the probable author of *The Chronicle of Queen Jane*, a contemporary eyewitness account of events, reported that 'Lord Robert and Lord Guildford' were given 'the liberty of the leads in the Bell Tower' where they were allowed to take their exercise on the roof.[24] By this time, Robert was the only one of the brothers who had not been condemned, but his time was fast approaching. It was not until Tuesday 22 January 1554 that he was 'brought out of the Tower to the Guildhall', a mile from his prison.[25] There he was 'arraigned and condemned' in the same manner as his brothers, and 'after his arraignment he confessed his treason'.[26] As such, his sentence was the prescribed death for a traitor: 'to be drawn, hanged, and quartered'.[27]

Robert's sentence looked to be nothing more than a formality, for Queen Mary made no further move against him. Like his brothers before him, he returned to the Tower, where he resumed his imprisonment alongside them. For his younger brother Guildford and Lady Jane Grey, however, their sentence was about to transpire into a devastating reality. Following the involvement of Jane's father in the Wyatt Rebellion, both were executed on 12 February, just a matter of weeks after Robert's condemnation. In only a few months, Robert had lost both his father and his younger brother to the executioner's axe: it was a crushing loss. Yet he was still alive, and Queen Mary made no further move to punish Robert or his three surviving brothers, John, Ambrose and Harry: for the time being, their lives appeared to be safe. Their lives, though, were all they had, for the brothers had lost everything and their family was in ruins.

Robert languished in the Tower for more than a year, during which time his mother, desperate to piece back together her fragmented family, had been 'doing her utmost to secure a pardon for her children'.[28] Her pleas had been ignored. Robert's signature can still be seen scratched into a wall of the Beauchamp Tower, a lasting reminder of the darkest period of his life. Similarly, the crest of the Dudley family with carved representations of Robert and his brothers also survives.[29] Robert was granted the privilege of visits from his wife, Amy, but this was one of his few comforts. The harrowing experience of imprisonment served as a further link to cement the bonds of friendship between Robert and Elizabeth, who arrived in the Tower as a prisoner less than a month after Lady Jane Grey and Guildford Dudley's execution. There is nothing to suggest, though, that they ever met during their time in the Tower, and it is rather unlikely that they did so. It is possible that they caught glimpses of one another, perhaps on the occasions when they were allowed to exercise outdoors, but this is probably as far as it went.

Once Lady Jane Grey and Robert's brother Guildford were dead, the threat that the remaining brothers were perceived to pose had been neutralized. As a result, it soon became clear that it was only a matter of time before they would be released. Through the clemency of Queen Mary and the persistent appeals of their mother, the surviving brothers, John, Ambrose, Robert and Harry, were eventually set at liberty on 18 October 1554. Robert was a free man, but his release was marred by yet more tragedy. Just three days after obtaining his freedom, his eldest brother John died at his sister Mary's home, Penshurst Place, in Kent.[30] The cause of his death is unknown, but it came as a bitter blow to the already-broken family. To add to the family's grief, as the new year of 1555 began, Robert's mother Jane also died.[31] It was now down to Robert to pick up the pieces.

ROBERT HAD SURVIVED the ordeal of imprisonment, and had endured all of the heartache that had been thrown at him. Though he was only twenty-two it would have been easy for him to fade into the background, passing away the rest of his days in peaceful obscurity. But Robert did no such thing. Rather than disappearing into the shadows, he and his two remaining brothers, Ambrose and Harry, were determined to claw back the Dudley family honour. Given the disgrace of their father and their own condemnations for treason, this was no easy task; despite everything, though, it was one that they managed to achieve. On 22 January 1555, Queen Mary pardoned the brothers, although they remained convicted traitors. In addition, they were gradually restored to royal favour, and began to build up the family fortunes once more. In September, almost a year after Robert's release from the Tower, Queen Mary's Spanish husband Philip left England and returned to the Continent. There has been speculation that Robert was a part of Philip's entourage, but there is no evidence for this. What is clear is that when Philip, now King of Spain, returned to England in the spring of 1557 in order to convince his wife to lend English support to Spain's war against France, Robert became attached to the King's party.[32] In July, he and his brothers, Ambrose and Harry, joined Philip in France as a part of his military campaign, where Robert was appointed to the prestigious position of Master of the Ordnance. The following month they were all together at the Battle of St Quentin in Picardy, when devastation fell upon the family once more. Before Robert's own eyes his youngest brother Harry, who was probably no more than twenty years old, was hit by a cannonball, and killed instantly.[33] Now just four of the original thirteen Dudley siblings survived: Robert, Ambrose and two sisters. Mary was married to Sir Henry Sidney, and Katherine had been wed to Henry Hastings, third Earl of Huntingdon, in the same ceremony that had witnessed the doomed wedding of their brother Guildford to Lady Jane Grey.[34] When Robert and Ambrose returned to England, it may have been some small comfort to them that, on 7 March 1558, they and their two sisters were 'restored in blood' by Parliament. Besides that, Robert's attainder was lifted: he was no longer a convicted traitor, and better days lay ahead.

THE ORIGINS OF Robert Dudley's relationship with Elizabeth are uncertain, but he later alluded to having known Elizabeth since she was eight years old. At this time, Elizabeth's father was married to Katherine Howard, who would be executed for adultery in 1542, and Robert's father was riding high at court. There has been some suggestion that he was part of the household of Prince Edward, Elizabeth's half-brother, but there is no evidence to support this. Given his father's presence at court, it may well be, perhaps, that Robert had seen Elizabeth there. They were also both pupils of the celebrated scholar Roger Ascham at one time, giving them another common link, although it is highly unlikely that they shared any of their lessons.[35] They had further contact during the reign of Edward VI, when Robert was a regular presence at court and Elizabeth often visited her half-brother. It may have been this period in Elizabeth's life that an English visitor was referring to when, in August 1562, the King of Sweden asked him why Robert was in such great favour with the Queen. The reply he received was that Robert 'had served the Queen when she was but Lady Elizabeth, and in her trouble did sell away a good piece of his land to aid her, which divers supposed to be the cause that the Queen so favoured him'.[36] If this was indeed the case then Robert had long since proven himself to be a good friend to Elizabeth. However they came to meet, the two struck up a friendship that would be central to both of their lives for many years. Indeed, Elizabeth's relationship with Robert was the most personally significant in her whole life, particularly on a romantic level. Robert's family had endured a turbulent past that was streaked with treason, but Elizabeth never held this against him. In reference to his father's plot to place Lady Jane Grey on the throne and remove both Mary and Elizabeth, Camden related that she 'heaped honours upon him, saving his life, whose father would have had her destroyed'.[37] In return Robert would, in most ways at least, remain utterly loyal to her for the rest of his life.

It seems unlikely that Robert had much contact with Elizabeth during the five years of Queen Mary's reign, but she certainly did not forget him. Immediately after her accession, he was appointed the Queen's Master of the Horse at her first meeting of the Privy Council at Hatfield. It was a prestigious post, and one that provided Robert with a regular salary, and a set of apartments at court. He also had four horses and his own servants, and the honours did not end there. On 23 April 1559, months after Elizabeth succeeded, she created him a Knight of the Garter, a great honour. That same year he was granted many lands, including a house at Kew, and on 24 November he was appointed Lieutenant of Windsor Castle and the park. Such posts ensured that he was well provided for, and now had a stream of steady income with which to maintain himself. Robert was not the only member of his family who was in receipt of the Queen's favour: Ambrose was made Master of the Ordnance, and their sister Mary was made a gentlewoman of the privy chamber. Mary was a great favourite of the Queen's, and her post would have placed her in daily contact with Lettice, her mother and her sister. The women would have come to know one another well.

From the very beginning of Elizabeth's reign the Dudleys were to be at the forefront of court life. Robert and Ambrose were the only surviving Dudley brothers, and their bond with the monarch was one that would never be broken. Although Ambrose, 'an excellent good man', was also close to the Queen, he never shared the same intimacy with her as his brother.[38] Similarly, although Ambrose was the eldest brother, Robert was the strongest character, and it was he who assumed the role of head of the family. Interestingly, this did not lead to tension between the two; rather, the opposite was true. Robert's accounts reveal that the brothers often dined together, and probably spent a great deal of time together besides.[39] Ambrose idolized Robert, often referring to him in letters as 'my loving brother', and Robert in turn worked to promote both of their interests.[40] Robert was also on good terms with Lettice's family, particularly her father. The two had known each other since the reign of Edward VI, and there are repeated references to the Knollys family in Robert's accounts.[41] He would later take Lettice's younger brother Francis into his service, and had continual contact with several of her other brothers besides.

⁘

ROBERT DUDLEY'S RELATIONSHIP with Elizabeth I was, in its time, as it is now, a cause of fascination. Their positions as monarch and favourite make it all the more complex when trying to unravel the threads that bound them together: although there is a great deal of contemporary evidence, the precise nature of what passed between them has continued to divide modern historians. They were undoubtedly physically attracted to one another, and often behaved more like lovers than monarch and subject, much to the shock of many of their contemporaries. Count de Feria was not alone when, in 1559, he relayed the court gossip that 'they say she is in love with Lord Robert and never lets him leave her'.[42] But it was not purely one-sided, for on Robert's side, too – though in 1559 he was a married man – there were genuine feelings for Elizabeth. Although many contemporaries were of the belief that Robert professed his love to her only in an attempt to promote his own interests, this was not so. They wrote to one another regularly, and his letters to her were written with heartfelt warmth. He often showed great concern for her welfare, and he was wholeheartedly loyal to Elizabeth. On one occasion, he wrote to 'confess how much I am tied to you by innumberable benefits' of which he was 'ashamed that I have deserved so little'. In return, though, 'I offer you a most faithful and loyal heart. God grant me no longer breath than it be most unspotted to you.'[43]

Using her ladies – Lettice may have been one – as intermediaries, Elizabeth continuously risked her reputation on Robert's behalf, visiting him in his chambers. This caused a great scandal, and throughout the course of her reign, tales emerged of Elizabeth and Robert having children together – one gentleman, known as Arthur Dudley, even claimed to be the couple's love child.[44] It was a claim that had no basis in fact, but in spite of this there is no doubt that Elizabeth and Robert's behaviour crossed the line of propriety. In 1559, Kate Ashley was so concerned for her mistress's reputation that she begged Elizabeth to marry and put an end to all of the rumours that were circulating. Though shaken by Kate's bold words, Elizabeth could not bear to be parted from Robert. It is highly unlikely, though, that they ever had a relationship in the full physical sense – despite her flirtatious nature, it has been suggested that the Queen had a fear of sexual intercourse, or that she had some medical condition that prevented her from indulging. Whatever the truth of the matter and however strong her feelings for Robert were, Elizabeth was too shrewd and politically astute to allow herself to get carried away by passion. Additionally, the issues of privacy and the constant presence of her ladies meant that she would have been unable to conduct a sexual relationship without anyone finding out. Even the spies of the hostile Bishop de Quadra could find no evidence of any such intimacies between the Queen and her favourite. Yet more compelling is Elizabeth's declaration when she lay dangerously ill with smallpox in 1562. Fearing that she might die, she swore that nothing improper had passed between herself and Robert. Afraid of death and thus looking towards the clearing of her conscience, there is every reason to believe that she spoke the truth. As such, Elizabeth's claim to be 'the Virgin Queen' is probably still justified.

The amount of time Elizabeth and Robert spent together was a testament to their mutual feelings for one another. Not only did Robert's duties as Master of the Horse bring him into daily contact with the Queen, but they also hunted, rode and danced together often. They shared jokes – Robert was among the few who were able to tease Elizabeth without causing offence, and in turn she affectionately nicknamed him her 'Eyes'; in his letters he often alluded to this when he signed himself ō ō. His intelligence also made him attractive, and he was able to engage the Queen in intellectual conversations on a number of topics – frequently talking with her for hours. Despite his marital status, Robert was utterly devoted to the Queen. He spent lavishly and freely on her, and often presented her with beautiful gifts. At New Year 1559, for example, he gave her 'a fair chain set with pearl', receiving a gilt bowl in return.[45] This was more than simply an attempt to win her favour – he genuinely cared for Elizabeth, and many of his gifts left him seriously out of pocket.

Given the Queen's feelings for him and as her favourite, Robert naturally attracted enemies and earned the jealousy and animosity of many of those at court. This worked both ways, and he in turn was equally jealous of those whom he felt had supplanted him in the Queen's affections. Though he was all courtesy to Elizabeth, he was good at making enemies. From the outset he and William Cecil were natural adversaries, constantly vying for power. In March 1559, the Imperial ambassador Count de Feria described Cecil as 'very clever but a mischievous man and a heretic', who governed the Queen.[46] Though she did not always take his advice, she relied on him heavily in matters of politics, and it was this that formed the basis of their relationship. It was therefore very different from the one that she shared with Robert: theirs was more pleasure than business, although Robert harboured strong opinions when it came to politics. Despite their differences, the two men did manage to maintain a working relationship. The Earl of Sussex also despised Robert, and the two men were often at loggerheads over matters of state. Equally, Bishop de Quadra held him in no high regard, describing him in scathing terms as 'the worst and most procrastinating young man I ever saw in my life, and not at all courageous or spirited'. To emphasize his point, he added that: 'Not a man in England but cries out at the top of his voice that this fellow is ruining the country with his vanity.'[47] De Quadra acknowledged, though, that 'the Duke of Norfolk was the chief of Lord Robert's enemies', and that the Duke had told him that if 'Lord Robert did not abandon his present pretensions and presumption he would not die in his bed. I think this hatred of Lord Robert will continue, as the Duke and the rest of them cannot put up with his being King.'[48] Norfolk was the Queen's second cousin, and his feelings reflected those of many at court, who were worried that the Queen and Robert would find some way of marrying in spite of Robert's wife. It was widely feared that the Queen was throwing away the prospects of making a good marriage because of Robert, and that her reputation would be permanently tarnished. In turn, Robert was against the idea of the Queen marrying because he feared that his own influence would wane, and he defiantly told the Duke of Norfolk that 'he was neither a good Englishman nor a loyal subject who advised the Queen to marry a foreigner'.[49]

The Queen was aware that Robert had enemies and did her best to protect him. He was completely dependent on her favour, and it was essential that he should keep it – without it he was vulnerable. He was fortunate that he also had the support of his sister, Lady Mary Sidney. The supremacy of a female monarch ensured that it was not just men who had the Queen's ear, but women too, and through her position in the Queen's household, Lady Sidney was able to exert her influence and keep her ears to the ground to Robert's advantage. So devoted to the Queen was Lady Sidney that when Elizabeth fell dangerously ill with smallpox in 1562, she nursed her through her illness. Although the Queen recovered, Lady Sidney's care for her was to come at a great personal cost. She herself contracted the sickness, and though she also survived she was left scarred for life. Her husband lamented sadly that 'I left her a full fair lady, in mine eyes at least the fairest, and when I returned I found her as foul a lady as the smallpox could make her', forcing her to retire into a life away from court.[50]

AS A MARRIED man, Robert's relationship with Elizabeth naturally attracted speculation and quickly drew comment, and as early as February or March 1559, rumours about their relationship began to circulate. By April 1559, the Spanish Count de Feria was writing disapprovingly to his royal master that

> *During the last few days Lord Robert has come so much into favour that he does whatever he likes with affairs and it is even said that her Majesty visits him in his chamber day and night. People talk of this so freely that they go so far as to say that his wife has a malady in one of her breasts and the Queen is only waiting for her to die to marry Lord Robert. I can assure your Majesty that matters have reached such a pass that I have been brought to consider whether it would not be well to approach Lord Robert on your Majesty's behalf, promising him your help and favour and coming to terms with him.[51]*

Much of this was malicious gossip, although the question of Amy's illness would later arise. The Queen was well aware of Amy's existence but she was never invited to court, and resided primarily in the country. For Elizabeth, her relationship with Robert allowed her to have the best of both worlds. Robert's marriage meant that he was unable to present himself to her as a suitor, thereby allowing Elizabeth to maintain her image as the Virgin Queen while still being able to flirt with and revel in his company. Since Elizabeth's accession Robert's presence was almost permanently required at court, and although the Queen knew that he was married, given his favour it was more politic for Amy to be kept away. Elizabeth was the shining star of her court, and demanded the full attention of her male courtiers – married or not. Robert was more than happy to comply.

Though Robert was largely occupied with affairs at court, he did not completely forget about Amy. He continued to send her letters and gifts, and she in turn busied herself with buying costly new clothes to add to her wardrobe of beautiful garments. On occasion she did visit London, and on one such visit Robert's accounts show that twelve horses were hired in order to convey her there.[52] Such visits were, though, a rarity. The couple did not have any children, and this has sometimes been interpreted as evidence of an estrangement, but this is not necessarily the case. When rumours about Robert and the Queen surfaced, it was maliciously reported that 'he thinks of divorcing his wife'.[53] Robert, however, never made any attempt to dissolve his marriage, and there is no other suggestion that it was unhappy.

By the summer of 1559, Robert and Elizabeth's relationship was the subject of much gossip, both in England and abroad. It was also widely rumoured that the couple were planning to marry if only Robert could rid himself of his wife. Cecil had already been spreading the word to this effect, for it was through him that Bishop de Quadra had informed the Duchess of Parma that 'Robert was thinking of killing his wife, who was publicly announced to be ill, although she was quite well, and would take very good care they did not poison her.'[54] In the late summer of 1560, de Quadra had heard that Amy was doomed.

———⟨∽⟩———

EARLIER IN THE year, Amy had taken up residence at Cumnor Place in Oxfordshire.[55] It was here that, on 8 September, she was found dead at the bottom of a staircase. She had sustained serious injuries that included a broken neck, and it was widely believed that her death was no accident, but murder. Robert was with the court at Windsor when the news of his wife's death was brought to him. Shocked, he immediately sent his chief household officer, Sir Thomas Blount, to Cumnor to find out what had happened. When the Queen heard the appalling news, she knew that it would have serious consequences for her relationship with Robert. Realizing that it would give their enemies a reason to slander them, she promptly ordered Robert to leave the court for his house at Kew while the matter was investigated. As suspected, Amy's death caused a scandal and blackened Robert's name – in an instant, Elizabeth tried to distance herself from the man with whom she had been spending much of her time. Gossip began to spread that Amy had been murdered on Robert's orders, and on 11 September Bishop de Quadra told the Duchess of Parma that 'Certainly this business is most shameful and scandalous, and withal I am not sure whether she will marry the man at once or even if she will marry at all, as I do not think she has her mind sufficiently fixed.'[56] Lettice may still have been at court at this time, and if so she would have witnessed at first-hand the scandal that Lady Dudley's death had caused, and heard the rumours of Robert's involvement. Did she suspect him, too?

Historians are still divided as to whether Amy's death was a tragic accident or murder. If it were murder, at whose hands was Amy killed? Her death left Robert free to marry again, but was it instigated on somebody else's orders? Cecil also had a motive for wanting Amy dead; he was concerned about Robert's relationship with the Queen, and fearful lest she did eventually consent to be his wife.[57] The nature and intensity of the rumours that spread following Amy's death served to ensure that a huge strain was placed on Robert's relationship with Elizabeth. Vicious gossip spread that Robert had killed his wife in order to marry the Queen, and was so injurious that it permanently damaged his reputation. This could only be to Cecil's advantage, for now any hopes that Robert may have harboured of eventual marriage to the Queen had been dashed – at least in the short term.

On 22 September, Amy's funeral was conducted at St Mary's Church in Oxford. No expense had been spared, although, as was customary for husbands, Robert did not attend.[58] Neither did he make any public display of grief for his wife. His private feelings are unknown, but it seems hard to believe that, whatever the circumstances of her death, he would not have felt some sorrow at the loss of the woman who had been his wife for the past decade.

It is evident that he was anxious to get to the bottom of the cause of Amy's death, and a number of letters between him and Thomas Blount in which they discussed the matter survive. Much to his relief, a verdict of accidental death was returned, clearing Robert of any involvement. Yet still suspicion loomed large over him. Mary, Queen of Scots, is reported to have remarked that 'The Queen of England is going to marry her horse keeper, who has killed his wife to make room for her.' In spite of these rumours, once the verdict was delivered Robert was immediately restored to royal favour and his place by the Queen's side, but any hopes of a royal marriage had been crushed – for the time being at least. Amy's death cast a dark cloud over Robert for the rest of his life, and his enemies never let him forget it. To this day the rumours that he was responsible have persisted, and the truth about what happened at Cumnor will never be fully known.

Following Amy's death, Robert's feelings for Elizabeth and their relationship intensified. When the matter of the mysterious events at Cumnor had died down, he would spend more than a decade attempting to convince Elizabeth to become his wife. Arguably, he came closer to achieving success than any of her other suitors. Though Elizabeth's feelings towards Robert had not changed, she found herself torn and in a quandary over what to do. Ultimately, however, it was the Queen and her head, rather than Elizabeth the woman and her heart, who won the game. She had made her decision, and she would not marry Robert. But he did not give up.

AS THE 1560S got underway, Robert tried to put the scandal of Amy's death behind him. He and his family continued to bask in Elizabeth's favour, and at Christmas 1561 Ambrose was created Earl of Warwick. It was the title that had once been given to their father, and that had belonged to their eldest brother John before his death. In addition, the following year Ambrose was granted Warwick Castle, also a former property of their father's. It was soon after this that he and Robert readopted the bear and ragged staff motif, made famous by the Beauchamp Earls of Warwick in the fifteenth century.[59] Having also had an ongoing family connection with the title of Earl of Warwick, the Dudley family had always proudly associated themselves with this house, and their father had also used it. From now on it would become a central part of their identity, and both Robert and Ambrose proudly displayed it in both their houses and their belongings.

Ambrose's promotion was just the tip of the iceberg. In October 1562 Robert, alongside the Queen's cousin the Duke of Norfolk, was admitted to the Queen's Privy Council. This was a sign of Elizabeth's trust in him, and the value she placed on his abilities in matters of state. But there was more to come. In 1560, François II of France, the husband of Elizabeth's cousin, Mary, Queen of Scots, died from an ear infection. Nine months later, in August 1561, the widowed eighteen-year-old Queen returned to Scotland. Many people considered the young Queen to be Elizabeth's heir, but Elizabeth herself refused to acknowledge Mary as such. However, she advised her cousin that when choosing a second husband, it ought to be someone who was on good terms with England. In March

1563, Elizabeth stunned one of Mary's ministers and those around her when she proposed a suitor for the Scottish Queen: her suggestion was Robert Dudley. If Mary married Dudley, Elizabeth in return would name Mary her heir. She claimed that Dudley was so noble that 'she would have herself married, had she ever minded to take a husband. But being determined to end her life in virginity, she wished that the Queen her sister might marry him'. Elizabeth's proposition caused both shock and amazement, not least to Mary.[60] She regarded it as an insult, for she had heard the rumours about Elizabeth and her favourite. She was also acutely conscious of the fact that Dudley was not of royal blood, rendering him an even more unsuitable match. Elizabeth's answer was to raise her favourite to the peerage, and she further suggested that once he and Mary were married the couple should live at the English court with her – perhaps as a way of keeping Robert close.

Having been granted the former royal castle of Kenilworth, close to Ambrose's castle of Warwick, on 9 June 1563, Robert was granted an earldom in the following year. No longer was he to be known as Lord Robert Dudley, for he was now the Earl of Leicester. It was a triumphant moment, but one that had another meaning. He was strongly opposed to Elizabeth's suggestion that he ought to marry her cousin, and had been astute enough to realize that the idea of the three of them living in England as a kind of *ménage à trois* was ill thought out. True it is that he harboured ambitions of a royal marriage, but not with Mary. He had no wish to leave behind England – or Elizabeth – for Scotland, and it was on Elizabeth that his hopes still rested firmly. Though the Queen had made up her mind, she and Leicester were still close, and he still hoped that she might eventually consent to wed him. To his immense relief, all thoughts of a marriage between him and the Scottish Queen came to nothing. Mary did take an English husband, but it was not one of Elizabeth's choosing. On 29 July 1565 she was married to her cousin Henry Stuart, Lord Darnley, the son of Lady Margaret Lennox, who Elizabeth had given permission to travel to Scotland in February.[61] Elizabeth was outraged, not least because both Mary and Darnley had a claim to the English throne, and married they posed a combined threat. But there was nothing that she could do.

Elizabeth's true intentions in regards to Mary and Leicester have long been a topic of debate. It has been suggested that she deliberately proposed Leicester as a suitor in order to insult Mary; there was probably an element of this, but it is unlikely to be the whole story. Mary, who understood Elizabeth's slight full well, made a show of pretending to consider Leicester's suit. Elizabeth had never expected this, and when confronted with the possibility of losing Leicester she panicked. Had negotiations progressed, it is probable that Elizabeth would ultimately have found the separation from her favourite too much to bear.

Robert Dudley was now Earl of Leicester, yet the ultimate prize of a marriage to Queen Elizabeth – the woman he was devoted to – still evaded him. It would not be long, though, before he aroused her anger, for there were rumours of him sharing a flirtation with another: Lettice.

CHAPTER 5

Flirting with the Viscountess

ETTICE DEVEREUX, THE new Viscountess Hereford, chose the occasion of her marriage to retire from court and the Queen's service for a time. In 1561 she stopped receiving royal wages, and at some point following her marriage she and her husband left London and her family behind.[1] The Queen had presumably – perhaps grudgingly – given her kinswoman permission to leave court, but in her usual way Lettice would have been in no doubt that by so doing she was causing Elizabeth great personal inconvenience. Bourchier Devereux claims that at this time 'her Majesty felt no great partiality' towards Lettice, but there is no evidence of this.[2] Lettice had never been as close to the Queen as her mother was, but that does not mean that Elizabeth was not fond of her – indeed, all contemporary evidence suggests that the contrary was true. After all, Bourchier Devereux was writing in the nineteenth century fully aware of what was to come.

Together the newlyweds travelled the 150 miles from London to Staffordshire, and Walter's main family seat, Chartley Manor. The journey was both long and arduous, but Lettice may have deemed that it had all been worth it when she caught her first glimpses of her new home. Situated a little over seven miles from Stafford, Chartley was an attractive moated timber manor house that had replaced the nearby crumbling Chartley Castle as the Devereux family home. Ranulph Blundeville, Earl of Chester, had built the castle in 1220 and Lettice would have become familiar with the sight of its decaying stones, which lay a short distance from the manor house. It had been abandoned in the 1480s when the more comfortable manor house had been built in its stead.[3] The house was set in nearly a thousand acres of parkland; John Leland remembered that 'There is a mighty large park', and it stood close to Needwood Forest.[4] The park provided excellent hunting, a hobby that Lettice became fond of, and was well stocked with red and fallow deer, as well as wild boar. Hunting was a popular sport that provided not only a form of exercise, but also socializing. Chartley Manor itself was a charming house; it was not overly large, but was two storeys high and had three wings built around a central courtyard. A seventeenth-century engraving shows that the courtyard contained an elaborate decorative fountain, and the house itself was half-timbered with gables.[5] In the windows and elsewhere throughout the house could be seen the emblazoned arms of the Devereux family, linked with those of the Ferrers and Garnishes, in a proud declaration of Chartley's past ownership.[6] To add further to its appeal, Chartley was also surrounded by a large and deep moat that still survives, giving it the semblance of a picturesque remote island.[7]

It was to this pleasant country retreat that Walter Devereux brought his new bride, and it was here that Lettice would spend much of her time in the coming years. Bourchier Devereux relates that in the first years of their marriage the couple lived in 'privacy and retirement', and that nothing was heard of them at court 'for several years'.[8] This is an exaggeration, for Lettice almost certainly visited the court in order to present her New Year's gift of 'a smock with a square collar and a rail wrought with black silk and gold' to the Queen in 1564 – the first occasion on which she is recorded as Viscountess of Hereford.[9] Such a gift shows that she still made an effort to retain her links with the Queen, and she may have visited on other occasions besides.[10] In addition, she probably wrote to her family, and they in turn would have kept her updated with the news from court. At Chartley, Lettice would have heard the continued gossip about the Queen and Leicester, and his candidature for the hand of the Scottish Queen in marriage.

Lettice was now mistress of Chartley, and as such Walter expected her to take responsibility for the good ordering of the household. It was with this in mind that she devoted her attentions to her wifely duties. The household at Chartley was largely self-sufficient, and it was Lettice's job to ensure that everything was run smoothly. When her husband was absent she was expected to manage the estate on his behalf.

Outwardly, Lettice's marriage was a happy one, and although no letters between the couple survive, there is no evidence to indicate otherwise. In 1574, when Walter was heavily engaged in affairs in Ireland, he would write to several lords of the Council instructing that, 'If I should die before the enterprise were achieved, the Queen's Majesty is to have of my lands a third part, my wife another third.'[11] Although it was not unusual for husbands to make provision for their wives, interestingly, just two years after writing this Walter's feelings about Lettice's welfare had changed, and the arrangements he made for her were not quite so generous. Walter was both handsome and intelligent; he was extremely ambitious, and this was an attractive quality for a girl of Lettice's temperament who wanted to do well in the world. However, his letters also show that he was hot-headed and blunt, and that he had a temper; he was not afraid to commit his outraged thoughts to paper, and he himself once referred to 'my plain and open nature'.[12] One wonders if, given Lettice's later strong-willed behaviour, such traits would have caused the couple to clash on occasion.

Lettice's other primary duty was to provide her husband with an heir, and by the spring of 1562 she was pregnant. She was at Chartley when, in January 1563, she gave birth to her first child. The baby was not the male heir that both she and her husband had hoped for, but a healthy daughter. All the same, she was Lettice and Walter's first child, and her parents' first grandchild, and as such she was a welcome addition to the family. The Queen was asked to stand as the baby's godmother, a role that she graciously accepted – much to her parents' delight. Unusually, though, the baby was not styled after her royal godmother, but was instead named Penelope. This was not a particularly common name at the time; it originated in Greek mythology with the wife of Odysseus, who was known for her marital fidelity – an example that would not be mirrored by Penelope Devereux. On 3 February baby Penelope was christened, perhaps in the nearby church at Stowe where Walter's grandfather lay entombed.

Unable to attend her new goddaughter's christening in person, as was customary the Queen sent both a representative and a gift on her behalf for 'the christening of Viscount Hereford his child'.[13] The gift was a fine 'gilt cup with a cover bought of the goldsmiths', a fitting present for the new arrival in Lettice's family.[14] Penelope bore many similarities to Lettice in appearance, with the same red-gold hair and beautiful dark eyes. She would grow to be 'the most celebrated beauty of the Elizabethan age', and a vivacious young woman who emulated her mother in many ways.[15]

Motherhood was a new experience for Lettice, and one in which she took great pleasure. She could at least draw on the knowledge she had acquired during her own childhood, when she had helped to raise her younger siblings at Greys Court. As she spent the next years of her life raising her family, she would prove herself to be an utterly devoted mother, who loved her children almost to the point of obsession. She was fiercely protective of them and was often overbearing, but in spite of this she remained close to them, and would do so for the rest of their lives. During their early years, at least, Lettice was the predominant influence in her children's lives, and she played a large part in shaping them. Little wonder, then, that similarities in their behaviour and their mother's would later emerge.

During the 1560s, Walter held no official post at court, and as such it is likely that he too spent much of his time at home with his growing family. Although estate business would have taken up a great deal of his time, he may nevertheless have been there to watch as Penelope took her first tentative steps, or uttered her first word. According to some accounts, the family spent some of their summers at Lamphey, the secluded spot in Wales where Walter is likely to have spent much of his time during childhood. There is no contemporary evidence to support this assertion, and given the distance – Lamphey was some two hundred miles from Chartley – it seems unlikely that they undertook this journey regularly every year. It is certainly possible that on occasion, however, the family did enjoy spending time at Lamphey, with its splendid deer park, fishponds and orchards. It is possible too that from time to time Lettice journeyed south to visit her family – frequently at court and Syon now rather than Greys.

The birth of Penelope was followed by that of another daughter, named Dorothy as a compliment to her paternal grandmother. Dorothy's birth is said to have taken place on 17 September 1564, also at Chartley.[16] The births of two surviving children in the space of just over eighteen months was an encouraging sign, and boded well for the future. Thus far, though, Lettice had yet to provide her husband with the male heir that he needed in order to continue the male Devereux line.

Although Lettice had much with which to occupy her time following the births of her two daughters, the vivacious Viscountess was unsuited to a life in the country. She loved her family, but she wanted more. She was still young – just shy of her twenty-first birthday at the time of Dorothy's birth – and she was still enticed by the intrigues of London and the court. Lettice may therefore have been delighted at the prospect of returning there in the summer of 1565, despite being pregnant with her third child. Leaving her two young daughters at Chartley in the care of the nursery staff, she and Walter journeyed south, her pregnancy ensuring that they travelled at a slower pace. Their visit was necessitated by the forthcoming nuptials of Lettice's elder brother, Henry, to Margaret Cave.

On 16 July, the wedding was hosted at Durham Place, and was a celebration of the utmost magnificence. Located on the fashionable Strand, Durham Place was now a Crown property that was given over to the use of the Queen's courtiers on occasion – from 1559 to 1565 it was used as the London residence of the Spanish ambassador, and it would later regularly be used by Walter. It was also a popular choice for entertaining, and it had been at Durham Place that the ill-fated Lady Jane Grey had been married to Guildford Dudley in May 1553. The wedding was not only a family celebration at which Lettice and her husband were present, but also a royal occasion. In a sign of her favour to the family, the Queen attended the wedding as the guest of honour. There had been some anxiety on the part of the bride's father, Sir Ambrose Cave, who was worried about issues of precedence; both the French and Imperial ambassadors – natural enemies – were in attendance, and a diplomatic incident was only narrowly avoided. The wedding was celebrated with great style, and the impressed Imperial ambassador observed that 'After supper there was a ball, a tourney, and two masques, the feast ending at half-past one.'[17] It is tempting to speculate that, given her relationship with the Queen, Lettice's wedding may have been conducted on a similar scale to that of her brother, but there is sadly no evidence to confirm this. Henry and Margaret's marriage was successful, and together the couple would have two daughters. The youngest was named Lettice as a compliment to her aunt.[18]

The festivities of Henry's wedding were a cause of great celebration within Lettice's family, and her attendance provided her with the opportunity to spend some time with both her parents and her siblings. The lively entertainments served as a reminder of the ones in which Lettice had once participated in at court, although in her pregnant state there was no opportunity for her to do so on this occasion. It is unclear where she resided during this time for Walter had no London home of his own, but they were in no rush to return to Chartley; instead they spent the rest of the summer at court. Here they were able to enjoy the amusements and diversions that were offered in abundance, and indulge in the opportunity to catch up with friends and family. The great topic of conversation at court that summer was the question of the Queen's marriage. Elizabeth was now thirty-one, and had been Queen for nearly seven years. Despite numerous attempts to coax her into matrimony with a number of suitors, she had remained unmarried. The Imperial ambassador, Guzmán de Silva, made his feelings on the matter clear in a report to his master:

I do not think anything is more enjoyable to this Queen than treating of marriage, although she assures me herself that nothing annoys her more. She is vain, and would like all the world to be running after her, but it will probably end in her remaining as she is, unless she marry Lord Robert, who is still doing his best to win her.[19]

The Earl of Leicester had not given up hope of obtaining the Queen's hand, but the name on everyone's lips at court that summer was not his. It was instead that of the Archduke Charles of Styria, the son of the Holy Roman Emperor, Ferdinand I.[20] This proposed match dominated court politics between 1564 and 1568, and would have been a topic that Lettice herself would have taken a great interest in.

Even so, the Queen's relationship with the Earl of Leicester remained the subject of gossip. Leicester still loved her, but for Elizabeth her former ardour for him had somewhat cooled: although she relied on Leicester and enjoyed his company, her sense of reason had now set in. As a prospective suitor, Leicester's candidature was unpopular, not least with Elizabeth's advisors. William Cecil, determined to pour cold water on the idea once and for all, had drawn up a list of reasons why Leicester was an unsuitable candidate. These included the accusation that he was believed to be 'inflamed by the death of his wife', that he 'is far in debt', and that he 'is like to prove unkind or jealous of the Queen's majesty'.[21] Cecil's feelings became even clearer when he compared Leicester with the Archduke Charles. While Charles was the 'brother of an Emperor' and 'an archduke born', Leicester was 'born a son of a knight' and 'an earl made'.[22] Where Charles was wealthy and had enjoyed an education 'amongst princes', Leicester's wealth was 'all of the Queen and in debt', and he had been educated 'always in England'.[23] Finally, in reputation Charles was 'honoured of all named to the empire', while Leicester was 'hated of many' by reason of 'his wife's death'.[24] In Cecil's eyes and those of many others, the ideal candidate for the Queen's hand in marriage was clear, and he was determined that it ought not to be Leicester. The Queen still expected to be the centre of Leicester's attentions, but, much to her irritation, his name was about to become associated with that of another lady.

⸺⸺⸺

IN AUGUST LETTICE was six months pregnant with her third child. As she whiled away the summer months back in the familiar surroundings of the court, listening to the Queen's musicians or indulging in the twitterings of the ladies, she could never have expected to become the topic of gossip – or to attract the attentions of the Earl of Leicester. Lettice was already acquainted with Leicester, but how well the two knew one another at this point is unclear. Well enough, it seems, for Leicester to use Lettice in an experiment designed to push the Queen into action.

The matter of the Queen's marriage had dragged on, and despite her hardened declaration to remain single at the time of her succession, she had since wavered in her resolve. Regardless of the talks and proposals that had been laid before her, though, she was still no nearer to taking a husband. Leicester's candidature as a suitor for the hand of Mary, Queen of Scots, had given him fresh reason to hope that Elizabeth would consider him a worthy husband for herself, and although in her head she may have made a decision, she gave him reason to retain his hope. He was impatient, however, for her to give him an answer. According to the Imperial ambassador, Guzmán de Silva, that summer Leicester had become engaged in a conversation with Sir Nicholas Throckmorton on the subject.[25] De Silva related that, on Throckmorton's advice Leicester had decided to 'devise some means to find out whether the Queen was really as much attached to him as she appeared to be, as his case was in danger'.[26] In order to ascertain the truth of the matter, Throckmorton had advised Leicester to pretend 'to fall in love himself with one of the ladies in the palace and watch how the Queen took it'.[27] Eager to ascertain Elizabeth's feelings once and for all, 'The Earl took his advice and showed attention to the Viscountess of Hereford, who is one of the best-looking ladies of the court and daughter of a first cousin to the Queen, with whom she is a favourite.'[28]

The origins of Lettice and Leicester's relationship are often placed at this point, but aside from the report of Guzmán de Silva there is no evidence to corroborate this, and it is highly unlikely. Though it is true that there is rarely no smoke without fire, this may have been one of those instances. That Leicester genuinely found Lettice attractive seems likely

– probable in fact, given their later relationship – but at this time she was a married woman whose pregnant state was obvious. Pregnant women were taboo, and were generally not considered to be desirable. Similarly, no matter what Lettice's physical appeal may have been, Leicester himself had his sights for the moment set very firmly in the Queen's direction. He doubtless flirted with Lettice and may have gained some enjoyment from doing so, but his true motives lay elsewhere. His intentions towards Lettice were harmless, and he was using her in order to establish the true nature of the Queen's feelings for him.

There is no indication as to how Lettice reacted to Leicester's attentiveness, but there is certainly no evidence to support the claim that 'Leicester's approaches were received with ardour'.[29] Elizabeth's reaction is far clearer. Predictably, 'The Queen was in a great temper and upbraided him' for his behaviour.[30] She was incensed, and admonished him for 'his flirting with the Viscountess in very bitter words'.[31] Leicester did not take kindly to this, and according to de Silva:

He went down to his apartments and stayed there for three or four days until the Queen sent for him, the Earl of Sussex and Cecil having tried to smooth the business over, although they are no friends of Lord Robert in their hearts. The result of the tiff was that both the Queen and Robert shed tears, and he has returned to his former favour.

Some writers have dismissed this story as nothing more than a rumour, but however exaggerated it may have been, there are likely to be some elements of truth to it. Elizabeth may not have wished to marry Leicester herself, but one thing was startlingly clear: she would not tolerate having to compete for his attention with any other woman. Historian Elizabeth Jenkins' claim that in order to resume the Queen's favour Leicester had to give up Lettice – 'some desirable objects cost too much' – is untrue, for it is highly unlikely that Leicester viewed Lettice as anything more than a harmless flirtation at this point.[32] Elizabeth assuredly had no need to fear that she had incurred a rival at this time: Leicester loved her, and though the nature of his feelings towards her may have changed over time, she would always come first.

How this episode affected Lettice and Walter is unknown. No mention is made of any hostility from the Queen towards Lettice, which suggests that her involvement in the scene was perceived to be minimal. From what would shortly transpire, however, it is evident that, before long, all was not well between Walter and Leicester. Whether Lettice was a factor in this is impossible to say.

AT THE END of the summer Lettice and Walter left the court and any gossip behind them, as Lettice prepared to begin her confinement. On 10 November, just days after her twenty-second birthday, she was triumphant; she had delivered her husband the best possible gift: a son. According to Bourchier Devereux, the baby was born at Netherwood in Herefordshire, a view that *The Complete Peerage* concurs with.[33] Netherwood was a Devereux holding, so it is possible that the child was born there.[34] There has been controversy over both the date and year of the birth of Lettice's first-born son, and other historians have variously cited it as 19 November 1566 and 10 November 1567, but 10 November 1565 is generally accepted to be the correct date.[35]

The proud parents of Walter's son and heir had also settled upon a godfather: Robert Dudley, Earl of Leicester, whom the baby was named after.[36] Given the summer's scandal, Leicester's selection may seem like an odd choice, but there was plainly no hostility between the two parties at this point. It may even have been a deliberate choice in order to highlight this to outsiders, firmly putting any gossip to bed. Leicester took an active interest in his godson, and it is probable that he sent him a christening gift. Although Leicester's accounts for the year of Robert's birth are missing, his surviving accounts reveal that he made christening gifts to other noble children. These were often silver salts or something comparable, and young Robert is likely to have received a similar token.[37] As Lettice's baby son lay in his cradle, she could have had no idea that in years to come both of them would become intimately linked to Robert's godfather.

The significance of Robert's birth was that, besides providing her husband with a male heir, Lettice had produced 'a well balanced Tudor family'.[38] She now had three children, and their care was to occupy much of her time over the coming years. At home, a nursery staff were employed to oversee the majority of the Devereux children's everyday care, which included wet-nurses to suckle them when they were babies, and perhaps a governess as they grew.[39] Lettice also played an active role in their upbringing. She doted on her children, and her strength of character meant that she was always going to take a keen interest in their welfare, as is attested to in the way in which she spoke about them in her letters. They were probably raised in a similar kind of environment to the one that she had enjoyed during her childhood, and the siblings grew to be close to one another. Penelope and Robert were particularly fond of one another and in adulthood would work closely together, while Dorothy signed her letters to her brother in the most affectionate of terms: 'your sister that faithfully loves you', she once wrote.[40]

All three of Lettice's children began their education at home, overseen by their mother. Their father was eager that they should be raised as fervent Protestants, a decision that met with the approval of their grandfather, Sir Francis Knollys. Walter and Lettice both appreciated the value of a good education, and as such they invested heavily in the lessons of their children.

Robert's first tutor was Thomas Ashton, a devoted Protestant who entered Walter's service in 1571. Ashton was a Cambridge scholar who had been appointed headmaster of Shrewsbury School in 1561, where his pupils included the Earl of Leicester's nephew, Sir Philip Sidney.[41] He was therefore an excellent choice of tutor for the Herefords' heir. Robert proved to be an apt pupil, and in 1576 Walter's secretary Edward Waterhouse informed Cecil, by then Lord Burghley, that Robert 'can express his mind in Latin and French, as well as in English, very courteous and modest, rather disposed to hear than to answer, given greatly to learning, weak and tender, but very comely and bashful'.[42] In his youth, a very deliberate decision was made to expose Robert to Puritan influences, and it had a marked effect upon his later beliefs. He would later invite Puritan ministers to preach at Essex House, his London residence.[43] Lettice herself would also have a noticeable impact on her son, and Robert's biographer Robert Lacey was not wrong when he wrote that 'The one adult who really shaped the young Earl of Essex, if anyone did, was his forceful, flirtatious mother Lettice.'[44]

Penelope and Dorothy did not share in their brother's lessons, but their parents considered their education to be equally important. Lettice in particular took her daughters' upbringing seriously, and another Cambridge scholar, Mathias Holmes, was employed to teach them. As Lettice herself later related, Holmes was the one 'that teacheth my daughters', and hath done since they began first to learn'.[45] Holmes had been in Lettice's household for some time – in 1577 Lettice informed Lord Burghley that he 'hath served my Lord and me these dozen or thirteen years', although in what capacity is unclear. Lettice held him in high regard, and she and Walter evidently knew him well enough to entrust him with their daughters' lessons.[46]

The girls' learning focused on all of the social skills that were required in aristocratic circles, and probably bore great similarities to the education Lettice had enjoyed. Penelope stood out as having an especially keen mind, and became fluent in both French and Spanish. She also understood some Italian. When the translator Bartholomew Young dedicated his translation of *Diana of de Montemayor* to Penelope in 1598, he wrote not only of her 'magnificent mind', but of her 'perfect knowledge' of French, and acknowledged that Spanish was a language that was 'so well known' to her.[47] Of Lettice's two daughters it was Penelope who was the darling; it was she who earned the admiration and praise of those who met her, for she could sing and dance beautifully, played the lute to perfection, and was applauded for her intellect. Even King James VI of Scotland was impressed, and later 'commended much the fineness of her wit'.[48] She was certainly a daughter to be proud of. Penelope would grow to be a great patron of the arts, and like the Earl of Leicester, would find herself the dedicatee of many works in return. Neither were they alone, for in 1570 Lettice would have been proudly able to show her children a work that had been dedicated to her.

Roger Edwardes made 'the Lady Lettice Viscountess of Hereford' the dedicatee of his *A Boke of Very Godly Psalmes and Prayers*, a book designed to 'increase the plenty of heavenly comforts'.[49] As Edwardes himself explained in the first line of his dedication, 'amongst many my gracious Lord your husband's bounden and faithful vassals, whom his Lordship's bounty and noble virtues do daily purchase abroad (unknown to your Honour) I am one'.[50] It is unclear how he was connected with the Devereux household, but he was not known to Lettice. Yet he continued to urge her to 'let my poor little labour, have liberty to bestow itself, where it would gladdest show the token of a thankful heart'.[51] He also hoped that Lettice would circulate his work, for he implored her to take the book 'to your use and tuition, that by your estimation of the same, it may grow common and acceptable amongst the virtuous sort of ladies and gentlewomen'.[52] Whether she did so or not is unknown, but she would at least have been gratified by the dedication.

FOR LETTICE, THE first half of the 1560s had been a whirlwind of domestic duties and childbearing, broken up by occasional visits to court. No further mention is made of her at this time in relation to the Earl of Leicester, and she and Walter, now with a growing family, had settled into a routine. But change was coming, and that not all of these changes would be welcome.

CHAPTER 6

Death with his Dart hath us Bereft

W HILE LETTICE REMAINED at Chartley with her husband and her three children, at court the Queen's marriage remained a talking point. Elizabeth continued to stall on the issue, and no doubt the court gossip wound its way from London to Chartley. Matters in England, though, were about to take a more serious turn, and Lettice's family were to become fully embroiled in them.

IN SCOTLAND, THE personal rule of Mary, Queen of Scots, had been a disaster. Having married Henry Darnley, the son of Lady Margaret Lennox, Mary's feelings towards him had quickly turned sour. She was appalled to discover that he was both a drunk and sexually promiscuous, and he in turn was outraged by her refusal to grant him the crown matrimonial – the right to rule equally alongside Mary. Had she done so, in the event of her dying childless, Darnley would have been able to succeed her in his own right. Mary's previous affection for her husband turned to a deep-seated hate when, on the evening of 9 March 1566, a group of the Queen's Scottish lords burst into her apartments at the Palace of Holyroodhouse. Mary was enjoying supper with a small group of friends, among whom was her Italian secretary, David Rizzio. Rizzio was unpopular, and Darnley had long been jealous of the influence the secretary exerted over his wife. Despite clinging desperately to his mistress's skirts, Rizzio was dragged out of the supper chamber and brutally stabbed fifty-six times.[1] Mary, who was heavily pregnant with her first child, was in fear for her life, and after witnessing this horrific scene was afraid of miscarrying.

It quickly became apparent that Darnley had colluded with the Scottish lords in the plot to kill Rizzio; Mary was horrified. Despite her personal feelings of distaste, she put on a show of reconciliation with her husband, and on 19 June she gave birth to a son at Edinburgh Castle. The baby was named James, and Queen Elizabeth was his godmother.

Matters in Scotland did not end there, and in February 1567 Darnley was murdered following an explosion at his house at Kirk o'Field in Edinburgh. The bodies of him and his servant were found in the garden, untouched by the explosion; they had probably been suffocated – Leicester later owned a print depicting the scene of the murder.[2] It was widely suspected that the Queen was implicated in the plot, and the situation was about to become infinitely worse. On 15 May, just months after Darnley's death, Mary married the man that most people suspected was guilty of his murder: James Hepburn, Earl of Bothwell. From then, events moved swiftly. Mary's Scottish lords rebelled and raised an army against her. The two forces met at Carberry Hill on 15 June, but there was no battle: the Queen was captured and taken to the remote Lochleven Castle in Kinross, while Bothwell was forced into exile abroad.[3] In July Mary miscarried of twins, and, taking advantage of her weakened state, the lords forced her to abdicate her throne in favour of her infant son, James. The following May, after nearly a year's imprisonment, Mary managed to escape from Lochleven and rallied her forces.[4] Her attempt to regain her throne was unsuccessful: she was defeated at the Battle of Langside on 13 May, and in desperation she fled across the border into England. Once there, she was hopeful of receiving aid from her cousin, Queen Elizabeth. Mary was immediately conducted to Carlisle Castle, and it was here that Elizabeth called upon the services of Lettice's father.

Sir Francis Knollys had been active in the Queen's service throughout the 1560s; in 1562 he had been made Governor of Portsmouth, necessitating several visits to the port, and in 1565 he was appointed Captain of the

Guard. In his role as Governor of Portsmouth, his duties included ensuring that the men of the Newhaven garrison received their wages and regular supplies – no mean task. The Queen had great confidence in his knowledge of military affairs, and it was here that he excelled. His work had required a great deal of travel, and he had journeyed to France, Scotland, the Channel Islands, the Isle of Wight and Ireland all in the Queen's service. It was while he was in the latter that he applied for the post of Treasurer of the Chamber, an appointment that he was awarded on 4 January 1567 at an annual salary of £133 (£22,500). He was later made Treasurer of the Household in 1570, an even more lucrative position. Francis had always been loyal to the Queen, to whom he often spoke with more frankness than many of her fawning courtiers. However, he was never elevated to the peerage, and it is difficult to believe that this would not have rankled, given his family's history with Elizabeth. Both she and Cecil trusted Francis's judgement, and so it was to him that she was about to thrust the ultimate responsibility.

WHEN NEWS OF the arrival of Mary, Queen of Scots, in England reached London, Elizabeth made the decision to send Sir Francis north to Carlisle to assume the role of her guardian. That he was stringently Puritan meant that he was unlikely to have any sympathy for the Catholic Mary, which in Elizabeth's eyes made him a good choice. For Francis this was completely new territory, and it was not an assignment he desired. He would later write that the Queen, by reason of her trust, 'putteth me to more pains, more careful perils, and more tedious grief's than she doth any other man'.[5] He had no choice, though, but to obey his orders. He was further disheartened when the Queen refused his request for permission to take his wife with him. The Queen could not bear to be parted from Lettice's mother, and to her dismay, Katherine was forced to remain at court. Accompanied by Lord Scrope and his twenty-three-year-old son William, Francis began to make the arduous journey north to Carlisle. He had been instructed to supervise the fallen Scottish Queen until Elizabeth had decided what to do next, but it was a task that Francis was deeply unhappy about. He felt sure that Mary was a threat to the security of the realm, and he constantly worried that she would escape from Carlisle. Even so, he found that, despite the great differences in their religious beliefs, he rather liked Mary. As her native tongues were both French and Scots, he even began to teach her English. Her first letter in that language, in which she begged him to 'excuse my evil writing', was addressed to him.[6] Mary took less notice, however, of Francis's attempts to lecture her on Protestantism, and remained a devoted Catholic. On one occasion she even sent a gift of 'a pretty chain of pomander beads, finely laced with gold wire' to Francis's wife, much to his distaste; 'see how she corrupts me', he complained to Cecil.[7] Security at Carlisle was still an issue, and in July Francis instigated the removal of Mary to Lord Scrope's stronghold of Bolton Castle. Situated in the heart of Wensleydale in Yorkshire, Bolton was a little over seventy-five miles south of Carlisle, and was a mighty medieval fortress.[8]

Francis was now slightly closer to London, but his pleas to return home fell on deaf ears. His desire may have been exacerbated by the fact that he had been informed that his wife had fallen ill. The nature of Katherine's malady is unclear, but news of it had reached Francis by 29 July. On that day he wrote to Katherine, and in his usual frank manner he came immediately to the point: 'I am very sorry to hear that you are fallen into a fever, I would to God I were so dispatched hence that I might only attend and care for your good recovery.'[9] He was genuinely concerned for her welfare and grieved not to be with her at this time, but added that 'I trust you shall shortly overcome this fever and recover good health again.'[10] For Lettice, ensconced at Chartley, the news that her mother was ill must have come as a concern too, and she is likely to have found a way to keep herself informed of her progress – perhaps by means of her sister Elizabeth, who was at court with their mother. She may even have written to her mother herself, perhaps in similar terms to Francis, who reminded his wife to take better care of herself. For, he admonished her, 'although in your health you do often forget to prevent sickness by due and precise order, yet when you are fallen into sickness, you will then (although it be late) observe very good order'.[11] Katherine had clearly suffered previous health problems, and since she had borne sixteen children this is hardly surprising.

It was not only Lettice's mother, but also her brother, twenty-one-year-old Edward, who was sick at this time. Suffering from 'an ague', it was this that had prevented him from joining his father in the north.[12] Edward's absence was not an issue, for as his father explained to his mother, he would not have used himself half so well as his brother William had done: 'for with his courtesy and good discretion he hath gotten here a very good opinion of all sorts'.[13] This included the Queen of Scots, with whom William had 'uttered his French tongue often times'.[14] Both Lettice's father and her younger brother William were trying to make the best of the situation in which they found themselves, but Francis was still desperate to return home. Katherine too was anxious to be reunited with her husband, and Francis informed Cecil that 'she is desirous to come hither if my return be not shortly'.[15] Once again, though, Elizabeth thwarted any such hopes, on the grounds that the journey 'might be to her danger or discommodity'.[16] Realizing that there was no hope of Katherine being permitted to travel north, Francis instead entreated his wife to 'help that I may be revoked and return again'.[17] There was little for him to do in any case, he claimed, and so he could very easily be spared. Signing himself 'your loving husband', Francis hoped for a favourable reply.[18]

Unbeknown to Francis, his wife had recovered from her illness. Much to his relief, he received word from two of his servants, Robert Bestney and Francis Fryer, that 'My Lady God be thanked is in ye way of recovering, having in effect altogether escaped her fit once or twice.'[19] This happy news was reiterated by the Earl of Leicester, who wrote to Francis on 7 August to inform him that 'my lady your wife is well again. But I fear her diet and order.'[20] Katherine's health had evidently plagued her before, to such an extent that it had attracted the notice of her contemporaries.

It is also clear that all of their years spent in the Queen's service had taken their toll on Lettice's family. While Lettice prepared to spend Christmas with her family at Chartley, her father was still no closer to returning home. Winter was never a good time to be away from court, particularly in the cold north, and Francis longed for his home comforts; 'we are utterly unprovided, as you know', he had complained to Cecil. Katherine had become ill once more, and once again she recovered. However, this had caused Francis such anxiety that, as he related to his wife on 30 December, he had almost written 'somewhat plainly to her Majesty in her own matters'.[21] He was disappointed by 'her Majesty's ungrateful denial of my coming to the Court this Christmas', and had been on the verge of informing her that he had been told that 'my wife is ready to die in discomfort and in miserable state towards her children even in your Majesty's Court'.[22] The only thing that had prevented him from doing so was his receiving word that Katherine was once more recovered.

LETTICE AND HER family spent the New Year of 1569 at Chartley. There is no record of either she or Walter sending a gift to court for the Queen, as Lettice had done on previous occasions. In 1567, for example, she had given her kinswoman a selection of pretty items, including 'a pair of ruffs and a pair of sleeves wrought with Venice gold and blue silk'.[23] In the north, meanwhile, there was still no word from court, and Lettice's father was forced to remain in his role as custodian to the Queen of Scots. He may have exchanged New Year's gifts with Lettice, for he informed his wife that he had sent their younger daughter Elizabeth, affectionately known as Bess, 'a new milled piece of gold to lay up in her store box', while she in turn had given him a pair of gloves.[24] By 17 January, Francis had had enough of the separation from his family, and in plain language he wrote to the Queen expressing his dissatisfaction: 'if your majesty think as I do, that you can never make me a good courtier, I most humbly beseech you dismiss me to the country, rather than aggravate my grief with noisome and fruitless service'.[25] That same day, he added a postscript to a letter to Cecil in which he wrote: 'Her majesty promised me I should shortly be rid of this Queen: but the resolution is long a coming. I trust you hasten it.'[26] Francis always spoke frankly to Elizabeth, and she in turn came to expect nothing less from him. As he himself once related to his wife, 'her Majesty sayeth she trusts me, and I believe she thinks me not false'.[27]

Unbeknown to Francis and probably also Lettice, at court all was not well with Lady Knollys. Despite her brief recoveries from the bouts of illness from which she had been suffering, after Christmas her health had rapidly declined. The court was in residence at Hampton Court, on the outskirts of London, and when Katherine once again fell ill she had been moved to a room closer to the Queen's. Nicholas White, a protégé of Cecil's, remarked that here Katherine 'was very often visited by her Majesty's own comfortable presence', but even this could not cure her.[28] The person she really craved was her husband, but despite his desperate pleas to be allowed to return home to her, Francis was not by his wife's side when she died on 15 January. Lettice's devoted parents, cruelly separated in the final months of Katherine's life, had never been reunited.

Following Lady Knollys's death, an unbearable sadness descended on Hampton Court. Given her place in the Queen's household, it is possible that Lettice's sister, nineteen-year-old Elizabeth, was by her mother's side at her end, but neither Lettice nor any of her other siblings were there to say their final farewells. The Queen was left heartbroken by Katherine's death, and fell into such 'passions of grief ... for the death of her kinswoman and good servant', that she fell ill; 'being forgetful of her own health, she took cold, wherewith she was much troubled'.[29] So affected was Elizabeth that, White noted soon afterwards, she could talk of nothing else. 'From this she returned back again to talk of my Lady Knollys.'[30]

The news of her mother's death took several days to reach Chartley. Four days later, at Bolton Castle, Francis was still oblivious, and complained to Cecil that 'It seems by your letter you cannot promise my wife that I shall be discharged.'[31] By now it had been decided that the Scottish Queen was to be moved further south, this time to Tutbury, a grim castle that stood not far from Lettice's home of Chartley.[32] Francis had taken this opportunity to inform Cecil that if he had not been relieved of his post by the time he had escorted Mary there, then 'I must repair to court and suffer any punishment her majesty pleases.'[33] However, word of his wife's death reached him on 20 January, when his brother Henry arrived at Bolton with the heavy tidings. It left him stunned, and the following day Henry informed Cecil that his brother was 'distracted with sorrow for his great loss'.[34] Francis was utterly devastated by the death of the woman that he had loved wholeheartedly for almost thirty years, and he would never remarry. In a letter to the Privy Council on 29 January, he complained that 'I am much disquieted with this service in these strange countries, which melancholy humour grows daily on me since my wife's death … My case is pitiful, for my wife disburdened me of many cares, kept all the monuments of my public charges, as well as my private accounts – now, my children, my servants and all other things, are loosely left without good order.'[35] Katherine had been the glue that had held the Knollys family together, and they were all thrown into deep mourning at her passing.

The Queen gave orders that Lettice's mother was to receive a costly funeral, and in April she charged the Earl of Leicester and the Duke of Norfolk with ensuring that this was done. By royal command the funeral took place in Westminster Abbey, and the total cost of £640 (£111,300) was borne entirely by the Queen.[36] The sum was staggering, and was a great deal more than Elizabeth would spend on burying other cousins, even those of royal birth. The funeral was conducted on an almost royal scale, and although the Queen and Katherine had been close this seems to indicate something more – perhaps an acknowledgement not only of kinship, but also of Katherine's royal blood.[37] The documents relating to her funeral were later discovered alongside those of seven monarchs and their consorts – significantly, Katherine was the only non-royal among them.[38]

There is no record of Lettice attending her mother's funeral, and once the ceremony had been concluded Lady Knollys 'was honourably buried in the floor of this chapel' – St Edmunds Chapel in Westminster Abbey, where her tomb can still be seen. Her elaborate marble and alabaster monument is decorated with a border of swans, a bull's head and a maiden's head, while among the four shields the arms of the families of Knollys, Boleyn and Carey appear. The epitaph on her tomb remembered Lady Knollys as 'Chief Lady of the Queen's Majesty's Bedchamber', and also contained a poignant Latin memorial:

O, Francis, she who was thy wife, behold, Catherine Knollys lies dead under the chilly marble. I know well that she will never depart from thy soul, though dead. Whilst alive she was always loved by thee: living, she bore thee, her husband, sixteen children, equally female and male (that is, both gentle and valiant). Would that she had lived many years with thee and thy wife was now an old lady. But God desired it not. But he willed that thou, O Catherine, should await thy husband in Heaven.

Given the emphasis on Francis, it is possible that the epitaph was commissioned on his orders. The touching words testify to the sadness that Katherine's death left in both his life and that of their children, and her passing also saddened many who had known her. She had been popular, and following her death Thomas Newton published an epitaph in her memory. It began with a verse that confirms the high regard in which her contemporaries had held Lettice's mother:

Death with his Dart hath us bereft,
A Gem of worthy fame,
A Pearl of price, an Ouche of praise,
The Lady Knollys by name.[39]

Now, though, Lady Knollys had gone, leaving the stage 'of this most wretched life, wherein she played a stately part'.[40] Following Katherine's death, the Queen remained on good terms with Francis, who, upon delivering the Queen of Scots to Tutbury on 4 February, was relieved of his role of custodian by the Earl of Shrewsbury. He left Tutbury four days later, leaving his brother Henry behind to support Shrewsbury in his new role.

The Queen was kind to Francis's children following the loss of their mother. Whether she made any attempt to reach out to Lettice during this time is uncertain, but it is likely that she condoled with her younger sister Elizabeth, who had by now been promoted to the role of lady of the privy chamber. However, Elizabeth typically viewed Katherine's death primarily as her own personal loss. It was at this time that Lettice's thirteen-year-old sister Anne became a paid member of the Royal Household, and throughout the course of her service the Queen gave her several gifts. With no mother to supervise her care and her father away from home, it is possible that the youngest surviving Knollys daughter, nine-year-old Katherine, went to live with her elder sister Lettice; Lettice and Katherine were always close, and this would not be the last occasion on which they would live together. In later life, probably in the 1590s, Katherine went to live with her older sister following the death of her second husband. At this time she was only a few years older than six-year-old Penelope and her younger sister Dorothy, and may have been seen as a suitable companion.

LETTICE'S MOTHER WAS now dead, and by this time Lettice was pregnant with her fourth child. She had had a successful, though exhausting, pregnancy record, having borne three children in the space of three years. This would not be a peaceful pregnancy, for later that same year events took a dangerous turn, threatening the security of the Queen on her throne. And Lettice's husband, Walter, was to be at the very centre of the action.

At the beginning of 1569, Mary, Queen of Scots, had been in England for more than six months. Following a conference at York the previous

October, at which Mary's half-brother the Earl of Moray had produced the infamous casket letters – proof, he said, of Mary's involvement in the murder of her second husband, Lord Darnley – Elizabeth was in a quandary of indecision about what to do next.[41] The letters were almost certainly forged, but still Elizabeth made no move to aid Mary in her hopes to be restored to her throne. As the Queen and her advisors pondered over what to do, it became apparent that Mary was now less Elizabeth's honoured guest, and more her prisoner. Mary longed for her freedom; she was well aware that her imprisonment was illegal, and she began making plans to escape.

The north of England was largely Catholic territory, and Mary's presence there had given rise to a new plot. The Northern Rebellion was the brainchild of Thomas Percy, seventh Earl of Northumberland, and Charles Neville, sixth Earl of Westmorland.[42] Its aim was to free Mary, and arrange for her marriage to the Duke of Norfolk, with whom Mary had been conversing on the subject.[43] More than that, the plot also aimed to depose Queen Elizabeth and set Mary on the throne in her place, thereby restoring England to Catholicism – despite the fact that Norfolk was a Protestant. When word of the uprising reached London, it caused panic, made worse when the Queen struggled to rally her forces. Moving Mary south was a priority, and with this in mind the Queen sought the assistance of Lettice's husband, Walter.

In September, Walter was at Chartley with his wife and children when he received an urgent message from the Queen. Together with his cousin, Henry Hastings, Earl of Huntingdon, he was commanded to assist the Earl of Shrewsbury at nearby Tutbury in securing Mary's person in order to prevent an escape attempt.[44] He had been ordered to keep a body of horsemen in readiness, and he prepared to take them to Tutbury. From Chartley, Walter bade his pregnant wife and children farewell as he began the sixteen-mile journey. It must have been difficult leaving Lettice at this time for she was fast approaching her confinement, but Walter's commission gave him an opportunity to shine in the Queen's service.

Tutbury had once been an important stronghold with royal associations, but it had since fallen into disrepair, and the Scottish Queen loathed it. Neither did she take kindly to the arrival of Walter and Huntingdon, especially when she learned of the reason for their visit. This was almost certainly the first occasion on which Walter had met Mary, and there is no evidence as to what his first impressions of her may have been. He was, however, intent on serving Queen Elizabeth, and in so doing did nothing to ingratiate himself with Mary. Both he and Huntingdon reported that they had searched Mary's coffers, but to no avail; anything incriminating she may have had was now gone, for Shrewsbury had informed Huntingdon that 'she did burn many papers'.[45] Mary took the search 'very grievously', complaining bitterly of her treatment.[46]

Interestingly, it was while Walter was at Tutbury that the first evidence of a rift with the Earl of Leicester appears. Having written to Cecil on 27 September to inform him of the search of the Scottish Queen's coffers, Huntingdon made reference to certain comments that had been made by John Leslie, Bishop of Ross, Mary's agent to Elizabeth.[47] Precisely what Leslie had said is unclear, but he had evidently made some remarks against both Huntingdon and Walter, which Huntingdon strenuously denied. Eager to defend himself, Walter had added a postscript. He was alarmed by the nature of Leslie's allegations, which were obviously concerned with the suits of both Leicester and the Duke of Norfolk for the Scottish Queen's hand in marriage. He felt obliged to answer them, and in so doing a different side to his character emerges. He indignantly claimed:

That which the Bishop of Ross hath reported of me, is most untrue; for any unfit speech, which hath passed from me, either of the Duke of Norfolk, or of the Earl of Leicester, I desire but to have it justified to my face, when time shall serve. I have spoken nothing which I will not say again; and yet that have I not said, which might give either of them cause of offence.[48]

Walter was vehement in his own defence, and felt that whatever charges Leslie had levelled at him had been blown out of proportion. He was a man who was not afraid to stand his ground, and to speak out when he felt that he had been wronged. If he is to be believed, then he bore no hard feelings against Leicester at this time. Yet this would later change.

WALTER RETURNED HOME to Chartley shortly afterwards, but there was little time for him to discuss his first impressions of Mary, Queen of Scots, with Lettice; her thoughts were elsewhere. On 31 October, All Hallows' Eve, she gave birth to her fourth child. To her delight and that of Walter, the baby was a boy. He was named Walter after his father, and it would later be rumoured that the boy was his father's favourite.[49] Walter would be the last of the Herefords' surviving children; a further son, named Francis, was born at a later unknown date. Sadly, no further details are known of him, and he died young.[50] He may have been laid to rest in the church at Stowe, perhaps close to Walter's grandfather. Lettice had now amply fulfilled her duty, providing her husband with two male heirs, and two beautiful daughters. She had every reason to be jubilant.

Just days after young Walter's birth, the precious time that Lettice's husband was able to spend with his family and his newborn son came to an abrupt end. The Northern Rebellion was posing an increasing threat, and in November the rebels' forces gathered in Durham. They defiantly ordered a Catholic Mass to be celebrated in the cathedral, and there was no doubt that they were intent on moving south. Their numbers were swelling daily, with more than four thousand men marching under their banner. Although Mary was now at Tutbury, Elizabeth's advisors began to fear that, with the rebels marching south, she would soon be freed if she remained there. It was with this in mind that Walter and Huntingdon were called upon once again, and ordered to move Mary further south. They escorted her to Coventry, from where extra guards were employed to ensure that she did not escape, while Walter and Huntingdon returned home to rally their troops.[51]

Walter's return to Chartley was of short duration. Having mustered 150 horsemen to add to the Queen's ranks, he prepared to leave his family once more. Knowing of the threat that the rebels posed was a cause of alarm for Walter, whose young family at Chartley was vulnerable; Lettice had only recently given birth and was probably not strong enough to travel, hence the reason why her husband did not send her further south. All that they could do was hope that the rebellion was crushed swiftly.

Having received orders to take his forces to Leicester, by the end of November Walter was ready to leave. On 27 November, he wrote to the Queen acknowledging his duty to her. He would, he assured her, 'repair with all the forces that I have levied, as speedily as it is possible unto Leicester, and so forward to what place it shall please them whom your Majesty hath appointed to have the government of your army'.[52] He also took the opportunity to profess his loyalty, declaring that 'I will most faithfully and truly serve your Majesty to the uttermost of my power.'[53] Leaving his wife and his four young children behind, Walter and his men marched towards Leicester. His first stop was Lichfield, where he managed to rally 3,000 men. When he arrived in Leicester, he joined the Queen's forces, which were assembled under the command of the Earl of Leicester's brother, Ambrose, Earl of Warwick. On 1 December, Ambrose advertised Cecil of Walter's arrival, informing him approvingly that 'My Lord of Hereford has been here with me, whom I find as willing to serve her Majesty as man can be.'[54] There was no hint of any animosity between the two families, and both men were intent upon serving the Queen. At the same time, Ambrose had pressed Walter to accept the post of Marshal of the army in the north, telling Cecil that although 'he took it very friendly at my hand for offering it', he was reluctant to accept the post.[55] He was worried, Ambrose explained, about his ignorance to 'discharge so great a burden', and Ambrose admired Walter's honesty.[56] Pressing him further, he finally convinced Walter to accept, admitting that 'I will love him the better while I live for this great forwardness which I find in him.'[57] That same year Walter was also made Lord Lieutenant of the county of Stafford in reward for his services.[58] Lettice's family had also been called upon to serve the Queen in the suppression of the rebellion, and among those who led a force were her father, her elder brother Henry, and her younger brother, William.

Lettice waited anxiously at Chartley for news of her husband and the rebellion. To her great relief, as well as that of Queen and country, support for the rebels melted away in the middle of December. As they proceeded to march south, the rebels found that their cause was less popular than they had hoped. When word reached them that the Earl of Sussex, Lord President of the North, was marching his force of 7,000 men towards them, the Earls of Northumberland and Westmorland disbanded their men and fled north.[59] On 26 December, the Queen wrote to Ambrose of her relief, 'Forasmuch as we are credibly advertised of the dispersing of this late rebellion by fleeing away of the two Earls, heads of the said rebellion'.[60] As a result, Ambrose could now disband his forces.

The rebellious Earls, meanwhile, managed to flee across the border into Scotland. From there Westmorland escaped abroad, living out the rest of his life in impoverished exile.[61] Northumberland was not so fortunate. He was captured in Scotland in 1572 and handed over to the Queen, who had him executed at York. Mary's intended bridegroom, the Duke of Norfolk, was arrested but was later pardoned. However, displaying staggering naivety, both he and Mary hoped that they would still be able to marry, and continued to make plans to this effect. With this in mind, another plot was hatched, under the auspices of the Florentine banker, Roberto Ridolfi. When the Ridolfi Plot came to the attention of the Queen and her advisors in 1571, Norfolk's luck ran out. In September, he was arrested once more while the evidence against him was compiled.

During the crisis posed by the threat of the Northern Rebellion, Walter had amply demonstrated his loyalty to the Queen. He had proven himself to be an able military leader who had earned the respect of his contemporaries, and having fulfilled his duty he was able to return to Chartley. In turn, the Queen was coming to hold Lettice's husband in increasingly high regard, and in dealing with the Duke of Norfolk's treason she once more requested his assistance. In January 1572, Walter arrived in London. He had brought Lettice with him, and with no London home of their own, the couple took up residence at Durham Place. This may have been Lettice's first visit to the capital in some time, but on this occasion the visit was more for business than pleasure. On 16 January, the Duke of Norfolk stood trial at Westminster Hall, and among the peers who presided over the trial was Walter. He probably discussed the proceedings with his wife, and if this were so then he would have been able to tell Lettice how the Duke's attitude had gone from one of proud defiance, to one of broken resignation following a guilty verdict. Norfolk was condemned for high treason, but in spite of his blatant guilt their ties of kinship – Norfolk was the Queen's second cousin – meant that Elizabeth was reluctant to order his execution. She also wanted to be seen as benevolent, but Norfolk's involvement in more than one plot made this difficult. Under pressure, she eventually signed the Duke's death warrant. On 2 June, Norfolk was executed, telling the crowd that had gathered to witness him die that 'he had never willingly offended the Queen'.[62]

Throughout these testing times Lettice's husband had distinguished himself, and proven that he was wholeheartedly loyal to the Queen. Her husband's success was a great source of pride for Lettice, but if she thought that life was about to resume its normal course then she was to be mistaken: Walter's star was now in the ascendant.

CHAPTER 7

Faithful, Faultless, Yet Someway Unfortunate, Yet Must Suffer

O N 23 APRIL 1572, much to Lettice's gratification and Walter's sense of family pride, his loyalty to Queen Elizabeth was rewarded. On that day he was made a Knight of the Garter, the highest order of chivalry in the land.[1] This was a great honour, and it did not end there.[2] In 1571, his cousin Anne Bourchier had died, securing him the title of Lord Bourchier.[3] Following the death of Anne's father the second Earl of Essex in 1540, the earldom of Essex had become extinct in the male line.[4] This title, one that had previously been invested in Walter's ancestors, was now to become his. On Sunday 4 May 1572, the Queen created Walter Earl of Essex in a splendid formal ceremony at Greenwich Palace. At the same time, Edward Clinton was created Earl of Lincoln.[5] The official account of the proceedings described how Walter,

> being apparelled in a kirtle of crimson velvet and having on his Robe of Estate of crimson velvet with a deep cape of ermine of three rows, and a hood of crimson velvet was conducted and led from the Closet where the chaplains remain to the Queen's presence between the Earl of Sussex on the right hand and the Earl of Huntingdon on the left hand they also having on their Robes of Estate. The Earl of Leicester on the right before the said Sir Walter bear the cap with the circlet. The Earl of Bedford on the left hand of the said Earl of Leicester before the said Sir Walter bear the sword the pommel upward.[6]

As Walter knelt before the Queen underneath her Canopy of Estate, she dubbed him Earl of Essex. It was a moment of great pride and triumph, and while Lettice was not there to witness it in person, she cannot have failed to exult that, through her husband, she was now the Countess of Essex. She was climbing up the social ladder, and such a title was indicative not only of the high favour in which the Queen held Walter, but also of her recognition of his faithfulness. It was probably in order to mark this momentous occasion that Walter's portrait was painted. Dated 1572, several copies of the same version survive, notably in Ulster Museum.[7] Walter can be seen wearing black armour, with his hand resting casually on his helmet. His armour is made richer by the adornment of gold embroidery and red trim. Notably, his wand of office also sports the Garter, which is highly visible in the portrait and was something of which he was immensely proud. On one of the portrait versions the motto *Virtutis, Comes Invidia* (Courage is Envied) is prominent, and this sentiment would be of the utmost importance: Walter was about to embark on a dangerous expedition that would put his own courage to the test.

Now that Walter was ennobled, he began to look towards furthering his career. Lettice had provided him with four living children, and his family were settled – it was time to concentrate his efforts elsewhere. Ireland had long been a source of concern, not just to Queen Elizabeth, but also to her predecessors. Despite being far from an impartial observer, Camden was firm in his presentation of the Irish as unruly, and though they were often divided among themselves, many were united in their hatred of the English. The inhabitants of Ulster in particular were prone to rebellion, the leaders of which were the O'Neill clan. Turlough Luineach O'Neill, who wielded control over several areas of Ireland, including Co. Tyrone, headed them, and he sometimes worked in collusion with the leader of Clandeboye, Sir Brian MacPhelim. MacPhelim, who had 'usurped a great part' of the county, had recently caused havoc in Ulster, burning the town of Knockfergus.[8] To add yet more complications, the Scots were also wielding some control there, creating further problems. For some time Sir Henry Sidney, the Earl of Leicester's brother-in-law, had been serving as Lord Deputy of Ireland, but in 1571 Sir William Fitzwilliam replaced him.[9] However, with few resources forthcoming from England it was a thankless task. The Irish needed to be brought to heel, and what was wanted was some fresh blood.

Camden claimed that Walter 'craved an expedition, following the counsel of those who desired above all things to have him further off, and to plunge him into dangers under colour of honour'.[10] The implication was that the Earl of Leicester wanted Walter out of the way, and that he had a strong motive to do so: Lettice. Leicester's romantic attentions at this time, though, were focused elsewhere. What is also clear is that the impetus for the expedition came from Walter. Camden recalled that he was a man who 'had acquainted his mind with warlike discipline even from his youth', and it was in Ireland that Walter perceived his path to future success: if he could successfully tame the Irish rabble and colonize Ulster, then he would surely earn the Queen's unending favour and great personal glory.[11] Perhaps he first discussed his plans with Lettice, for she would have had some knowledge of what was afoot. Given her ambition, there is likely to have been truth in the claim that 'she encouraged her first husband in his Irish enterprise, in the hopes of sharing in the fame and fortune to be won'.[12] In the spring of 1573, Walter put his proposal to the Queen. He was convincing enough to earn her confidence, for Elizabeth agreed to back him. If he were successful, she would grant him almost the entirety of the territory of Clandeboye. Little wonder that he was enthusiastic, but he appeared oblivious to the obstacles that lay ahead of him. Chief among them was that Walter had to finance the whole expedition himself. This was to be the price of his potential success – if he wanted glory, Ulster would have to be a private enterprise.

It was a high price, but this did not deter Walter and he moved quickly to consolidate his plans. Despite his increased status, though, he did not have the funds to necessitate such an enterprise. The Queen consented to loan him £10,000 (£1,740,000) at a 10 per cent interest rate, but even this was not enough. In order to cover some of the costs, Walter was forced to mortgage some of his lands, chiefly in Essex, but also in Buckinghamshire and Wales. He must have felt confident that the income these estates rendered would not affect the cost of maintaining his wife and children, although this would have been a concern to Lettice, for whom money – as later evidence shows – was always a worry. This may even have been something she broached with her husband, but Walter was driven by other considerations. Money aside, he began to throw himself into the preparations for his mission with enthusiasm.

By the summer he was in London, residing in Durham Place where he and Lettice had previously enjoyed the wedding celebrations of her brother Henry. Due to the nature of his business, it is unlikely that Lettice or their children were with him at this time; they had probably remained at Chartley. Durham Place provided easy access to the court, whose headquarters were at the Palace of Whitehall, and which Walter was frequenting at this time in order to further his plans.[13] It was from Durham Place that Walter wrote to Burghley, on 22 June, desirous for the 'delivery of the money unto me' – the Queen's loan.[14] He had received instructions from Burghley in regards to Ireland and 'the government of the country for a time, and of those I carry with me', but he was now anxious to be on his way.[15] He had much to do before he left England, and he was eager to leave London, for 'I have very great business to do in the country after I have done here; and therefore would I be gladly despatched hence.'[16] Presumably this reference was to his affairs at Chartley, which included his wife and children. Interestingly, Walter also made reference to those at court who spoke unfavourably of his commission, remarking that 'I look for to find enemies enough to this enterprise, and I feel of some of them already.'[17] It is just possible that he was referring to the Earl of Leicester. Whatever his thoughts, he prayed that Burghley would commend him to Sir Henry Sidney, the former Lord Deputy. He did greatly 'desire his favour and furtherance to me in this enterprise', for he was 'a gentleman who I have ever loved, and liked well of'.[18] He was anxious to obtain Sidney's support, and even more so because he was worried that Sidney was against him 'by reason of some speech that hath passed from his near friends'. What this was is unclear.[19]

On 20 July, Walter, still at Durham Place, was preparing to depart from the capital. He had just taken his leave of the Queen, and as he informed Burghley, he was feeling confident: 'I am departed from Her Majesty with very good words, and promise of her favour and furtherance to this enterprise.'[20] With this, Walter also bade farewell to Burghley, and leaving London behind, he made his way to Chartley. He was only there for a short time, and as he said goodbye to his wife and his four young children, none of them could have had any idea when he would return, and what success his mission might bring.

It was in high hopes and confident of success that Walter set sail for Ireland from Liverpool on 16 August. Always a realist and more practical than many of his contemporaries, Lettice's father had expressed doubts over the viability of the mission, but this did not prevent four of his sons from accompanying Walter. Also with the party was Lord Rich, whose son would later play an integral part in the story of Walter and Lettice's eldest daughter, Penelope.[21] It was not a smooth crossing, and heavy gales scattered the ships. According to Walter's own account, some arrived 'to the Isle of Man, some to Cork' in the south.[22] His was one of the few that made it to the port of Carrickfergus; it was not a good start, and things were about to become worse.

───── ⁃◦⁃ ─────

WHILE HER HUSBAND sought to tame Ireland, Lettice was left at home with her four children. They were all growing up fast; Penelope was now ten, Dorothy nine, Robert was just short of his eighth birthday, and Walter was three. Their care, and the management of Chartley and her husband's estates during his absence, occupied much of her time, and there is no clue as to how often – if at all – she corresponded with her husband. Her feelings about his absence are unknown, but what is clear is that Walter soon had concerns about Lettice's behaviour towards their children. She was a somewhat overbearing mother who smothered her children, but they nevertheless adored her. In April 1574, however, while ensconced in Ireland, Walter had written to Burghley to ask if he would consider allowing his heir, Robert, to join his household in order to remove him from 'his mother's wing'. Lettice mollycoddled Robert more than was usual, and this is borne out by his behaviour as he grew into adulthood: he could be both petulant and spoilt.

UPON HIS ARRIVAL in Ireland, Walter had declared to the inhabitants who had gathered to greet him that he and his army were there to 'defend such of the country as had disposition to live dutifully under Her Highness's obedience'.[23] It was not long before word reached Sir Brian MacPhelim that Walter had landed and had made his way to Knockfergus, and it stirred him into action. He wrote to Walter, informing him that he knew of the army that he had brought with him, and had heard that reinforcements were forthcoming. With this in mind, he wanted to know under 'what conditions I would receive him, if he should return to Her Majesty's service'.[24] Shortly afterwards, Walter responded, advising MacPhelim to submit himself to the Queen's mercy, and the following day MacPhelim duly did so. Within days, though, seeing that the English force were at a disadvantage due to their limited knowledge of the terrain, MacPhelim had relented and joined forces with Turlough Luineach O'Neill. In dismay, on 29 September Walter wrote to the Privy Council in London that MacPhelim, 'contrary to my opinion of him, is again revolted'.[25] It was this betrayal that led him to declare that 'they have given me just cause to govern such as shall inhabit with us in the most severe manner' – a warning, it turned out, of what was to come.[26]

ABOVE: Lettice Knollys. Described as 'one of the best-looking ladies of the court', Lettice was favoured by Elizabeth I until she dared to wed the Queen's favourite.

ABOVE: Robert Dudley, Earl of Leicester. Lettice's second husband was the love of her life and the reason she became Elizabeth I's rival.

LEFT: Elizabeth I at the age of fourteen. Elizabeth had been close to Lettice's mother since childhood, and Lettice is also likely to have spent time with the future queen during her youth.

ABOVE: Sir Francis Knollys. Lettice's father was a man of great principle and was devoted to his children. He was one of the few witnesses at Lettice and Leicester's wedding.

RIGHT: Lady Katherine Knollys. The only surviving portrait of Lettice's mother shows her in the final months of pregnancy. In total she would bear her husband sixteen children.

ABOVE: Greys Court, Oxfordshire. It was at Greys that Lettice was born and passed the majority of her childhood.

A·DÑ·1572·
Æ·SVÆ·32·

HONI·SOIT·QVI·MAL·Y·PENSE

VIRTVTIS·COMES·INVIDIA·

ABOVE: Walter Devereux, first Earl of Essex. Created in the year of his ennoblement, this painting shows Lettice's first husband and father of her children, who died while on campaign in Ireland.

ABOVE: Penelope (right) and Dorothy (left) Devereux. Lettice was close to her two daughters, and both girls spent a great deal of their time with their mother in adulthood.

DESPITE HIS ABSENCE and the nature of affairs in Ireland, Walter's family were still very much in his thoughts. He had barely settled in Knockfergus before he was writing to Burghley with a proposition; once again, it concerned his son Robert. It was November, and Robert had just turned eight years old. Walter was in regular contact with Burghley about events in Ireland, but on this occasion his letter assumed a different tone. He began by expressing his heartfelt thanks for the 'love and favour' that Burghley had shown to him, before moving to the main subject of his letter.[27] It was Burghley's friendship, he said, that had prompted him to make him a pledge of 'the direction, education, and marriage of mine eldest son, whom if you can like to match with your daughter, I will presently assure him 2000 marks by the year in England, besides my houses, domains, and parks'.[28] The marital prospects of noble children were always a primary consideration for their parents – particularly in the case of the family heir – and Walter was no different. It would not have been considered unusual for him and Lettice to have given Robert's future marriage some thought, despite the boy's youth. However, as the head of the family it was Walter who had the final say on the matter, and it seems unlikely that he had informed his headstrong wife that he was about to make Burghley such an offer. Lettice would have wished to have been consulted, but she would also have been aware that given Burghley's position with the Queen, a match for her son with his daughter was advantageous. Despite Walter's assurances that 'from myself you shall most assuredly look and ever find as firm, as constant friendship, as your Lordship shall receive by any other alliance in England', it came to nothing.[29]

Back in Ireland, it was not long after their arrival that Walter's followers began to return home. Lord Rich – never enthusiastic about the mission – left within a month, and after only a few months' service Lettice's elder brother, Henry, was sent home. On 2 November, Walter explained to the Queen that 'my brother Henry Knollys, compelled by sickness, is now persuaded by me to pass into England for the recovery of his health, meaning to return in the spring; he hath showed himself here very forward and discreet in all his doing, having escaped very narrowly to have been slain with a shot'.[30]

Thus far his Irish mission had achieved nothing, and to make matters worse he was quickly running out of money and supplies. Similarly, plague and sickness were spreading through his camp, killing his men. The Queen had promised to send more, but as of yet nothing had materialized. Walter's frustrations intensified, and according to Camden he 'grievously complained to the Queen and his friends by letters'.[31] To make matters worse, Sir William Fitzwilliam, the Queen's Lord Deputy, was doing all that he could in order to ensure that the expedition ended in failure. He refused to offer Walter any assistance; behaviour that was based entirely on jealousy. Five years previously, in 1568, Fitzwilliam himself had headed a failed expedition to Ulster, and he believed that if Walter were successful he 'would eclipse his glory in Ireland'.[32] He also worried that the process of colonization in Ulster would lead to rebellion from the citizens – a rebellion that he himself would have to suppress. With dwindling supplies and little support, the mission that had, just months ago, been so enticing for Walter, was beginning to lose its appeal.

In January 1574, the Council wrote to Fitzwilliam urging him to offer Walter his support. The Queen was not impressed by Fitzwilliam's behaviour, and was seriously considering replacing him. It was rumoured that Walter himself would be appointed in his stead, but Lettice's father quashed this theory, informing Burghley that 'Her Majesty hath said that in no wise she will allow my Lord of Essex shall be Deputy of Ireland'.[33] Following the advice of the Earl of Leicester, the Queen had opted to allow Fitzwilliam to remain in his post, while Walter was promised the position of Earl Marshal of Ireland and Governor of Ulster. Fitzwilliam continued though to hinder Walter's progress, and after a lack of support from him following an attempt to bring Turlough Luineach O'Neill to heel, Walter was forced to conclude a truce with the clan chief on 16 March. He could now see that the task he was faced with was becoming increasingly complex, and there were rumours that the Queen was about to recall him home.

In June, Walter journeyed to Dublin, there to consult with the Council as to his next steps. His mind had, however, been much occupied by a quarrel with someone at home: the Earl of Leicester. Conducted through letters that sadly no longer survive, it is clear that hostility had recently broken out between the two men. There has been speculation that this centred on Leicester's interest in Lettice, but there is no evidence that this was the case. The surviving evidence shows that it was actually very much politically based: Walter seems to have been fed false information that led him to believe that Leicester was working against his enterprise from home. He had written to Leicester demanding answers, and in his usual frank manner had made his feelings of betrayal clear. Leicester, in turn, had sent a reply refuting any wrongdoing, and for good measure he had also sent a servant to relate his version of events. Walter appears to have accepted this case of crossed wires, and acknowledged the letter in his response that October. He felt the need, though, to explain that this misinformation had come from a source that he had thought he was able to trust:

> *And finding then, as I conceived by his words, a declination in you, and that joined with your Lordship's ill opinion of me when I thought myself most assured of it, I took this undeserved alteration so unkindly, as I must confess I was not satisfied until I had revealed it unto your Lordship; the manner whereof I trust with friendly interpretation cannot be ill taken, for I am sure it appeared how loath I was to lose your Lordship, and I named both the causes of my grief, and the reporter.*[34]

This, Walter hoped, would be an end to the matter, and he continued to assure the Earl that 'from henceforward no one man's tale shall make me conceive doubtfully of any friend of far meaner calling than your Lordship, of whose good affection towards me I do now see sufficient cause to judge'.[35] Signing himself 'your assured friend and kinsman',

Walter's letter made no reference to his wife: hostility between the two men had been purely political.[36] Matters might now have been resolved, but beneath the surface tension simmered; it was not the last time that antagonism between the two Earls would arise.

WALTER MAY HAVE been gone, but at home Lettice did not spend all of her time pining after her husband – the Countess of Essex had her own life to lead, and she was determined to enjoy it. Presumably leaving her children at home, in the summer of 1574 she travelled to Buxton in Derbyshire. Buxton was fast becoming a fashionable and popular spa resort among the nobility, many of whom travelled there in order to take the medicinal waters to ease ailments. Among others, the captive Mary, Queen of Scots, had been taken to Buxton the previous year by her gaolers, the Earl and Countess of Shrewsbury, in order to take the waters for her rheumatism. Buxton had been famed as a spa town as far back as Roman times, but its prominence had only recently come to the fore. In 1572, the physician John Jones had written a treatise, dedicated to the Earl of Shrewsbury, in which he extolled the benefits of taking Buxton's healing waters. Taking the waters consisted of either drinking them, or bathing in them, and Jones explained that both of these methods could be employed by 'women that by reason of overmuch moisture, or contrary distemperature be unapt to conceive and weak men that be unfruitful'.[37] Buxton also provided a perfect centre to socialize, and in many ways adopted the role of a holiday retreat, where entertainments were staged for the enjoyment of the visiting nobility.

It is possible that some medical ailment necessitated Lettice's visit, but it is more likely that she had travelled there to enjoy the company, for she was part of a large group of friends. On 3 August, Thomas Greves, a servant of the Earl of Shrewsbury's, informed his master that among 'The strangers which be at Buxton at this present' alongside Lady Essex, were Lady Norris, Lady Mildmay, Lady Gresham and Margaret, the Earl of

Bedford's daughter.[38] Listed as Lettice's most particular travel companions were Sir George Digby and his wife Abigail, who hailed from Coleshill in Warwickshire.[39] Theirs was a close friendship, and George had once been the ward of Lettice's father.[40] Lettice would therefore have come to know him well, and not only did she visit him and his wife at Coleshill on several occasions, but later the two families also cemented their allegiance to one another with a marriage. In April 1598, the Digby's son and heir, Robert, was married to Lettice's niece and namesake, the daughter of her youngest sister Katherine and her husband, Gerald FitzGerald, Lord Offaly.[41] It was a happy union that would produce ten children.[42]

While Lettice was at Buxton she and her friends resided at the Old Hall, a house that had been recently built by the Earl of Shrewsbury to accommodate noble guests to the spa town.[43] As a memento of their visit, many visitors scratched their names into the window panes; Lettice's brother William, the Earl of Leicester, and apparently also Lettice herself, did the same. The message she left supposedly read, 'Faithful, faultless, yet someway unfortunate, yet must suffer. L. Essex.'[44] If Lettice did indeed leave this inscription, it gives us some indication as to her state of mind at this time, and perhaps tells us something of her relationship with her husband. Faithful and faultless clearly refer to how she perceived herself, while the latter half of the inscription could be interpreted in several ways. Perhaps it referred to the suffering Lettice was forced to endure on account of Walter's absence; alternatively, she may have been intimating that her unfortunate circumstances were *because* of Walter. By complete contrast, it is just possible that Lettice was not referring to Walter at all; perhaps she was thinking of someone, or something else entirely. She would doubtless have heard of the misunderstanding between her husband and the Earl of Leicester that summer, and her husband's outburst may have been a source of embarrassment to her. Alternatively, according to gossip that will be examined in due course, Lettice had taken the opportunity of her husband's absence to conduct an adulterous affair with the Earl of Leicester – the same man who had been accused of flirting with her at court in 1565. The gossip was almost certainly untrue – in the physical sense at least. It is just possible that Leicester may indeed have been on Lettice's mind at this time.

Leicester, nonetheless, most certainly was conducting a romantic affair at this time, but it was not with Lettice. Though he may have found the Countess of Essex attractive, she was off limits – for the time being at least. The object of Leicester's affection was another, and one whom Lettice would have good cause to resent in the future.

CHAPTER 8

His Paramour, or his Wife

O N 7 AUGUST 1574, the Earl of Leicester became the proud father of a son.[1] He was elated at the birth of his first child, though he was on progress with the Queen when the news was brought to him. However, there was just one problem: the child was illegitimate, for the Earl was not married to his mother; or was he?

Following the death of his first wife, Amy Robsart, in 1560, Leicester had not remarried. His aspirations of marrying the Queen had thus far come to nothing, but whatever his personal feelings towards Elizabeth, he was still a man with desires. They were desires that he had been largely forced to suppress due to his standing and feelings towards the Queen, but as time passed this became more difficult. He later wrote that 'I will not justify myself for being a sinner and flesh and blood as others be', and so it was that at some time in the early 1570s he began an affair with Lady Douglas Sheffield, one of the Queen's ladies.[2] In May 1573, Gilbert Talbot had written to his father from court, 'There are two sisters in ye court that are very far in love with him [Leicester], as they have been long; my Lady Sheffield and Frances Howard. They, of like striving who shall win him better, are at great war together, and the Queen thinketh not well of them, and not the better of him.'[3] Gilbert's news was not fresh, for by now the affair had been going on for some time. Even so, he had certainly accurately related the strength of Douglas's feelings towards Leicester, as well as the Queen's evident disapproval. Though the affair was conducted relatively discreetly, the Queen had become aware of it. She probably did not view Douglas as a threat to her own relationship with Leicester, hence why she seems to have been unusually tolerant – though disapproving – of the situation.

Douglas Sheffield was of an age with Lettice, and was the eldest daughter of William Howard, first Baron Howard of Effingham, and his second wife, Margaret Gammage.[4] Like Lettice, she was also related to the Queen, for her father had been a son of the second Duke of Norfolk, Elizabeth's maternal great-grandfather.[5] Douglas and her family had been well favoured by the Queen in the same way as the Knollyses had, and her father was the Lord Chamberlain of Elizabeth's household. As such, he was a colleague of Lettice's father, who had once been the Queen's Vice-Chamberlain. Douglas herself would have been well known to Lettice, for by the time of the Queen's coronation in 1559, she and her younger sister Mary were also maids of honour. She would therefore have come into regular contact with Lettice, but it is unlikely that they became close friends, for, like Lettice, Douglas was not in the Queen's service for long. In 1560, potentially the same year that Lettice had married Walter Devereux, Douglas was also wedded.[6] Her husband was John Sheffield, second Baron Sheffield, who hailed from a family of Lincolnshire origin.[7] Following the wedding, in the same manner as many ladies, Douglas chose the occasion to retire from court and devote herself to domestic matters. She and her husband produced two children, Edmund and Elizabeth, but the marriage was sadly cut short. On 10 December 1568, Douglas's husband died, leaving his young son to succeed to his title as third Baron Sheffield. It was this that prompted Lady Sheffield to return to court and resume her place in the Queen's household, this time as a gentlewoman of the privy chamber. She was well regarded by her mistress, and she had not been back at court long before she caught the Earl of Leicester's eye. Years of frustration over the Queen's refusal to marry him were taking their toll, and Leicester was a notorious flirt. He and Douglas soon became involved in an affair that would later take a very serious turn.

The circumstances of how the relationship was conducted are unknown, save that it went on for several years and attracted court gossip.

What is certain is that Douglas's feelings towards her lover were stronger than those he harboured for her – and she wanted more from him than he was prepared to give. More than anything, it shows 'the attraction that his personality exercised over women'.[8]

Douglas and Leicester's relationship provided the hostile anonymous authors of *Leicester's Commonwealth* with plenty of fuel with which to slander the Earl, and they took full advantage. The affair features heavily in the tract, and is the source of many false myths on the subject. According to the *Commonwealth*, the couple's relationship began during the lifetime of Douglas's husband. It asserted that long after the death of Leicester's wife Amy, 'he fell in love with the Lady Sheffield', but she being married, the Earl arranged for her husband to 'die quickly with an extreme rheum in his head (as it was given out), but as others say of an artificial catarrh that stopped his breath'.[9] This was a ridiculous claim with no basis in truth, and it was not the only time the *Commonwealth* would level such an accusation. Neither would it be the only time that Leicester would be accused of arranging for the murder of a love rival.

The *Commonwealth* continued to assert that Leicester's 'lust compelling him to another place, he would needs make a postcontract with the Lady Sheffield, and so he did, begetting two children upon her, the one a boy called Robin Sheffield now living, some time brought up at Newington, and the other a daughter, born (as is known) at Dudley Castle'.[10] There is no evidence of a daughter. The son, named Robin Sheffield, was born on 7 August 1574, but Douglas herself would later insist that he was her only child by Leicester, and no further mention is made of this rumour. Leicester duly acknowledged and accepted young Robin as his son, and was eager to make provision for him. The baby remained with his mother for no more than two years, when his father made other plans for the boy, and he was sent to live with a relative of Leicester's, John Dudley, in Stoke Newington. Leicester cared for his son, and as he grew Leicester also made plans for young Robin's education: on 17 May 1588, at the age of fourteen, he would enter Christ Church, Oxford.[11]

The question of whether or not Leicester and Douglas were married is a crucial one, and continues to perplex to this day. In time, it would also come to have potentially damaging consequences for Lettice. Even Camden, who was hostile to the Earl, wrote that 'whether his paramour, or his wife I cannot say'.[12] However, he could not resist stressing that Leicester was 'given awhile to women and in his latter days doting above measure on wiving'.[13] Leicester himself vehemently denied that any such marriage had ever taken place, a claim that he would continue to uphold until his death. Similarly, when rumours later began to surface, Douglas also denied them. When news of Leicester's later marriage became public in around 1579, she still made no word of protest. Even when the Queen questioned her on the matter, she responded 'with great vows, grief and passion that she had trusted the said Earl too much to have anything to show to constrain him to marry her'.[14] Should she have wished to voice her objections she could certainly have done so, for she was single at this time, and it was not until 28 November 1579 that Douglas remarried. Additionally, Douglas's brother, Charles Howard, later wrote to Leicester asking to 'let me be humbly commended unto my honourable good Lady [Lettice], God send you both long to live and love together' – something he is unlikely to have done if he had believed that the Earl had wed and wronged his sister.[15] It was not until 1604, long after Leicester's death, that Douglas changed her story. As will become clear in due course, by then she had a very clear motive for doing so.

The best evidence on the matter comes in the form of a letter, written by none other than Leicester himself. The recipient, though, has been debated: it was either Lettice, or, as is more probable, Douglas. The lady in question was a widow, but frustratingly the date of when it was written is unknown: this detail would have probably settled the matter once and for all.[16] What is clear is that Leicester was on intimate terms with the lady, telling her that 'I have, as you well know, long both loved and liked you.'[17] At the time of writing, he had resolved not to marry her in case it affected his position with the Queen: 'If I should marry, I am sure never to have favour of them [the Queen] that I had rather yet never have wife than lose them.'[18] This in itself lends credence to the recipient of the letter being Douglas, for later Leicester was prepared to risk this and more for the honour of becoming Lettice's husband. By the time his relationship with Lettice had evolved, he had abandoned all hopes of marrying the Queen.

The letter tells the story of the couple's relationship, and it is clear that the lady in question was pushing Leicester for marriage. She had made her feelings for him plain, and her dissatisfaction at the state of their relationship was evident.[19] However, in his letter Leicester took the opportunity to remind the lady that 'This good will of mine, whatsoever you have thought, hath not changed from that it was at the beginning towards you.'[20] Douglas later testified that she and Leicester had been betrothed in 1571 at a house in Canon Row, Westminster, and that when she had discovered herself pregnant with his child in 1573, he had agreed to marry her.[21] The ceremony had, she claimed, taken place that May, but Leicester had insisted that it must remain secret. As a symbol of their union, Douglas recalled that the Earl had given her a diamond ring, and written her numerous letters in which he had addressed her as his wife.[22] Crucially, she was unable to produce either of these elements to support her case. Douglas also claimed that there had been ten witnesses at her wedding, most of whom were her servants. One of these did provide a testimony in support of her claims, but naturally cannot be viewed as a reliable source. Even more suspiciously, she could not remember the name of the minister who had performed the ceremony.[23]

In Leicester's letter the Earl makes clear that he had certainly once cared for Douglas, but his feelings were not strong enough to propel him into matrimony. He reminded her that she had agreed to be his mistress, knowing that he was unable to offer her more:

And I trust, after your widowhood began, upon the first occasion of my coming to you, I did plainly and truly open unto you in what sort my good will should and might always remain to you, and showing you such reasons as then I had for the performance of mine intent, as well as ever since. It seemed that you had fully resolved with yourself to dispose yourself accordingly, without any further expectation or hope of other dealing.[24]

This did not prevent many of Leicester's contemporaries from believing the opposite to be true. Rumours continued to circulate for many years after Leicester's death; in the early seventeenth century, Thomas Rogers, a poet from Bryanstone, composed a poem based on *Leicester's Commonwealth*, called *Leicester's Ghost*, in which he claimed that,

> *When death by happ my first wife's neck had cracked*
> *And that my suit unto the Queen ill sped,*
> *It chanced that I made a postcontract,*
> *And did in sort the Lady Sheffield wed,*
> *Of whom I had two goodly children bred.*[25]

More than four hundred years later, it is difficult to ascertain the truth of the matter. Leicester certainly acknowledged Douglas's son as his own, and made no secret of his existence, but even after the death of his legitimate son in 1584, which left him without a legitimate male heir, he continued to refer to Robin Sheffield as 'my base son'.[26] Neither did Leicester raise any qualms following Douglas's marriage to Edward Stafford in 1579. He may perhaps have made her a promise of marriage, but it seems improbable that this led to anything more. Camden may have been correct in asserting that when Leicester had tired of her, probably upon learning of her pregnancy, he put Douglas away 'with money and great promises'.[27] When, later, in 1583, Douglas's husband was appointed ambassador to France, taking his wife with him, Leicester probably hoped that that would be an end to the matter.[28] Unfortunately, it was not to be. Ultimately the summary of historian Anne Somerset is quite accurate: 'It would take Lettice Knollys, a woman of infinitely stronger character than the lightweight Lady Douglas, to make Leicester prepared to risk jeopardizing his position with the Queen by remarrying.'[29]

BY THE AUTUMN of 1574, more than a year had passed since Lettice had last seen her husband. Walter's time and energy were very much absorbed by affairs in Ireland, and there was little opportunity for him to think of much else. Frustratingly, after a year-long campaign he was forced to accept that his enterprise had achieved none of the glory that he had anticipated. His forces were by now greatly depleted, and though the Queen had sent some reinforcements, many had deserted. Those that did remain were largely suffering from disease and famine – on one occasion Walter had written to the Council that in twenty days his men 'had neither bread, drink, fish, nor flesh, but were forced to beg, and lay their arms, pieces, and garments in gage for to buy them food'.[30] Conditions were appalling, and there was no end in sight.

In an attempt to bring the rebels to heel, Walter had led an expedition to Lough Foyle in Munster. He then offered Turlough Luineach O'Neill safe conduct into his camp in order to discuss terms, but the Irishman 'refused it utterly'. Walter responded by sending him word that 'if he did break with me I would invade his country'.[31] The following evening, O'Neill, accompanied by 200 horsemen and 600 Scots, came close to Walter's camp, but 'being discovered by the scout that gave the alarm, bestowed three or four shot, but, upon the sound of the drum, they took their flight, leaving sixty of their bows behind them, and many of their arrows, and many skulls, which, in the morning, the soldiers found and brought away'.[32] Walter was determined to confront the enemy, and pressed on, marching his men to Omagh, 'putting out of my horsemen to spoil and burn, without having any sight of the enemy'.

But conditions for Walter and his men were still hard, prompting Walter to inform the Council that 'I never had a beef, or any thing else for my household, but at such extreme penny worths as hath not been heard of in this country.'[33] Hearing of the appalling state of the Queen's army, the contemporary poet Edmund Spenser later wrote of the land that

> *Was brought to such wretchedness, that the most stony heart would have rued the same; out of every corner of the woods and glens they came creeping forth on their hands, for their legs would not bear them; they looked like anatomies of death; they spake like ghosts crying out of their graves; they did eat the dead carcasses, they spared not to scrape out of their graves.*[34]

It was all very bleak, and Walter was getting nowhere. Despite his efforts, he had still not brought O'Neill or Sir Brian MacPhelim to heel, and he was determined to do something about it.

Hearing that MacPhelim was contemplating raising another revolt, Walter decided to play dirty. Having journeyed from Dublin to Belfast, in November, he invited MacPhelim there to discuss politics with him. MacPhelim was unaware that Walter had discovered his intent, and was therefore not at all suspicious when he travelled to Belfast, taking his wife with him. Upon their arrival, the unsuspecting guests sat down to a feast, hosted by Walter. Suddenly, Walter's men burst into the room, and set about mercilessly killing MacPhelim's supporters. MacPhelim himself, his wife and his brother were all seized and taken to Dublin Castle, where on Walter's orders they were executed. Such underhand behaviour and brutal dealings reveal another side to Walter's character – one that Lettice herself may have witnessed on occasion. These traits in his personality contrast a good deal with the other image of him as an honourable man who had earned the respect and admiration of many of his contemporaries. Even by contemporary standards, Walter's treatment of MacPhelim and his family was shocking – Lettice could not have failed to have been sickened by the execution of MacPhelim's wife, an order given by her own husband and the father of her children. Walter viewed the situation differently, and seems to have felt that in executing MacPhelim he had made important progress in his mission. Despite the problems he had been faced with, he seems to have enjoyed wreaking havoc across the Irish land, and he was not above continuously threatening his enemies. If he thought that that would be an end to the matter, though, he was to be badly mistaken.

By March 1575, Walter had progressed no further, and by now the Queen had come to the decision to call the expedition off. Walter was fearful that she would order his recall, and it was with this in mind that he wrote her a long letter, begging that 'being now altogether private, I do desire your Majesty's good licence so to live in a corner of Ulster, which I hire for my money; where though I may seem to pass my time somewhat obscurely, a life, my case considered, fittest for me'.[35] Despite the expedition having proved to be a failure, as well as a huge drain on his resources, his enthusiasm for Ireland had not wavered. Had the Queen concurred with his request that he remain in Ulster as a private individual, then Walter would presumably have sent for his wife and children to join him. He may have been content to live thus, but it is highly unlikely that Lettice would have shared his feelings. His reasons for wishing to remain in Ireland are likely to have been motivated by several factors. Although the Queen and those at home could see that he was getting nowhere, Walter himself was still eager to achieve success – after all, there was his sense of pride to consider, and the thought of returning home after a failed campaign was a humiliating one. He had also become fond of the country in which he had spent the past year, and liked the control that he had been given. If Ulster could be colonized, he perhaps perceived more power and a better future for himself there. Walter held no position in England at Elizabeth's court, and with men such as Leicester and Burghley at the forefront of affairs, it was unlikely that he would ever gain any influence with the Queen. Ireland, then, provided him with the best possible opportunity for prestige and control – it was a chance that Walter was determined to grasp with both hands.

The Queen was impressed with Walter's hard work, and on 12 April she had praised his efforts to Sir Peter Carew, an English adventurer who was also in Ireland: 'Considering of the great zeal and noble courage of our cousin the Earl of Essex towards our service and the reducing of the province of Ulster to due obedience and good order.'[36] She evidently held him in high regard, so much so that she wrote to him, calling him 'a rare treasure of our realm, and a principal ornament of our nobility'.[37] It was this that led her to declare that the Ulster enterprise must not be abandoned after all, and to Walter's gratification, his work continued.

THE DAYS OF Walter's absence from home were growing ever longer, leaving Lettice to oversee the development of her children. She had also made some trips of her own. In addition to Buxton the previous year she had also taken the opportunity to visit the court. Residing at Durham Place once more, in January 1575 Lettice had exchanged New Year's gifts with the Queen. On this occasion she had given her kinswoman 'a waistcoat of white satin all over embroidered with Venice gold and silver', and had received three gilt bowls with a cover in return.[38] Her younger sister Elizabeth, still one of the Queen's ladies, had also presented the monarch with a gift, and it is probable that while she was at court Lettice had had the opportunity to spend some time with her while they participated in the traditional New Year's entertainments. But there was someone else who Lettice would also have spent time with.

That New Year, the Earl of Leicester had presented the Queen with a magnificent gift. It was 'a fair gown of black taffeta with a fair border of Venice gold and silver, lined with sarcenet'.[39] It came with a kirtle [a gown] and a doublet, which was garnished with goldsmith's work containing diamonds and rubies. It was a costly gift, and one intended to showcase Leicester's continuing devotion to Elizabeth. But was his attention also captured by another?

The hostile *Commonwealth* claimed that while her husband was in Ireland, the path was now clear for the relationship between the Countess of Essex and Leicester to develop. What is evident is that during Walter's absence, Lettice did indeed have some contact with Leicester. Exactly how much is unclear, but the Kenilworth Game Book confirms that in 1573 – the year Walter left for Ireland – she received the gift of a hind from Leicester.[40] Additionally, the following year she was given three out of nineteen bucks that had been killed. Out of the sixteen named recipients, Lettice was the only one to receive three. In 1575, she would receive yet more game from him, but the significance of this ought not to be overestimated, for there is nothing to suggest that this was anything other than usual practice. Such gifts were normal among members of the aristocracy and Lettice was just one of many to whom Leicester sent such things.[41] Lettice and Leicester did, however, clearly have a friendship at this time – hardly surprising given that they would have seen one another at court, and the relationship between their two families – and he may have grown fonder of her as it became progressively clearer that his relationship with Elizabeth was becoming more platonic. Although they may have been mutually attracted to one another, and could have flirted in the courtly fashion, things are unlikely to have progressed any further at this time. After all, despite her husband's absence Lettice was still very much a married woman. A lady's reputation was of the utmost importance, and with a father as stringent as Sir Francis Knollys when it came to codes of moral behaviour, Lettice knew this well. It is certainly possible that with her husband away she had become lonely, and perhaps sought male company and attention. She would also have been aware of Leicester's relationship with Douglas Sheffield, and as a mother of four she was not a giddy young maid, but old enough to know better.

In character, Leicester and Walter were also wildly different. Though on occasion they argued, Leicester and the Queen were extremely close, and he spoke to her in the manner dictated by courtly love. Walter had no time for such frills, and although courteous, always spoke plainly. He enjoyed the idea of military warfare, and although his Irish campaign was going disastrously, he was a strong man who would handle events very differently from Leicester when he too was placed in a military position.

Leicester blended in well with the fineries of the court, and was both intelligent and polished – a finesse that Walter seems to have lacked.

Leicester, meanwhile, had made his feelings about marriage very clear in his letter to Douglas Sheffield. But that did not mean that he could not give his attempts to marry the Queen one last throw of the dice.

————⟨⟩————

AS THE SUMMER heat of 1575 intensified in London, the Queen began her annual progress. Every summer she left the capital in order to avoid the disease that often spread, and to visit some of the country homes of her nobles. It was also a good opportunity for her to be seen by her subjects, who always delighted in any chance to catch a glimpse of their beloved Queen. On this occasion, Elizabeth journeyed towards the Midlands via Oxfordshire, where a number of hosts were preparing to welcome her. The preparations for such visits were always treated with the utmost seriousness, and a great deal of care was taken over the presentation of both the houses in which the Queen would stay, and the entertainments that would be provided. There was one host in particular who was waiting to make a dazzling impression on the Queen, and he had a very specific agenda.

During the course of her progress, the Queen visited Warwick Castle, where Ambrose Dudley and his third wife, Anne, entertained her. The couple had been married in November 1565, and Anne was a great favourite of the Queen's.[42] The visit was of short duration, and before long Elizabeth and the court set out for their next destination. The journey was short, and on 9 July the Queen arrived at Kenilworth Castle, where the air was 'sweet and wholesome'.[43] Situated just a few miles from Warwick, Kenilworth was the magnificent residence of the Earl of Leicester. The castle stood on the outskirts of the town, which by this time was a well-inhabited market town that hosted regular cattle fairs. This was not the first of the Queen's visits, for she had called on Leicester there several times previously, and neither would it be her last.[44] Yet it was this visit that would be remembered by history, and this visit that has been interpreted as serving a very specific purpose. Many of the ladies and gentlemen of the court were present, and given that she herself was to be involved in that summer's progress, Lettice is likely to have been there to witness the whole sensational spectacle.

Kenilworth was a castle that was steeped in royal history. Begun in the Norman period, the castle had enjoyed a whole host of royal owners and was an important medieval stronghold.[45] When Leicester was granted Kenilworth in 1563, it was in desperate need of modernizing, and the Earl immediately began a vast rebuilding programme. The work had cost him an eye-watering sum of £60,000 (£10,433,000), and had only been completed earlier that year.[46] As a result, Kenilworth had been transformed from a medieval castle into a splendid Renaissance home – one of the great Elizabethan prodigy houses.[47]

The majority of the information concerning the visit, and by far the most detailed, comes in the form of a letter from Robert Laneham. Laneham had been employed as Leicester's Gentleman Usher at court, and therefore knew the Queen's host well. It is likely that he was employed by Leicester to write an account of the visit, with the view to publication and wide distribution. It was intended to paint Leicester in a good light, and it certainly succeeded. Similarly, another contemporary account, written by George Gascoigne, also praised the Earl's efforts. Like Laneham, Gascoigne was also in Leicester's employ, working as both a poet and an actor. On this occasion, he had been called upon to use all of his skills, for it was he who was responsible for devising many of the entertainments that were to be staged.

Many have viewed the 1575 visit as Leicester's final attempt to convince Elizabeth to marry him. There was probably an element of this, but the likelihood is that he had realized by now that his hopes would not bear fruit. Even so, the matter of the Queen's marriage was one that had once again become the topic on everybody's lips, and Leicester was determined to have his say. He was still one of the Queen's closest advisors and friends, and Elizabeth listened to his advice and opinions. Years of proposals from a variety of suitors had come to nothing, but in the 1570s there was reason to believe that a French marriage could be on the cards, for the Queen was once again wavering in her resolve. In January 1571, the Queen's ambassador in France, Sir Francis Walsingham, who would later become her principal secretary, had travelled to Paris in order to make enquiries, for the Queen appeared to be considering a match with Catherine de Medici's son, Henri, who would later succeed as Henri III of France.[48] By the following year, however, the plan had been abandoned, and instead the possibility of a marriage to Henri's younger brother, François, Duc d'Anjou had been raised.[49] Religion would prove to be a sticking point, for Anjou was fervently Catholic, but talks and negotiations were to continue until 1578. Perhaps Elizabeth was seriously considering marriage after all.

WHEN THE QUEEN arrived at Kenilworth, a magnificent entrance had been prepared for her. Mythology was to be a common theme for the visit, and the Queen entered via a bridge that was decorated with gifts from Roman gods and goddesses, including bowls of fish and live fowl which were offered to her. As she was conducted inside Kenilworth's walls, the Queen was greeted by 'the Lady of the Lake with two nymphs', who had come to attend on her.[50] She cannot have failed to have noticed Leicester's bear and ragged staff badge which appeared everywhere, proudly proclaiming Dudley ownership of this once royal stronghold. There were large windows full of costly glass, and many pieces from Leicester's splendid picture collection were also on display.

Eight surviving inventories detail Leicester's paintings at Kenilworth, and among the portraits – numbering more than fifty – were likenesses of both himself and the Queen, as well as one of the Countess of Essex. As historian Elizabeth Goldring highlights, all of the inventories of the Kenilworth portraits were compiled from 1578 onwards, by which time the nature of Lettice and Leicester's relationship had significantly changed.

Lettice was then consistently referred to as the Countess of Leicester in the inventories.[51] That she was referred to as the Countess of Essex in this particular portrait indicates that it was painted, and owned, by Leicester during the time of Lettice's first marriage. The portrait was full-length, and had perhaps been given to him as a gift.[52]

Kenilworth was lavishly furnished, and the surviving inventories bear testament to the wealth and splendour that Leicester had acquired by the time of his death. There were magnificent tapestries, including nine pieces depicting 'hawking and hunting', footstools of 'purple cloth of silver fringed with purple silk and gold', and endless pieces of costly plate and glass.[53] There were also twenty-three maps – yet another of the Earl's interests. Leicester's initials appeared throughout in another visual reminder of his ownership, including on the 'chair of crimson velvet' that was 'embroidered with R.L. in cloth of gold, and the bear and ragged staff in cloth of silver'.[54]

In preparation for the Queen's visit, Leicester's attention had been dedicated not just to the interior of his home, but also to the exterior. A unique garden had been created especially for the Queen, laden with Elizabethan symbolism. Influenced by ideas from abroad and one of the first examples of an English classical garden, it contained an array of fruit trees, including pears, apples and cherries – the Queen's favourite, which were symbolic of heaven. The garden also contained exotic birds in aviaries, and an opulent fountain. Obelisks and spheres were featured, as was the white bear that had been associated with Leicester's ancestors, the Earls of Warwick, since the fourteenth century. It was a brilliant display, encapsulating Leicester's character, achievements and lineage.

The Queen's visit, which would be remembered as the Princely Pleasures for its dazzling splendour, was destined to last for nineteen days. This was the longest stay that Elizabeth made at any of her courtiers' houses, and as such was a testament to the favour in which Leicester was held. Elizabeth was lodged in the same accommodation that she had used during her most recent visit in 1572, although Leicester had significantly improved it especially. There is no indication as to where Lettice was lodged during her stay, and neither is there any mention of her in the ensuing festivities. Nevertheless, she cannot have failed to have been impressed by the spectacular show that Leicester had prepared, and is likely to have participated in the 'dancing of lords and ladies' that took place.[55]

Every day the Queen was entertained by something new that Leicester had devised, whether it be hunting, a masque, dancing or fireworks. The Earl also showered his royal mistress with gifts, but if he had indeed been hoping that his efforts would coerce Elizabeth into reconsidering his suit, then he was to be sadly disappointed. Despite his lavish hospitality, as he bade farewell to his royal guest at the end of the month, Leicester must now have known for certain that a marriage with Elizabeth was never going to transpire: she would never agree to be his bride.

Leaving the magnificence of Kenilworth behind her, the Queen continued with her progress. Travelling via Lichfield, she journeyed further into the leafy Staffordshire countryside. Having presumably travelled ahead while the festivities at Kenilworth were still underway, Lettice was busy ordering the last frantic preparations in her household. On 6 August, she was honoured to be able to welcome her kinswoman to Chartley, and during her brief stay the Queen would also have met Lettice's children – probably for the first time.[56] Her goddaughter Penelope was now twelve, Dorothy was eleven, Robert was nearly ten, and Walter was five. They were all handsome children, and the importance of the royal visit would have been heavily imprinted on them. Compared to the splendour of Kenilworth, Chartley had little to offer, and the Queen's visit lasted for just a night. Regardless, it was still a significant honour, and a sign of the Queen's continued favour towards Lettice. In spite of the rumours that had once surfaced about her and Leicester, the kinswomen were still close, and it was with pride – and also great cost given the state of her finances, thanks to her husband's campaign – that Lettice was able to extend her hospitality.

The Queen's visit was also a sign of the high regard in which she held Walter. Despite his absence, she did find the time to write to him during her short stay in his house. He would have been disappointed to have missed the Queen's visit to his family home, but her letter was one that Walter was delighted to receive, for the Queen praised him for his loyal service. Much to his relief, he had recently had some success in 'taming Ulster', and the Queen acknowledged that 'we understand your painful travails in Ulster and good success. With as small effusion of blood as may be, you have brought Ulster into obedience and quiet.'[57] There was better news to come, for she also informed him that she had decided to send Sir Henry Sidney back to resume his former role as Deputy, in place of the difficult Sir William FitzWilliam. Best of all, the Queen informed Walter that she was creating him Earl Marshal, an office that he was to hold 'during life'.[58] In a postscript written in her own hand, Elizabeth added a more personal note: 'the search of your honour, with the danger of your breath, hath not been bestowed on so ungrateful a Prince that will not both consider the one and reward the other'.[59]

Lettice must have been told of her husband's new post while the Queen was at Chartley – news that came as a source of great pride. As the Queen bade farewell to her kinswoman and her home, she made her way the short distance to Stafford Castle, where Lord Stafford was her host. Lettice remained at home, where before long there was more news of her husband.

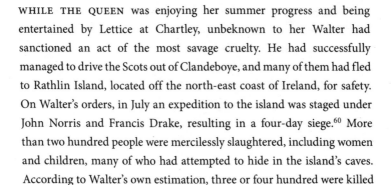

WHILE THE QUEEN was enjoying her summer progress and being entertained by Lettice at Chartley, unbeknown to her Walter had sanctioned an act of the most savage cruelty. He had successfully managed to drive the Scots out of Clandeboye, and many of them had fled to Rathlin Island, located off the north-east coast of Ireland, for safety. On Walter's orders, in July an expedition to the island was staged under John Norris and Francis Drake, resulting in a four-day siege.[60] More than two hundred people were mercilessly slaughtered, including women and children, many of who had attempted to hide in the island's caves. According to Walter's own estimation, three or four hundred were killed in the caves alone, as he proudly informed the Queen.[61] It is difficult to find any justification for such an act of barbarity, showcasing Walter's ruthless nature. Far from being appalled by Walter's violent methods, both he and the Queen viewed his actions as necessary in order to tame the unruly nation. It was to be his last act in Ireland, and it was one that made a lasting impression.

That autumn, Sir Henry Sidney returned to Ireland. In spite of the recent atrocities, he was full of praise for Walter, who he described as 'so noble and worthy a personage', and 'complete a gentleman'.[62] There were many at home who had taken the opportunity of Walter's absence to criticize his actions in Ireland, but Sidney was not among them. Instead, he commended Walter on his 'painful travels in the hardest part of this miserable county'.[63] Nevertheless, it was time for him to abandon Ireland, for he had been summoned home. Almost two years in Ireland had achieved very little, and had drained all of his resources, leaving him heavily in debt. It had always been an ambitious enterprise, but one that was fraught with a great number of difficulties: lack of resources, continued opposition both at home and in Ireland, not to mention the rugged determination of the Irish rebels, meant that Walter was faced with a gruelling task. In spite of this he had persevered, but he realized that his priorities now lay elsewhere, chiefly in the replenishing of his empty coffers.

Leaving Ireland behind, Walter set sail for home, landing in October. He would soon be reunited with his wife and his children, something that filled him with anticipation. However, it was not long before gossip of an unsavoury nature began to reach his ears: it involved both the Earl of Leicester and his wife, and was far from the homecoming that Walter could have hoped for.

CHAPTER 9

Great Enmity

T HE REVELRIES OF Kenilworth and the Queen's visit to Chartley seemed all but forgotten when Walter landed in South Wales in October 1575. Having 'much wasted his patrimony' in Ireland, after an arduous journey he quickly proceeded to Lamphey.[1] Upon his arrival he was 'very much weather-beaten, where he is driven to stay to recover himself, and to attend his servants' arrival, who were by the same tempest dispersed from his company'.[2] From Lamphey he may have journeyed to Chartley to be reunited with his family, whom he was eager to see. It had been more than two years since Lettice had last seen her husband, and there is no reason to believe that it was anything other than a warm and friendly reunion. Much had changed during Walter's absence: his eldest daughter, Penelope, was approaching her thirteenth birthday, and was growing into a beautiful young woman. Her father had high hopes for her, and in due course he confidently expected to arrange a marriage for her with Sir Philip Sidney, son of the Lord Deputy of Ireland, and nephew of the Earl of Leicester. Dorothy was also a pretty creature, and then there were his sons. Robert and Walter were both continuing their education at home, where their mother doted on them.

Pleasant though this family reunion may have been, it was not long before Walter's thoughts had once again returned to business. On 10 November, Sir Francis Walsingham wrote to Burghley from Windsor that 'I met with a messenger sent from the Earl of Essex with letters to Her Majesty, by the which he did give Her Majesty to understand that he hath arrived within this country, and that he presently desired that he might have leave to come to see Her Majesty.'[3] Walter was already eager to return to court; he was feeling deflated from the disastrous Irish campaign, and was heavily in debt. It was for this reason that he was keen to obtain an audience with the Queen, and plead his case in person. Elizabeth had responded to his letters, telling him that 'she was glad of his arrival, and was well pleased that he should repair to the court, with condition that with over much haste he did not distemper his body'.[4]

The Queen's reply gave Walter all of the encouragement he needed, and he wasted no time in preparing to journey south to London, taking Lettice, and also possibly his children, with him. He was, he said, residing in the capital 'partly in view of my own poor estate, which I find far altered from that it was at my departure into Ireland'.[5] Walter's comment can be interpreted in one of two ways. It is beyond question that his finances had been severely depleted in the Queen's service, and his remark could, therefore, have been an attempt to highlight this to the Queen in order to incur her sympathy, in the hope of gaining financial recompense. It is unclear whether he was referring to the physical state of Chartley, or the broader issue of his finances. In either scenario, Chartley and the running of Walter's estates had been entrusted to Lettice's care in his absence, and the other explanation is that he was genuinely unhappy with what he found upon his return. At the point of his departure into Ireland he had felt confident that – though financially stretched – enough provision had been set aside for Lettice and their children. Neither he nor Lettice could have predicted the length of his absence, and it may be the case that, finding that Walter was away for longer than she anticipated, Lettice had genuinely struggled to maintain her husband's estate on a limited income. In such circumstances, the past two years would have been both stressful and full of uncertainty for Lettice, who would have been forced to make many decisions about her husband's estate alone. The past two years had been demanding for Walter, but Lettice, also, is likely to have faced challenges of her own.

With or without their children, the Earl and Countess of Essex spent Christmas in the capital, almost certainly residing at Durham Place. The return to London may have come as a welcome change to Lettice, although as the court was in residence at Hampton Court on the outskirts of the city, she is unlikely to have participated in any of the celebrations there. It is probable, however, that they travelled there for New Year in order to present their gifts to the Queen. Walter gave his mistress 'one whole piece of black velvet, the ground white satin fringed with black knots', while Lettice presented 'a forepart of a kirtle, a pair of sleeves and a partlet of green satin cast over with net work'.[6] Revelries, though, were very far from Walter's mind, and he was instead busy seeking financial compensation for his losses in Ireland. Whether Lettice accompanied him on each of the many occasions that saw Walter travelling back and forth from the court to Durham Place is unknown, but in any case she would certainly not have lacked for company or entertainment.

Walter recognized that 'this Christmas time [was] altogether dedicated to pastimes, and, therefore unapt for such as be suitors', but he could not resist talking about business.[7] In his letter to the Privy Council on 29 December, written from Durham Place, he claimed that since his return he had conferred with those to whom he had entrusted the management of his estates. It was through them, he said, that 'I find how heavy mine Ireland service hath been to me, by consideration of mine expenses past, my debts present, and the danger that my lineage resteth in, if order be not presently taken in it.'[8] Furthermore, 'my servants in household' were many, and 'more than I am willing to continue about me'.[9] His plea suggests that he and Lettice were living an extravagant lifestyle that was beyond their means, but was almost certainly exaggerated in order to obtain sympathy. Trips to Buxton and the court were not cheap, and the funds for Lettice's outings while Walter was away had come directly from his coffers. Walter begged the lords of the Council to 'be suitors with Her Majesty to grow to some speedy resolution in that which shall be determined concerning me; for upon that determination resteth the course of my life hereafter'.[10]

Unhappily, there was to be no quick fix and, with no money forthcoming, Walter instead turned his attentions to petitioning the Queen.

Lettice was still with her husband at Durham Place, when he wrote to the Queen on 13 January 1576. By now she was aware that her husband's debts were increasing, as was his distress that the matter was being dragged out by the Queen's failure to compensate him. It would no doubt have been a constant topic of conversation between the couple, as they waited to hear what Walter's future would hold. He implored the Queen for her intervention, telling her honestly that

finding that my ability to serve you, or to maintain that estate whereunto your Majesty hath called me, resteth much upon your gracious dealings with me for my charge past, I have, upon the comfort of your Majesty's former favourable writings and speeches, been bold to press the Lords of your Privy Council to be earnest with your Majesty for your speedy resolution concerning me.[11]

He had received no answer from the Privy Council, and as such was becoming increasingly irritated. To make matters worse, it seems that in order to ease his worries the Queen had made him several offers, all of which he had rejected. This left Elizabeth offended, and Burghley exasperated. Precisely what these offers were is unknown, but Walter felt that they were not good enough to compensate him and held out for more. Following Burghley's counsel, he had written a draft of a letter to the Queen in which he explained his reasons for declining. Having sent the letter first to Burghley for his perusal, he was annoyed when 'he hath added many things to humiliate my style'.[12] He was a proud man, and was determined to stand his ground – he would not grovel. Given Lettice's later behaviour and the tone she exercised in her extant letters, it seems likely that she encouraged her husband in this. Such behaviour towards the Queen, though, was unwise, and, perhaps realizing that he had pushed her too far, by 5 February Walter had changed his tune. By this time he and Lettice were preparing to leave London, for they were so indebted that 'no man will give me credit for any money'.[13] A later inventory of Lettice's possessions shows ample examples of finery, all appropriate to her rank, and as such she would not have taken kindly to having been deprived of her luxuries. Walter wrote to Sir Francis Walsingham, asking him to deliver a letter to the Queen, and 'to promise in my behalf that I will ever be ready to adventure my life, and to spend in Her Majesty's service every thing that her highness shall think good to bestow on me'.[14] Above all, 'my desire is, that you will labour to keep me in Her Majesty's good favour, which I more regard than all that I have spent'.[15] Having done all that he could and hoping to retain the Queen's good grace, Walter and Lettice left London behind and returned home to Chartley.

Fortunately for Walter and his family, in March he received word that he was to return to Ireland. Quite what prompted the Queen to send him back is unclear, as is Walter's initial reaction. He was, however, persuaded to resume his post once more, and his spirits were bolstered when in May the Queen granted him an additional three hundred soldiers, of which a hundred were cavalry.[16] For Lettice and her children, Walter's acceptance meant that he would once more be leaving home, and though she may have been dismayed to be losing his company, Lettice was relieved at the prospect of resolving their financial problems. For Walter, it appeared that all of his campaigning and hard work in Ireland had not been in vain, and it was with a renewed sense of vigour that he began to make preparations to leave home once more.

IN WALTER'S ABSENCE, rumours about the nature of the relationship between Lettice and the Earl of Leicester had been circulating; according to the hostile authors of *Leicester's Commonwealth*, an affair was now in full swing, resulting in unbearable tension between Lettice's husband and her supposed lover. The *Commonwealth* was not released until after Walter's death, but it nevertheless reflected the rumours that were current in

London at the time. Chief among these, as reported by a Spanish agent, was that 'whilst Essex was in Ireland his wife had two children by Leicester'.[17] Such a notion was absurd and had no basis in fact – to start with, for at least part of Walter's absence Leicester had been conducting a relationship with Lady Douglas Sheffield. It is also unlikely that a woman of Lettice's standing would have allowed herself to become embroiled in an affair by which she was forced to conceal two children. Such a liaison could not have been hushed up, and would have caused a great scandal. The authors of the *Commonwealth* later related a similar story, claiming that Walter had returned from Ireland 'with intent to revenge himself upon my Lord of Leicester for begetting his wife with child in his absence'.[18] Although the authors mention one child rather than two, they went further by claiming that the child that Lettice bore was a daughter, who was raised by Lady Dorothy Chandos, the wife of Lettice's brother William.[19]

The gossip was both damaging and scandalous, but it was probably not the reason that the Spanish agent wrote of the 'great enmity which exists between the Earl of Leicester and the Earl of Essex'.[20] Neither was it the reason that 'great discord is expected in consequence'.[21] Similarly, Walter had certainly not returned from Ireland 'openly threatening Leicester', as Camden claimed, 'whom he suspected to have done him injuries'.[22]

In recent years, Walter and Leicester had not had the easiest of relationships, and there is no doubt that the rumours about the Earl and his wife would have reached Walter's ears. They were humiliating for all parties – particularly Walter, and there was little that they could do in order to stop the rumours circulating. Retaining a dignified silence, they chose not to respond and instead waited for the gossip to die down. Whether the rumours placed a strain on the couple is unknown, but if Walter did harbour suspicions about his wife and Leicester, they did not concern him unduly – at least not on the surface. After all, he had another Irish campaign to prepare for, and it was one that required all of his energies.

CAMDEN INSINUATED THAT it was Leicester who contrived to have Walter returned to Ireland 'by his cunning court tricks', but there is no evidence of this.[23] In the time that had passed since Walter and Lettice's departure from London, Walter had been busy sorting out his affairs. As he informed Walsingham, 'I have made some disposition of my lands, one part of the conveyance remaineth with myself, the other, my desire is, shall rest in your keeping.'[24] He had entrusted a servant to deliver the necessary paperwork to Walsingham, and with 'the conveyance of my lands there is also my will; my earnest desire is, that you will take them into your custody'.[25] It is interesting that though he had left her in charge of his lands, he chose not to entrust his will into Lettice's safe-keeping – when its contents later emerged, his reason became abundantly clear.

Lettice had been reunited with her husband for a little over six months, when she had to bid farewell to him once more. In distant Staffordshire, the rumours that had been circulating about her in London seemed to be nothing but a dull and unpleasant memory. Nevertheless, it may have been a cause of both relief and concern to her when her husband left home. If the rumours had caused tension in her marriage, she would have been relieved to have had some space from Walter in order to allow things to heal; his absence, however, left Lettice vulnerable to further gossip. Whatever the state of matters between them, as Walter left Chartley and England behind once more, he can have had no idea that he would never see his wife and children again.

Walter left Chartley in mid-July, and after a smooth crossing he arrived in Dublin on 23 July. He received a 'good welcome the same day by the citizens of Dublin, and the gentlemen of the country that came to him at his landing'.[26] Back in Ireland with a renewed sense of vigour, Walter spent much of the rest of July and August in pleasantries and entertainments: on 24 July the Chancellor, with whom he resided in Dublin until 9 August, hosted a splendid feast for him. He was also 'invited to sundry of his friends', including the Archbishop of Dublin and the Countess of Kildare.[27] While he was there, the Lord Deputy, Sir Henry Sidney, joined him. It was Sidney who 'solemnly caused my Lord's patents of Earl Marshal' to be read and published, and 'invested my Lord in his office'.[28] Walter was once again Earl Marshal of Ireland. Despite Camden's claims that it was a 'vain title', for Walter it was a great honour, and served as some small reward for his services.[29] Sadly, he was not to enjoy it for long.

THE KENILWORTH GAME Book, in which Lettice features regularly, shows that in 1576 she visited the Earl of Leicester's estate to enjoy the hunt. Hunting was a passion shared by both Lettice and Leicester, and on this occasion there was 'killed by my Lady Essex a buck'.[30] It is unclear whether this visit took place before or after Walter's departure for Ireland, or whether indeed Leicester was present – it was not unusual for his friends and family to hunt on his estate in his absence – but in either circumstance, given the whispers about Lettice and Leicester, the timing of the visit is interesting. Equally interesting is that on two other undated occasions that year, Leicester sent 'to my Lady to the court' – Lettice – two separate gifts of game.[31] That they were friends is certain, but was there more than friendship on their minds? By this time Leicester's relationship with Douglas Sheffield was well and truly over, and he had realized that the Queen would never be able to offer him anything more than friendship. Lettice was an attractive woman who he had known for many years, and he had flirted with her before. In turn, though Lettice certainly had once loved her husband and probably still did in many ways, their enforced separation meant that for several years they had spent very little time together. As such, it is perfectly plausible that they had grown apart, and that Lettice had become lonely. Leicester may even have become her confidant. That she and Leicester now began to view one another in a romantic capacity is not beyond the bounds of possibility, but Lettice was still a married woman. Even so, Kenilworth was not too great a distance from Chartley, so it is certainly possible that when Lettice journeyed there in order to hunt, she also met with Leicester, perhaps on more than one occasion. The gifts of game he sent to her at court could have been nothing more than a friendly gesture, or maybe something more. Given what later transpired, an affair of some sorts between the pair is possible at this time, but if this was the case then given Lettice's marriage neither of them had any reason to believe that matters between them would develop any further.

———⌒∾———

ACCORDING TO THE account of Walter's trusted servant, Edward Waterhouse, on the evening of Thursday 30 August, 'having dined and supped at his own house, he [Walter] was seized with a flux [diarrhoea]'.[32] At first there seemed to be no cause for alarm, but in the coming days Walter's illness continued to plague him. Matters were made worse by the fact that 'he travelled rapidly', but although he 'ate as usual' he occasionally complained of 'grief in his belly', and would say that he never had hearty grief of mind but a flux must accompany it'.[33] Initially, he was suspicious of the cause of his illness, for his servant had also fallen sick, and he wrote to his lawyer, Richard Broughton, that this 'maketh me suspect of some evil received in my drink'.[34] However, when his servant recovered, both he and those around him quickly dismissed that notion.

Eventually returning to his own lodgings in Dublin, Walter began to grow gradually weaker. A contemporary informant wrote to Walsingham to advise him that since 8 September, Walter had been 'marvellously tormented with pains in the stomach' that were becoming worse.[35] Edward Waterhouse described his master's symptoms in detail, relating that he had been passing 'twenty or thirty stools everyday, and is already many times bloody and the rest of his stools black burnt colour'.[36] In an attempt to affect a cure Walter had tried many remedies, including the popular 'unicorn's horn which has made him vomit many times'.[37]

With no signs of improvement, Walter had resolved to return home in order to promote his recovery. Not wishing to make the whole laborious journey home to Chartley, he instead planned to embark for Milford

Haven and 'repose myself at my house at Lamphey til I shall understand how God will work his will in me'.[38] His physician, Dr Peny, had been instructed to meet him there, and Waterhouse had advised the doctor to 'bring all things necessary for this disease'.[39] Walter would also have sent word to Lettice of his plans, although it is unlikely that he would have expected her to travel the long distance to Lamphey to meet him. Sadly, he never made it home.

Although Walter and those around him had optimistically expected him to recover, as September progressed he grew weaker; it soon became clear that he was dying. He himself had accepted this, and looking to the future he began to put his affairs in order. On 20 September, he wrote to the Queen, calmly informing her that the hour of his death was approaching. He begged her forgiveness for any offence he had ever caused her: 'not only for my last letters wherewith I hear your Majesty was much grieved but also with all other actions of mine that have been offensively conceived by your Majesty'.[40] This proud man was now much humbled, and in his final days he sought forgiveness of the whole world, and looked only to God. He commended his 'poor children' to the Queen, begging that 'since God doth now make them fatherless', she should be 'as a mother', and ensure that they continued to receive a good education.[41] He was concerned that, thanks to his dwindling resources, as a widow Lettice would not have the means to support the children herself, hence his petition to the Queen. Walter also implored his royal mistress to allow his heir, Robert, 'upon whom the continuance of my house remaineth', to inherit some of his lands.[42] There was one point, though, on which he was adamant: 'I do not wish him mine office of Earl Marshal here [Ireland].'[43] His worries in this quarter were understandable, so it is little wonder that he ended thus: 'he is my son, and may be fit for more in his life than his unfortunate father hath in his possession at his death'.[44] For the time being, his wishes would be granted, but in the future Robert and Ireland would come to be closely entwined.

The welfare of his heir continued to trouble Walter, and the following day he wrote to Burghley. Commending Robert to him, he once again expressed his hope that his son ought to be allowed to join his household for the continuation of his education. If he were able to divide his time during his minority between Burghley and Thomas Radcliffe, Earl of Sussex,

> to the end that as he might frame himself to the example of my Lord of Sussex in all the actions of his life tending either to the war or to the institution of a nobleman, so he might also reverence your Lordship for your wisdom and gravity, and lay up your counsels and advices in the treasury of his heart.[45]

Having done all that he could, Walter ended his letter with a final farewell: 'And so to the Lord I commit you, sequestering myself from henceforth from all worldly causes.'[46] Walter's letter to Burghley may have been the last he ever wrote; if he did write a final letter of farewell to Lettice then it has not survived. His letters to the Queen and Burghley reveal that he was more concerned for his children's welfare than that of his wife – Lettice would have to take care of herself. Certainly, for the most part, children were the primary concern of parents who were approaching their end, and Walter could feel confident that Lettice, as a resilient woman who had coped with his long periods of absence from home thus far, would be able to do so again.

At eleven o'clock on the morning of 22 September, Walter died at Dublin Castle. He was thirty-seven years old. The previous evening he had called for his musician, William Hewes, to sing and play the virginals for him, and from there he had gone rapidly downhill.[47] Whispers of a suspicious death caused by poisoning immediately surfaced, and though he was not directly accused, the Earl of Leicester was the prime suspect. Camden later wrote that 'This death of so noble a man, was not without suspicion of poison amongst the vulgar sort', an assertion that was influenced by *Leicester's Commonwealth*, whose authors claimed that Walter died 'of an extreme flux, caused by an Italian *recipe*, as all his friends are well assured'.[48] This, they said, was the work of a surgeon, 'A cunning man and sure in operation', who had been employed by Lettice.[49] In their scandalous claim, the authors asserted that

> *if the good lady had been sooner acquainted and used his help [the surgeon], she should not have needed to have sitten so pensive at home and fearful of her husband's former return out of the same country, but might have spared the young child in her belly, which she was enforced to make away for clearing the house against the goodman's arrival.*[50]

The claims that Lettice had had a child by Leicester have already been quashed, but the *Commonwealth* now portrayed her as a murderess.

These assertions did not, however, emerge until later. It is therefore important to recognize that when rumours that Walter had been poisoned began to circulate, nobody pointed the finger in Lettice's direction. *Leicester's Commonwealth* was printed eight years after Walter's death, and its authors were the only source that directly accused her of having any involvement in the decease of her first husband. At the time, she was not suspected – at least not openly – of having had any involvement in Walter's demise, and for good reason.

In order to quell suspicions of poison, the Lord Deputy, Sir Henry Sidney, with 'diligent inquisition' immediately ordered that a post-mortem be conducted on the late Earl's body.[51] Sidney held Walter in high regard, asserting that he was 'a lusty, strong, and pleasant man', whose 'breath was out of his body' completely unexpectedly.[52] Sidney was in no doubt that Walter's soul was 'in Heaven; for in my life I never heard of a man to die, in such perfectness'.[53] As such, the post-mortem was taken with the utmost seriousness, but as Sidney himself announced, 'there was no appearance or cause of suspicion, that could be gathered that he died of poison'.[54] The Earl of Essex, it was declared, had died of natural causes. The results of the post-mortem report were also supported by the account of Walter's secretary, Edward Waterhouse, and his chaplain Thomas Knell, 'an honest preacher in this city', declared the same.[55] It is thus clear that despite the rumours, in reality few of Walter's contemporaries believed that he had been poisoned. The likeliest cause of his death is dysentery. Even Camden, who was hostile to Leicester, had to admit that although he believed that Walter was 'pining away with grief and sorrow', it was unlikely that he was poisoned.[56] As he had heard it, in the Earl's final moments, he

> piously rendered his soul to Christ, dying of a flux with most grievous torments, after he had prayed standers by, to warn his son being then scarce ten years old, to set always before his eyes the six and thirtieth year of his age, as the uttermost scope of his life, which neither he nor his father had passed.[57]

The circumstances of how Lettice learned of her husband's death are unknown, as is her reaction. Sir Henry Sidney later revealed that in his final hours Walter 'forgot not to send weighty warnings to some of his absent friends by message', but whether this included a final message for Lettice is unclear.[58] Outwardly, she displayed all of the signs of grief that would have been expected of her. A later inventory of Leicester House records a portrait of her during her tenure as Countess of Essex, dressed in mourning; it is reasonable to assume that this was for Walter, and such portraits were not uncommon.[59] However far apart they may have drifted in recent years, a circumstance caused by Walter's absence, she had loved him once, and in many ways probably still did. Walter's death had also left her four young children fatherless, and his loss was keenly felt.

Following the completion of the post-mortem, Walter's body was returned home for burial. It was taken to Carmarthen, the town of his birth, although it was not, by all accounts, an easy journey. When the party landed in Wales, they were forced to travel to their destination 'with most painful labour of his servants in extreme tempestuous weather upon their backs, where horses with litters could not go'.[60] Waterhouse had been sent to Chartley 'to have attended on my Lord of Essex to the burial of his father', and it may indeed have been he who broke the news of Walter's death to his family.[61] He related that the young Earl was unable to travel to Carmarthen, for having 'conferred with such as are about the Earl, and understood by them the tenderness of his body, I durst not consent to take him from hence in this extreme cold weather, to so long a journey'.[62] Lettice was among those to whom Waterhouse referred, and her concern for her young son is understandable. Robert does appear to have been genuinely ill at this time, and he himself wrote to Lord Burghley begging to be excused.[63] As such, the role of chief mourner at Walter's funeral was assigned to his brother, George Devereux.[64]

On 26 November, Walter was laid to rest in the chancel of St Peter's Church in Carmarthen, the sermon being preached by Richard Davies, Bishop of St David's.[65] In accordance with custom, Lettice did not attend her husband's funeral, and Walter's grave is unmarked.

At thirty-three, Lettice was now a widowed mother with four young children to support. Knowing the debts that her husband had incurred during his time in Ireland, this was a source of great concern to her, as would shortly become clear. Walter's final will, entrusted to Sir Francis Walsingham before his final journey to Ireland, had been made on 14 June.[66] His primary concern had been the welfare and provision of his children: at his death, Lettice's eleven-year-old son Robert succeeded his father as the second Earl of Essex. In monetary terms, thanks to Walter's Irish campaign it was a poor inheritance, and 'Young Robert was the poorest Earl in England.'[67] On his deathbed, Walter had vested the responsibility for 'the burden and care of the now young Earl of Essex causes during the Earl's minority' to his lawyer, Richard Broughton of the Inner Temple.[68] He felt that Broughton could manage them better than Lettice. Robert was Walter's main concern, and much of his will was taken up with his thoughts for his future. He had also expressed his cherished hope that his eldest daughter Penelope, now thirteen, would be married to

Leicester's nephew and heir, Sir Philip Sidney. He was so desirous of the match that he had started referring to Philip as 'son'. Sadly for Walter, it was a wish that was never to be fulfilled.

Walter's will made few mentions of Lettice. On the occasions her name does appear, there is nothing to suggest that his feelings for her were anything other than affectionate. He referred to her as 'my right well beloved wife the Lady Lettice Countess of Essex', and made provision for her jointure – the lands and estates that would be settled on her for the time during which she survived Walter.[69] These included properties in Essex, and manors in the counties of Hertford, Gloucester, Pembroke and Brecknock. He also gave her the use of 'my said manor and park of Benington', a house that he had inherited from Anne Bourchier.[70] It was a house that Lettice would make use of in later years. These estates rendered a total of £550 (£95,600) a year: it was a reasonable, if not a sizeable income for a woman of Lettice's status. In addition, though, Walter also ordered that 'the disposition of my goods, jewels, plate and household stuff I will and bequeath that my said wife the Countess of Essex shall have'.[71] This boosted her income in terms of moveable goods, although she would later complain bitterly that it was not enough. There was, however, one other major problem with Walter's will: it made no provision for Lettice to remain at Chartley. While her son Robert would now inherit the property, he was a minor who had no jurisdiction over who remained in his house and who would live elsewhere until he attained his majority, so she would be forced to move out. It was only through the good graces of Lord Burghley, who now assumed Robert's care, that she and her children were allowed to remain there until Christmas. This meant that Lettice now not only had to contend with finding a new home, but also had to deal with the many financial issues that needed to be addressed following Walter's death. It was certainly not a situation to be envied, and it was one that Lettice greatly resented.

With Walter now dead, had Lettice and the Earl of Leicester wished to be together they were now at liberty to do so. They were both widowers who had experienced the loss of a spouse, and there was a spark of attraction between them. Just one obstacle remained: the Queen's jealousy. After all, it was Elizabeth's 'Sweet Robin' that Lettice was on the verge of seducing. For the time being, neither she nor Leicester made any move: there may have been a spark, but it had yet to develop into a burning flame.

CHAPTER 10

Up and Down the Country

A T THE TIME of their father's death, Lettice's children were with their mother at Chartley. On 14 November 1576, Edward Waterhouse arrived at the house, where Lettice's eleven-year-old son Robert, now Earl of Essex, impressed him. Feeling a natural loyalty to the boy on behalf of his late father, Waterhouse wrote to Sir Henry Sidney to inform him that 'I do not think that there is at this day so strong a man in England of friends, as the little Earl of Essex, nor any man more lamented than his father, since the death of King Edward.'[1] Given his affinity to Walter, it is little wonder that Waterhouse had exaggerated the effects of his death, but nevertheless it is clear that the welfare of his heir was considered to be of great importance.

Just days before Walter's funeral, Lord Burghley had written to the young Earl, acknowledging that his 'father commended me to your Lordship on his deathbed for your Lordship's wisdom'.[2] It was a responsibility that Burghley took seriously, and at the turn of the new year, on 11 January 1577, young Robert left Chartley behind as he journeyed to join Burghley's household in accordance with his father's wishes. He travelled to Cecil House, Burghley's London residence, and over the next few months his time was divided between there and Theobalds, Burghley's Hertfordshire estate.[3] While he was there, he was given the opportunity to mix with other young boys, including Burghley's heir, also called Robert – all may have been harmonious between the two boys now, but that would later change.[4] This would have been a new experience for Robert, who had never been away from home before, and had previously relied on his sisters and his younger brother for company. It was also the first time that he had not been under his mother's watchful supervision, and instead Burghley's wife, Lady Mildred, oversaw his care. Mildred was herself a great scholar who had been praised as one of the most learned women in the kingdom, and Lettice could not but be impressed by the positive influence she would wield over her son.[5] She herself later wrote to Burghley, giving 'thanks for the great goodness and fatherly love and friendship it pleaseth you to show to my son, who may say he hath happily met with a second father instead of a guardian'.[6] Although Robert had now been removed from her protective care, she did at least appreciate the opportunity he was being given. She may also have taken the chance to visit him upon his arrival at Cecil House, for she herself was already in the south.

WITH WALTER LAID to rest, Lettice moved forward with her life. Having been forced to remove herself from Chartley after Christmas in accordance with the terms of Walter's will – her home for more than a decade – she had no option but to turn to her family for support. She had arranged to stay with her father at her childhood home of Greys Court, and at some time shortly after Christmas she began her journey south, taking her daughters and her younger son Walter with her. Given the circumstances, she could have been forgiven for omitting to send a New Year's gift to the Queen, but she did not. Now more than ever she needed her royal kinswoman's support, and so in January 1577, less than four months after Walter's death, she almost certainly paid a visit to court before travelling to Greys. The Queen was at Hampton Court, and listed among her numerous sumptuous New Year's gifts from her courtiers was one from Lettice: 'the forepart and bodice of a kirtle of ash colour covered with a net of silk and gold, lined with crimson sarcenet'.[7] It was a thoughtful gift, and one that was perhaps also intended to remind the Queen that Lettice was now a poor widow who faced an uncertain future.

Given the favour in which the Queen had held Walter and her fondness for Lettice, she took the opportunity to condole her kinswoman on her loss, but there is no indication that she offered Lettice any practical help at this time.

Unsurprisingly, Walter had died deeply in debt, and it was not long before his creditors came knocking at Lettice's door. Not only did he owe £6,190 (£1,000,000) to the Queen, but he had also accrued large debts elsewhere.[8] Besides this, Lettice already had enough to deal with, for she and her children had lost their home and she resented the small jointure which Walter had assigned to her. This rankled so much that she 'by some forward advice did utterly renounce and refuse the jointure to her assigned by her late husband'.[9] But Lettice was no meek widow; rather than accepting what Walter had felt that she should have, she was determined to pursue what she believed to be rightfully hers: in short, she wanted more. She was at her father's home, Greys Court, when on 22 January she took up her pen and wrote to Lord Burghley and the lords of the Council, voicing her contestation of her jointure. In the first of her surviving letters, she made her feelings clear in no uncertain terms:

My very good Lords,

Remembering my hearty commendations to you, forasmuch as I do sufficiently understand by the estate wherein my late Lord, my husband, hath left his son, that my demands of dower of all the possessions his Lord was seized of would be sundry ways very prejudicial unto my son, and considering withal that the portion devised unto me by my Lord his will is over small for the maintenance of mine own estate, a reasonable mean between both would be used whereunto your Lordships shall find me willing to yield, so far as shall appertain to the natural care that a mother ought to have of her son. My demand is, to have by your Lordships' consent such lands annexed to my jointure (somewhat to further my maintenance withal), as are not mentioned in my Lords will, and are most convenient to be spared, until my son shall come to his full age, wherein as I have already made request to my father to deal with your Lordships.[10]

Claiming that her income was so pitiful that it did not provide enough to live on, Lettice had already sought her father's intervention to help resolve the matter. Her demands amounted to a claim that she was entitled to a third of the revenues from Walter's lands, but she was also concerned by the debts that her son Robert had inherited by right of his father. It was this that caused her to continue,

supposing you will not deal so straightly with me as to urge me to prosecute my right of dower already brought only for the recording my refuse of jointure, I am not unmindful of the great debts wherein my son is left, which I trust by your Lordships' good order will be well mitigated during his minority with the revenues of the lands and leases left for the discharging thereof, chiefly if her Majesty vouchsafe to deal graciously with him touching the debt due unto her (as I trust she will).[11]

Evidently believing that all of her requests were with her children's best interests in mind, she insisted that 'I am content to respect my children more than myself, which is seldom done by any in my case.'[12] Her appeals, however, were not at an end. Remembering that 'I am now to provide for a house of mine own for my abode', something which she was 'by no means able' to achieve by reason of 'being so hard and barely left of all manner of furniture', she sought the lords' assistance.[13]

I must rather become a suitor unto your lordships to let me have some such things of my late Lord's as he hath left meet to supply my wants therein, otherwise I must be unwillingly driven to seek my friends houses from time to time as presently I do, for that my portion is scant able to find me and my company meat and drink.[14]

For some reason, she had not been permitted to take the household goods that Walter had willed her, and she was now feeling desperate. She ended her letter with a plea that the lords would 'see me somewhat like a noble woman used in these respects', hoping to receive a favourable outcome to her suit.[15]

While she waited on the 'good considerations' of the Council, the following month Lettice had returned to Hampton Court, where the court was still in residence.[16] Perhaps she hoped for some news about her jointure, and she may also have been seeking the Queen's favour for her suit. During her stay she took the opportunity to let loose and enjoy the frivolities of court life, something of which she had been largely deprived for more than a decade. Alongside the dancing and the Queen's musicians, a payment was made to the Countess of Essex's players 'for presenting a play before her Majesty on Shrove Tuesday at night'.[17] This is the only mention of Lettice employing a company of actors, and their association with her suggests that she patronized and employed them regularly. There is also a further indication of the favour in which she was held by the Queen at this time; significantly, on the same Shrove Tuesday evening, the Earl of Leicester's players had also made their 'repair to the court with their whole company and furniture to present a play before her Majesty', but 'the play by her Majesty's commandment was supplied by others'.[18] That the Queen chose to be entertained by Lettice's players rather than those provided by her favourite is a sign of her esteem for her kinswoman.[19]

While she was at court, Lettice had the opportunity to socialize and catch up with her friends, but her problems had yet to be resolved, and by the end of February she was still residing at Greys Court. Once again she wrote to Lord Burghley, and although she was 'sorry that I have cause to be yet more troublesome unto you', she was again seeking his help – this time with some troublesome tenants.[20] Yet again, she complained of her 'slender allowance', and hoped that Burghley would provide her with a 'friendly answer' to her suit, as well as to her request for the 'import for wines'.[21] She had no issue with bewailing her circumstances in order to illicit sympathy, but unfortunately for Lettice there was bad news to come, and her claim to receive a third of Walter's lands was eventually refuted. Though she was furious, this left her with no choice but to make do with what she had been assigned, with an additional £60 (£10,000) per annum 'by her demanded'.[22] Perhaps sensing that Lettice's complaints were not at an end, as a compromise, in April she was also granted a life interest in Benington, her husband's former Hertfordshire estate. It may have been here that she eventually chose to settle, but if this was the case then her movements show that she probably did not take up residence there until early the following year.

As the spring of 1577 got underway, Lettice and her daughters left the familiar surroundings of Greys Court and travelled to the Midlands. Her son Walter was no longer with her, for in his will her husband had left instructions that his younger son and two daughters were to join the household of his cousin, Henry Hastings, third Earl of Huntingdon, 'for maintenance'.[23] In accordance with his father's wishes, little Walter had gone on ahead, so was therefore not with Lettice and her daughters when they arrived at Coleshill, the Warwickshire home of her friends, the Digbys. As they were close friends, Lettice intended to stay with the Digbys for some time; they had small children, and so Penelope and Dorothy would not have lacked for young company.[24] Meanwhile, Lettice still had other things on her mind, and it was from Coleshill that, on 30 April, she once more wrote to Burghley about financial matters. She did, this time, take the time to be courteous, thanking him for 'your friendship both to my son and me'.[25]

Coleshill was just ten miles from Kenilworth, the Earl of Leicester's magnificent home that had witnessed the Princely Pleasures of 1575. During her stay with the Digbys, Lettice took the opportunity to ride to Kenilworth on several occasions, there to participate in the regular hunting parties that gathered in Leicester's deer park. The hunting at Kenilworth was exceptional, and it was not the first time that she had hunted there, or received the gifts of the kill from its owner. On this occasion, though, there may have been a difference. In June, nine months had elapsed since Walter's death, and with her affairs settled – albeit not to her satisfaction – life was beginning to resume its normal course. As she arrived at Kenilworth, Lettice's thoughts were once more turned towards its owner.

That same month, Leicester spent two weeks at Kenilworth with his brother, Ambrose, as they journeyed towards Buxton in order to take the waters for their health. While he was there, he had the pleasure of welcoming the Countess of Essex and her eldest daughter, Penelope, to hunt in his park. Lettice's hosts, the Digbys, who were also close friends of the Earl, joined them. Lettice's brother William and his wife Dorothy had likewise seized on the opportunity of a summer holiday, and were determined to join the party. Lettice was an expert huntswoman, and with her bow and arrow she had managed to kill nine deer that season.[26] However, hunting deer may not have been the only thing on her mind, and it is possible that it was during this time that Lettice and Leicester's romance began to kindle.

Immediately after Walter's death, Camden claimed that Leicester 'more openly made love to Lettice', whom he had used 'at his good liking before, for satisfying of his own lust', during her husband's lifetime.[27] Whether the couple were having an affair or not, they were attracted to one another, and it is clear that at some point in 1577 their friendship developed into something more. Witnesses later confirmed that Leicester had been talking of a marriage with Lettice for almost a year prior to their wedding, which took place in September 1578.[28] Further evidence to corroborate this comes in the form of orders that Lettice gave for three bucks, killed by others at Kenilworth, to be sent to two of her friends.[29] Given that they were not her bucks to bestow, that she did so suggests that her relationship with the master of Kenilworth had become more significant.

Walter had been dead for less than a year, and so the assertion of *Leicester's Commonwealth* that his demise led to Leicester's 'hasty snatching up of the widow' can be partially justified.[30] By contemporary standards, however, this was not necessarily unusual. Exactly two weeks after the execution of her first husband in 1554, Frances Brandon, Duchess of Suffolk, had wed Adrian Stokes, her Master of Horse. And she was not alone.[31] Moreover, in the summer of 1577 there is no indication that Lettice and Leicester had even spoken of marriage, let alone anything more. Prior to this, Lettice had more pressing issues to deal with, chiefly the perilous state of her finances.

Lettice and Leicester's initial relationship was conducted with such secrecy that we have no indication as to how or where it was conducted. That it was staged away from London and the court is a given, for in the capital gossip was always rife, and it would have been impossible to keep their romance under wraps. Kenilworth and the Midlands seem like the likeliest locations, and here Lettice and Leicester would have been afforded relative privacy. Equally uncertain is whether or not it was consummated at this stage, although it was later intimated that it was. Sadly, no letters between the couple have survived – they certainly once did, but may have been burned in an attempt to maintain secrecy. Secrecy was vital, for not only was Lettice in official mourning for Walter, but Leicester was also still the Queen's favourite – Elizabeth did not like to share. Relationships, sexual or otherwise, were often hidden from the Queen, and both Lettice and Leicester were aware that Elizabeth was likely to fall into a jealous rage if she discovered the truth. According to *Leicester's Commonwealth*, in order to manage their relationship, Leicester sent Lettice 'up and down the country from house to house by privy ways, thereby to avoid the sight and knowledge of the Queen's Majesty'.[32] There are elements of this that have a ring of truth about them. Given that Lettice spent most of 1577 travelling between houses, it is possible that she managed to arrange meetings with Leicester. As mutual friends, it is also likely that the Digbys were aware of their relationship, and may have contrived to help Lettice in this quarter – Coleshill might even have been used as a location for trysts. If they did so, though, they would have been taking a considerable personal risk. Nobody, especially the Queen, could ever find out.

ELSEWHERE, IN MAY, after only a few months in Lord Burghley's household, Lettice's son Robert was sent to Trinity College Cambridge, to continue his studies. It was from here that he wrote to Burghley, acknowledging 'your Lordship's great care of placing me here in the University, where, for your Lordship's sake, I have been very well entertained, both of the University and the town'.[33] The Master of Trinity was the 'pious and learned' Dr John Whitgift, who would later become Queen Elizabeth's Archbishop of Canterbury, and was by her side at the time of her death.[34] Robert's tutor, Robert Wright, himself a former Cambridge student, accompanied him, and it was he who recorded the young Earl's expenses. By the summer Robert was in 'extreme necessity of apparel', and Wright petitioned Richard Broughton to speak to Burghley about releasing funds.[35] The response was positive, and Wright recorded that among a multitude of other items, gloves, a hat, a velvet cap and lace for the Earl's stockings had been purchased.[36] Robert would remain at Cambridge for the next four years, diligently applying himself to his studies, much to Lettice's pride. However, the plague often visited the city during the summer months, and on these occasions Robert abandoned Cambridge, perhaps taking the opportunity to visit his mother.[37]

BY THE AUTUMN, the time was fast approaching for Lettice to send her daughters north to join her younger son in the Earl of Huntingdon's household. Determined to spend one more Christmas with them, she left the hunting parties of Kenilworth and her friends the Digbys behind as, together with Penelope and Dorothy, she travelled to London. Winter was no time to be in the country, for everyone usually gathered at court to enjoy the season's entertainment – including Leicester.

It was late October by the time Lettice and her daughters arrived in the capital, for on 5 November Richard Broughton related that 'My lady of Essex came to Hackney a week past.' Hackney was then a fashionable hamlet on the outskirts of the city, where many members of the nobility owned properties. It is unclear exactly where in Hackney Lettice and her daughters were residing, and it has been suggested that she may have been the guest of the Queen's cousin, Lady Margaret Lennox.[38] Lady Lennox was the mother of Mary, Queen of Scots' murdered husband, Henry Darnley, and she was also a friend of the Earl of Leicester.[39] It is possible that Lettice may have stayed with Lady Lennox, who was by now in her sixties, but aside from their common connection in Queen Elizabeth there is no evidence of a friendship between the two women.

By December, Lettice and her daughters had removed from Hackney, and were now staying in Bedford House on the Strand. They were the guests of Bridget Russell, Countess of Bedford, and here they would remain to celebrate the New Year.[40] It is unlikely that Lettice would have confided in the Countess about her relationship with Leicester, for it would have been considered too risky. She would have had an opportunity to see him when she presented her New Year's gift of 'ruffs of lawn white work edged with seed pearl' to the Queen.[41] But the couple would have been careful to keep their distance to avoid the sharp tongues of the court gossips.[42]

———

SHORTLY AFTER THE New Year's celebrations of 1578 had been concluded, Lettice was forced to say goodbye to her daughters. It was time for Penelope and Dorothy to join the Earl of Huntingdon's household, and they duly set out for the north. Described by the Spanish Bishop de Quadra as 'a great heretic', Huntingdon was a zealous Protestant.[43] He was also married to the Earl of Leicester's youngest sister, Katherine, who, like her husband, was stringently religious. The couple had no children, but were responsible for overseeing the education of several children from noble families. In 1572, Huntingdon had been appointed president of the

Council of the North, and had established his household at the King's Manor in York.[44] It was here that Penelope and Dorothy were to travel to meet their brother and their new guardians, bidding farewell to both London and their mother.

While in Huntingdon's household the Devereux children were to live by a strict moral code of behaviour. All three of them continued with their lessons, and it was also expected that their guardian would arrange marriages for them. Although the elder of Lettice's two sons did not spend as much time with him as his younger siblings, when Huntingdon died in 1595 Essex would declare that he was one 'whose name without sorrow I shall never mention'.[45] Walter had been hopeful that Penelope would wed Sir Philip Sidney, and it is a pairing that Lettice is also likely to have had high hopes of. Sidney was a good match for Penelope, and he was also Leicester's nephew. He had spent several years travelling in Europe, and when he returned he was a cultured young man, skilled at poetry.[46] Given Leicester's lack of legitimate issue, Philip was also his heir. Ultimately, though, all hopes of a marriage between Philip and Penelope would come to nothing.

With the departure of her daughters for the north, Lettice no longer had any children in her care. She felt their loss keenly. However, that year there were plenty of other matters to occupy her mind. Her movements are unclear; it is possible that, having spent a year travelling around the country staying with friends and family, she finally established herself at Benington, the Hertfordshire home that had been settled on her the previous year. If this were true, then she would have been well placed for attending court, bringing her into regular contact with the Earl of Leicester. Perhaps significantly, Benington was just a little over thirty miles from Wanstead, the Essex home that Leicester had purchased in 1577. He would soon put it to good use. No matter how their relationship may have started out, and whatever Leicester's initial intentions towards Lettice had been, one thing was certain: Lettice had seen the way that Leicester had cast away his former lover, Douglas Sheffield, and was determined that she would not go the same way. What was more, by now she had fallen deeply in love with Leicester, and he in turn with her. As such there was no longer any question of them continuing their relationship under the guise of friendship, or arranging clandestine meetings. They both wanted more, and only marriage would do. It was a momentous decision for Leicester, who had avoided such a commitment for almost two decades following the death of his first wife – all on the Queen's behalf. Though the Queen did not know it, she now had a rival.

⁂

ON 10 MAY, Lettice's younger sister Elizabeth was married. Elizabeth had been a member of the Queen's household since almost the beginning of her reign, and she was well favoured by her royal mistress. Given the Queen's general attitude to the marriages of her ladies, Elizabeth was fortunate, for her groom met with the Queen's approval. Thomas Leighton was a great friend of Leicester's – the hostile *Leicester's Commonwealth* described him as one of Leicester's 'most obliged dependents' – and he was on good terms with Lettice's father.[47] The couple's wedding took place at court in the Chapel Royal. Elizabeth was close to her family and as she is likely to have been residing in the south, it seems probable that Lettice would have attended. If she did, she could not have failed to notice the Queen's generosity to the happy couple, for she made them a wedding gift of a 67 oz gilt cup.[48]

Lettice's sister was not the only one who had been thinking about matrimony: Lettice, too, was preparing to marry.

CHAPTER 11

A Marriage in Secret

F OLLOWING THE DEATH of his first wife, Amy Robsart, in 1560, Leicester had spent more than a decade trying everything in his power to persuade the Queen to marry him. He had come closer than any Englishman ever would. The Queen had encouraged him to hope, and many of her advisors had worried that it was a strong possibility. However, Leicester had long since come to the realization that such a marriage would never transpire, and he had given up all hope. As time had progressed, the nature of the relationship between them had changed from that of courting lovers, to good friends who were genuinely fond of one another. Even so, in order to retain the Queen's favour Leicester had also avoided marrying elsewhere – until now.

There is no way of knowing where the impetus for marriage came from, but by the beginning of 1578, if not before, Leicester and Lettice made an agreement to wed. While they certainly loved one another, risking the Queen's wrath in their determination to marry, there were other advantages to a marriage. From Lettice's perspective, Leicester was an undeniable catch: he was well favoured by the Queen, he had a good income, numerous estates and cultured interests. His patronage of the arts was famous; Leicester's Men, the company of players he had founded, were performing regularly at court, where they were popular, and after 1576 they had also begun to appear at the theatre – in 1587 they even performed at the Danish court.[1] He could also provide her with a home and valuable support when it came to settling her finances. For Leicester, too, the prospect of marrying Lettice held appeal. She came from a good

Protestant family, and he was on friendly terms with both her father and her brothers; her younger brother, Francis, was a member of his household, and he was well acquainted with several of the others. Like him, Lettice was also a widower who was thirty-two at the time of her husband's death, but crucially, she had also proven that she was capable of producing children – an important consideration for a man who was in his forties and had yet to produce a legitimate heir. In addition, not only had the Queen shown great favour to Lettice, but she was also her close kinswoman. If Leicester could not marry the Queen, then Lettice, as her kinswoman with royal blood in her veins – something of which she was inwardly proud – was the next best thing.

Both Lettice and Leicester realized that they were highly unlikely to obtain the Queen's consent for their marriage. But they were in love and determined to be together; a secret marriage was therefore their only option. They were playing a dangerous game, though; and what was more, they both knew it. Numerous examples of the Queen's displeasure upon discovering that her courtiers had married without her consent loomed in front of them. In 1562, it had been Leicester himself who had informed the Queen of the secret marriage of her cousin, Lady Katherine Grey, and the Earl of Hertford.[2] So outraged was the Queen that she had Lady Katherine, the younger sister of the ill-fated Lady Jane, and her husband cast into the Tower. To make matters worse, Katherine was pregnant, and gave birth to a son while still imprisoned. Katherine's story was not destined to have a happy ending, and having given birth to another son in the Tower, she was permanently separated from her family. She died in house imprisonment on 26 January 1568.[3] The Queen's treatment of Katherine Grey was extreme, and fuelled by the fact that she had a claim to the throne. Nevertheless, over the years her attitude had not thawed. Katherine's youngest sister, Mary, had faced similar treatment for a similar crime – she had been clandestinely married on the same day as the wedding of Lettice's brother in 1565 – and it did not end there.[4] In January 1576, Eleanor Brydges, the daughter of Lord Chandos, had informed the Earl of Rutland that 'The Queen has used Mary Shelton very ill for her marriage.' She claimed that the Queen was liberal 'both with blows and evil words, and hath not yet granted her consent'.[5] It was little wonder that many of her ladies and courtiers were afraid to tell their royal mistress the truth, forcing them to marry in secret. By doing so, however, they risked her wrath. As historian Tracy Borman accurately summarized, 'It was without doubt the surest way to lose the Queen's favour.'[6]

Although Lettice did not have a claim to the throne like Katherine and Mary Grey, she had enough experience of her kinswoman to realize that if Elizabeth discovered that she had married her favourite then there would be serious consequences: for Leicester the outcome could surely be much worse. Elizabeth had once been in love with him, and still harboured strong feelings for him. Despite the arrival of another favourite on the scene in the form of Sir Christopher Hatton, and talks of a French marriage with François, formerly the Duc d'Alençon and now Duc d'Anjou, Leicester and Elizabeth still had a unique and strong bond.[7] She would not marry him, but that did not mean she was happy for him to marry elsewhere, and Leicester knew it. He was the one man in her life who was completely off limits: he was taboo. He in turn had once loved her, too, but his feelings towards her had changed, and while he still cared about her deeply he now loved another. Though there were numerous examples before them, and in spite of the likely ramifications that news of their marriage would create, Leicester and Lettice were by now too emotionally involved to contemplate abandoning each other. They were in love – so much so that they agreed that the risk was worth the reward.

It was probably shortly before or shortly after the wedding of Lettice's sister, Elizabeth, that they were either secretly betrothed, or underwent some kind of marriage ceremony. It is believed that the ceremony took place at Kenilworth, but no details are known.[8] Neither is it clear how long the couple intended to keep their vows a secret, but what is certain is that before long Lettice's father, Sir Francis Knollys, discovered it. Several reports later circulated relating the news. These detailed that following Walter's death,

> the Earl of Leicester, with a great sum of money, and large promises, put away Douglas Sheffield, his wife, and openly married Essex's widow. For although it was given out, that he was privately married to her, yet Sir Francis Knollys, her father, who was well acquainted with Leicester's roving loves, would not believe it, unless he himself was at the marriage, and had it testified by a public notary.[9]

Camden told a similar tale, reporting that Leicester 'joined himself in a double marriage', while Leicester's Commonwealth said that he 'married and remarried her for the contention of her friends'.[10] Lettice herself may have chosen to confide in her father, but whatever the circumstances, Francis was deeply concerned. If there had been no witnesses to the marriage then it could easily be denied or annulled by either party, should they so wish. Francis resolved to take action, 'fearing lest he [Leicester] should deceive his daughter'.[11] He had a strict sense of morality and upright principles, and if Lettice and Leicester were to be man and wife, then the union needed to be binding.

RICHARD, LORD RICH, had built Wanstead House, recently acquired by Leicester, in the 1550s. It was a traditional Elizabethan house enclosed around a quadrangle, and among its sumptuous rooms were a hall, a great chamber, twenty bedrooms and a chapel. There was also a 'great gallery', where many pieces from Leicester's splendid portrait collection were hung. These included paintings of the Queen, her half-sister Mary, and Lady Margaret Lennox, and were all proud declarations of Leicester's loyalties and friendships, both past and present.[12] There was also stabling for fifty-eight horses, and beautiful gardens that the Earl was proud of.[13] Situated just ten miles from London, it provided easy access to court, and yet was located at a convenient enough distance to allow the Earl some privacy. In the autumn of 1578, that was exactly what Leicester was hoping for.

All was quiet at Wanstead on the morning of Sunday 21 September 1578. The preparations for the day's event had been finalized just the previous day, when Leicester had approached his chaplain, Humphrey Tyndall, and asked him to perform a marriage ceremony for him. Tyndall later testified that Leicester had spoken to him earnestly about the fact that 'he had for a good season forborne marriage in respect of her Majesty's displeasure', but that he was now 'for the better quieting of his own conscience determined to marry with the right honourable Countess of Essex'.[14] His feelings for Lettice had had plenty of time to grow, and there was no question of her being his mistress. Leicester, however, was careful to inform Tyndall that the marriage 'might not be publicly known without great damage of his estate', and therefore asked him 'to solemnise a marriage in secret between them'.[15] Tyndall was a 'full minister', having been ordained by the Bishop of Peterborough in 1572, and was happy to comply with Leicester's request.[16]

That same evening, Leicester's good friend Roger Lord North arrived at Wanstead. After the friends had eaten, Leicester divulged to North that 'he intended to be married next morning, by the leave of God, and therefore prayed this deponent to rise somewhat betimes for the purpose'. North readily agreed to witness his friend's nuptials, and when he rose the following morning he discovered Leicester 'walking in a little gallery, looking towards the garden'.[17] The day had now come.

When Tyndall arrived at Wanstead between seven and eight o'clock that morning he was met by Lord North. Conveying him to 'a little gallery of Wanstead House opening upon the garden', before long they were joined by Leicester himself.[18] His brother Ambrose, Lettice's father and Henry Herbert, second Earl of Pembroke, accompanied him. Like Lord North, the Earl of Pembroke was a close friend of Leicester's, and the bonds of friendship between them had been further cemented when, in

1577, Pembroke had married Lady Mary Sidney, Leicester's niece.[19] Also present was Lettice's younger brother, Richard. He was close to his sister and well trusted, and was therefore an obvious choice of witness. They were all painfully aware that there would be consequences for them if the Queen were to discover what was taking place, but they were determined to support the couple. After the men had gathered, 'within a little after' a hush descended as Lettice entered the room. Dressed, as Tyndall remembered, in 'a loose gown', she was escorted by her father towards her groom.[20] They had both been here before, but gone were the pomp, the festivities, the gawping onlookers. The morning's ceremony was a most personal and quiet affair, quite at odds with what it heralded for both bride and groom.

Much has been made of Tyndall's reference to Lettice's 'loose gown', which has been interpreted as a sign of pregnancy. Similarly, Leicester's comments about 'the better quieting of his own conscience' have been taken as an implication that he and Lettice had consummated their relationship before they were married.[21] There is no way of knowing the truth of the matter; it is possible that Lettice was in the early stages of pregnancy at this time. This may explain why a marriage ceremony with witnesses was required, in order to safeguard the legitimacy of their child. This is, indeed, the precise reason why depositions providing details of the ceremony were taken in 1581, when Lettice was pregnant with the couple's son. However, the reference to her 'loose gown' is the only indication that this was the case; certainly no child was born, and it is hardly conclusive proof. If Lettice had indeed been pregnant, then it is surprising that none of her contemporaries made reference to it. Loose fitted clothing was also fashionable for women at this time, so Tyndall's comment may have amounted to nothing more than a complimentary observation about Lettice's appearance.

The witnesses watched as Tyndall 'did with the free consent of them both marry the said Earl and Countess together in such manner and form as is prescribed by the communion book, and did pronounce them lawful man and wife before God and the world according to the usual order at solemnization of marriages'.[22] Lettice was now officially Leicester's wife, and from the moment she took her wedding vows, her relationship with Queen Elizabeth had changed forever.

Camden claimed that this second ceremony was performed 'a year or two after' the first, but this would be impossible – the ceremony at Wanstead was conducted almost exactly two years to the day after the death of Walter Devereux.[23] More probable is that the wedding at Wanstead took place within a matter of months of the secret ceremony that may have been hosted at Kenilworth.

Leicester's feelings as he encountered his bride were those of a man who was besotted. Unlike her royal kinswoman, Lettice was not reluctant to enter into matrimony, and instead felt quite the opposite. She loved him, and she would be a proper wife to him – she wanted to marry him, and she had not played the games that her cousin had become so eloquent at. Theirs was a marriage that would prove to be both happy and enduring. For her part, she was now married to one of the most powerful men in the realm. Even so, no matter how much happiness her marriage brought her on a personal level, hers was a dangerous position.

THE NEWLYWEDS' HONEYMOON was destined to be of short duration, for two days after the ceremony the Queen descended on Wanstead. A portrait of Elizabeth by the Flemish artist Marcus Gheeraerts, known as the Wanstead portrait or the Peace portrait, supposedly portrays the Queen at her favourite's home with the beautiful gardens of Wanstead in the background. Two women and a gentleman can be seen in the background, and it has been conjectured that one of these women was Lettice. With no idea of what had so recently taken place at Wanstead, Elizabeth chose to visit the home of her favourite in order to mark the end of her summer progress. On this occasion, her travels had taken her to Cambridgeshire, Suffolk and Norfolk, and when she arrived at Leicester's

Essex home her host ordered a magnificent feast in her honour. While she dined with him, a meal at which Lettice was almost certainly present, the Queen remained oblivious to the fact that her favourite was now a married man. Neither did she have any inkling that her kinswoman was no longer the Countess of Essex, but was instead the Countess of Leicester. As the couple ate their meal in the Queen's company, they would doubtless have been on edge, and with good reason. Their happy news was not destined to remain a secret for long, and what they were now experiencing was the calm before the storm.

CHAPTER 12

One Queen in England

WITHIN WEEKS OF Lettice's wedding and the sumptuous feast at Wanstead, the badly kept secret, which had been the subject of servants' gossip, was out. Whispers of Lettice's 'secret marriage' had begun circulating almost immediately, and it was not long before they reached the ears of those at court. In November 1578, two months after the wedding, the Earl of Sussex had informed the French ambassador, Michel de Castelnau, that Leicester was married to the Countess, and before long many of those at court were aware of the couple's nuptials. Sussex was an enemy of Leicester's, and had heard of the marriage through the gossip that had been spread via the Earl's servants. Even the captive Queen of Scots, imprisoned in the north of England, knew of the marriage. It was, therefore, only a matter of time before the Queen found out. The storm was brewing. The only question was: who would be the one to tell her?

AS THE NEW Year of 1579 began, Lettice exchanged the customary gifts with the Queen in the same pleasant manner that she had always done. On this occasion she made her royal mistress a rich gift of 'a great chain of amber garnished with gold and pearl', and though her name was listed among the recipients who received a gift in return, the exact nature of her present was unrecorded.[1] The Queen received her kinswoman at court that season with as much favour as she had on previous occasions, unaware that Lettice was harbouring a secret. However, it was to be the last occasion that Lettice's name would appear on the New Year's gift rolls. Leicester, whom Elizabeth believed to be as devoted to her as ever, gave the monarch several costly presents of jewels, including 'a very great topaz set in gold enamelled, with eight pearls pendant', as well as a gift of a far more personal nature: a set of buttons gorgeously inlaid with diamonds and rubies, with the bear and ragged staff that formed the crest of the Earl's family and, even more significantly, lovers' knots.[2] The symbolism was clear, but it was not a suggestion that Leicester was at liberty to make.

ON 5 JANUARY 1579, the personal envoy of the French Duc d'Anjou arrived in London. Monsieur Jean de Simier, 'a most choice courtier, exquisitely skilled in love toys, pleasant conceits and court dalliances', was a close friend of the Duc's, and had a charm that quickly won him great favour with Elizabeth.[3] Simier also had an extremely shady past, for he had murdered his own brother after he discovered that he had been having an affair with his wife – a crime for which he miraculously went unpunished.[4] Simier's task was simple: he was to pay suit to the Queen on behalf of his master and sue for her hand in marriage. If Simier were successful, Anjou would have triumphed where all of Elizabeth's other suitors, including Leicester, had failed. Lettice was almost certainly at court in order to be close to her new husband, and would therefore have been a witness to the fact that, within no time, Elizabeth had given Simier the nickname of 'Monkey'. It was also observed that the Queen 'is best disposed and pleasanteth when she talketh with him'. Elizabeth enjoyed the notion and language of courtship, and Simier played the game and flattered her with dazzling effect.

However, though for many years Elizabeth's councillors had been eager for her to marry, there were those who were now concerned for her health. She was forty-five, and by contemporary standards she was old to be considering a first marriage with the view to begetting heirs – although her doctors informed her that it was still possible. Lord Burghley was one of those who expressed the opinion that 'it would have been better for her and the realm also' if the Queen had married earlier. The idea of Elizabeth making a French marriage was deeply unpopular in England, primarily due to the fact that France was a Catholic nation and had been embroiled in the civil Wars of Religion for the past seventeen years. Only seven years prior to Simier's arrival, the English people had been appalled to hear of the massacre of three thousand Huguenots (French Protestants) in Paris, in a sickening attack that is remembered as the St Bartholomew's Day Massacre.[5] When she was told of the news, the Queen and her ladies had dressed in black, and when Elizabeth later received the French ambassador it was in silence; although, politically, the alliance was fully maintained.

Seven years on, the scars had still not faded; as a French Catholic, Simier naturally earned the dislike of many of the men at court. Lettice, too, was not a fan. An ardent Protestant, she was among those who found the idea of the Queen's marriage to a Frenchman abhorrent – but her opinion was of little matter; and increasingly so. For Lettice would soon discover that there were more pressing matters than the Queen's courtships – her own relationship with her royal mistress was about to take a drastic turn.

Simier himself was intimately involved in Lettice's change of fortunes. Within a short space of time, the French courtier became convinced that the Earl of Leicester was foremost among his enemies. Simier was well aware that the Earl had harboured ambitions of matrimony with the Queen himself, and rightly believed that Leicester was doing all that he could to dissuade Elizabeth from making a French marriage alliance. Even so, the portrait of Anjou that now hangs in the National Gallery of Art, Washington, DC, once hung in Leicester House in the 1570s and Wanstead in the 1580s – perhaps a diplomatic gift. Behind the scenes, Leicester was determined to prevent the Queen's marriage to Anjou, yet his motivation seems to have been based on political and religious rather than personal motives. He had been spreading rumours that Simier had used 'amorous potions and unlawful arts', and had 'crept into the

Queen's mind and insisted her to the love of [Monsieur]' in his attempts to woo Elizabeth.[6] He was playing a dangerous game. Simier had heard the whispers and was himself aware of the Earl's marriage – and he was determined to use the knowledge to his advantage at the most opportune moment. It was not long before that moment arrived.

In July, after being persuaded by Simier's smooth words, the Queen signed a passport which allowed Anjou to come to England. Leicester was horrified by this development, and in an act of protest immediately retired to Wanstead where he sent word that he was ill. Lettice was not with him at this time, for shortly after his departure the Queen arrived to visit him – perhaps to reassure herself of the legitimacy of his 'sickness'. It was an anxious time for Lettice, as she was aware that the French ambassador had urged her husband 'to confess to the Queen that he was married'.[7] She waited to hear whether the Earl would act on the ambassador's advice, but Leicester did no such thing. Within three days, Elizabeth was back in London, where Lettice almost certainly was too. But any cosy reunion between the couple would be short-lived.

Soon after her return to the capital – with Leicester, now fully recovered, not far behind her – the Queen was found on the afternoon of 17 July travelling down the Thames on the Royal Barge to Greenwich Palace. The summer heat had set in, and as the Queen enjoyed the sunshine and the cool breeze that emanated from the river, she also had the pleasure of the company of her 'Monkey' Simier, Leicester and the affable Sir Christopher Hatton. The pleasant serenity of the summer afternoon was shattered when, out of nowhere, a gunshot was fired at the barge. For a moment, panic spread among those on board as the shot came within inches of the Queen. A second later the bargeman began 'to cry and screech out piteously' as it became apparent that he had been hit. As those around the Queen scrambled to ensure that the monarch was protected and strove to help the injured man, on land the would-be assassin was seized.[8] Though he had escaped unscathed, it was believed that Simier had been the target, for his presence in London was well known and unpopular.

Simier himself was convinced that the shot had been intended for him, and that the assassination attempt had been Leicester's doing.[9] It was this that prompted him to take action against the Earl – and play his winning hand.

The precise circumstances are unknown, but without pause Simier delivered to Elizabeth the poisonous news. The Earl of Leicester, he told her, was unworthy of the Queen's friendship, and had no right to try and prevent her marriage to the Duc d'Anjou – especially since he himself had been recently married, in secret, to the Queen's own kinswoman, the Lady Lettice, Countess of Essex. As Elizabeth heard the news, her outward reaction was one of shock and utter fury. It was the ultimate betrayal: for many years Leicester had been her closest male friend and ally, and she had come to rely on him heavily. More than that, she had loved and cared for him deeply, and had once given him the impression that she had strongly considered him as a suitor for her own hand. Though all notions of her marrying Leicester had long since vanished from her mind, she now no longer wielded the same power over him – a realization that shook Elizabeth to the core.

As if his marriage without her consent were not enough, Leicester had then kept it from her for months, in a shocking betrayal of her trust. His bride was her own kinswoman, making the wound all the more painful for Elizabeth. Nobody could fail to notice the physical resemblance between Lettice and the Queen; Lettice too had the dark and sensual eyes so characteristic of the Boleyn family, and the beautiful flame-red hair that marked Elizabeth out as a Tudor. And the similarities did not end there, for like Elizabeth, Lettice had also demonstrated that she was a strong and forceful character, determined to have her way whatever the cost – and it seemed that she had got it.

From Lettice's point of view, at the time of her wedding at Wanstead she had been a widow for almost two years to the day, and had therefore fulfilled the customary period of mourning that society expected of her. For a woman of her beauty and sensuality, it had always been likely that she would wish to remarry. Elizabeth had heard the rumours that had once circulated about the flirtation between Lettice and her favourite, but she had made her feelings about this perfectly clear, by flying into 'a great temper' and upbraiding Leicester in 'very bitter words' back in 1565. She had never imagined that the scurrilous whispers would evolve into an appalling reality. The court gossip of a mere flirtation had transformed into something so much worse, and though Elizabeth did not want to face it, Lettice was now the Countess of Leicester, and there was nothing she could do about it.

According to Camden, Elizabeth's initial reaction was to have Leicester 'committed to the Tower of London, which his enemies much desired'. However, 'The Earl of Sussex, though his greatest and deadliest adversary, dissuaded her. For he was of the opinion that no man was to be troubled with lawful marriage, which estate among all men hath ever been held in honour and esteem.'[10] Elizabeth clearly felt otherwise.

Sussex was a man of great courage and honesty – almost to the point of tactlessness – and while he was no friend of Leicester and perceived no advantage in the situation for himself, he knew that it would be beneath the Queen's dignity to send the Earl to the Tower for such a personal issue. He had persuaded his mistress to be merciful, and Leicester and Lettice were fortunate that she was. After all, both of them would have been painfully conscious of the pitiful fate of Lady Katherine Grey among others.[11]

And so the couple were spared a spell in prison, but it was clear that Elizabeth was by no means prepared to let Leicester and Lettice go completely unpunished; they had broken no law, but in the Queen's eyes they had still committed a heinous crime. With no opportunity to speak to the Queen personally, Leicester was immediately told to absent himself from court; without seeing Lettice he slipped quietly away to Wanstead, where he laid low to wait on events. Ultimately, though, it was Lettice who bore the brunt of Elizabeth's anger. Was it because she was a woman? This almost certainly was a significant factor in the affair, for Elizabeth was notoriously jealous of younger members of her own sex. This was exacerbated by Lettice's personal qualities: she was both strikingly beautiful and ten years younger than the Queen, which added an element of resentment. To add insult to injury, she had been fond of Lettice, who had once been a member of her household and attended to her most personal of needs. Lettice had probably been by Elizabeth's side since her girlhood and they had shared many important moments. She had witnessed at first-hand her kinswoman's intense relationship with Leicester, and was aware of how deeply she cared for him. It was, therefore, no wonder that the Queen considered Lettice's actions to be such a great betrayal. By contrast, Elizabeth's deep-rooted fondness for Leicester and her reliance on him prevented her from punishing him; she could not bear to lose him from her life altogether.

But that still left Lettice, who was probably in London at this time, although her precise whereabouts are unclear; for the time being there was nothing her husband could do to protect her from the Queen's wrath. However, Lettice was soon to prove that she was perfectly capable of taking care of herself. It was now that she chose to demonstrate her true strength of character, for rather than being apologetic for her actions, throwing herself on her knees to beg the Queen's forgiveness, Lettice instead appeared to be defiant. In her eyes, she had done nothing of which she ought to be ashamed and she was determined not to hide away. According to one contemporary report, though not at court, 'She now demeaned herself like a princess, vied in dress with the Queen.'[12] Lettice was acutely conscious of her status and her close blood ties with her royal mistress – not to mention her own Tudor blood – and she had always been headstrong. She was adamant that she would not bow down – not even to the Queen. This was unwise behaviour, and did nothing but antagonize Elizabeth further. Quickly, and sharply, Lettice was given a reminder that it was Elizabeth who was Queen of England – not her.

Shortly after the Queen's discovery of Leicester and Lettice's betrayal – and with it having become clear that Lettice, at least, was not prepared to ask for her mercy – a dramatic confrontation between the two women took place within the privacy of the Queen's apartments at the Palace of Whitehall. It is unclear how this interview came about, but the gossips soon seized upon it. Even before the two women were left alone, the atmosphere was tense and frosty as 'Her Majesty, after sundry admonitions, told her [Lettice] as but one sun lightened the earth, she would have but one Queen in England, boxed her ears, and forbade her the court.'[13] This was not the first occasion on which Elizabeth had apparently resorted to violence in a burst of temper, but if true it was shocking nevertheless. She clearly felt threatened by Lettice, and her simmering jealousy came bubbling to the fore.

It says much about Elizabeth's attitudes towards women that she was prepared to abandon and punish a woman with whom she had shared so much. Similarly, it also says much about Elizabeth's reaction to betrayal. However much she had loved Lettice's mother, the days when Elizabeth shared the same warmth of feeling for her daughter were over.

All vestiges of a close relationship between the two kinswomen now vanished. As Lettice was aware, from the moment she said her wedding vows in the chapel at Wanstead, she effectively forfeited the Queen's favour and goodwill. After her death, her granddaughter's husband would write that Lettice was 'content to quit her favour for her favourite'.[14] The Countess, who loved Leicester deeply, felt that the sacrifice was one worth making, for whatever her private feelings may have been at her disgrace and the loss of the Queen's friendship, outwardly she was determined not to show them. Rather than the humiliating meeting with Elizabeth serving to humble her and curb her displays, as was doubtless intended, Lettice too was angry, and vowed not to cower away and hide as if overridden with guilt. This feisty attitude met with astonishment from her contemporaries, and her behaviour drew further disapproving comment, as the observations of the Spanish ambassador reveal:

Yet still she is as proud as ever, rides through Cheapside drawn by four milk-white steeds, with four footmen in black velvet jackets, and silver bears on their backs and breasts, two knights and thirty gentlemen before her, and coaches of gentlewomen, pages, and servants behind, so that it might be supposed to be the Queen, or some foreign Prince or ambassador.[15]

This is precisely what Lettice would have intended, for it was normally only the Queen whose carriage was drawn by white horses. The livery of her footmen, which displayed the bear that formed part of her husband's family crest, was a clear declaration to the world that Lettice was now an integral and legitimate part of that family – it was an alliance that not even the Queen could break. Lettice was proud of her marriage, and in the portrait that now hangs at Longleat, commissioned several years later by the artist George Gower, she took care to ensure that part of the Earl's family crest was embroidered on to her rich dress in a further, permanent reminder of her new identity.

If these reports of Lettice's behaviour are accurate, it demonstrates her blatant disregard for the Queen's feelings. This was, though, incredibly foolish. Everyone, both at court and in the capital, knew that Leicester and his new wife were in disgrace; the authors of *Leicester's Commonwealth* wrote that 'by his known marriage with his Minion Dame Lettice of Essex, [Leicester] hath declared manifestly his own most impudent and disloyal dealing with his sovereign in this report', while also declaring that he had 'denied he the same by solemn oath to her Majesty and received the holy communion thereupon'.[16]

The effects of their marriage were keenly felt elsewhere, too. Lady Mary Sidney, Leicester's sister and the Queen's friend, found the scandal surrounding the situation so unbearable that she laid low at her home at Penshurst Place, there to wait until the affair had died down. Lettice and Mary had always been on friendly terms, but the discovery of the clandestine marriage pushed their friendship to the limit, as Mary struggled to absorb the news. It was a slight that Lettice took to heart, and their relationship seems never to have fully recovered.

In a report that was doubtless highly exaggerated by *Leicester's Commonwealth*, Lettice's family are portrayed as exacerbating the situation. The authors reported that her brother Robert had 'danced disgraciously and scornfully before the Queen in the presence of the French', for which behaviour the Queen had berated him with 'a reproachful word or two'. To make matters worse, Lettice's sister Anne then added fuel to the fire by saying that 'she nothing doubted but that one day she should see her sister, upon whom the Queen railed now so much, to sit in her place and throne, being much worthier of the same for her qualities and rare virtues than was the other'.[17] These comments fortunately never reached the ears of the Queen, and no other contemporary report makes any mention of them. It would have been unwise for Lettice's family to voice such thoughts, for they were treasonous, but the report does at least lend credence to the notion that Lettice's family were behind her. With her husband at Wanstead, Lettice probably resided with one of them while she remained in London. Her time in the capital was to be short.

In direct contrast to Lettice's defiant displays, her husband greatly lamented incurring the Queen's displeasure. After all, as her close favourite he had far more to lose. But he also resented Elizabeth's rage, and in a bitter letter to his colleague Lord Burghley complained that 'I have lost both youth and liberty and all my fortune reposed in her'.[18] He had loved Elizabeth, and had spent many years trying to persuade the Queen to marry him, to no avail. Lettice could offer him everything that Elizabeth could not: marriage, with the possibility of begetting heirs, and a stable life of domesticity. According to the Earl's friend Lord North, this was precisely what Leicester craved, for in his later deposition about the couple's marriage, North claimed that 'There was nothing in this life he more desired than to be joined with some godly gentlewoman, with whom he might lead his life to the glory of God, the comfort of his soul, and to the faithful service of Her Majesty.'[19] There is no way of knowing precisely how Leicester felt about his wife's behaviour towards their sovereign – later accounts suggest that he was greatly in awe of her, and was happy to go where she led.

IT WAS NOT long after her disastrous meeting with Elizabeth that Lettice realized that her presence in London served only to inflame the Queen's anger towards her – and towards Leicester, too. It was one thing for her, the Queen's own relative and lady, to lose her favour, but it would be quite another if Leicester should permanently do so. He needed the protection of his sovereign, and his new wife's residence in the city gave his enemies at court further venom to drip into Elizabeth's ear.

Whether of her own accord, or at her husband's instigation, Lettice decided that it would be best to retire from London. Having had time to think since her shocking confrontation with the monarch, she hoped that with some distance between them, Elizabeth's fury would soon be quelled, and that there was a possibility that she might be forgiven. Once the first flushes of anger and pride had cooled, Lettice was able to think more logically. She realized that it would be foolish to abandon all hope of being restored to royal favour, a thought that Leicester also encouraged. In what may have been a further desperate attempt to placate the Queen, although she was now legally entitled to style herself Countess of Leicester, Lettice curiously refrained from doing so. Instead, for several years, she continued to refer to herself as the Countess of Essex – perhaps more for her husband's sake than for her own. In Elizabeth's eyes, however, it was a case of too little too late: the damage had been done.

So it was that the newly married Lettice left London under a dark cloud of disgrace that showed no signs of clearing. Her destination is unclear – a year later she was at her childhood home at Rotherfield Greys with her father, awaiting the birth of her first child with Leicester, and it is plausible that it was to this place of familial sanctuary that she came on this occasion, too. The other possibility is Benington, the Hertfordshire residence that had once belonged to Walter. She certainly did not travel to any of Leicester's estates at this time, for the Queen had made it clear that she loathed the idea of the couple spending time together either in London or elsewhere – thus far their meetings had been discreet, and for the next year they would continue in a similar vein. Elizabeth was not used to having to share her favourite and, in spite of his marriage, she clearly did not expect to have to start now. In the early days of her queenship she had known that Leicester was married, but with his wife Amy living in the remote Oxfordshire countryside the unseen spouse had blended quietly into the background of his life, and was no obstacle to the Queen's flirtations. Though Lettice had retreated to the country, she could not be trusted to remain there indefinitely. Neither did Lettice have any intention of doing so.

If Lettice did indeed travel the forty miles from London to Rotherfield Greys to be with her family, she would at least have been met with a show of love and support. At the risk of losing his own standing with the Queen, her father, Sir Francis Knollys, had shown himself to be both thoughtful and concerned for her welfare. Despite his being one of the six witnesses at his daughter's wedding, Elizabeth did not blame Sir Francis in any way for the displeasing union, and he retained her favour. Similarly, her brother Richard, another witness to her nuptials, and Lettice's other siblings also remained in the Queen's good graces. It was Lettice, and Lettice alone, who was forced to accept the consequences of her disgrace.

Lettice's family was an unusually close one, and if she were with them at this time then her father probably advised her to keep a low profile. This was indeed the course of action that Lettice now chose; but it did not come naturally to her. In the storm that followed the discovery of her marriage, she resumed a lifestyle similar to that which she had adopted during her first marriage, throwing herself into the role of a wife whose primary concern was her household and family, living in the seclusion of the countryside. It was not, perhaps, the life that she had ultimately envisaged for her marriage with Leicester, but for the moment she had few options. At least she was happy in her choice of husband, and that must have kept her partly content through the lonely months away from court and Leicester. In order to win back the Queen's favour, Leicester realized that it was more prudent to keep his wife in the background. Even so, their love for one another had survived the moment that they had both been dreading. Lettice, though, could and would not be content to remain in the shadows forever – the Queen would have to accept that Lettice and Leicester were man and wife, whether she liked it or not.

CHAPTER 13

A She-Wolf

D
ESPITE LETTICE'S RETREAT from London, as time passed the Queen still showed no signs of thawing. It was not long, however, before Leicester was once more restored to favour. As Elizabeth Jenkins surmised, 'certain aspects of the landscape had been irreparably altered, but the ground was still firm beneath Leicester's feet'.[1] His relationship with Elizabeth held strong, and Leicester was free to show himself at court. For Lettice there was no such clemency. She was forced to remain in the shadows, living quietly in the hope that the Queen's temper would eventually cool. This meant that she was unable to officially take up residence with her husband. Consequently she spent the majority of 1580 at Greys Court, apologizing to Lord Burghley in October for detaining her younger brother Francis, who was expected at court. While in the country she missed company, and longed for news from court. She still received visits from her husband, although the frequency of these is unknown. Their passion for one another was still strong, and by the end of the year it was clear that the situation could not continue in this vein: by then, Lettice would have known that she was pregnant.

Despite the malicious reports that Lettice and Leicester had had children born out of wedlock, this was nothing more than scandalous gossip, and there is no evidence of any children prior to their marriage. In February 1580, the French ambassador, Mauvissière, had heard that Lettice was heavily pregnant, but nothing more is heard of this. It may well be the case that – possibly not for the first time – she had experienced the tragedy of a miscarriage. If so, it would have made the child that she and

Leicester conceived later in 1580 doubly precious. Leicester was delighted by the news of his wife's pregnancy: he had long craved a legitimate child, and in his earlier letter to Douglas Sheffield, he had claimed that besides the Queen's favour, 'there is nothing in the world next that favour that I would not give to be in hope of leaving some children behind me, being now the last of our house'.[2]

It was with the arrival of their child in mind that both Leicester and Lettice realized that the situation had to change. There was to be no doubt in anybody's mind that the child that Lettice was carrying was legitimate, and it was this that prompted the recorded testimonies of the witnesses who had attended their wedding. Leicester had also determined that his child ought to be born in his house, and so at some time between the end of 1580 and the spring of 1581, Lettice took up residence at Leicester House, her husband's townhouse on the Strand.

Formerly the property of Lord Paget, who named it Paget Place, the house had been acquired by Leicester in January 1570. He immediately renamed it in recognition of his title, and it became his London base when he was not residing at court. The Queen visited Leicester there on a number of occasions, even after his marriage to Lettice – presumably the Countess was either absent or required to remain out of sight.[3] Leicester House lay immediately opposite the church of St Clement Danes, and was an imposing house with a Tudor gatehouse.[4] Built around four sides of an inner court and with an open forecourt, it boasted a number of lavishly furnished rooms, and four beautifully laid-out knot gardens. Within them was a two-storey banqueting house that Leicester had built by the river, perfect for entertaining guests.[5] A contemporary report noted that 'There was a chapel where now the porter's lodge is at the outer-gate, appertaining to St Clement's Danes', and this was something that both Leicester and Lettice made regular use of.[6] Inside, it was full of the beautiful objects that Leicester adored, and that he had spent many years acquiring. By the time that Lettice arrived these included 'a pair of playing tables of black ebony and white bone', silver-gilt plate which proudly displayed

Leicester's bear badge, 'a little treble lute in a case', and 'a globe of all the world standing in a frame'.[7] In addition, forty-two pieces from Leicester's portrait collection were on display, including two of the Duc d'Anjou – the Queen's suitor – which may have been given as gifts in an attempt to curry Leicester's support, one of 'Venus and Cupid', and interestingly, one of Lettice's daughter, 'my Lady Dorothy'.[8] More surprising, perhaps, was the presence of a 'picture of my Lady Sheffield enclosed in a wainscot case' – a piece that Lettice must have been none too pleased about, but which nevertheless was still there after Leicester's death.[9]

It would not be long before Lettice put her own stamp on Leicester's residences – particularly Leicester House, where in addition to the apartments that were provided for members of Leicester's family, a number were also set aside for Lettice's children. Her own bedchamber in the house was sumptuously furnished in a reflection of her status; there was a fine bed of walnut which was adorned with curtains of luxurious scarlet, and a set of furniture that included coffers for storing her lavish wardrobe. Curiously, sculptures of Leicester and the Queen were on display in Leicester House in the late 1570s and 1580s, but after that they disappear. Elizabeth Goldring suggests that this may have been due to Lettice's influence.[10]

IT HAD BEEN around a decade since the birth of Lettice's last child – the short-lived Francis. As she was now thirty-seven years old, the risks that came with childbirth were significantly higher, something which both Lettice and her husband would have been all too aware of. It therefore made good sense for her to remain in London, where both midwives and physicians were easily at hand, ensuring Lettice received the best possible care as she entered her confinement. Meanwhile, her husband was still needed at court in order to support the Queen: though Lettice was now his wife whom he loved, there was no doubting that Elizabeth still remained Leicester's greatest priority. He was first and foremost a courtier.

Lettice began her confinement at Leicester House in the spring. It is possible that during this time she had the company of her two maids, Bridget Fettiplace and Lettice Barrett, although exactly when they entered her service is unclear.[11] She had a particularly good relationship with the latter, who in 1588 would become her sister-in-law when she wed Lettice's younger brother, Francis. It was during this time that the couple became well acquainted, for Francis was a member of Leicester's entourage. Lettice was both relieved and overjoyed when, on 6 June 1581, she was safely delivered of a son. On both a personal and a practical level, their son's birth was a joyous moment for the couple, who probably saw it as a sign that their union was blessed. Leicester was elated: thanks to Lettice, he finally had a legitimate male heir. The boy was named Robert after his father, and was immediately given the title of Lord Denbigh.[12] He may have been christened in nearby St Clement Danes shortly after his birth. There is no indication as to the identity of his godparents – given the circumstances, neither Leicester nor Lettice dared to invite the Queen to assume this role. More probable is that Leicester's brother, Ambrose, and perhaps also Lettice's father or one of her siblings filled these positions. What is clear is that the boy's parents doted on him, and he was raised in the utmost splendour within the luxurious trappings of Leicester's homes. At Leicester House, his cradle was covered with costly crimson velvet, and he had a fine little chair that was upholstered in green.[13]

There is no reference to the Queen's reaction upon learning of the birth of Lettice and Leicester's son. Unsurprisingly, however, it did nothing to warm her to Lettice; indeed, it may have served to heighten the dislike and jealousy that Elizabeth felt towards her kinswoman. After all, in effect Lettice now had many of the things that the Queen may arguably have wanted – a marriage with Leicester that was cemented by love on both sides, and a son. In the immediate aftermath of her son's birth, though, Lettice probably cared little about Elizabeth's feelings, and threw herself into caring for her baby.

Although the usual team of nursery staff were employed to oversee the infant Lord Denbigh's everyday needs, Lettice, devoted mother that she was, also played an active role in her son's life. It had been twelve years since she had had a newborn to care for, and given that she was still banned from attending court, her son's care gave her something to focus her energies upon.

BESIDES LORD DENBIGH, Lettice also had her four children from her first marriage. With the exception of her eldest son, three of her children were still residing in York in the Earl of Huntingdon's household. There is no contemporary evidence as to how these children reacted upon learning of their mother's remarriage to the Earl of Leicester. Judging by the relationships that they all came to share with him, though, it is safe to say that any teething problems were quickly smoothed over. Not only did Lettice still dote on her elder children, but Leicester would also prove himself to be a caring stepfather who took an interest in all of their lives – particularly his wife's eldest son, Robert.

By the summer of 1581, Robert, Earl of Essex, had completed his MA at Trinity at Cambridge. He had paid a brief visit to Leicester House, where he had perhaps met his baby half-brother for the first time. Lettice would surely have been delighted at having been reunited with her eldest son, her 'Sweet Robin' who she had probably not seen for some time. Essex had met the Earl of Leicester before, but this was the first occasion on which he would have been introduced to him as his stepfather. In the same way that Lettice had once done, Essex was able to travel from London to Kenilworth, there to take advantage of the hunting that his stepfather's country residence offered. From there he returned to the south, taking up residence with his grandfather, Sir Francis Knollys, at Greys Court. Francis took a great interest in his grandchildren, and certainly did his best to guide his eldest grandson. However, on this occasion Essex's stay with his strict grandfather was of short duration, and from Greys he continued to his father's former estate at Lamphey. It was here that he would largely remain over the course of the next few years, where he did 'very honourably and bountifully keep house with many servants in livery and the repair of most gentlemen of those parts'.[14]

Meanwhile, Lettice's disgrace had no bearing on the Queen's attitude towards her goddaughter Penelope, who she welcomed to court in January 1581. Penelope had just turned eighteen, and had been escorted south by her guardian, the Earl of Huntingdon. It is possible that she took the opportunity to visit her pregnant mother while she was in the capital, for mother and daughter were close. Beautiful, vivacious and intelligent, Penelope was an instant hit at court in the same way that Lettice had once been. Though she had washed her hands of Lettice, Elizabeth now showed that she bore Penelope no grudge, offering her a place in her household. Penelope thus began her career at court, following in the footsteps of her grandmother, her aunts and her disgraced mother: hers was to be a more active career than Lettice's had been. Her daughter's success with the Queen and her popularity at court may have filled Lettice with optimism; perhaps, in time, she too would be the recipient of the Queen's favour once more.

The court was a world away from the quiet seclusion of the north that Penelope had been raised in, and had much to offer a girl of her vitality. It was all the more splendid given that, at this time, there were a host of entertainments staged in honour of the proposal of the Queen's marriage to the Duc d'Anjou – plans that would, like those of all of Elizabeth's previous suitors, come to nothing as once again the Queen got cold feet. By 1583 everyone – fifty-year-old Elizabeth included – was under no illusions that she would ever marry. Her love for Leicester, and her diplomatic negotiations elsewhere, had all come to nothing. There would be no royal marriage.

In no time at all, Penelope had earned the admiration of many of her contemporaries, including Leicester's nephew, Sir Philip Sidney. Her father, Walter, had cherished hopes that the couple would marry. Later, Philip would make her the inspiration for his famous poem, *Astrophil and Stella*. Probably written in the summer of 1582, just months after Penelope's marriage to Lord Rich, the verses were intended for private rather than public pleasure, and were not published until 1591. About a love affair that was never consummated, the references to Penelope as Stella are blatant. Sidney consistently played on Penelope's marital name, Rich, referring to her as 'The richest gem of love and life', and making reference to Cupid's shield, 'Where red roses are show on a silver field' in the same manner as the Devereux crest. Among other things, the poet also refers to her 'joyful face'.[15] There is no evidence to support the suggestion that Philip and Penelope became lovers, and her father's aspirations for a marriage between the pair would never transpire; Penelope's guardian, Huntingdon, had found a replacement.

When Lettice's first husband had left instructions for his children to join the household of the Earl of Huntingdon, he had also given him control of their futures. Lettice's daughters and her younger son, Walter, were completely dependent on him, and relied on him in order to secure their future prospects. Penelope had barely settled at court when Huntingdon began looking towards her marital prospects. In March, he believed that he had found the perfect candidate.

On 27 February, Robert Rich, second Baron Rich, died. His heir was his second son, also called Robert, for whom the succession to the barony of Rich had come as something of a surprise.[16] Only the previous year, in 1580, Robert's elder brother had died, and the death of his father in quick succession meant that in a short space of time Robert had had the title of third Lord Rich thrust upon him. Robert was three years older than Penelope, and hailed from Essex, where his family estate was the former monastery of Leez Priory, near Chelmsford.[17] He had also inherited a vast number of other estates, mainly in Essex, rendering him an annual income of £5,000 (£746,500). This eye-watering sum rendered the as-of-yet-unmarried Lord Rich one of the most wealthy and eligible bachelors in the country – little wonder that the Earl of Huntingdon saw him as a great prize for Penelope.

Besides his wealth, though, Lord Rich had little to commend him. His grandfather, Sir Richard Rich, was an unpleasant character, who had gained notoriety during the reign of Henry VIII for supplying false evidence against Sir Thomas More.[18] His father did not have much more to recommend him, for although he had been among the gentlemen who had accompanied Penelope's father to Ireland in 1573, it had not been long before he craved his home comforts and returned to England. Robert had not been educated to anywhere near the same standard as Penelope, but Huntingdon approved of the fact that he was a vociferous Puritan. He was also an unsavoury character who had a reputation as a bully – he had once resorted to violence when attempting to evict a family from his lands, and his underhand tactics were well known.

A match between Penelope and Lord Rich is unlikely to have been one that either Lettice or Walter would have considered – especially since both parents had probably had their hearts set elsewhere. However, Lettice no longer had any legal say in the matter, and given that she was at this time awaiting the outcome of Lord Denbigh's birth, her mind was occupied elsewhere. Huntingdon swiftly took matters into his own hands, without first consulting Lettice or Penelope. Just eleven days after Lord Rich had succeeded to his father's title, Huntingdon wrote to Sir Francis Walsingham, explaining that Rich was 'one in years very fit for my Lady Penelope Devereux', and asking him to intervene for 'the favour and liking of her Majesty' to the match.[19] The Queen duly gave her blessing, perhaps perceiving that, with her father dead and her mother in disgrace, Penelope's fortunes rested on her ability to make a good marriage. Although Penelope had little in terms of material wealth, she was born of good family, something that Rich could not have failed to value.

There is no record of how Lettice felt about her daughter's impending marriage, but Penelope's feelings on the matter are clear. She was expected to obey the arrangements that her guardian had put in place, but, like her mother, Penelope had spirit. Rather than accepting the husband that had been chosen for her, she bravely defied the conventions of the day by voicing her objections even as she stood at the altar: sadly, her feelings of despair were paid little heed. On 1 November, Lord Rich and Penelope were married. Lettice was not there to witness this unhappy moment in Penelope's life, which was probably conducted at court. However, her son Essex was certainly in attendance, splashing out on a lavish new suit of clothes for the occasion. For Penelope, it was not a cause for celebration; Lettice no doubt heard first-hand an account of her eldest daughter's wedding day, later recorded by Penelope's second husband. He wrote that, 'A lady of great birth and virtue, being in the power of her friends, was by them married against her will unto one against whom she did protest at the very solemnity and ever after.'[20]

Lettice must have been distressed to hear of her daughter's unhappiness, and matters did not get any better. Following her marriage, although Penelope remained in the Queen's service she now chose to spend much of her time with her family, particularly her mother, in order to avoid Lord Rich as far as possible. She did not bother to hide her feelings, and her marriage would prove to be notoriously miserable. It was, furthermore, one that would force her to seek comfort in the arms of another.

IN SEPTEMBER 1582, three years had elapsed since Lettice and Leicester's Wanstead wedding. At this time, the French ambassador Mauvissière claimed to have heard that Lettice was once again expecting a child ('*grosse de son segond enfant*'), but if this was the case then nothing more is heard of it.[21] While Lettice had continued to keep a low profile, she had by the summer of 1583 established herself firmly – and permanently – as Countess of Leicester at Leicester House. Perhaps both she and her husband expected that by now the Queen's anger would have cooled; if so, they were both very much mistaken. Although Leicester had by now been restored to his former favour, the matter of his marriage was still raw. Elizabeth was not in a forgiving mood, and it was probably upon hearing that Lettice had installed herself in Leicester's homes as his wife that her anger flared. It was reported that she was once again furious with the Earl 'about his marriage, for he opened the same more plainly than ever before'.[22] But Lettice was determined not to hide away any more.

THE MARRIAGE OF Lettice's eldest daughter had now been settled, but there was still her youngest, Dorothy, to consider. In January 1582, Leicester had made a will in order to set out the provisions for his young son and heir. However, he also made reference to the marriage of his stepdaughter. Penelope's marriage to Lord Rich had put an end to all thoughts of a match between her and Sir Philip Sidney, but it seems that Leicester, and possibly also Lettice, had considered Sidney as a husband for Dorothy instead. Dorothy was now seventeen years old, and, like her elder sister, had joined the Queen's household as one of her ladies. As her guardian, it was Huntingdon who bore the responsibility for arranging a husband for her, but Leicester had also shown an interest in the marriage of his stepdaughter. He was keen to ally Lettice's family with his own, and in his will he had noted that there had been 'some talk of marriage between my well beloved nephew Philip Sidney and the Lady Dorothy Devereux'. In a confirmation of his fondness for them, he continued, 'my hearty and earnest wish was and is that it be so, for the great good will and liking I have to each party'.[23] His final desire in the matter was 'that such love and liking might be between them as might bring a marriage'.[24] Sidney had spent some time residing with his uncle at Leicester House in the early days of Leicester's marriage to Lettice, and it is possible that talk of a union with one of the Devereuxs was raised then. Unfortunately, by early 1583, if not before, all of Leicester's hopes were dashed. On 21 September, Philip married elsewhere – to Frances, the daughter of Sir Francis Walsingham. A matching pair of portraits of the newlyweds, which may have been commissioned to mark their marriage, now hangs at Parham House in Sussex. It was not what either Leicester or his wife had hoped for, but in the coming years they would both show themselves to be kind to the new Lady Sidney.

According to the Spanish ambassador, when it came to finding a husband for Dorothy, by 1583 both Leicester and Lettice had raised their hopes even higher than Sir Philip Sidney. On 17 March, Bernardino de Mendoza was reporting to his master that Robert Bowes, Queen Elizabeth's ambassador in Scotland, had been tasked with a mission. He had, according to Mendoza, been instructed to speak to King James, the son of the deposed Mary, Queen of Scots, on the matter of a potential marriage with Lettice's daughter. Under directions from Leicester and Walsingham, Bowes had told the King of Scots that

> *if he will marry Dorothy, daughter of the Earl of Essex (who, they say, was poisoned by order of Leicester so that the latter might marry his wife, the present Countess of Leicester), and will assure them that he will not change religion, on his being acknowledged by the English Catholics, they, Leicester and Walsingham, will have him declared by the judges to be the heir to the Crown of England.*[25]

There is very little real evidence that Leicester had attempted to do any such thing: although the Queen had not named or acknowledged an heir, most people were now of the opinion that she would never marry, and that King James would be her successor. Nevertheless, the rumours about Dorothy's marriage were not helpful, and once more served to intensify Elizabeth's feelings of rage towards Lettice. In June, Mendoza reported that the Queen had begged the King of Scots' representative to tell her 'whether it was true that Leicester had negotiated through Davison for the marriage of the King of Scotland with the daughter of his wife'.[26] The King's representative denied it, yet

> *the Queen became so excited about it as to say that she would rather allow the King to take her crown away than see him married to the daughter of such a she-wolf, and, if she could find no other way to repress her ambition and that of the traitor Leicester, she would*

proclaim her all over Christendom for the bad woman she was, and prove that her husband was a cuckold. She said much more to the same effect; and, in order to mollify her, Leicester is now making great efforts to marry the girl to a private gentleman.[27]

Parts of this report were undoubtedly exaggerated, but what it does show is the intensity of the Queen's hostility towards her kinswoman. Considering that this episode supposedly took place almost five years after Lettice's marriage, the wounds caused by her betrayal of the Queen were still felt deeply. The comment about Lettice's ambition also suggests that the Queen perceived their rivalry to be more than personal – that she perhaps felt that now that Lettice had managed to ensnare Leicester, she was beginning to turn her attentions elsewhere by planning to ally her daughter with a king. Either way her venomous words were scathing indeed, and whether there was any truth in the rumours or not, the Queen was not even prepared to entertain the prospect of a reconciliation with Lettice.

Prior to, and even during this episode, the Queen appears to have been fond of Dorothy Devereux in the same way that she favoured Penelope. However, that was all about to change. In July, Dorothy took the matter of her marriage into her own hands. Sir Thomas Perrot was the son of Sir John Perrot and Anne Cheyne; like Dorothy's father, Sir Thomas had served in Ireland under his father, who was later appointed Lord Deputy. He frequently participated in tournaments at court, and it was certainly here that he had encountered Dorothy for the first time. In order to promote his suit, Sir Thomas had sought the help of Dorothy's sister, Penelope, writing to her in complimentary terms and seeking her assistance in the pursuit of obtaining Dorothy's consent to marry him. 'I know my Lady Dorothy to be worthy of all titles that may be given to any lady, and one whom the greatest and proudest minded in England may think himself happy to serve,' he wrote.[28] Penelope had clearly given the match her blessing, for he continued, 'I understand by my cousin

Taseborow how great a happiness it hath pleased your ladyship to wish me.'[29] It is highly improbable, though, that Sir Thomas had sought the permission of either Lettice, Leicester or Dorothy's guardian the Earl of Huntingdon when pressing his suit.

The circumstances of what happened next are confusing, but Dorothy had evidently accepted Sir Thomas's proposal. However, repeating Lettice's experience, neither party felt able to approach the Queen to ask for her consent to their marriage. As a result, the couple eloped to Broxbourne in Hertfordshire, close to Lettice's home at Wanstead. Once they were there, it was probably in the church of St Augustine's that 'a strange minister' married them. This same minister had approached the church vicar that morning, in order to ask for both the keys to the church and the communion book.[30] The whole scene had been conducted rather bizarrely, with 'two men guarding the church door with swords and daggers under their cloaks, as also had the rest of the company, five or six in number', and numerous interruptions from the local vicar, who warned them of the peril that they risked in conducting the service.[31]

Lettice was less than impressed by her daughter's behaviour, and even less impressed by her choice of husband – with good reason, for Perrot's father would later die in the Tower having been condemned for high treason – but there was little that she could do.[32] A portrait of Dorothy, now at Syon House, dates from this period of her life. Like her mother and her sister, she had been blessed with good looks, and in a play on her new marital name, a parrot is perched on her hand.[33] Described by her father-in-law as 'that virtuous and gracious lady', she had the same determined character as her mother, and what was more, history was about to repeat itself.[34] Precisely when or how the Queen learned of Dorothy's marriage is uncertain, but her reaction was predictable: utter outrage. Dorothy was immediately banished from court, but for Sir Thomas the price of marrying without the Queen's consent was worse. In a clear sign of his disgrace, he was sent to the notorious Fleet Prison, along with the chaplain who had performed the marriage ceremony.[35] Thanks to the intervention of Lord Burghley both men were later released, but that was not an end to the newlywed's troubles. They were plagued by financial woes, which, like her mother before her, Dorothy begged for Burghley's help to solve. He duly obliged, but still the Queen refused to forgive her. In despair, Dorothy wrote to Burghley that 'our infection is a like a pleurisy that have need of present remedy'.[36] The result was that Dorothy and her husband were forced to retire to the Perrot family residence, Carew Castle in Pembrokeshire, where they were to spend much of their time.[37] The parallels between Dorothy's and Lettice's stories were remarkable, and her daughter's feelings were ones that Lettice knew all too well.

CHAPTER 14

My Sorrowful Wife

THE EARL OF Leicester's primary residences were Leicester House, Wanstead and Kenilworth, and it was at the former two that Lettice spent the majority of her time. In the years that she was married to Leicester, there is evidence of her having visited Kenilworth just the once, as part of a holiday in 1585. Leicester's surviving accounts show that all three households were in constant communication with one another, and items were regularly moved between residences.[1] Though Lettice and Leicester were married for ten years, it is just for the years from 1584 to 1586 that the accounts survive, but much can be gleaned.[2] Eleven volumes of his household inventories are still available to us, a staggering number and the largest surviving collection of any Elizabethan.[3] They provide unique and illuminating glimpses into the luxury in which Lettice and her family lived, and the ways in which they spent their time.

Although Lettice does feature in her husband's accounts, her appearances are not as frequent as one might expect. The most logical explanation for this is that her household was maintained by the income she received as dowager Countess of Essex, but it is likely that her accounts would have contained some similar entries to those that can be found in her husband's. For example, members of the nobility were expected to be charitable, and Leicester's accounts reveal regular payments to the poor; on 24 October 1584, he gave money to the poor people of Witney, Abingdon and Burford Bridge, and Lettice would have distributed money in a similar way. Certainly after her death, her epitaph praised the fact that in her later years 'the poor that lived near, death nor famine could not fear'.

Leicester's payments also record items that Lettice would have enjoyed, such as white wine, the services of a harpist, and rewards to Leicester's Players for performing at Leicester House.[4] On the occasions that she does appear, it was often when her husband covered her travel expenses. In 1584 and 1585 she travelled fairly regularly by water, and Leicester's waterman was often rewarded for transporting her in her husband's barge. On 26 September 1585, for example, he was paid for 'carrying my lady to Baynard's Castle and back again to Leicester House'.[5] Though she had been forbidden from attending court, this did not prevent Lettice from mixing with other friends and members of high society in the capital, and Baynard's Castle was the London residence of the Earl of Pembroke, one of the witnesses at her wedding.[6]

Lettice's life with Leicester was full of luxury. She was mistress of an expanding household, with 150 people working at both Leicester House and Wanstead. There were gardeners, musicians and a fisherman at Wanstead.[7] In addition, Lettice had her own footman, whose duties would have included admitting Lettice's visitors into her presence. He was known only as Dampard.[8]

At Leicester House she was surrounded by a variety of gold and silver objects, including gold plate, bowls, cups, spice boxes, spoons and candlesticks, most of which were engraved with Leicester's bear symbol.[9] There was Venetian glass as well as numerous costly tapestries – Leicester even patronized the Sheldon tapestry workshop in Warwickshire, and a tapestry believed to have been made for the banqueting house at Leicester House still survives in the Victoria and Albert Museum. The floors were covered in fine carpets, while there was also a painted table 'with an ape, owls, fish, flies and birds in a gilt frame with a case of black leather'.[10] Lettice slept in one of the many elaborate beds, perhaps with one of the 'silk quilts' that could be found among Leicester's belongings – at New Year 1585, she even made a gift of a fine bed to her husband: beds being among the prize possessions of the nobility.

Elsewhere in the house, 'A pair of harp virginals covered with yellow leather', and 'a white bone horn' conveyed the couple's love of music, while 'A map of the north part of England in vellum', a map of Sir Francis Drake's voyage, and 'two maps of the kingdom of France' demonstrated Leicester's love of maps.[11] Lettice's husband's passion for books meant that he also had a vast library, filled with books that were covered in crimson velvet and stamped with Leicester's crest in gold – one of which still survives in Lambeth Palace Library.[12] By the time of his death he had amassed several hundred volumes, some of which were written in Italian and Latin.[13] Lettice's father would have approved of the copy of 'An book of Common Prayer, stamped with my Lord's arms', as well as 'a bible covered with yellow leather'.[14] By 1584 there was also a copy of Foxe's *Acts and Monuments*, which immortalized the sufferings that Protestants had been forced to endure during the reign of Queen Mary.[15] Lettice had access to all of these items, and may even have taken the time to read some of her husband's books. This does seem likely, as an inventory of her possessions taken after her death reveals that she too owned many books.[16]

When she was at home, Lettice had plenty of things with which to occupy her time. She certainly spent some of it engaged in needlework, and in 1586, for example, there is a note that 'a fair saddle cloth very richly embroidered with gold, pearl, turquoises, two counterfeit rubies' had 'all the pearl taken off by my Lady' on 19 March.[17] She also made cushions from her old gowns. Leicester House was the scene of regular entertainments, and, as mentioned, her husband's accounts record frequent payments to Leicester's Players. Formed in 1559, the group of actors were at the peak of their popularity between 1570 and 1583, so much so that the Queen had granted them a royal patent. One of their most prestigious members was William Kempe, who gained fame as a popular Elizabethan clown who danced to jigs. Another of their players, James Burbage, was responsible for building the first theatre in England in 1576, known simply as The Theatre in Shoreditch.[18] The Players performed a variety of plays of varying genres, including a comedy called *Delight*, and another called *The Greek Maid*. Leicester also patronized the poet Edmund Spenser, whom he had made his secretary in 1579.[19] Despite his employment Spenser continued with his literary works, and it was at Leicester House that he wrote his first major work, *The Shepherd's Calendar*.[20] Significantly, it contains a less than flattering reference to Lettice – it was instead highly complimentary to the Queen. The shepherd, speaking to his friend, explains that as spring is approaching

> *Then shall we sporten in delight*
> *And learn with Lettice to wax light.*

This impertinent phrase referred to the Leicesters' relationship, and was a slight, referring to the way in which Leicester had used Lettice for sexual gratification. Though it was a blatant dig at Lettice's reputation, there is no evidence of a rift or any repercussions for the poet.

The Leicesters were also very sociable, and regularly exchanged gifts with other members of the nobility, all of whom now accepted them as a married couple; the inventories record two small salts given by Lady Burghley in 1583, while the following year Sir Walter Ralegh gave an elaborate gift of 'the body of a strange shell of a fish garnished with silver and gilt'.[21] Lettice's father once presented a buck, while Sir Francis Walsingham gave a stag's head.[22] Presumably Leicester and Lettice reciprocated in similar terms. Also in 1583, the French ambassador Mauvissière informed his master Henri III that he had been invited to dine at Leicester House by the Earl: 'He has especially invited me to dine with him and his wife, who has much influence over him, and whom he introduces only to those to whom he wishes to show a particular mark of attention.' Whether this was true or not, it is interesting to note that this was the way in which one of Lettice's contemporaries chose to view the situation. Interestingly, Mauvissière wrote of the same dinner to the captive Queen of Scots. He told her that he had dined with Leicester 'and his lady to whom he is much attached. They both received me very kindly.' The couple had also, according to Mauvissière, 'expressed a wish that the Countess and my wife should be on intimate terms'.[23] Lettice would have been aware that the French were supporters of Mary, Queen of Scots, making her kindness towards one who was on good terms with the woman who had shown herself to be an enemy to Elizabeth even more intriguing.

LEICESTER HAD ALWAYS been an avid collector of art, and by 1588 he owned almost two hundred pieces. While the only connection with Lettice in 1580 was the portrait of her daughter Dorothy, by 1584 this had all changed, and her family was in greater evidence. Francis Knollys's picture had been added to the collection, as well as one of her younger brother, Thomas, 'leaning on a halberd with his armour lying by him', and her niece Lettice Fitzgerald.[24] Lettice Fitzgerald was the daughter of the youngest of Lettice's sisters, Katherine, of whom there was also a portrait, and her husband Gerald Fitzgerald. Their daughter was their only surviving child, named after her aunt who was probably also her godmother. It was at around this time that a double portrait of Lettice's daughters, which now hangs in Longleat House, was completed. Originally it was wrongly called 'Frances and Dorothy Devereux', but it shows that Lettice's daughters were growing into attractive young women.[25] It was almost certainly this portrait that was also hanging at Leicester House in 1590, described as 'two ladies in one picture, my Lady Rich and my Lady Dorothy'.[26] Most importantly, Lettice herself now appeared in the Leicester House collection, as 'The picture of my Lady with blackamores by her'.[27] Presumably the blackamoor's mentioned in relation to Lettice's portrait were black servants; if this was the case then the Leicesters were not alone, for the Queen also employed a young black boy in her household. This was just one of several portraits of Lettice, and as time progressed more pieces were added to the collection. Two years later, two great portraits of the Queen and two of Leicester had also been added, as well as one of Lettice that cost forty shillings.[28]

It is possible that this latter portrait was the one completed by George Gower in 1585, which now hangs at Longleat. That it was painted after Lettice's marriage to Leicester is clear, for sewn into the elaborate design on her richly embroidered dress is the ragged staff which formed part of the badge of the Dudley family. Roses from the Knollys family crest also feature, highlighting Lettice's proud association with both of these houses, which had now been joined together through her marriage. In her splendid portrait several ropes of costly pearls adorn her neck, as well as her ears and her hair. Gower was also responsible for painting Lettice's sister Elizabeth in 1577, to whom her portrait bears a strong similarity – so much so that for some time it was believed to represent Lettice.[29] Interestingly, since 1581 Gower had been Serjeant Painter to the Queen, but he was also popular with the nobility.[30] Clearly, he did not see Lettice's disgrace with the monarch as a reason not to accept the commission for her portrait.

Another portrait that is likely to be of Lettice also dates from this period. Sold at Sotheby's in 2010, the location of the image is now sadly unknown. It is a miniature completed by the famous miniaturist Nicholas Hilliard, executed in delicate watercolour on vellum and set in an emerald and diamond frame. Facially, the sitter does bear a resemblance to the Gower portrait of Lettice. Hilliard was well favoured by the Queen, and Lettice was also a known patron of his; one of his two daughters was named in her honour.[31] This lends support to an identification of Lettice, as does the fact that the artist also painted members of her family. There are three surviving miniatures of Leicester, and Hilliard painted Lettice's beautiful daughter, Penelope, on at least four separate occasions.[32] Later, Hilliard would also be patronized by Lettice's eldest son, Essex, who sat for his portrait with the artist at least eight times.[33] A little picture of Lettice did once survive among Leicester's collection, so it is possible that if the sitter in the miniature was Lettice then it may have been the same one.

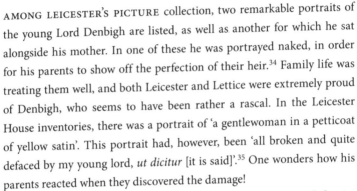

AMONG LEICESTER'S PICTURE collection, two remarkable portraits of the young Lord Denbigh are listed, as well as another for which he sat alongside his mother. In one of these he was portrayed naked, in order for his parents to show off the perfection of their heir.[34] Family life was treating them well, and both Leicester and Lettice were extremely proud of Denbigh, who seems to have been rather a rascal. In the Leicester House inventories, there was a portrait of 'a gentlewoman in a petticoat of yellow satin'. This portrait had, however, been 'all broken and quite defaced by my young lord, *ut dicitur* [it is said]'.[35] One wonders how his parents reacted when they discovered the damage!

Lettice and her husband had high hopes for their son, and despite his youth they had apparently entertained thoughts of his marriage. In March 1583, at the same time as the rumour of Dorothy's marriage to the King of Scots was circulating, the Spanish ambassador Mendoza also made reference to Lord Denbigh's marriage: 'Leicester still perseveres in the marriage I mentioned, of his son with the granddaughter of the Countess of Shrewsbury, who, after the queen of England, they say, is the nearest heiress. With Walsingham's aid he is thus trying to get his son made King in right of his wife.'[36] The girl to whom he referred was Lady Arbella Stuart, the granddaughter of Leicester's good friend the Countess of Shrewsbury – better known as Bess of Hardwick. The orphaned Arbella had royal blood in her veins, for her father, Charles Stuart, had been the brother of Mary, Queen of Scots' murdered husband, Lord Darnley. Darnley and Charles were the grandsons of Henry VIII's elder sister, Margaret Tudor, and thus through her Arbella had a claim to the English throne. Leicester and Bess may well have discussed such a marriage, and the following spring, the rumours surfaced once more. The evidence for this comes in the form of a letter from the captive Mary,

Queen of Scots, who had met Leicester in 1577.[37] In the spring of 1584 Mary had been Elizabeth's prisoner for sixteen years, and was still under the custodianship of the Earl of Shrewsbury, who had inherited the role from Lettice's father. That spring, Mary wrote to the French ambassador, claiming that the Countess of Shrewsbury 'has conceived of settling the crown of England on the head of her little girl, Arbella, and this by means of marrying her to a son of the Earl of Leicester. These children are also educated in this idea, and their portraits have been sent to each other.'[38] According to *Leicester's Commonwealth*, such a desire demonstrated that 'the disposition of this man [Leicester] bent wholly to a sceptre'.[39] The Leicesters would have realized that the Queen would never consent to such a marriage. The matter, in any case, would soon be taken entirely out of their hands.

ON 19 JULY 1584, just months after the captive Queen of Scots had referred to Lord Denbigh's potential marriage, 'the Noble Imp' – as he was referred to on his tomb – died at Wanstead. The nature of his malady is unknown, and in all likelihood he had suffered from one of the common ailments that often claimed the young. The assertion that he was deformed is false – a theory based on a suit of armour once believed to be Denbigh's, now at Warwick Castle, which shows one leg piece longer than the other.[40] It has now been proven that the armour dates from around 1625, long after Denbigh's death. There is certainly no evidence in favour of the absurd – and frankly cruel – claim made by *Leicester's Commonwealth* that Denbigh was seized by 'such a strange calamity of the falling sickness in his infancy as well may be a witness of the parents' sin and wickedness and of both their wasted natures in iniquity'.[41] The 'falling sickness' refers to epilepsy, but there is no evidence that Denbigh was suffering from this. Such slanders – when the Leicesters heard of them – would have been incredibly painful. Denbigh had just passed his third birthday, and although Lettice was present, Leicester was with the court at Nonsuch Palace. A message was immediately sent to him, conveying the devastating news. When it reached him, Leicester's first thoughts were for Lettice – for once, the Queen was not his first priority, and he fled the court without waiting for her permission. Asking Sir Christopher Hatton to explain his absence, he hurried to Wanstead to be by Lettice's side. Their happy family life had been shattered, and both parents felt their son's death keenly. Lettice's sorrow was heightened, for she had already experienced the loss of a son with her first husband – young Francis. For Leicester, though, it was a completely new and heart-wrenching experience that left him a broken man. He later wrote sadly of 'the loss of my only little son, whom God has lately taken from us'.[42] Now, the only reminders the couple had of their son were the portraits that adorned the walls of their homes.

When the Queen was informed of the Leicesters' tragedy, she immediately sent a message of condolence via Sir Henry Killigrew, a court diplomat who had been patronized by Leicester. However, it was Leicester whom the Queen wished to comfort, not Lettice. The following day a letter arrived from Hatton, in which he urged Leicester to take solace, for

if the love of a child be dear, which is now taken from you, the love of God is ten thousand times more dear, which you can never lack nor lose. Of men's hearts you enjoy more than millions, which, on my soul, do love you no less than children or brethren. Leave sorrow, therefore, my good Lord, and be glad with us, which much rejoice in you.[43]

Leicester responded to this touching letter on 23 July, thanking Hatton for 'your careful and most godly advice at this time'.[44] As he continued, his words conveyed the feelings of a man who was utterly distraught: 'I must confess I have received many afflictions within these few years, but not a greater, next her Majesty's displeasure: and, if it pleased God, I would the sacrifice of this poor innocent might satisfy.' He went on: 'The afflictions I have suffered may satisfy such as are offended, at least appease their long hard conceits.' He had been touched by the Queen's message, and finished his letter in his praise of her: 'She shall never comfort a more true and faithful man to her, for I have lived and so will die only hers.'[45] If Lettice had seen these words, they would have done little to comfort her at this difficult time. The truth of them would not have been lost on her either; she and Leicester were married – and in love – but Elizabeth would always be the most important woman in his life. Perhaps even the true love of his life. Elizabeth still mattered greatly to him, and her words had brought him much solace.

While the Queen and Hatton consoled Leicester, there was nothing for Lettice: she and Elizabeth remained estranged. It seems that she was, nevertheless, remembered by her old friend Lord Burghley, who had offered the grieving couple the use of his house, Theobalds, in order to give them a break. This was not lost on Leicester, who took the opportunity to write to Burghley on 31 July, expressing his thanks for his 'kindness towards his poor wife, who is hardly dealt with. God only must help it with Her Majesty.'[46] Though the Queen's words of comfort towards him had genuinely touched Leicester, her attitude towards Lettice was clearly starting to rankle, and it says something about Elizabeth's animosity towards her kinswoman that she was not even prepared to condole with her on the loss of her child. Leicester evidently felt the same way.

The visit to Theobalds did little to distract Leicester and Lettice from their sadness. When Leicester apologized to his absent host for their 'unceremonious visit' to his home, he also explained that while they had hunted they had made 'some of his stags afraid, but killed none'.[47] They had wanted to escape from Wanstead before their son's funeral, which was conducted on 1 August and which, as was custom, neither of them attended. From there, the child's body was conveyed to St Mary's Church, Warwick, where he was buried on the south side of the Beauchamp Chapel. A life-sized effigy was erected to his memory, and his tomb was decorated with his father's heraldic devices. In a further sign of his youth, his effigy was dressed in a sexless gown. His epitaph made no mention of

Lettice, but instead referred to Leicester and the noble ancestry that the child had acquired through him:

Here resteth the body of the noble imp Robert Dudley, Baron of Denbigh, son of Robert Earl of Leicester, nephew and heir unto Ambrose Dudley Earl of Warwick, brethren, both sons of the most mighty Prince, John, late Duke of Northumberland, herein interred, a child of great parentage but far greater hope and towardness, taken from this transitory world unto everlasting life, in his tender age at Wanstead in Essex on Sunday, 19th of July, in the year of our Lord God 1584 ... and in this place laid up among his noble ancestors, in assured hope of the general resurrection.

The rawness of Leicester and Lettice's grief was evident on the day following the funeral. Leicester had written to thank William Davison, the Queen's secretary, for his letter of condolence, which 'found me from the court, whence I have been absent these fifteen days to comfort my sorrowful wife for the loss of my only little son, whom God has lately taken from us'.[48] They drew solace from one another, but the couple must have felt mixed emotions when, in early October, Joan Heigham, the wife of Lettice's brother Richard, gave birth to a child. Even so, on 12 October Leicester gave a reward to the nurse and midwife.[49]

In what would come as a further bitter blow, Leicester and Lettice would have no more children. At the time of Denbigh's death Leicester was fifty-two, while Lettice was approaching forty-one – '*fort agée*' to bear another child, according to the French ambassador, Mauvissière.[50] From now on, Leicester vested his hopes in his 'base son' by Douglas Sheffield, but perhaps more prominently, in Lettice's eldest son, the Earl of Essex.

Lettice and Leicester spent most of the rest of 1584 in company with their friends and family. At the end of the month they decided to leave London behind, and travelled to the peaceful serenity of Greys Court. The time spent at Greys was a welcome distraction from their grief, but it could not last forever. It was probably soon after this that Leicester, with his wife's encouragement, had other matters to occupy his mind.

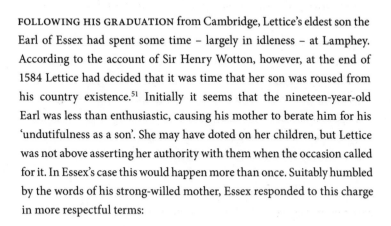

FOLLOWING HIS GRADUATION from Cambridge, Lettice's eldest son the Earl of Essex had spent some time – largely in idleness – at Lamphey. According to the account of Sir Henry Wotton, however, at the end of 1584 Lettice had decided that it was time that her son was roused from his country existence.[51] Initially it seems that the nineteen-year-old Earl was less than enthusiastic, causing his mother to berate him for his 'undutifulness as a son'. She may have doted on her children, but Lettice was not above asserting her authority with them when the occasion called for it. In Essex's case this would happen more than once. Suitably humbled by the words of his strong-willed mother, Essex responded to this charge in more respectful terms:

> *My very good Lady and mother,*
>
> *If I find by your Ladyship's displeasure conceived, that I am thought in sort to have offended, so I desire to deliver myself either wholly, or in some part from the same fault. The which some will hardly term undutifulness to your Ladyship, others carefulness of mine own good, and many think me inconsiderate, in not making your Ladyship more acquainted with my determinations. The name of undutifulness as a son I utterly abhor, my purposed course to do well I hope shall deliver me from the suspicion of carefulness of mine own estate, and if in your Ladyship's wise censure I be thought inconsiderate, I plead as a young man pardon for that fault whereto of all others our age is most subject.[52]*

He ended, 'humbly craving your Ladyship's blessing I daily pray for your Ladyship's most honourable and happy estate', before signing himself, 'Your Ladyship's most obedient son'.[53] It was almost certainly later that year that, under the auspices of his stepfather, Lettice's son was presented at court. His mother actively encouraged him, perceiving her children's futures to be at court. The young Earl made an instant impression.[54]

Lettice's son was an attractive young man: tall, with a full head of hair and a beard and moustache, Essex also had charisma and charm that he knew how to use to effect – something that he had inherited from his mother. Beneath the surface, though, he could be petulant, and was prone to sulking and rages when he did not get his own way. The fifty-one-year-old Queen liked his youth, and was immediately very taken with him. She would later, however, have good justification for berating his bad behaviour, declaring that 'He held it from his mother's side.'[55] The court was the perfect place for Essex to seek his fortune, and to attempt to restore some of the family coffers that had been so heavily squandered by his father. So successful was he that he was raised to heights not achieved by either of his parents. The arrival of a new potential favourite at court naturally earned the jealousy of others who craved the Queen's favour. In particular, the Devon-born Sir Walter Ralegh, whose rise had also been meteoric. He and Essex despised each other: theirs was a rivalry that would continue for the next two decades.

Lettice was gratified by her son's warm reception from the Queen, and was grateful to her husband for his influence in that quarter. Leicester did his best to mentor his stepson, and the two men began to spend a great deal of time together. But as time went on, it became apparent that stepfather and stepson were very different in their treatment of their royal lady – Essex was, after all, his mother's son.

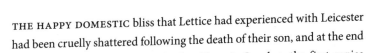

THE HAPPY DOMESTIC bliss that Lettice had experienced with Leicester had been cruelly shattered following the death of their son, and at the end of 1584 the couple received a further blow. In London, the first copies of *The Copy of a Letter Written by a Master of Art of Cambridge*, better known as *Leicester's Commonwealth*, began to circulate, placing both

Leicester and Lettice under considerable strain. Though anonymously published, the scandalous tract was the work of several authors, all of whom cast Leicester in a less than flattering light. They hated the influence that Leicester wielded over the Queen, and as Catholics, felt that she would be better advised by one of their number. As such, the authors urged the Queen to withdraw her favour from Leicester. They were also eager for Elizabeth to recognize the captive Queen of Scots as her heir, and Leicester's support of other Protestant candidates only increased their loathing of him. The claims the tract made against him and Lettice, chiefly of their roles in the deaths of their previous spouses, were extremely damaging. Among other libellous assertions, the authors cast doubt on the validity of the Leicesters' marriage: 'And for the widow of Essex, I marvel, Sir, how you call her his wife, seeing the canon law standeth yet in force touching matters of marriage within the realm.'[56] Though it was full of inaccuracies, the *Commonwealth* had a devastating effect on Leicester, who tried desperately to suppress it. It was damning to both his and Lettice's reputations – and there was nothing that they could do about it. Equally offended was the Queen, although only on behalf of her favourite. She not only sent letters to the Mayor, Sheriffs and Aldermen of London defending Leicester's innocence, but also demanded that they put all of their resources into suppressing as many copies as possible.[57] The true effects of the *Commonwealth* would not be felt until later, and it has had an alarming impact on the way Leicester has been viewed by historians over the centuries; William Camden was just one of many who contributed to his blackened reputation. In response, Leicester's nephew Sir Philip Sidney wrote a defence of his uncle, in which he claimed that 'my chiefest honour is to be a Dudley'.[58] The damage had nevertheless been done and it is true to say that the year 1584 had been the most devastating one of both Leicester and Lettice's lives.

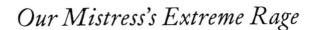

CHAPTER 15

Our Mistress's Extreme Rage

EW YEAR 1585 was a fresh start for Lettice and Leicester. Their year had begun at Greys Court, where once again Leicester had lost money in play – this time at dice – and had given money both to the poor, and in reward to the servants of Greys for their hospitality.[1] Having spent a few days travelling around Oxfordshire, the Leicesters had returned to Greys later in January, before making their way back to Leicester House. In February, Lettice's daughter Dorothy had given birth to a child, and Leicester had rewarded her nurse, but nothing further is heard of this baby – presumably it died young.[2]

With all the heartache that the couple had been forced to endure the previous year, it was little wonder that Leicester sought some fresh occupation with which to busy his mind. He had always been a great advocate of Protestantism, and he had also taken a great interest in the Netherlands. Since the abdication of the Emperor Charles V in 1555, the Netherlands had come under the rule of his successor, Philip II of Spain.[3] Philip, formerly married to Elizabeth's half-sister Mary, was devotedly Catholic, and was alarmed that Protestantism in the Netherlands was starting to spread. After a number of armed rebellions against Spanish Catholic rule, Philip retaliated by sending a large force of both Spanish and Italian soldiers to the Netherlands. This provoked further resistance, and across the Channel, Queen Elizabeth was becoming increasingly wary of the threat posed by Catholic Spanish soldiers who were now just a short distance from England. In 1575, the Spanish government lost control, and though four years later the southern provinces of the Netherlands made peace with Spain, the northern provinces refused to do so. Spain would spend many years trying to regain control.

On 10 July 1584, William 'the Silent', the Prince of Orange, was shot in the chest by a Catholic assassin at Delft.[4] William was a champion of the reformed faith, and had led the Dutch resistance against Spain. His death therefore came as a huge blow to the Dutch Protestants, who were becoming overwhelmed by the might of the Catholic Spanish Empire. In desperation, they now cast around for support. They looked in Queen Elizabeth's direction, offering her the Dutch throne in return for aid. Meanwhile, the Spanish commander Alessandro Farnese, Duke of Parma, began besieging Antwerp.[5] This rang alarm bells in England, and the Queen realized that in order to prevent the Netherlands from collapsing, she needed to offer them her support. Though she ultimately refused the sovereignty of the country, she was nevertheless keen to offer military aid to her co-religionists. It was decided that a force ought to be sent to the Netherlands, and it was clear that a person of great eminence should head the Queen's army, but who should fill that role was not yet decided.

By February 1585, Leicester had made it known that he was enthusiastic to lead the Queen's forces, but Elizabeth and her councillors deliberated over the best course of action. As they pondered, at home Lettice and her husband spent much of the earlier part of the year occupied in the usual domestic matters. On 25 March there was a payment to 'the French cook at Leicester House', while on 2 April William the fool was rewarded for travelling from Wanstead to the Earl of Essex.[6] On 26 April, 'Luck the fool of Wickham' was rewarded for 'presenting a cheese', as was a servant of Sir Walter Ralegh's for bringing a gift of oysters.[7] Lettice seems to have busied herself with ordering clothes for her husband, for on 3 June one Mrs Barker was paid eight shillings (£60) 'for ruffs for eleven shirts that my lady bought for your lordship'.[8] Five days later, Leicester gave her money, presumably to cover her costs 'when she played with my Lord of Derby at cards'.[9] As the summer approached, however, the couple decided that they needed a holiday.

In August, the Leicesters left the disease-ridden air of London behind them, and began their journey to Kenilworth. They travelled with a party of sixty via Abingdon, where on 16 August a reward was given to three singers that sang 'under my lady's window in the morning the same day'.[10] Their journey onwards was a sociable one, and gave them the opportunity to spend some time with their friends and family. Having stopped at Cornbury – a house of Leicester's near Oxford – and Woodstock on the way, the couple finally reached Kenilworth on 20 August. This seems to have been the first occasion on which Lettice had visited the ancient stronghold in her capacity as Leicester's wife, and it must have been a source of great satisfaction to her to consider that she was now mistress of the castle's treasures. It may also have stirred fond memories of the hunting parties that she had once enjoyed in the park, and Leicester's courtship of her – and of their possible first secret exchange of vows.

Even at Kenilworth, though, there was no escaping from the Queen, whose portraits hung from the castle's walls.[11] There were also two portraits of Leicester 'in whole proportion, the one in armour, the other in a suit of russet satin and velvet', and another in half proportion, as well as another of Lettice's sister, Elizabeth.[12] A likeness of the captive Mary, Queen of Scots, could also be seen, and significantly, so too could that of Philip of Spain.[13] The King as a show of friendship may have given this in the 1560s, when Philip believed that Leicester was a contender for the Queen's hand in marriage.[14] There were, however, few traces of Lettice.

Kenilworth provided a welcome change of scene. Unfortunately, their holiday was destined to be of short duration. As Leicester informed Burghley at the end of August, 'I have got a shrewd wrench on my foot by the fall of my horse, which drives me to my couch, and more rest than here I would have had.'[15] He was writing from nearby Stoneleigh, the home of Sir Thomas Leigh, and it was while he was here that he received word from the Queen.[16] His request to lead the Queen's forces in the Netherlands had been successful: Elizabeth had decided that her favourite would head the campaign.

There was no time to be wasted, and with all holiday thoughts now forgotten, Leicester left Lettice at Kenilworth as he began the journey back to London. Lettice was used to her husband being called away in the Queen's service, but this time she was determined to join him. She followed Leicester back to London at a more leisurely pace, probably arriving at Leicester House in early September – much to the Queen's annoyance. Elizabeth was fearful lest Lettice should try to travel abroad with her husband, something that she was determined to prevent. Writing from the court on 5 September, Walsingham informed William Davison that 'I see not her Majesty disposed to use the service of the Earl of Leicester. There is great offence taken in the carrying down of his lady.'[17] Leicester and Lettice had now been married for seven years, yet still the Queen raged against her kinswoman. This placed an intolerable strain upon Lettice, but there was nothing that she could do. Everyone knew that the Queen came first.

Meanwhile, Leicester began making preparations for his journey. By necessity this required him to spend much of his time with the Queen, with the inevitable consequence that Lettice was neglected. He thus asked Walsingham to 'send my wife word in the morning that I cannot come before Thursday to London'. His plans took on many different aspects, and on 27 September he told Walsingham that he had instructed those friends and servants who were accompanying him to prepare themselves 'with all the speed possible, to serve her majesty, under me, in the Low Countries'.[18] His arrangements had included taking up 'both armours and steel saddles, as many as must cost me a good piece of money. I have set in hand sundry furniture also for myself.'[19] He had also stressed that the Dutch representatives at court were eager for him to be on his way, and were doing all that they could to press him to leave. It was not just Leicester who was employed in preparations, but Lettice's son Essex, too. Essex was now twenty years old, and was a handsome youth with dark hair and eyes. Although Leicester and Lettice's young son was now dead and Leicester's official heir was his nephew, Sir Philip Sidney, this did not prevent him from taking an active interest in his stepchildren. This endeared Lettice further to her husband, and she watched as he primed Essex to take centre stage at court, where he had first been presented the previous year. Now about to receive his first taste of military action, the young Earl enthusiastically began recruiting men for the campaign, running up huge debts in the process. This earned the reproach of his grandfather, Sir Francis Knollys, who hoped that 'youthful wilfulness and wasteful youth do not consume you before experienced wisdom shall have reformed you'.[20] Although Sir Francis acknowledged that he liked 'very well your desire to see the wars, for your learning', he did not approve of his grandson's 'wasteful consumption' of his limited resources.[21] Essex paid no heed.

In other matters, Essex was dismayed to learn that his childhood home of Chartley – now his primary estate – had been chosen as the latest prison of Mary, Queen of Scots. He worried that the trees on his estate would be cut down in order to provide firewood for the fallen Queen, and was concerned that damage would be caused to the interior. So anxious was he that he gave orders to his steward, Thomas Newport, to 'remove all the bedding, hangings, and such like stuffs'.[22] Mary had now been Elizabeth's prisoner for seventeen long years, and despite numerous plans for her escape, none had been successful. As such, it had been agreed that she should be moved, and with its surrounding moat Chartley was deemed to be the ideal place. At the same time a new custodian was appointed to guard her: Sir Amyas Paulet. Like Francis Knollys, Paulet was a militant Puritan, and Mary loathed him. Leicester had evidently attempted to intervene on his stepson's behalf, warranting the response from Walsingham that 'I will do what I can to stay the intended removal thither'.[23] However, he feared that none of the suggested alternatives would be found 'so apt' as Chartley.[24] Essex even petitioned his grandfather, Sir Francis Knollys, to intervene to prevent his 'poor and only house' being put to 'inconvenience'.[25] Sir Francis responded, stressing to Walsingham that Chartley was the only one of his grandson's residences that had no debt attached to it. In his usual candid fashion, he added that 'It is no policy for her Majesty to lodge the Queen of Scots in so young a man's house as he is.'[26] Their arguments had no effect, and in due course Mary was removed to Chartley. It was while she was there that her fate would be sealed.

Back in London, Lettice watched as her husband busily planned his mission. His preparations included sitting for his portrait, for one completed at this time was later recorded in the Leicester House inventory.[27]

In December, Leicester received the official instructions for his mission. These included using 'all good means to redress the confused government of those countries, and that some better form might be established amongst them'.[28] Later that same month, 'with good preparation, and goodly show', Leicester bade farewell to Lettice and set out for the Netherlands, taking his stepson and many others with him.[29] These included Lettice's brothers William, who was to serve as one of Leicester's captains, Thomas and Francis, as well as two of her brothers-in-law and her son-in-law, Thomas Perrot.[30] According to Camden, the Earl had accepted the mission 'out of a ticking desire of command and glory', but the reality was very different: he knew that the task he faced would not be an easy one.[31] Lettice was forced to say goodbye to her beloved husband and her son, as well as three of her brothers, and this understandably caused her great concern; who knew what dangers they might face? Nevertheless, Leicester demonstrated his faith in her by tasking her with the administration of his lands during his absence, and she was determined not to let him down.

After a smooth and speedy crossing, Leicester landed at Flushing in the southwest of the Netherlands on 10 December with almost a hundred ships. His nephew Sir Philip Sidney, who was Governor of the town, greeted him, and the locals welcomed him and his men enthusiastically, 'with all manner of honour, hearty well-wishings, triumphing arches' and such like.[32] It was an encouraging start; Leicester himself reported that the cries of '"God save Queen Elizabeth"' were plentiful, and added that 'I believe she never bestowed her favour upon more thankful people than these countries of Holland'.[33] His journey into Holland, however, was marred by bad weather, including heavy fog. This inevitably impacted upon letters travelling to and from England, and Lettice waited anxiously to hear word of her husband and her son, and the Queen also grew concerned. Unfortunately, there is no surviving record of a correspondence between Lettice and either Leicester or Essex during this time, but at one point there certainly was: the following March Sir Thomas Sherley, who was serving under Leicester but had returned home to deliver news, reported to Leicester that 'My lady your wife is well, but had no new cause to write. I waited upon her yesterday to know her pleasure.'[34] Given the gravity of the task that Leicester faced, it nevertheless seems unlikely that he and Lettice communicated frequently during this time.

DESPITE THE PROBLEMS he had encountered in reaching his destination of the Hague, it is difficult to believe that, given his love of display and finery, Leicester did not enjoy the revelries and entertainments that had been laid on for his benefit as he travelled. The Dutch people were exceptionally grateful for the help that they were receiving from England, and Leicester was the natural figurehead for this. It was because of this that the Dutch leaders urged him to accept a position as head of their government, a role that he eventually felt obliged to accept. Though he deliberated and sent desperate letters to England seeking the Queen's instructions, the poor weather conditions meant that he received no word of reply. By January 1586, the Dutch leaders were pressing Leicester for an answer, and he felt that he had no option but to give them one.

On 15 January, Leicester accepted the position of Governor General of the Netherlands, and was sworn in that same day. Having still received no word from England, it was a warily made decision, and one that Leicester knew risked incurring the Queen's wrath. Although he immediately despatched William Davison to break the news to the Queen, by the time that Davison arrived at court he was dismayed to discover that word had leaked out and the Queen already knew. What was more, she was utterly incensed. It was to Leicester's 'great discomfort' that he received word from the Council of 'her Majesty's great mislike of my acceptance of this government'.[35] He tried to explain himself and the reasons that have 'moved me to do this I have done, above her commission or commandment'.[36] His actions, he claimed, were borne out of doing 'her Majesty acceptable service', rather than 'to do myself either honour or good'.[37] Leicester hoped that Davison would have presented to 'her Majesty my own letter', and 'acquainted all your lordships with such reasons as have moved me to deal as I have done', and now sought their understanding in the matter.[38] He was deeply troubled, and wrote further to Walsingham attempting to justify his actions further. Nevertheless, he confessed that 'I find myself most deeply wounded' by 'her Majesty's good favour and good opinion drawn from me'.[39] Not for the first time, the Queen was furious with him, and on 10 February she wrote to her favourite, not bothering to mask her rage. The letter was delivered by Sir Thomas Heneage, and the Queen's words were scathing: 'How contemptuously we conceive ourself to have been used by you, you shall by this bearer understand, whom we have expressly sent unto you to charge you withal', she began.[40] In fury, she continued to express that 'We could never have imagined had we not seen it fall out in experience that a man raised up by ourself and extraordinarily favoured by us above any other subject of this land, would have in so contemptible a sort broken our commandment.'[41] There could be no doubt that, once again, the Queen felt utterly betrayed by her favourite. She ended her letter with a chilling warning: from now on he was to follow his commandment, 'whereof fail you not, as you will answer the contrary at your uttermost peril'.[42] Leicester was deeply troubled when he read these words, but the bad news did not end there.

There was another reason for Elizabeth's anger. Lettice had by now accepted that a reconciliation with the Queen was unlikely: she and Leicester had been married for more than seven years, and Elizabeth's attitude towards her had still not shown any signs of thawing. As such, she had no position at court and her young son was dead, ensuring that all of her time was her own. Her husband was abroad where he was highly favoured; why should she not join him? It may have been a tempting prospect, but it was one that both Lettice and her husband realized could not become a reality: the Queen would never permit it. Malicious gossip, though, declared the contrary. On 11 February, Thomas Dudley, a distant relative who served in the Earl's household, reported to Leicester that 'It was told her Majesty that my lady was prepared presently to come over to your excellency.'[43] It had been said that Lettice planned to join her husband in the Netherlands, 'with such a train of ladies and gentlewomen, and such rich coaches, litters and side-saddles as her majesty had none such'.[44] As if this were not bad enough, the gossips continued to assert that Lettice was arranging to establish herself at the head of 'such a court of ladies as should far pass her majesty's court': in short, that Lettice was preparing herself to become Elizabeth's rival in more than just personal terms.[45] It had seemed that her relationship with the Queen could not get any worse, but this gossip once more served to heighten Elizabeth's anger towards her kinswoman. Though Thomas Dudley asserted that this information was 'most false', it 'did not a little stir her Majesty to extreme choler and dislike of all your doings there'.[46] She had responded, so Dudley reported, 'with great oaths, she would have no more courts under her obeisance but her own, and would revoke you from thence with all speed'.[47] Several councillors had recounted this to Leicester, including Lettice's father, and to all of them he responded by saying that 'the information was most false in every degree, and that there was no such preparation made by my lady, nor any intention in her to go over, neither had your lordship any intention to send for her'.[48] When Sir Francis Knollys had related this to the Queen, given his relationship to those involved she trusted his word, and thus it 'did greatly pacify her stomach'.[49] Thomas Dudley assured Leicester that in this, Knollys 'dealt most honourably and friendly for your lordship to her Majesty, both to satisfy her highness in this report, as in the other great action'.[50] Lettice heard of this episode first-hand, for Dudley had written to Leicester from Leicester House.

There is unlikely to have been any truth in the rumour, but that did not matter. The fact that it was circulating is evidence enough of the

222

malice that Elizabeth still bore Lettice. It is unclear where it originated, but the Queen's hatred of Leicester's wife was well known, and it did not take much for those at court to stir the situation up once more. In all probability it was a story that had been invented both to discredit Leicester and to continue the Queen's animosity towards Lettice. Whether true or not, the Queen made it clear that she expressly forbade Lettice to leave England, but rumours continued to circulate. Even those close to Leicester believed that there was some truth in it, and in the Netherlands Sir Philip Sidney expressed the hope that 'some way might be taken to stay my lady there'.[51]

LEICESTER FELT THOROUGHLY disheartened by his loss of royal favour, and he was not alone. William Davison, who had returned to England on his orders, had also been sent to visit Lettice. Presumably he conveyed letters to her from her husband, but though he had not seen her 'these ten or twelve days', when he visited her at the end of February he reported that 'I found her greatly troubled with the tempestuous news she received from court.'[52] Fortunately, she was in better spirits 'when she understood how I have proceeded with her Majesty'.[53] Lettice's anxiety was understandable, but Davison had evidently managed to soothe the Queen's fears and reassure them both. In addition, he told Leicester that he had got to the bottom of the matter:

> It hath been assured unto me by some great ones, that it was put into her Majesty's head that your lordship had sent for her, and that she made her preparation for the journey, which added to a number of other things, cast in by such as affect neither your lordship nor the cause, did not a little increase the heat of her Majesty's offence against you.[54]

At least the couple had friends at court, who they were able to trust to work in their best interests.

The Queen had been assured that the gossip concerning Lettice was nothing but a baseless rumour, but by March her temper had still not cooled. She remained furious with Leicester for accepting the position of governor, and his brother Ambrose wrote to warn him. 'Our mistress's extreme rage doth increase rather than any way diminish and [she] giveth out great, threatening words against you,' he wrote.[55] In sentiments that doubtless reflected Lettice's own feelings, Ambrose continued to reassure him that among all of his friends, 'you were never so honoured and loved in your life amongst all good people as you are at this day, only for dealing so nobly and wisely in this action as you have done, so that whatsoever cometh of it, you have done your part'.[56]

By the end of March, much to Leicester's relief the storm had largely passed and the Queen's temper had subsided. She wrote to him with warmth once more, albeit formally. Nevertheless, she could not resist the opportunity of having a dig at Lettice: 'We think meet to forbear to dwell upon a matter wherein we ourselves do find so little comfort, assuring you that whosoever professeth to love you best taketh not more comfort of your well doing, or discomfort of your evil doing, than ourself.'[57] Lettice might be his wife, but the Queen wanted Leicester to be left in no doubt that it was she who loved him best, and had the greatest concern for his welfare.

WITH LEICESTER RESTORED to the Queen's favour, he was able to breathe a sigh of relief as he continued with his mission. In July, the Queen wrote to him in her usual warm tone. Addressing him informally as 'Rob', she prayed that 'God bless you from all harm and save you from all foes, with my million and legion of thanks for your pains and cares.'[58] Harmony might have been restored between Queen and favourite, but elsewhere trouble was brewing. The English were hopeful of capturing Zutphen, an important town in Gelderland that had been commandeered by Spanish troops. On 13 September, Leicester's forces began to lay siege to the town, but nine days later disaster struck. Sir Philip Sidney, 'a most valiant and towardly gentleman', had his horse shot from under him.[59] As he was mounting a fresh one, he was 'shot into the thigh' by a musket ball.[60] Initially, it seemed as though he would recover, and Leicester wrote confidently to Walsingham, Sidney's father-in-law, that he was 'well amending as ever any man hath done for so short time'.[61] Aside from the injuries his nephew had sustained, Leicester would claim that at Zutphen 'we had had a most famous day', thanks to the defeat of the Spanish cavalry by the Earl of Essex's force.[62] His optimism for Sidney's recovery, however, was misplaced. It was not long before gangrene set in, and on 17 October he died at the age of thirty-one, leaving his uncle devastated. Leicester expressed his sorrow to Walsingham, lamenting that 'the grief I have taken for the loss of my dear son and yours would not suffer me to write sooner of those ill news unto you'.[63] He continued to bemoan that 'For mine own part, I have lost, beside the comfort of my life, a most principal stay and help in my service here.'[64] Though Zutphen had come at a great personal cost to Leicester, his stepson Essex had excelled. He had thrown himself into the fight with bravery, and as a result was commended by his stepfather. When Lettice heard of how her son had distinguished himself, her already great motherly pride swelled. It was bolstered by the news that it would not be long before she was reunited with both her son and her husband.

During her husband's absence Lettice had had plenty of things with which to occupy her mind. She remained close to both of her daughters, especially Penelope. By now she was also a grandmother, for despite the unhappiness of her marriage Penelope and Lord Rich had managed to produce children. The first of these was a daughter, named Lettice in honour of her grandmother, and born either in late 1582 or early 1583. Lettice was especially proud of her grandchildren, and as they grew would show as much interest in them as she had done with her own children. Additionally, Lettice seems to have spent some time with her sister Katherine, to whom she was close. Katherine's first husband had died in

1580, and she was now married to Philip Boteler, by whom she had four sons. Katherine also had her daughter, Lettice, from her first marriage, and her aunt was particularly fond of her niece.

IN ENGLAND POLITICAL matters had taken a dramatic turn. The Babington Plot, which aimed to assassinate the Queen and replace her with Mary, Queen of Scots, had been uncovered, and it would have dire consequences for Mary. Hatched by a group of Catholic noblemen headed by Anthony Babington, the plot had Mary's full knowledge and approval.[65] Though the fallen queen was imprisoned at Chartley, the plotters had found a way to communicate with her by means of hiding letters in a beer barrel.[66] Unbeknown to them, however, Walsingham, who was employed as the Queen's spymaster, knew exactly what was going on. In August 1586, the conspirators were arrested, and the following month they were 'hanged, bowelled, and quartered' for their treason.[67] Walsingham also had vital written evidence that Mary had approved of the plot, and it was this that led to her arrest and removal from Chartley. She was taken to the former royal stronghold of Fotheringhay Castle in Northamptonshire – birthplace of Richard III – and it was here that she stood trial in October.[68] When word of the Babington Plot reached Leicester, his instinct was to punish Mary in the harshest possible terms, and he wrote to Walsingham, urging 'the furtherance of justice on the queen of Scots'.[69] Elizabeth herself had written to Mary, stating, 'You have in various ways and manners attempted to take my life and to bring my kingdom to destruction by bloodshed. I have never proceeded so harshly against you, but have, on the contrary, protected and maintained you like myself.'[70]

On 25 October, Mary was found guilty of treason and sentenced to death. Yet the Queen hesitated when it came to implementing the sentence against her royal cousin, and her reaction was understandable: there was no precedent for the execution of an anointed monarch, and Elizabeth did not want to be the one to set it. After all, if killing Mary was legal, why should she herself not also become a target? What she needed was some persuasion, and who better than her favourite, the Earl of Leicester? It was with this in mind that, bringing the body of his dead nephew with him, Leicester began the journey home to England and Lettice.

CHAPTER 16

A Continual Fever

L
ETTICE WAS DELIGHTED at being reunited with her husband, who was home in time to celebrate Christmas. There were, though, many political matters that occupied Leicester's mind, and there was little of the merriment that the couple had enjoyed on previous occasions. Adding further tragedy to her life, Sir Philip Sidney's widow had given birth to a dead child, and the Queen was in a quandary over the fate of Mary, Queen of Scots. Her councillors were eager to force her into a decision, and in the minds of most there was only one option. According to Elizabeth, matters were later taken out of her hands.

A death warrant for the Queen of Scots had been prepared, but at court the atmosphere was unbearable, as Elizabeth refused to sign it. As the New Year of 1587 began, the Queen was still no closer to making a decision, and tension continued to mount. Finally, on 1 February, Elizabeth summoned William Davison – the same man who had tried to defuse the situation between the Queen and Lettice while Leicester was in the Netherlands, and into whose hands the death warrant had been given for safe-keeping. According to Davison, the Queen had finally made the momentous decision to sign the death warrant of her fellow queen. He claimed that Elizabeth signed the warrant, ordering him to send word to Fotheringhay immediately that the sentence was to be carried out. Her councillors were relieved, and eager for Mary to be executed as quickly as possible in order to prevent Elizabeth from changing her mind. But there was no time for that. Lettice and Leicester were at Wanstead when, on 8 February, Mary, Queen of Scots, was executed in a shocking scene at

Fotheringhay. It was a brutal death, and it took three strokes of the dull axe to sever the Queen's head from her body.[1] Her death caused shockwaves throughout Europe, and Queen Elizabeth immediately relinquished all responsibility for the demise of her cousin. Though she had signed Mary's death warrant, her version of events unsurprisingly differed from that of William Davison. Davison, she claimed, had despatched it without her consent. Immediately, she sent Lettice's cousin Robert Carey 'to the King of Scots, to make known her innocence of her sister's death, with letters of credence from herself to assure all that I should affirm'.[2] The unfortunate Davison, meanwhile, was sent to the Tower, and only escaped with his life thanks to the intervention of Burghley.

For Leicester there were other matters to consider, chiefly the funeral of his nephew. On 16 February, he and his brother joined the funeral procession of Sir Philip Sidney, whose body had been returned to England for burial. It was a huge state funeral that was staged at St Paul's Cathedral, where the young poet was later 'honourably buried'.[3] Sadly, his grave and monument were later lost when the Great Fire of London destroyed Old St Paul's in 1666.[4] Prominent among the procession was Lettice's son, the Earl of Essex. The two young men had become great friends, and in his will Sidney had left Essex 'my best sword'. It is likely that Lettice also mourned the passing of this bright young star, particularly given the hopes that her first husband had had of a marriage between Sidney and Penelope. It would not be long, though, before Sidney's widow, Frances Walsingham, would become closely linked with Lettice's family.

LETTICE MAY HAVE hoped that the return of her husband was permanent, but if this was the case then she was to be sadly mistaken. Although Leicester was in no rush to return to the Netherlands, matters there were far from resolved. Under orders from King Philip, Parma had intensified his efforts to bring the Netherlands to heel, in order to use it as a platform from which to invade England. Philip's rage had swelled when, in April, Sir Francis

Drake had burned thirty-seven Spanish ships in the harbour of Cadiz, and had plundered and acquired a whole host of Spanish treasure from ships in the Azores. That Drake dared to do so in Philip's own realm incensed the Spanish King, who was determined to have his revenge. Thus, Leicester would need to return to the Netherlands, in order to resist Parma's attack. By now his health was greatly troubling him, and in April he travelled to Bath in order to take the waters. Though he acknowledged to Burghley that his brother had received some benefit from doing so, he himself had failed to notice any improvement.[5] It is unclear whether Lettice travelled with him, but it is certainly possible that she did. She knew that he would soon be leaving, and was eager to spend time with him before he did so. He was busying levying more men for his campaign when, in early June, news had reached him that his Master of Horse, Sir Christopher Blount, had been wounded in the hand. Blount had accompanied him on his initial trip to the Netherlands, and had remained there following his departure. Blount's injuries were not serious, but a concerned Leicester wrote to him that he was sorry 'for your hurt', reassuring him that his own return to the Low Countries would be imminent. Given his place in Leicester's household, Blount was a man who was well known to Lettice, and whom she would, in the future, become better acquainted.

Shortly afterwards, Lettice bade farewell to her husband once more. She was relieved to find that her son was not to accompany him on this occasion, for he was needed elsewhere. When Essex returned home from the Netherlands in triumph following his bravery at Zutphen, Leicester had done his best to push his stepson to the forefront at court in order to catch the Queen's eye. By May, Lettice and Leicester were gratified to see that Essex had firmly established himself as the Queen's new favourite. His rise put Sir Walter Ralegh's nose firmly out of joint, as was Leicester's intention. Essex was utterly devoted and wholeheartedly loyal to his stepfather, referring to himself as 'your son' in his letters, and Leicester could therefore be confident that while he was away, Essex would do all that he could to safeguard his and his family's interests. He could not have chosen better. Essex and the Queen began to spend an increasing amount of time with one another; they danced, hunted, and the Queen whispered intimately to her favourite. With his charm and good looks, he made her feel youthful, and he in turn grew in confidence. A contemporary observed that the Queen was constantly in Essex's company, for 'at night my Lord is at cards, or one game or another with her, that he cometh not to his own lodging till birds sing in the morning'.[6]

The Queen seemed to be oblivious to the fact that Essex was the son of her rival, and this did not prevent her from heaping favours upon him. With the intervention of his stepfather, on 18 June Essex succeeded him as the Queen's Master of Horse. This position brought with it a healthy income to help boost the young Earl's dwindling finances, and was a remarkable sign of favour. But just weeks later, his whole position would be in jeopardy.

While Leicester returned to the Netherlands and Lettice remained at home, throughout the summer Essex remained by the Queen's side, loyally doing all that he could in order to boost the superiority of his own faction and family. However, it was not long before it became clear that he had inherited many of his parents' traits; unlike his mother, there was only so much of the Queen's attitude and tantrums that he would tolerate.

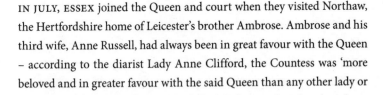

IN JULY, ESSEX joined the Queen and court when they visited Northaw, the Hertfordshire home of Leicester's brother Ambrose. Ambrose and his third wife, Anne Russell, had always been in great favour with the Queen – according to the diarist Lady Anne Clifford, the Countess was 'more beloved and in greater favour with the said Queen than any other lady or woman in the kingdom'.[7] She and her husband must, therefore, have been disappointed when their home became the scene of an eruption between Essex and their royal visitor.

Lettice's younger daughter, Dorothy, had been married to Sir Thomas Perrot for several years. Like her mother before her, the Queen's attitude towards Dorothy had not warmed, and she was still furious about her marriage. Essex admitted that initially he 'knew not at first' that his sister was the Earl and Countess of Warwick's guest at Northaw, 'yet to prevent the worst, I made my Aunt Leighton [Elizabeth Knollys] signify so much unto the Queen' when she planned to visit the house from Theobalds.[8] He did so in order that 'this matter might not seem strange unto her. She seemed to be well pleased and well contented, and promised to use her well.'[9] The Queen's promises, though, were quickly forgotten. When she arrived at Northaw, although she 'knew my sister was in the house, she commanded my Lady of Warwick that my sister should keep her chamber'.[10] Essex was greatly troubled by this, and after supper he confronted the Queen. 'Her excuse was, first, she knew not of my sister's coming', but Essex was not satisfied.[11] Perceiving the Queen's refusal to meet with his sister as a great insult that had been encouraged by his rival, Sir Walter Ralegh, Essex was incensed. He berated the Queen, demanding to know 'why she would offer this disgrace both to me and to my sister, which was only to please that knave Ralegh'.[12] Knowing of the Queen's anger at Dorothy's marriage, Ralegh had indeed encouraged her to believe that Dorothy's presence at Northaw was a deliberate slight from Essex. Family honour was integral, and the petulant Essex was not prepared to let the Queen's slight pass. Like his father, he was hot-headed, and like his mother, he had spirit. And as such, he always found it difficult to curb his temper.

Ignoring the respect that was due to the Queen, he determinedly defended his sister. The Queen was not used to such behaviour from her favourites, and neither did she take kindly to it. A fierce confrontation between the pair ensued, during the course of which Essex remembered that 'she came to speak bitterly against my mother, which, because I could not endure to see me and my house disgraced, I told her, for my sister she should not any longer disquiet her'.[13] Though it was almost midnight, Essex 'had no joy to be in any place', and after sending 'my men away with my sister', he too fled from Northaw in a furious rage.[14] The Queen's venom for Lettice was still as poisonous as ever, and the latter certainly came to hear of the episode; Essex ended his account of the fraught exchange by urging its recipient that if he were to show anybody, 'let it be to my mother'.[15] Although Lettice would have supported her son in his defence of his sister, she was astute enough to realize that such outbursts were dangerous. Essex would have to watch his step.

On this occasion he was fortunate. He was determined to re-join his stepfather in the Netherlands, and having fled Northaw he began to make his way towards the coast. However, the Queen sent Lettice's cousin, Robert Carey, to prevent him from leaving the country and to persuade him to return to court. He did so, and within a few days he and the Queen had patched up their differences, and he once more basked in her favour. All signs of any animosity between them had disappeared; be that as it may, the rivalry between Essex and Ralegh had not.

<hr />

AS THE SUMMER and autumn drew to a close, Lettice was delighted to learn that her husband would soon be home once again. Aside from Zutphen, his military mission had achieved very little, and his return to the Netherlands had been plagued with problems. The Dutch captains refused to cooperate with him, and as such he and his allies had lost the opportunity to relieve the town of Sluys that was besieged by Parma, much to Leicester's frustration. Matters between him and his Dutch allies deteriorated so much that Leicester informed the Queen that he felt he could progress no further in her service there. On 10 November, Elizabeth recalled him, and this time his return home would be permanent. Before he left, he had a silver medal struck to commemorate his time there. On the reverse is an image of a sheepdog leaving his flock, inscribed with the words 'Unwillingly I forsake … not the flock, but the unthankful.'[16] For Lettice's brothers, though, in personal terms the campaign had been a success. William had been knighted at Zutphen, and in 1586 Thomas had distinguished himself so far that he was made Governor of Ostend. It was while he was abroad that, in 1588, he met and fell in love with Odelia, the daughter of the Duke of Bergen. The couple were married, and together had a daughter, Penelope.

On 4 December, it was reported from Flushing that 'The Earl of Leicester is leaving for England, his baggage being already shipped. He is on bad terms with the rebels.'[17] Three days later, before embarking for home Leicester took the time to knight his brother-in-law, Francis, who joined him on his return journey. For some months the Earl had been suffering from bouts of ill health, which was a cause of concern to Lettice. When he returned home later that month, she was shocked to discover just how much his health had deteriorated. He was worn down from the constant anxiety he had suffered during his mission, and suffered from gout, for the relief of which he had travelled to Buxton on several occasions. While abroad he had also complained of 'the stone', which could indicate any manner of stomach problems, or even kidney stones.

Although Leicester's time in the Netherlands had achieved little, he had now done his duty for Queen and country. He was exhausted, and at fifty-five years old it was time for him to content himself with his domestic duties. The recovery of his health was now a primary concern. However, as 1587 came to a close and the new year set in, neither he nor Lettice can have had any idea that matters in England were about to take a drastic turn.

⁓

IT HAD BEEN nearly a year since the execution of Mary, Queen of Scots, but the former queen's death had not been forgotten, least of all by Catholic Europe. Queen Elizabeth's support of the Dutch against Spain had also served to further fuel Philip II's hostility towards England. Most people in England, Lettice included, were aware of the increasing threat posed by Spain; the time had now come for Philip to act.

Sure enough, Philip planned an invasion of England that aimed to depose Elizabeth and reinstate Catholicism throughout the land. The threat posed by Spain was of great concern to the Queen and her councillors, and even more worrying was the fact that Philip's campaign had the blessing of Pope Sixtus V, who actively supported the King's plans. Philip began to assemble a mighty fleet of ships, which totalled 130 and carried a huge crew and mass of weaponry. On 28 May, Philip's Spanish Armada set sail from Lisbon and began its journey to England – and invasion.

When word of the Armada reached the Queen, she and her Council deliberated over the best course of action. Leicester was no longer a young man, and coupled with his illness, he did not possess the same enthusiastic energy that he had once had. Even so, he had been by the Queen's side for the entirety of her reign, and he was not prepared to abandon her now. In spite of his own personal circumstances, he was actively involved in the military preparations that were underway, and threw himself into the creation of a military camp at Tilbury across the Thames. This was as far as his contribution went, and on this occasion others would be at the forefront. Nevertheless, he knew that his advice was still of great importance to Elizabeth, and on 27 July he wrote to her from Gravesend. The priority, he believed, was for the Queen to 'gather her army about her in the strongest manner possible, some special nobleman to be placed at the head of it, and to be officered with the oldest and best assured captains'.[18] Following this, the Queen, 'the most dainty and sacred thing we have in this world to care for', ought to retire to Havering in order to secure her safety.[19] He ended by professing that he would 'offer his body, life, and all to do her service'.[20] They were heartfelt sentiments, but ones that would not be necessary.

Although the fleet was delayed by bad weather, on 19 July the Armada was sighted off the coast of Cornwall. The news was hurriedly conveyed to London, and as Robert Carey noted apprehensively in his memoirs, 'the King of Spain's great Armada came upon our coast, thinking to devour us all'.[21] Two days later, under the command of Lord Howard of Effingham and the Vice Admiral Sir Francis Drake, the English fleet engaged the Armada off the coast of Plymouth. Though the Spanish ships soon retreated to Calais where they dropped anchor, the English moved quickly and engaged them in battle at Gravelines on 29 July. By this time the Spanish had lost many of their ships, due largely to adverse weather conditions. But this did not lessen their determination to fight. Even so, it was the English who now had the upper hand, for it was they who had the larger force. In the course of the fighting, fifty Englishmen were killed, as opposed to two thousand Spanish. It was the weather, though, that eventually determined the outcome. Shortly after the battle at Gravelines, the wind changed, forcing the Spanish fleet off course and scattering the remaining Spanish ships. While Lord Howard initially pursued the broken fleet as they retreated, there was no need for him to do anything more: the result was conclusive. As Robert Carey joyfully noted, much to everyone's great relief and against all odds, after much indecisive action 'Thus did God bless us, and gave victory over this invincible navy.'[22] Many viewed the winds that had scattered the Spanish ships as a sign from God, who had intervened to prevent England's ruin. The Armada had been defeated, and the crippled fleet attempted to return to their native land. Both the ships and the men were in a poor condition, and only sixty-seven of Philip's original imposing fleet survived; some of the ships were driven on to the rocks on the coast of Ireland, where many of the men drowned or were killed as they made their way on to the shore. Others were subjected to strong North Atlantic storms and ran out of food and water, resulting in many of the crewmen dying of cold, starvation or disease thanks to the cramped conditions. The Spanish Armada posed one of the most serious threats of Elizabeth's reign, and the danger had not entirely passed: when Philip learned that his fleet had been defeated, despite his humiliation he made it clear that this was not the end. He was true to his word, but two further armadas in 1596 and 1597 both failed due to perilous weather.

THROUGHOUT THE DAYS of danger and uncertainty, Lettice had remained in London. Leicester, meanwhile, had been by the Queen's side, facilitating a trip to Tilbury for her on 8 and 9 August. It was here that, on 9 August, Elizabeth delivered a memorable speech to the land troops who had assembled in preparation to fight the Armada. Sat on her horse with Leicester to her right and Essex on her left, the Queen bravely told her men that 'I have the body of a weak, feeble woman; but I have the heart and stomach of a king, and of a king of England too, and think foul scorn that Parma or Spain, or any prince of Europe, should dare to invade the borders of my realm.'[23] At this most critical of points in her reign, though she was estranged from Lettice, it is at least significant that the two men who were by Elizabeth's side – the most important in her life – were also beloved by Lettice. Whether the two women liked it or not, blood ties aside, their relationships with Leicester and Essex would ensure that they were always closely bound.

By now Leicester was thoroughly exhausted, but he returned to London with the Queen where a host of celebrations were staged to mark the defeat of the Armada. He was determined to be by her side in order to share in this most triumphant of moments with her, and she was happy to have him there. He was there when a joust was staged at which his stepson, Essex, ran 'two tilts' against the Earl of Cumberland. Here it was observed that 'As they are two of the best horsemen in the country the spectators were much pleased at this.'[24] Leicester's stay at court was brief, and, in need of a break, on 27 August he left London and the Queen behind. He intended to spend the remainder of the summer and the autumn regaining his health, and enjoying some much needed quality time with Lettice. As he had bade the Queen farewell in his usual fond terms, though he was exhausted his health gave Elizabeth no cause for alarm; she fully expected him to return to her side again soon, in the same way that he always had done. Neither she nor Leicester had any idea that they would never see one another again.

In the hope of finding the 'perfect cure' for his illness, Leicester and Lettice planned to travel to Buxton in order that the Earl might take the restorative waters. They intended to break their journey at Kenilworth, where three years previously their summer holiday had been brought to a sudden end. Two days after leaving London, the couple had made it as far as Rycote, the beautiful Oxfordshire home of Sir Henry Norris. Norris had a close connection with Lettice's family, for his father had been one of those who had been executed for his alleged adultery with Anne Boleyn, Lettice's great-aunt.[25] He was a good friend of Leicester's, and his wife Marjory was close to the Queen.[26] While Leicester and Lettice enjoyed the Norris's hospitality, Leicester's health remained troublesome to him. The Queen had sent him some medicine, and he wrote to her assuring her of its benefits: 'For my own poor case, I continue still your medicine and find that [it] amends much better than any other thing that hath been given me. Thus hoping to find perfect cure at the bath, with the continuance of my wonted prayer for your Majesty's most happy preservation, I humbly kiss your foot.'[27] His adoration for her was still strong, but it would be the last occasion on which he would ever write to her. The Queen would later endorse it sadly as 'his last letter'.[28]

At the time he wrote, Leicester's illness drew no further cause for alarm, and he felt well enough to continue travelling. Both he and Lettice were gratified when Essex wrote to his stepfather from the court, informing him of his great favour with the Queen: 'Since your lordship's departure her Majesty hath been earnest with me to lie in the court, and this morning she sent to me that I might lie in your lordship's lodging.'[29] Given that Leicester's lodgings lay close to the Queen's own, this was a sign of the utmost favour, although Essex hurried to assure his stepfather that he had forborne to accept until he received his permission.

From Rycote, the Leicesters travelled the twenty-five miles to the former royal hunting lodge of Cornbury Park, when it became clear that the Earl's illness was of a serious nature. Cornbury was located just a short distance from Wychwood Forest, and Leicester had occasionally used it for hunting parties. Now was no time for hunting, and instead Leicester took to his bed. It is evident that those around him – including Lettice – expected him to recover. Word of his illness reached court, and it was from here that on 2 September, Lettice's father wrote to him. He was clearly not unduly concerned by his son-in-law's fragile health, for the main topic of Sir Francis's letter was business. Nevertheless, 'I have heard since that your lordship hath been troubled and stayed with an ague at Cornbury Park whereof I am very sorry,' he wrote.[30] Taking the opportunity to advise Leicester as to the best course to take in order to restore his health, Knollys continued, 'I trust in God that through your lordship's foresight and good order of diet, that you will easily and soon dispatch yourself thereof with good recovery of your health again in short time.'[31] Tragically it was not to be.

On 4 September, Lettice was by her husband's side when Leicester passed away at Cornbury.[32] Commissioned on her orders, his epitaph describes her as his 'most sorrowful wife', and his death came as a devastating blow to her. They had only been married for ten years, and theirs had been a marriage that was based on friendship, love and mutual respect. With Leicester now gone, Lettice had not only lost her husband but also her protector.

According to Camden, the fifty-six-year-old Leicester had died 'of a continual fever', which is likely to have been malaria.[33] A Spanish report, though, recorded that on his way to Buxton, 'in the house of a gentleman near Oxford, it is said he supped heavily, and being troubled with distress in the stomach during the night he forced himself to vomit. This brought on a tertian fever, which increased to such an extent on the third day that on Wednesday, fourth instant, at ten o'clock in the morning, he expired.'[34] The same observer continued to report on his memories of the Earl, as well as the reaction at his death:

The last time I saw him was at the Earl of Essex's review, at the window with the Queen. On the previous week I had seen him go all through the city, accompanied by as many gentlemen as if he were a king, and followed by his household and a troop of light horse. He was going from a country house of his (Wanstead) to St James's, and was quite alone in his coach. He had gone through a few days before on horseback, even more splendidly accompanied, and showed every appearance of perfect health, as if he would have lived for years. For

the last few months he has usually dined with the Queen, a thing,
they say, such as has never been seen in this country before. He was
a man of great authority and following, and his death will be much
felt; but, on the other hand, the general opinion is that the conclusion
of peace will be much easier than before, as he was usually in favour
of war. God decree all for His greater glory![35]

The reporter was right in thinking that the Earl's death would be much felt, for it was not only Lettice and her family who were left heartbroken by Leicester's loss. His death shocked the court, even more so because it came so unexpectedly. The other woman in Leicester's life, Elizabeth, was completely grief-stricken when the news of her favourite's death was broken to her, causing the celebrations that had been staged for the defeat of the Armada to come grinding to a halt. Her sorrow was all genuine, for in Leicester she had lost not only her closest companion, but also the man who she had truly loved. In the blink of an eye the happiness that she had been experiencing after her recent victory had been taken from her. No other man had ever come close to supplanting him in her affections: it had always been Leicester. Elizabeth was so heartbroken that on 17 September, nearly two weeks after his death, a Spanish report recorded the extent of her grief:

The Queen is sorry for his death, but no other person in the country.
She was so grieved that for some days she shut herself in her chamber
alone, and refused to speak to anyone until the Treasurer and other
Councillors had the doors broken open and entered to see her.[36]

Leicester had been a constant figure for much of Elizabeth's life, and for the entirety of her reign he had been by her side to offer her advice, friendship, support and love. Although a marriage between them had never transpired, their love for one another had remained mutual – despite the form that this took changing over time – and he had been wholeheartedly loyal to her. For the past decade she had been forced to share his heart and his affections with a member of her own family, but had ultimately – in her eyes at least – remained his first priority. But perhaps Leicester's marriage to Lettice had left Elizabeth wondering what might have been – the very nature of her role as sovereign ensured that the dynamics of their relationship were different from that shared by Leicester and Lettice, but Elizabeth may have been left thinking that they could still have found happiness. In an attempt to treasure his memory, Elizabeth kept Leicester's last letter in a locked casket for the rest of her life. She was left utterly bereft by his loss, but even now she could not bring herself to reconcile with Leicester's widow. As is so often the case in times of grief, the feelings that Elizabeth experienced towards Lettice could have involved fresh anger, jealousy and blame at all that had passed between them. In her Sweet Robin's final moments, it had been Lettice, rather than Elizabeth, who had been by his side, and never again would Elizabeth be able to look upon him, or to talk with him and share one of their private jokes. Elizabeth had no thought for Lettice's feelings, and Leicester's wife remained banished with no word of condolence; the Queen felt that the loss was all hers. It was as if Lettice simply did not exist.

On a political level, Leicester's death could not have come at a worse moment. The threat posed by Philip of Spain still loomed large, and the Queen needed all of the support that she could get. Already, though, there were those at court who were eager to fill his shoes. Just days after his death it was observed that 'The Lord Chancellor [Sir Christopher Hatton], now that Leicester is dead, has much more power than before, and is helped by Secretary Walsingham, with whom he is very friendly.'[37] In reality, however, Lettice's son Essex remained the favourite.

———⟡———

DESPITE THE SHOCK that was felt by many at Leicester's death, in retrospect it is evident that his health had long been in decline. Though he died from natural causes – almost certainly malaria – this did not prevent whispers of something more sinister. A Spanish contemporary reported that 'The Earl of Leicester died almost suddenly on his way to the baths, and in the same house as that in which he had caused his wife to be killed, the master of it having invited him to dinner.'[38] He had evidently got Cumnor and Cornbury mixed up, but he was not the only one to hint that Leicester's death may have been caused by something other than a natural illness. It was later rumoured that Lettice had been responsible for poisoning her husband, and that a servant had witnessed 'the Lady Lettice give the fatal cup to the Earl'.[39] The playwright and poet Ben Jonson gave a slightly different version. He supposedly related that Leicester had given Lettice 'a bottle of liquor which he willed her to use in any faintness, which she, not knowing it was poison, gave him, and so he died'.[40] Both of these tales are completely baseless, and it is perfectly clear that Lettice had no reason for wanting her husband dead. In fact, precisely the opposite was true; not only did she love Leicester deeply, but while he was alive he also served as her protector, and had helped to advance her children. That rumours of poison were circulating for the second time in her life following the death of Lettice's husbands must have been devastating for her. It is nevertheless easy to see why such rumours came about. Not only had Leicester apparently died suddenly, but he had also given orders that the sole executor of his will was to be his 'most dear well beloved wife'.[41] He had rewritten his will on three occasions, and two days after his death his final will was proved: by its terms, when it came to property and material goods Lettice was left an extremely wealthy widow. This was in stark contrast to the condition in which she had been left following the death of her first husband, who had bequeathed her very little. The main reason for this was Walter's spiralling debts, but it transpired that in terms of cash, Leicester's situation was no better.

Leicester had taken much time and great care when composing his will, and he had discussed one of his primary desires with Lettice: 'I have always wished, as my dear wife doth know, and some of my friends, that it might be at Warwick, where sundry of my ancestors do lie', he wrote, concerning where he hoped to be buried.[42] His choice was hardly surprising, for it was here that the ornate Beauchamp Chapel that housed the remains of Richard Beauchamp, Earl of Warwick, stood – a man of great renown with whom Leicester wished to be associated.[43] More poignantly, it was also here that the 'Noble Imp' lay entombed. If for whatever reason it were not possible for Leicester to be buried there, he had requested that he should instead be laid to rest, 'where the Queen's Majesty shall command, for as it was when it had life, a most faithful, true, loving servant unto her, so living, and so dead, let the body be at her gracious determination, if it shall so please her'.[44] Like his love for Lettice, his loyalty and devotion to Elizabeth had endured until the end, and he referred to her as his 'most gracious sovereign, whose creature under God I have been, and who hath been a most beautiful, and most princely mistress unto me'.[45] In material terms, though he acknowledged that he had little to give her, he did bequeath the Queen

> the jewel with the three great emeralds with a fair large table diamond in the middest, without a foil, and set about with many diamonds without foil, and a rope of fair white pearls, to the number six hundred, to hang the said jewel at; which pearl and jewel was once purposed for her Majesty, against a coming to Wanstead, but it must now thus be disposed, which I do pray you, my dear wife, see performed, and delivered to some of those whom I shall hereafter nominate and appoint to be my overseers for her Majesty.[46]

Perhaps Leicester thought that Lettice might be reluctant to part with such a jewel, hence his request for her to ensure that his wish was carried out. He had even asked her to deliver the jewel to someone at court, knowing that Elizabeth was unlikely to grant his wife a personal audience. Lettice did carry out his wish, however, for when the Queen was painted by George Gower – a magnificent portrait that celebrated her victory over Spain, and became known as the Armada Portrait, she was wearing

Leicester's pearls.[47] In Leicester's eyes the Queen had, and by needs must, always come first, but 'Next her Majesty I will now return to my dear wife, and set down that for her, which cannot be so well as I would wish it, but shall be as well as I am able to make it, having always found her a faithful, loving, and a very obedient, careful wife.'[48]

In her husband's eyes, Lettice had always conformed to the behaviour that was expected of a good wife. The will was also a testament to his love for her, which was still strong after ten years of marriage, and the admiration that he had for her. He did not doubt that she would be willing 'every way to the utmost of her power, to do all I have committed to her charge, not thinking good to trouble any other of my friends, but herself, with my hard and broken estate'.[49]

The Earl was well aware that he had 'many debts', and knowing that it would be a weighty task to satisfy them, he exhorted his wife to take on the burden of overseeing that they were paid: 'for all love between us, that she will not only be content to take it upon her, but also to see it faithfully and carefully performed'.[50] His trust in Lettice was evident, although he knew what a huge weight of obligation he was placing upon her shoulders. This says much for his belief in her abilities, but it was a task that would cause Lettice a great deal of stress and worry. And the Queen was determined to make things worse.

IN ACCORDANCE WITH his wishes, on 10 October Leicester's funeral took place in Our Lady Chapel of St Mary's Church, Warwick, 'a fine large building'.[51] As was customary, Lettice did not attend, and it was her son, the Earl of Essex, who played the role of chief mourner – a duty that he had been unable to assume for his own father. The funeral party was several hundred people strong, and was attended by a whole host of relatives and courtiers, including Lettice's son-in-law, Lord Rich, her brothers William and Francis, and the Earl of Huntingdon. Despite Leicester's request that he be buried with 'little pomp or vain expenses of the world', it was a costly affair that amounted to £4,000 (£597,000).[52] Leicester's remains were 'honourably interred' in the Beauchamp Chapel, close to the tomb of his young son.[53] On Lettice's orders, an epitaph commemorating her husband's achievements was placed there: 'to her best and dearest husband on account of her love and faith as his wife'. She would later erect a splendid monument to his memory, which she also intended to share. Another tangible reminder of Leicester's presence in Warwick and the contribution he had made to the town was Lord Leycester's Hospital, which he had founded in 1571, and for which he left provision in his will. It was later intended to care for soldiers who had been injured during the Netherlands campaign, and its presence ensured that the association with his memory in the town endured. The hospital still survives, and is now a retirement home for ex-servicemen.

Leicester's death was not universally mourned, though. Ben Jonson is supposed to have penned the following epitaph to honour Leicester:

> Here lies a valiant warrior, who never drew a sword;
> Here lies a noble courtier, who never kept his word;
> Here lies the Earl of Leicester, who governed the Estates,
> Whom the earth could never, living, love, and the just heaven now
>   hates.[54]

This may well have accurately described the way in which some of his contemporaries viewed him – particularly his enemies at court – but the same could certainly not be said of Lettice and the Earl's family. Not only was Lettice devastated by his loss, but her children – Leicester's stepchildren – were equally distraught. For the second time in her life, Lettice – now forty-five years old – was a widow. Also for the second time, she now attempted to pick up the broken pieces of her life and carry on. She did so with remarkable speed.

CHAPTER 17

My Best Friend

ETTICE MAY HAVE been disappointed that Leicester's death did
nothing to heal the breach between herself and the Queen, but
matters were about to become a whole lot worse. Although Leicester
had been a wealthy man and Lettice had been left well provided for in
terms of land, his debts to the Crown were extensive. As he had himself
acknowledged in his will, he was 'I know not how many thousand, above
twenty in debt; and, at this present, not having in the world five hundred
pounds towards it.'[1] The Queen was not prepared to let this pass, and
in a move doubtless intended to hurt Lettice, quickly seized some of his
estates in order to ensure that they were paid. Her venom towards her
kinswoman was as potent as ever, and there was nothing that the helpless
Lettice could do about it.

For the second time, Lettice found herself dealing with the financial
worries and debts that a husband had left her with. Leicester may not
have realized that the actual amount he owed totalled around £50,000
(£7,465,000) – an exorbitant sum. He had been aware that he was
shouldering his wife with a huge burden, and Lettice in turn had even
been advised that it may not be wise to accept the role of executor for this
reason; however, she paid little heed.[2] Once again, her determined spirit
shone through. The result was that she was unsurprisingly inundated with
requests for money from those who were worried that the debts owed to
them would not be repaid. Many of these debts stretched back several years,
including one from Elizabeth Sutton, who urged Lettice to settle 'the great
charge I was at when you with the young lord and other your honour's

friends and company lay with me', amounting to £393 (£58,700).[3] The young lord to whom Elizabeth Sutton referred was Lettice's young son, Lord Denbigh. Lettice dealt with these matters as best she could, and once again she turned to her friend, Lord Burghley, for assistance. On 20 November, just two months after Leicester's death, she wrote to him from Leicester House about her attempts to convince the Queen to take a valuable ship from her as part of a deal whereby she also sold her interests in the Fine Office. The ship lay at 'a continual charge' to her, but the servant whom she had sent to convey the request had returned 'without any mention or motion of it'.[4] She begged for Burghley's intercession, but no further reference to it is made. Burghley had been a constant friend, and in 1590, recognizing all that he had done for her over the years, she thanked him for his 'compassion' towards 'distressed debtors', bewailing 'the misery into which she is likely to fall without his help'.[5] Lettice also received some assistance from her brother-in-law, Ambrose, who, as his brother's heir, had inherited many of his lands. Nonetheless, raising the funds to meet Leicester's debts was a thankless task, and caused Lettice no end of stress.

Although Leicester was dead, the Queen continued to make life as difficult as possible for Lettice, showing a ruthless and cruel side to her character that had perhaps been exacerbated by her grief. Even with the favour in which Elizabeth held her son, Essex, Lettice was powerless to resist her malevolence. She needed a protector – a partner – and in the same way as she had always done, she took matters into her own hands.

IN THE WARM summer days of July 1589 – ten months after Leicester's death – Lettice took her third set of marriage vows.[6] On this occasion her groom was not an earl or a member of the nobility, but was instead a former member of the Earl of Leicester's household: Sir Christopher Blount.

Sir Christopher Blount was the second son of Thomas Blount of Kidderminster, and his wife Margery Poley.[7] Unlike Leicester, he was a

Catholic, and it was a faith to which he was utterly devoted. This in itself made him a curious choice of husband, for Lettice and her family were all stringently Protestant. It was also a dangerous time to be a Catholic in England: following her excommunication from the Church of Rome and the Papal Bull of 1570, the Queen and her government were making life increasingly difficult for English Catholics. In the 1580s the government's treatment of them became harsher still, as a result of the numerous plots against the Queen's life: the Throckmorton Plot in 1583 and the Babington Plot in 1587 were just two of many. As a result, many had now resorted to worshipping in secret, and a growing number of priest holes were being built into Catholic households across the country.[8] Blount, though, had managed to avoid persecution, having spent many of his formative years abroad. He had been educated primarily at Louvain, where his tutor was the English Cardinal William Allen, who had supported Philip II in his plans for the Spanish Armada.[9] Allen's tutelage naturally brought Blount under many Catholic influences, but at some point he got mixed up in other affairs: it appears that, despite his faith, he had begun working as a double agent for Sir Francis Walsingham in the plot to secure the fall of Mary, Queen of Scots. His motives for doing so are unclear – many Catholics joined Walsingham's ranks in order to avoid the religious persecution in England and to protect their families, while also benefiting materially. This is likely to have been Blount's motivation too, and he does not seem to have been naturally duplicitous in character. Moreover, his later declarations would reveal that he remained a devout Catholic.

Blount was a younger son, and as such his fortune rested on his own shoulders. Alongside working for Walsingham he had also entered the entourage of the Earl of Leicester, who was probably aware of his double-dealings. Employed as his Master of Horse, Blount had been well favoured by his master, and this was little surprise; frequent references to Blount family members appear in Leicester's accounts, and Christopher's employment followed on from many of his relatives who had been a part of the Earl's household. His father, for example, may have been the same Thomas Blount who Leicester had once tasked with ascertaining the truth of the mysterious events at Cumnor. Christopher had accompanied Leicester to the Netherlands, and it was there that Lord Willoughby had knighted him for his bravery. Following his injury, however – the very same which had once caused Leicester great concern – Blount had returned home to recover. His presence in Leicester's household brought him into regular contact with Lettice, and it is plausible that the two would have got to know each other reasonably well during this time. This certainly never went beyond the bounds of decorum, and Blount's name was not mentioned in relation to Lettice's until after his master's death.

There is no way of knowing if Blount was attracted to Lettice prior to Leicester's death, but if he was then it was not reciprocated. Lettice was utterly devoted to her husband, and probably paid Blount little heed. He was also twelve or thirteen years her junior, having been born around 1555 or 1556. Hence, her decision to marry him came as a surprise to her contemporaries and caused a sensation – not least because of the speed with which it took place following Leicester's death. There is no surviving information that allows us to ascertain how their relationship took shape, or when it began. The motivations for the marriage probably stemmed from two factors. As a widow Lettice was certainly under no obligation to marry if she did not so wish, but all of the evidence suggests that the couple were happy; she would later refer to Blount as 'my best friend'.[10] Clearly, then, there was a genuine physical attraction and warmth of feeling between the pair. At around thirty-four, Blount was known to be handsome; his contemporary Thomas Morgan described him as a 'tall gentleman and valiant', and Lettice, while being older at forty-five, was still an attractive woman.[11] It is interesting, though, to consider that she never referred to him as her husband, nor he to her as his wife. It is possible that, as her daughter Penelope's biographer Sylvia Freedman suggests, this was because Blount 'retained a most respectful attitude to his late master's widow even after he married her'.[12] The second factor that may have prompted their marriage was the matter of Leicester's former debts to the Crown. Lettice was struggling to pay the balance, and though Blount did not have the financial means to aid her, or any known standing with the Queen, he would at least have been able to provide her with essential male support. A husband by her side provided Lettice with a strong figure who could alleviate some of the burden – who could deal with creditors, sell items to raise funds without being ripped off, and take control of the situation. As a member of Leicester's household, Blount also had some understanding of his former master's affairs, which Lettice may have deemed helpful. For Blount, the advantages of marrying Lettice were obvious. Aside from her personal qualities, he had now acquired a wealthy wife and a prestigious family connection.

Lettice was not the first woman of her class to marry a man beneath her in social status. She was following a precedent that had long since been set by other noble women: Frances Brandon, Duchess of Suffolk, had also married her Master of Horse, and her stepmother Katherine Willoughby had done the same.[13] There is no record of how the Queen reacted upon hearing of Lettice's marriage, nor is it clear when she was informed. By this point, though, Lettice had long since realized that Elizabeth would not approve of any of her actions. Similarly, the reaction of Lettice's father Sir Francis Knollys is unknown, but as a stringent Protestant he would have disapproved of Blount's religious motivations. By contrast, others made their feelings about the newlyweds very clear. Lettice's son the Earl of Essex was initially deeply suspicious of the marriage, referring to it as an 'unhappy choice'.[14] But Blount was determined to win him over, and as time progressed he proved himself to be both a useful ally and a loyal stepfather who eventually earned Essex's trust. In one letter to his stepson he signed himself 'wholly your Honour's most faithful servant', words that Lettice was gratified to see.[15]

Blount is the only one of Lettice's three husbands for whom one of her letters survives. The undated note is short, and she entreats Blount to 'do what in reason you may' for a gentleman who was facing a case in the Star Chamber.[16] Although the reason for writing concerned business, the letter does show signs of affection. 'So hoping to see you shortly,' she wrote, before signing herself 'Your most faithful wife'.[17]

Lettice was instrumental in smoothing the ground between her new husband and her son, and in her letters to Essex she commonly referred to Blount as 'your friend', or to herself and her husband as 'your friends', and as time went on, relations between the two men became easier.[18] Later, Essex even urged Robert Cecil, whom Blount had approached in order to procure a favour, 'I pray you have for my sake the more affection to satisfy him.'[19]

Just months after her wedding, in December Lettice was writing to Essex on behalf of herself and Blount to enquire after his welfare:

Your poor friends here, my dear son, are in great longing to know how you fare, to which purpose we have addressed this bearer to bring us true word thereof. For although our ears are fed with many flying reports, yet we believe nothing but what we receive from the oracle of truth, wherefore relieve us, if it please you, with some of your occurrents.[20]

She signed herself 'Your mother that more than affectionately loveth you', a phrase that she employed frequently.[21] She had always been a fiercely protective mother, and this is particularly apparent in her letters to Essex. Given his position at court he was the one she saw the least often. She regularly enquired after his health and badgered him for news, chiding him gently when she did not receive a response: 'Your Lordship is grown, I will not say slothful, but somewhat sparing of your pen,' she once wrote to him.[22] Essex found her attentions somewhat overbearing, but there is no evidence that he complained of them – indeed, on one occasion she wrote that it was 'her greatest happiness to have for the staff of her age so worthy and loving a son'.[23]

She rarely made any direct references to the Queen, but on one occasion she wrote that 'It seems, the time approacheth wherein it will be seen what a jewel your prince and country hath of you. The Lord turn all to the best for England's good and your honour.'[24] On another she could not resist adding her hope that 'your mistress makes of you as her best servant, and chiefest hand to defend her against that wicked generation [the Spanish]'.[25] Both of these comments referred to the situation in which England now found itself, for at the time of writing, the 'wicked generation' to whom Lettice referred were the Spaniards. Following the defeat of the Armada, Philip had been busy rebuilding his navy in preparation for a fresh attack. In 1589, Essex had gone against the Queen's orders when he joined an expedition to Portugal headed by Sir Francis Drake, which was an attempt to crush Spanish naval strength. The expedition was a failure, and planning for the Anglo–Spanish war continued. It was only a matter of time before Philip launched another attack.

Sadly, none of Lettice's letters to her daughters or her youngest son Walter have survived, but they may have been written in a similar vein. Leicester had been a particularly attentive stepfather, and it would be difficult to match him, but Lettice was now eager for all of her children to accept Blount. Aside from Essex's initial qualms, there is no evidence to suggest that her children disliked him. Blount actually appears to have shared a relatively good relationship with his new stepchildren. In 1597, he would write to Essex on behalf of his stepdaughter Dorothy, informing him that 'I am entreated by your sister to let you know that she hopeth your care will be no less for her means of living ladylike than your endeavour has been earnest to bestow on her a ladyship.'[26] Evidently Dorothy felt comfortable enough around Blount to ask him to convey messages.

Her marriage made her Lady Blount, but both she and those around her continued to refer to her as the Countess of Leicester. For the rest of her life she would sign herself 'L Leicester', in a permanent reminder both of her second husband and the title that he had brought her. At the onset of her third marriage, Lettice and Blount initially spent some time at Benington, the home that had come into her possession following the death of her first husband. Before long, though, they left the south behind them, instead installing themselves more permanently at Drayton Bassett, a property that had been purchased by Leicester in 1578. He had stipulated in his will that Lettice was to enjoy full use of Drayton, but her right had initially been disputed, and it took the intervention of her son Essex to settle the matter. Set in the countryside of her native Staffordshire, Drayton Bassett was also just twenty-five miles from her former home of Chartley. Today, the pretty village shows no signs of the house that was once occupied by Lettice and her third husband, for this was sadly demolished in 1929.[27] An inventory of Drayton taken in 1601 shows that although it was lavishly furnished, it was not to the same standard as Leicester House, Wanstead or Kenilworth. It was nevertheless a comfortable home with a three-storey banqueting house, ideal for entertaining guests. Lettice used it often, and her daughter Penelope was a regular visitor.[28]

Additionally, Drayton also contained a drawing room in which hung a canopy of damask, which was where Lettice sat.[29] There were numerous bedchambers, including one reserved for the use of Lettice's sister, Katherine, who moved into Drayton at some point in the 1590s following the death of her second husband. There was a hall, a parlour, rooms for the servants, and a kitchen complex.[30] All of these facilities would have ensured that Lettice's lifestyle was extremely comfortable. At fifty years old, she may have been attracted by the quietness of the countryside, and with Blount by her side she turned to focus on domestic matters. Blount, meanwhile, was able to use his association with Essex to his advantage. In 1593 he sat in Parliament on behalf of Staffordshire, and four years later he would do the same.[31] The life of country gentry, however, was one to which they were both poorly suited.

BEFORE LONG, LETTICE discovered that marrying Blount did not help to ease her financial woes. He worsened matters when, in an attempt to improve their circumstances, he began selling off pieces from her extensive jewel collection: 'The first year Sir Christopher Blount was married he sold many great jewels, and hath continued the same course almost every year since.'[32] Several pieces were sold to her son, the Earl of Essex, including 'a great chain of pearl, a fair table diamond and a pointed ruby, for the which Sir Christopher Blount received three thousand pounds [£376,000]'.[33] Her daughter Dorothy also bought 'two fair pendant pearls', but the funds were not enough to solve the problem.[34] Before long, Blount had even resorted to selling off some of Lettice's properties that he had got 'into his own hands'.[35] Later, Lettice complained bitterly about his handling of her estates, but there is no evidence that she did so at this time. In November 1593, it was reported that Lady Leicester still owed the Queen the balance due to her from Leicester, and it had not been forthcoming.[36] It was not just Blount who had resorted to selling her belongings to cover the costs, but Lettice, too. A contemporary report stated that 'At my Lady's last being at London was sold two fair collars, and other jewels of pearl and stone.' Though the Queen loathed her she was not averse to buying her jewels, and it was noted that 'Her Majesty had two fair pearls and a jewel of opals made fast to the seals of a letter.'[37] The result, according to the report, was that 'It is well known my Lady hath paid of my Lord of Leicester's debt at the least fifty thousand pounds.'[38]

LETTICE'S WAS NOT the only wedding that took place in 1589. The same year her youngest son, nineteen-year-old Walter, was also married. Like his sisters, Walter had spent much of his childhood in the household of the Earl and Countess of Huntingdon at King's Manor, York. From 1585 he had then been studying at Oxford, but the time had now come for his marital prospects to be settled. As his guardian, Huntingdon had the right to choose Walter's bride, and he needed to look no further than his own household. Margaret Dakins was the only daughter of a good Yorkshire family, and, like Walter, she had been placed in the Huntingdons'

household in order to complete her education. The youngsters had therefore known one another for many years, and in 1588 Huntingdon had started negotiations for their marriage. Although it was a good match on both sides, it is, once again, unlikely that Lettice was consulted.

No details of the wedding are known, but it is certainly possible that Lettice attended. When it was over, the newlyweds set up home together, and were given an estate at Hackness in Yorkshire, the money for which was raised by Margaret's father, Huntingdon, and Lettice's eldest son, Essex.[39] Like his elder brother, young Walter was spirited, and found his wife to be dull in comparison. Her company bored him, but Huntingdon was determined to ensure that the marriage was a success. He urged his lively ward 'that your good wife, for so I may rightly term her, may receive that comfort of your coming to her, as in right, and by her desert is due unto her'.[40] Walter seems to have taken no notice.

AS THE NEXT decade began, great changes started to take place within Lettice's circle. On 21 February 1590, her brother-in-law, Ambrose, Earl of Warwick, died at Bedford House on the Strand. Camden described how he had 'departed this life, as full of virtue, as empty of issue'.[41] Though Lettice had got along harmoniously with Ambrose during Leicester's lifetime, and he had indeed supported her when it came to executing Leicester's will, there is no evidence to suggest that the two had any other contact with one another. In the latter months of Ambrose's life there is unlikely to have been any warmth of feeling between them, because they had for some time been embroiled in a property dispute. Several months after Ambrose's death, the matter had still not been settled, and it was left to Ambrose's widow, the feisty Anne Russell, to take up the reins. Both Anne and Lettice were strong women, and in her usual stubborn manner Lettice refused to back down. However, unlike Lettice, Anne had the support of the Queen and this was destined to be a battle that Lettice would not win. Given the circumstances it is hardly surprising that no mention of Lettice or her family was made in Ambrose's will, although he made bequests to many others.[42] Like Leicester, he too was laid to rest in the Beauchamp Chapel of St Mary's, Warwick. His elaborate tomb can still be seen alongside that of his brother and his young nephew, and was presumably erected on the orders of his widow.

Ambrose's death did, nonetheless, have important consequences for Lettice. Like his brother before him, Ambrose had died without any legitimate heirs. Sir Philip Sidney, the nephew that both he and Leicester had once considered to be their heir, was now dead. As such, many of Leicester's former lands that had passed to Ambrose on his death now passed, in turn, to Leicester's 'base son', Robin Sheffield. This included Kenilworth, much to Lettice's great annoyance. She was determined not to allow Leicester's bastard to take possession of what she believed should have passed to her, and in a desperate bid to assert herself, Blount forcibly took control of Kenilworth. The law, though, was not on her side, and to her chagrin she was forced to hand Kenilworth over to Robin Sheffield.[43] This grated on her, for Robin was the only person who stood in the way of her son, Essex, inheriting Leicester's former lands. For the time being there was little that she could do, but it would not be the last occasion on which Robin Sheffield's name would return to haunt her.

ON A BRIGHTER note, that summer Lettice's daughter Penelope gave birth to her final child by Lord Rich. Theirs had been a notoriously unhappy marriage, and over the years matters had deteriorated further. When their son Henry was baptized on 19 August, there was no point in keeping up the pretence any longer. Penelope had provided her husband with two male heirs, and by now it was well known that she had taken a lover.

Charles Blount was the son of James Blount and Catherine Leigh, both of whom stemmed from minor gentry families; despite their shared surname, Charles was only distantly related to Lettice's husband Christopher.[44] Charles was one of three children, and had been sent to

ABOVE: Elizabeth Knollys, Lady Leighton. Lettice and her younger sister resembled one another so closely that for many years this portrait was believed to be Lettice.

ABOVE: The magnificent ruins of Kenilworth Castle, Warwickshire. This once mighty stronghold may have been the setting for the origins of Lettice and Leicester's relationship.

BELOW: Leicester House. Once one of the grandest houses on the Strand, Leicester House was the main seat of Robert Dudley. It was here that Lettice would spend a great deal of her time during their marriage.

LEFT: The bear and ragged staff that formed the family crest of the Dudleys. This representation can be seen in the entrance to the Beauchamp Chapel in St Mary's Church, Warwick.

BELOW: Detail from the tomb of Lettice and Leicester's only son, 'the Noble Imp', in St Mary's Church, Warwick.

LEFT: A miniature thought to be of Lettice. The physical resemblance she bore to Elizabeth I was striking.

RIGHT: The kneeling effigy of Lettice as seen on her parents' tomb in St Nicholas's Church, Rotherfield Greys.

ABOVE: Elizabeth I. This famous portrait was painted in celebration of England's victory over the Spanish Armada.

ABOVE: Robert Devereux, second Earl of Essex. 'Sweet Robin', Lettice's eldest son, was her pride and joy.

ABOVE: William Cecil, Lord Burghley. Cecil was Elizabeth I's chief advisor, and Lettice also sought Cecil's advice on numerous occasions when attempting to settle her financial affairs.

ABOVE: The tomb of Lettice and her second husband, Robert Dudley, Earl of Leicester, in St Mary's Church, Warwick.

Oxford where he received a magnificent education.[45] He was later awarded an MA.[46] Having graduated, Charles travelled to London where he had every intention of starting a career in law. He entered the Inner Temple, but he did not remain there for long. His brother was already at court, and before long Charles had joined him. He quickly became a favourite with the Queen, to the extent that the Earl of Essex considered him a potential rival. Although the Queen showed Charles her steady favour, Essex had nothing to fear, and continued to reign supreme. Charles had also been among those who had accompanied Leicester on his campaign to the Netherlands, and it was not the last time he would see military action. Upon his return to England, however, the handsome, dark-haired Charles had other matters on his mind, for he had attracted the notice of an admirer: Penelope.

It was probably at some time in 1590 that Charles and Penelope began a passionate affair. It quickly became serious, and by November the relationship was common knowledge at court. In a strange twist, Penelope's husband Lord Rich was fully aware of his wife's extramarital activities, and was curiously happy to tolerate them. The Queen also knew of and condoned this *ménage à trois* – a sure sign of her favour towards Penelope. The Richs had always had an unhappy marriage, and Penelope had amply fulfilled her duty to her husband by providing him with four surviving children.[47] In private the couple ceased to have relations, but in public they maintained a show of unity, even though Penelope's relationship with Charles Blount was well known. Consequently, when Penelope and Charles's first child, a daughter named Penelope, was born in 1592, in an attempt to save face and avoid public humiliation, the child took Lord Rich's name and was brought up alongside his children for many years.[48] Penelope and Charles's relationship would endure for the rest of their lives, and Charles remained completely devoted to her. Together they would have six children, five of whom survived infancy. Penelope's birth was followed by that of Mountjoy, a son named in honour of the title that Charles had inherited in 1594 when his elder brother William died just a few months after their father. Charles, St John and Isabella completed the family.

Lettice knew of her eldest daughter's affair from the very beginning, and appears not to have been concerned – after all, there were few in her family who had much time for the unpleasant Lord Rich, and the dashing Charles Blount must have seemed like a pleasing alternative. She also adored her grandchildren, and came to spend a great deal of time with them in the coming years. Penelope doted on her children; in an undated letter to her son Essex who had been unable to attend a family gathering, Lettice wrote to him of Penelope's concern over the health of one of her daughters: 'Your excuse is so reasonable, sweet Robin, as it must be taken, but if you had come this night you had found a knot of good company here together and the idle housewife your sister in one of her worst humours, solemnly disposed in doubt that her best beloved daughter should be a little sick.'[49] This, it seems, was a trait that Penelope had inherited from her mother.

LIKE PENELOPE, LETTICE'S son Essex had also inherited many of his mother's characteristics. Having learned nothing from her example, on an unknown date in early 1590 he made a risky decision: he married in secret without obtaining the Queen's permission. His bride was Frances Walsingham, the daughter of the Queen's spymaster, and the widow of Essex's friend and Leicester's nephew, Sir Philip Sidney. Frances's father had died in April that year, and the marriage was conducted either shortly before or soon after his death – almost certainly with his knowledge and approval.[50] Frances already had a five-year-old daughter, Elizabeth, by Sidney, and given that their first child was born in January 1591, she and Essex had probably been indulging in a sexual affair before their marriage. Frances was besotted with her second husband, referring to him as her 'dear life', and she hated to be parted from him.[51]

Given how close she was to her son, it is probable that Lettice was aware of his secret nuptials, although there is no evidence that she attended the wedding. Her feelings about the match are unknown, but she shared a reasonable relationship with her new daughter-in-law. Penelope was certainly close to Frances, and the two women would come to spend a great deal of their time with one another. Lettice, though, was all too painfully aware of the consequences of clandestine marriages, and was fearful of the Queen's reaction towards her son when she learned the truth. She had good reason to be. By October the secret was out and predictably, given her reaction on so many previous occasions, Elizabeth was seething with anger. She was enraged not only that 'it was contracted without her consent', but also because Frances was 'considered by Her Majesty as below the dignity of his family'.[52] Essex was in disgrace, but unlike Lettice, it was to be a temporary state. The Queen could not bear to be parted from her favourite for long, and though she refused to receive the new Countess of Essex at court, the Earl soon basked in her favour once more. That same year, the Queen granted him the lease of all of the sweet wines imported into England, and this provided him with a generous source of income. Meanwhile, like her mother-in-law before her, Frances was banished into private life. She was quite content with this arrangement, and spent much of her time living with her mother at Walsingham House, her parents' London residence in Seething Lane.[53] Yet again, the Queen's inability to live without her male favourites was in evidence. As usual, she apportioned all blame to the female party.

<hr />

TO LETTICE'S DELIGHT, on 11 January 1591 her son became a father for the first time. The Countess of Essex gave birth to a healthy son at Walsingham House, and the child was baptized there three days later.[54] Lettice was asked to stand as godmother, and she attended his baptism alongside the baby's great-grandfather, Sir Francis Knollys. Frances's 'little jewel' was named Robert after his father, and from the start Lettice was extremely fond of 'little Robin'.[55] He would be her favourite grandchild, and as he grew, young Robert would spend much of his time with his grandmother.

The birth of her grandson was a cause for great celebration for Lettice, but the infant Robert was not the only child his father would sire that year. Essex's marriage did not prevent him from indulging in extramarital affairs, and he was sexually promiscuous. As a result, he was responsible for the pregnancy of Elizabeth Southwell, one of the Queen's ladies, and he flirted with many others.[56] However, Essex realised that if the Queen learned the truth he could risk losing her favour. When the Queen was informed of Elizabeth's pregnancy and reacted in her usual manner, Essex did nothing. Instead, in an attempt to protect Essex and his standing with the Queen, the blame and punishment was initially acknowledged by Sir Thomas Vavasour, one of Essex's loyal followers.[57] When Elizabeth gave birth to a son named Walter – a compliment to Essex's father – Essex said nothing. It has been suggested that this child was sent to live with Lettice at Drayton Bassett, but this is highly unlikely, for had he done so then the true identity of Walter's father would have become immediately apparent. And so it was not until May 1595 that the Queen discovered the truth of the matter, forcing Essex to acknowledge Elizabeth Southwell's son as his own. From then on he referred to Walter as 'his natural son', and Lettice also took an interest in his welfare.[58] So much so that in her will she later left him £50 (£4,460) and 'a diamond ring with God's blessing'.[59]

Elizabeth Southwell was not the only woman who caught Essex's eye, and in the mid-1590s he also began an affair with Elizabeth Stanley, the daughter of the Earl of Oxford.[60] Other names were also linked with his, and although each of these provoked the Queen's fury when they came to light, Essex knew all too well that her anger would soon cool: his confidence was staggering. His wife, meanwhile, was so devoted to him that she turned a blind eye to his infidelities, and Lettice probably did the same. His promiscuity certainly did nothing to diminish her love for her beloved son.

THE LOVE THAT Lettice bore for her children knew no bounds, and she was therefore left devastated when, in the autumn of 1591, tragedy again struck the family. Earlier that year, Essex had been given command of the Queen's forces, which were sent to Normandy to support the French King, Henri IV. France had long been in a state of civil war – in 1585 the eighth civil religious war had begun during the reign of Henri IV's predecessor, Henri III. This was still being fought when Henri IV, a Huguenot, succeeded to the throne in 1589, but his claim was not recognized by many of his Catholic subjects. In 1576, the Catholic League had been formed, and with the support of Spain it was causing havoc. In 1590, Spanish troops landed in Brittany and Normandy, leaving Henri with no choice but to take military action. He had appealed to Elizabeth for her support, but she had stalled for some time, not wanting to commit money or resources to the enterprise. Essex had persistently urged her to act, and finally, alarmed at the thought of Spain taking control so close to England, the Queen agreed. Essex had landed at Dieppe on 2 August at the head of a four-thousand-strong army that included his younger brother, Walter. Walter was just shy of his twenty-second birthday, and idolized his elder brother. The expedition was to be his first experience of military warfare, but it would also be his last.

On 8 September, a skirmish took place at Rouen. As Lettice's cousin Robert Carey sadly recorded in his memoirs, 'unfortunately we lost Mr Walter Devereux, my Lord's only brother, with a shot in the head, so we returned that night to Pavilly, the whole army being full of sorrow for the loss of so worthy a gentleman'.[61] Essex was devastated by the death of his younger brother, for he was 'dearer to me than ever I was to myself'.[62] Sir Christopher Hatton was one of those who wrote to him with his condolences, expressing his sorrow at the death of 'your noble brother, who hath so valiantly and honourably spent his life in his Prince's and country's service'.[63] These were touching sentiments, but nothing could detract from the family's loss. There is no record of how or when the news of the death of her youngest son was communicated to Lettice, but whatever the case his death came as a shattering blow to her. It was the second time in less than a decade that she had lost a child, and in total three of her sons had died. Essex was now her only surviving one, and as such he became all the more precious to her.

Aside from the tragedy that his brother's death brought, Essex's campaign in France was a disaster: he ignored the Queen's orders, and wasted both time and money on frivolity. The Queen was not impressed, and commanded him to return home. He arrived in January 1592, bringing the body of young Walter with him. The casket was conveyed to Carmarthen for burial, where Walter was laid to rest in the same church as his father, although, as with him, there is no surviving monument to mark his memory. Walter's death was the subject of an elegy by Madame de Maulette, a Frenchwoman residing in England.[64] It was coupled with a remembrance of the death of Henri III of France, and was translated by Gervase Markham and published in 1597. Markham dedicated his work to Lettice's daughters, and among the words extolling Walter's virtues can be found,

> *And now I come to thee most blessed Saint,*
> *Thou sweetest nightingale in the heavenly choir,*
> *Noble born Walter Devereux.*[65]

His mother and his siblings never forgot him, and when Essex's wife gave birth to a son in 1592, the boy was named in honour of his deceased uncle.[66]

Following the death of her husband, Margaret Dakins returned to Huntingdon's household, but her time there was to be brief. Just three months after Walter's death she married for a second time, her groom being Thomas Sidney.[67] She and Walter had never been happily married, but even so Lettice and her family were highly offended by the speed with which she had moved on. Never again would Margaret be welcomed by the Devereux family.[68]

THE LETTERS WRITTEN by Lettice and her family members to one another make for pleasant reading. Here were a family who were all genuinely fond of one another, and in Lettice's letters in particular we see a change in her style and character. When writing to Burghley, for example, her letters were to the point, even blunt on occasion. But the love she bore her children is unmistakeable. In one such letter she took care to remind Essex that 'You are much beloved and greatly honoured in this desolate corner, not according to the fashion of your courtly mistresses but in our true country sincerity we will ever pray for the height of your happiness.'[69] The latter part was perhaps an indication of the disapproval she felt about her son's infidelities. She still complained that she did not get to see him nearly enough, and chided him for failing to 'grace this ill-favoured cottage', Drayton Bassett.[70] She told him in no uncertain terms that 'We wish you often with us to ease your burdened mind with some country sports; for we think of no enemies [the Spanish] till you remember [remind] us, so far are we from hearing foreign news.'[71]

Lettice's youngest son was now dead, and her daughter Dorothy remained in disgrace with the Queen. By contrast, the stars of Essex and Penelope were still rising high at court, and it was left to them to promote the family's interests. The Queen best loved Essex, and Penelope actively used her favour with the monarch in order to advance her brother. The siblings were extremely close, and Essex and Penelope spent a great deal of their time with one another. In his two surviving letters to his sister, it is clear that Essex depended on Penelope greatly. He recognized her intelligence and valued her advice and opinions not only as a sister, but also as a friend. Though Essex and Penelope worked together, there were those in the family who did not. Lettice's sister, Lady Leighton, still a presence at court and in high favour with the Queen, was not active on her nephew's behalf. Neither does she appear to have made any attempt to intercede with the monarch on Lettice's behalf, although the sisters were still very much in contact. To do so, she realized, was pointless, and she had no wish to risk losing the Queen's favour towards herself and her family.

Lettice was naturally ambitious for her son, and actively encouraged Penelope's efforts to support him. Although she and those around her were left in no doubt of Essex's position, the Queen did not have the same confidence in him that she once had in Leicester. He did not share the same history with her that Leicester had done, and his character was wildly different from that of his stepfather. He could not control his petulance, but time and again the Queen forgave this. Proud Essex, however, did not learn from his mistakes.

CHAPTER 18

Disgraced Persons

THOUGH LETTICE CONTINUED to be styled Countess of Leicester despite her third marriage, in all other aspects her life had drastically changed since Leicester's death. In 1593, she relinquished Leicester House – her home for the past decade and more – to her son Essex. It was renamed Essex House, but in the same way as it had been during Leicester's lifetime, it remained a hub of social activity and artistic patronage. There were also constant reminders of Lettice's presence, including her portrait which adorned the walls of the dining chamber, ensuring that her son would not forget about her. Likewise, in acknowledgement of 'divers debts of the late Earl of Leicester due to Her Majesty' that 'remain still unpaid by Sir Christopher Blount, and the Countess of Leicester, his wife, executrix of the said Earl', it had been agreed that Wanstead, 'by lawful conveyance', should also pass to Essex.[1] This latter transaction was something that the Queen actively encouraged, for she was fond of Wanstead, and eager to return there as Essex's guest.

Lettice's children now took centre stage at Essex House, where the Earl hosted a great variety of regular entertainments. Penelope had a chamber there, preferring to reside there than at her husband's Smithfield residence at St Bartholomew's while she was in the capital, and it was at Essex House that much of her relationship with Charles Blount was conducted. She was a regular visitor, and held more eminence than Essex's own wife. Lettice also visited her children and grandchildren at Essex House, but she was no longer a permanent presence, and was more than content for her son and eldest daughter to bask in the limelight.

IN FEBRUARY 1594, Sir Thomas Perrot, Dorothy's husband, died. Two years earlier, his father, Sir John Perrot, had died in the Tower having been condemned for treason – it was rumoured that he had been poisoned.[2] Despite his attainder, with the support of Essex an Act of Parliament had restored the majority of his father's lands to Thomas in March 1593. He was sadly not to enjoy them for long. More than ten years of marriage had produced just one surviving child, a daughter named Penelope.[3] As such, when Thomas died his lands were divided between his wife and daughter.[4]

Thomas's death came as a blow to Dorothy, who, like her mother, was still in disgrace with the Queen. Nevertheless, it was not long before she had found herself a replacement. Later that same year, thirty-year-old Dorothy married for a second time – a marriage that may have been arranged by her brother. Her groom was Henry Percy, who had succeeded his father as the ninth Earl of Northumberland in 1585. The Percy family were an ancient and noble family, but Henry's father had died in the Tower under a cloud of suspicion, after allegedly having become embroiled in the treasonable dealings surrounding Mary, Queen of Scots. The scandal did not end there, for six months after his imprisonment, the eighth Earl was found dead in his bed – he had been shot through the heart. A verdict of suicide was delivered – considered to be a mortal sin – and the Percy family were left to deal with the aftermath.[5] The family were great landowners, particularly in the north of England, though their primary residence was Petworth in Sussex, and later Syon where Dorothy and her children would spend a great deal of their time.[6] By 1594, the scandal surrounding the suspicious death of the eighth Earl had died down, and so when Dorothy married Henry Percy, who was the same age as her, Lettice heartily approved of the match. Northumberland provided all of the prestige that Lord Rich, the husband of her eldest daughter, lacked.

The wedding took place in London, and at Essex House, Essex hosted and paid for the entertainments, including a performance from a company of players.[7] Lettice was almost certainly present at her younger daughter's wedding, but the Queen was not: Dorothy, the new Countess of Northumberland, remained banished. Though relations between the two women were never fully restored, at some point Dorothy was received back to court, but the timing of this is unclear. Her marriage, on the other hand, was destined to be rocky.

Dorothy and her husband often quarrelled furiously, to the point that she left him in October 1599. Telling those around her that her husband had thrown her out, Dorothy began to rent a house in Putney, and for some time they remained estranged.[8] Like her mother, Dorothy was headstrong, and was determined to assert herself as a strong woman in her own right. Even her brother wrote of her 'passions'. It was left to him to try and resolve the situation, and he duly did his best. 'Since I knew of the breach betwixt your husband and you, my first desire was that you might be both thoroughly reconciled; and my second if the first might not be, that it might appear to the world it was his fault and not yours', he wrote to her, and he even drafted a letter to Northumberland on his sister's behalf: 'I will believe that your honour, wisdom, and discretion, will hold you from wronging both yourself and me, and then I will promise myself a more happy life and prove my love and desert both to you and the world, which doth constantly bind me to be, your faithful wife.'[9] This played a part in reconciling the couple, and in December 1601 they were reunited. In spite of whatever problems they had encountered, the rest of their marriage proved to be happy and was solidified by the births of two sons: Algernon and Henry.

———⌇———

ELSEWHERE THE CIRCLE surrounding Essex was growing, and among his close friends were Henry Wriothesley, third Earl of Southampton.[10] Southampton idolized Essex, but in years to come their friendship would lead him into troubled waters. Both men were great patrons of the arts, and poets and playwrights gathered around them. Shakespeare's *Love's*

Labour's Lost, written in around 1594, contains many allusions to people and events that were contemporary, and probably relates to many of those who were included in Essex's circle.[11] Essex's political influence was also growing, and he had been admitted to the Privy Council on 25 February 1593. Although Lord Burghley remained the Queen's primary advisor, he was now in his seventies, plagued with gout and desperate to retire, and the twenty-seven-year-old Essex was hopeful that when the time came he would be able to take his place. Unlike his former stepfather the Earl of Leicester, Essex had always been exceedingly popular, but he did not have the same kind of relationship with the Queen that Leicester had once shared. Neither did he have the same humility, and though Elizabeth was fond of Essex, she quickly tired of his moods.

In the countryside, Blount was occupying himself with the management of his wife's affairs. Both he and Lettice wrote frequently to Essex, often concerning business. On one such occasion, however, Blount added a postscript on behalf of his wife: 'Your Lordship's mother greets you, and craves her excuse in accompanying your sisters.'[12] Lettice seized upon any opportunity to communicate with her son, and it is from this period of her life that the largest number of her letters survives. Twenty are addressed to her son, who she often referred to as 'My dear son', 'My dear and most noble child', or 'Sweet Robin'.[13] It is interesting to note that the latter was one of the same fond terms that the Queen had once used to address Leicester. The nature of Lettice's letters varied, and she did on occasion take the opportunity to ask for favours for herself and her friends. For example, she begged for her son to find a place for a servant of hers, named Gawdy, who was 'so honest and so thankful a man'.[14] Unfortunately for Gawdy, Essex chose not to employ him.

At Drayton Bassett Lettice was often visited by Penelope, who usually brought her children with her. It seems likely that Dorothy also travelled to see her mother, and the three women had remained close. In September 1595, for example, Penelope had been staying with Lettice, and when she returned to London her mother travelled with her. On 7 November,

Rowland White, the agent of Sir Robert Sidney, wrote to his master that 'Lady Leicester and Lady Rich are yesterday come to London', where they presumably stayed at Essex House.[15] Penelope rarely stayed at her husband's London home, viewing her brother's house and the company of her family as infinitely preferable. Neither does Lettice appear to have put any pressure on her to reconcile with Lord Rich; indeed, she had great sympathy with her daughter's marital woes.

Upon her return to the capital, Penelope had expressed an interest in purchasing some hangings from Sir Robert Sidney, 'a piece or two of the story of Cyrus'.[16] On 13 November, Rowland White was able to report that 'Lady Rich likes the piece of hanging', although 'Lady Leicester thought the price high, but wishes you had sent her friend Sir Christopher some.'[17] Lettice was clearly thrifty with money and liked a bargain, for three days later White noted that 'Lady Leicester said that if it be above ten shillings [£62] the stick it is too dear. I answered that it seemed hangings were good cheap when she bought any.'[18] In any case, Penelope liked the hangings and chose to buy them.

WHILE LETTICE BUSIED herself with spending time with her daughter, the Queen and Essex had other matters with which to occupy themselves. The threat posed by Spain as part of the ongoing Anglo–Spanish war was still present, and was becoming more alarming. In July 1595, several Spanish ships had made it into English waters, attacking the Cornish coast and burning Penzance. The Queen and her advisors were well aware that King Philip was still rebuilding his navy, in preparation for a further attempt at invasion. In turn, the Queen was readying her own fleet, and on 3 June 1596, the Earl of Essex set sail from Plymouth at the head of an expedition bound for Cadiz. It was not the first time he had journeyed abroad, but this time he faced infinitely more danger. In anticipation of Philip's forthcoming Armada, Elizabeth hoped that her force would beat him to it, and crush the Spanish King's fleet. Lettice was worried for her son, and wrote to him of 'how fearfully we harken after the Spaniards, whose malice God bless us all from'.[19] Blount was planning on joining his stepson, and Lettice assured Essex that he 'prepares his arms and himself in readiness to do you service when time is. And so the Almighty bless you, and send, if they dare come, you may be a scourge to them.'[20] Before long she had bid farewell to her husband and, much to Penelope's relief, her husband, Lord Rich, who did not approach the mission with enthusiasm, joined them, too.

When Essex's ships reached the wealthy Spanish port of Cadiz, his men rampaged through the city for two weeks, during which time they ruthlessly sacked and plundered, and took many important hostages. More importantly, they also ravaged some of the Spanish King's ships, which were being kept there in preparation for the Armada. A Venetian envoy reported that

> *It is said that they have burned the five ships of the West India fleet which were ready to sail, fourteen beautiful galleons, and about twenty-five other ships, and rumour adds five guard ships besides. The loss is estimated at four millions of gold, including the value of the vessels that have been burned; a serious reduction of the naval forces belonging to his Majesty.*[21]

The mission was an overwhelming triumph for Essex. So much so that it marked the peak of his career and popularity, and when he returned home it was as a hero. Essex revelled in his own glory, but the Queen, though delighted, never enjoyed sharing the limelight, and was jealous of his popularity. She was also disappointed that he came bearing little in terms of plunder to add to her coffers. Nevertheless, the raid on Cadiz had a great impact, and the Venetian ambassador in France wrote to his master, 'The English have inflicted a very heavy blow upon Spain at Cadiz. It will be some time before his Catholic Majesty can put another fleet on the sea.'[22] The Spanish King was naturally furious, and bent on vengeance.

Lettice beamed with pride when she heard of her son's success, but her joy was tinged with sadness.

The month after Essex left England, on 19 July, Lettice's father, Sir Francis Knollys, died. He was in his eighties, but his age had not prevented him from continuing in his loyal service to Queen Elizabeth. By way of reward, three years previously she had made him a Knight of the Garter, and she too was left saddened by his loss. His death had not been wholly unexpected, for in March he had made his will. In this he touchingly acknowledged the fact that he had been blessed 'with many children, whose advancement I am in fatherly care to regard and provide for'.[23] He left the Queen a gold diamond ring worth £40 (£5,000), 'as a poor remembrance of my humble duty to Her Majesty'.[24] His foremost concern besides asserting his religious faith was the welfare of his children. Lettice's brother William was his heir, and it was to him that the greater part of Francis's estates, including Greys Court, now passed.

Sir Francis had also assigned lands to his four surviving sons; Robert, Thomas, Richard and Francis, though Richard did not live long enough to enjoy his – he died within days of his father, and was buried at Rotherfield Greys three days after Sir Francis. Neither were Francis's daughters forgotten. Lettice and her sisters each received a piece of gold plate, weighing 30 oz, and there were likewise bequests to his grandchildren and loyal servants.[25] Francis had been the constant figure in the lives of Lettice and her siblings, and he had also taken an active interest in the affairs of his grandchildren. For Lettice he had been a source of support through some of the most testing periods of her life, and had not wavered even when he risked the Queen's displeasure. Now the Knollys family figurehead was gone, leaving a void in Lettice's life that would never be filled.

Four days after Francis's death, Lettice's uncle, Henry Carey, also died.[26] Camden asserted that he was 'a man of great stomach, but very choleric, and somewhat discontented, that being somewhat of kin to the Queen, he attained but mean honours, and wealth, departed also'.[27]

The epitaph on his tomb commended him as 'the best of fathers and dearest of husbands'. His kinship and closeness to the Queen ensured that he was given a funeral in Westminster Abbey that was paid for by Elizabeth in the same manner as for his sister; despite the regard in which he was held, Francis was to be afforded no such special treatment. On 18 August, Francis's funeral procession, including his Lord Treasurer's staff, helmet, coat and sword, made its way from Greys Court to the nearby church of St Nicholas. There Dr Holland, who had once served as Leicester's chaplain in the Netherlands, conducted the service.[28] Lettice's brother William played the role of chief mourner, but it is unlikely that Lettice herself was present. Sir Francis was laid to rest in the church, but if he had cherished any hopes of his wife's remains being moved to join him, he would have been sadly disappointed. The Queen made no attempt to move the remains of her kinswoman from Westminster Abbey, and therefore the couple who had been cruelly separated in the final months of Katherine's life were also to remain separated in death; thus, the magnificent tomb that was later erected to the couple's memory contains only the bones of Sir Francis. Nevertheless, the monument reflects the way in which Francis would have chosen to be remembered: a devoted husband and father, next to his wife and flanked by his children.

William Knollys was now the head of the family, and, as with his father, the Queen had ample faith in his abilities. Just days after his father died, William had heard that she intended to appoint him either Comptroller of the Royal Household or Vice-Chamberlain, and he informed Burghley's son, Robert Cecil, honestly that 'I wish rather to be Controller than Vice-Chamberlain. For as I desire to continue my father's place if it be possible, so will I by all the means I may shun to be Vice-Chamberlain; persuading myself rather to a solitary country life than to remain a courtier in that place.'[29] His wish was granted, and on 30 August he was made Comptroller and a Privy Councillor. In 1602, he would also be appointed Treasurer of the Household, although as time would reveal, this came at a price. William, though, was to prove himself a loyal and able advisor to the Queen.

THROUGHOUT THE 1590S Lettice had occupied herself with domestic matters in the countryside, and had taken pleasure in spending time with her children and grandchildren. In the aftermath of Cadiz, Essex was at the peak of his power and influence with the Queen. As the year turned to 1597 England was still at war with Spain, from where they were expecting an invasion fleet that summer. As usual, Essex urged the Queen to action, and she agreed that he would lead an expedition against them. Lettice watched as, once again, her son left home to brave danger. When Essex, accompanied by Blount, set sail in July the gales were so bad that the fleet was forced to return to Plymouth. They had no choice but to remain there until the weather turned, but the gales had caused Lettice alarm. Assured that her 'dearest Robin' was safe, such news 'doth more joy me than to have the King of Spain's Indies'. She was still concerned, and expressed her feelings that

And much gladder shall I be if, with your contentment, her Majesty might stay you upon good terms for this year, the time being so far passed, and sea travel in winter so troublesome and dangerous. I can no more, but pray unto God to bless and prosper all your noble attempts and actions, now and whensoever.[30]

Her hopes of delay were not to be realized, and in August the fleet set sail once more. Penelope shared her mother's worries, writing to Robert Cecil of who she longed 'to hear that all the troubles of this voyage were past and some hope of his speedy return'.[31] It was greatly hoped that the expedition would amount to, or surpass, the glory of Cadiz. However, the weather meant that the English fleet was unable to reach the port of Ferrol, where the Armada force was docked. Deciding to take the opportunity to win further plunder, Essex instead sailed for the Azores. But there was to be none of the success of Cadiz, for thanks to furious arguments with his rival, Sir Walter Ralegh, and Essex's own ill-advised tactics, they missed the Spanish treasure fleet. As a result, Essex was forced to return to England both empty-handed and having failed to destroy the Armada. The Queen was angry at his disobedience, and at his having left England vulnerable to attack once more through his failure to obliterate the Spanish force. What she had not realized was that Philip, having heard that the English were sailing from the Azores, ordered the Armada to follow them, hoping to intercept them before they reached England. Once again, though, the weather intervened, and the Spanish ships were shipwrecked and scattered as a result of heavy storms. Three Armada attempts to invade England had now failed, and, feeling utterly broken and in a state of financial ruin, Philip was left with no choice but to permanently abandon his plans of invasion.

When Essex arrived in England at the end of October, the Queen's fury at his failure meant that he retired from court under a dark cloud. But it was not long before Elizabeth forgave him and, for the time being at least, he was the favourite once more. In what became known as the Islands Voyage, the expedition left Essex deeply in debt, but that was the least of the family's problems. That same year Penelope fell sick with smallpox, and although she survived it was greatly feared that she would be scarred for life. Much to the relief of Lettice and her family, Penelope recovered 'without blemish to her beautiful face'.[32] In December, she gave birth to Charles Blount's son, Scipio, whose unusual name – taken from an ancient Roman general – was chosen in recognition of his father's military prowess. The baby was baptized at Essex House on 8 December, but he is never mentioned again, presumably dying shortly after.

Lettice had now been estranged from the Queen for nearly twenty years, with neither hope nor indication of reconciliation. For many years she had accepted this state of affairs, but her letters to her son signify that she was hopeful of achieving a return to favour. Though in Staffordshire

Lettice was miles from London, this did not deter her from writing to Essex regularly. She may have been optimistic that his position with Elizabeth, which was still strong, would translate into a thawing of the Queen's attitude towards his mother. Whatever the truth of the matter, she had become restless and longed to return to London. She was fifty-four – old by contemporary standards – but she informed Essex that she would gladly come to the capital 'to obtain that favour without which I live there as you know with greater disgrace'.[33]

Essex certainly did his best to convince the Queen to receive his mother, and while it is unclear how long he had been working on her behalf, by December 1597 his efforts had produced some results. He was then able to deliver Lettice the heartening news that 'Her Majesty is very well prepared to hearken to terms of pacification'. It says much for his charm and powers of persuasion that after almost twenty years of estrangement between the two women, he had succeeded in some degree where others had failed. Essex had in that same month been appointed Earl Marshal of England – he believed that he was invincible.

These words of encouragement were all that Lettice needed to hear, and eager to seize upon the opportunity, she informed her son that she was prepared to set out for the court immediately. It was now winter and the roads were perilous, but Lettice was so desperate to be restored to Elizabeth's favour that she had determined to brave the 'foul travelling' that the arduous journey between Staffordshire and London provided. She relayed her optimism to her son, declaring that she was ready to travel: 'especially if matters stood so well as you might hope to obtain some favour for us, then would I come also presently up, otherwise a country life is fittest for disgraced persons,' she wrote sadly.[34] But, she added, 'if you find reason to wish my coming then you must presently send some coach horses to fetch me for my own will never be able to draw me out of the mire'.[35]

With a renewed sense of confidence and full of expectation, Lettice left Drayton Bassett behind as she began her journey to London. There is no mention of Blount travelling with her, and it is safe to assume that he remained in Staffordshire during this time. She arrived in January 1598, and immediately took up residence with her son and his family at Essex House. On 14 January, it was observed that 'My Lady Leicester is now come to town, and many went to meet her.'[36] In addition to his eldest son Robert and the tragically short-lived Walter, Essex and his wife had also sired a daughter, Penelope, and a son named Henry, who had died in 1596.[37] Lettice was therefore able to spend some time with her beloved grandson and granddaughter while she waited anxiously for Essex to play his part.

January passed, and while she waited she was able to participate in the magnificent party thrown by Essex on Valentine's Day. It was a huge celebration, during which the Earl and his friends and family enjoyed a splendid banquet, followed by 'two plays which kept them up till one o'clock after midnight'.[38] All of Lettice's children were in attendance, as was her daughter-in-law and Penelope's lover Charles Blount, Lord Mountjoy. Shortly after the festivities, Lettice was delighted when her son delivered her some welcome news; after years of rivalry and estrangement, the Queen had at last agreed to grant her an audience. For Lettice this seemed to be the culmination of all of her recent hopes: she was willing to put the past behind them, but the question still remained: was Elizabeth?

CHAPTER 19

Some Wonted Unkind Words

O N 27 FEBRUARY, Lettice arrived at court for the first time in nearly two decades. She was full of optimism about her meeting with the Queen, but her hopes were about to be cruelly shattered. 'I acquainted you with the care to bring Lady Leicester to the Queen's presence,' Rowland White wrote to Sir Robert Sidney: 'it was granted, but the Queen found occasion not to come.'[1] It is clear that Elizabeth had only agreed to meet with Lettice at Essex's request rather than through her own desire, and at the last minute – in a style that was so typical of her – she changed her mind. Perhaps she had planned on doing so all along, for the result was that Lettice was left waiting in a snub that was humiliatingly public: nobody was left in any doubt that despite her presence at court, she was still in disgrace.

Lettice was disappointed, but determined not to give up. After all, she had braved the bitter winter weather for an opportunity to meet with her kinswoman, and she was resolved on doing so. By contrast, Elizabeth was equally eager to avoid Lettice's longed-for meeting. The cancelled audience at court was not a one-off, for White reported to his master that

Upon Shrove Monday, the Queen was persuaded to go to Mr Controller's at the Tilt End, there was my Lady Leicester with a fair jewel of £300 [£37,600]. A great dinner was prepared by my Lady Chandos, the Queen's coach ready and all the world expecting her Majesty's own coming; when upon a sudden she resolved not to go and so sent word.[2]

Essex was not there to witness this second snub to his mother, but when he heard of it he made it clear that he was not prepared to let the matter lie. He had defended his sister Dorothy before, and now prepared to do the same for his mother. White observed that the Earl 'kept his chamber the day before, in his night gown went up to the Queen the privy way; but all would not prevail and as yet my Lady Leicester hath not seen the Queen'. Even his persuasive words could not move his royal mistress, and White was concerned, for by Essex 'importuning in unpleasing matters loses opportunity to do good to his friends'.[3] Elizabeth's attitude towards Lettice was extraordinary, and her ability to hold a grudge astonishing – the anger she had felt towards her in 1579 was as fresh as ever. It is even more remarkable when one considers that Leicester – the cause of the women's rivalry – had now been dead for a decade.

Surprisingly, Essex's smooth words had some effect on the Queen. After much encouragement, he convinced her to agree to meet his mother on 2 March. Both Lettice and her son were anxious that Elizabeth might once more change her mind, but nevertheless Lettice dutifully arrived at court – perhaps more apprehensive than she had been before. On this occasion, though, whatever her reservations, the Queen was true to her word. After many years, 'My Lady Leicester' had finally been given the opportunity to speak to the Queen.[4]

What the two women felt as they observed one another can only be imagined, for in appearance they were much changed. At sixty-four, Elizabeth was no longer the most beautiful Queen in Europe, with tumbling red locks. She now wore a wig and heavy lead makeup, and her teeth had rotted from eating the sugary confectionaries of which she was so fond. Lettice was a decade younger, and though no descriptions of her appearance survive at this time, this can only have increased the Queen's jealousy and animosity towards her.

The meeting was short – as Elizabeth no doubt intended. There is no record of the words that were spoken between the two kinswomen, but it was believed that after many years in disgrace, Lettice 'kissed the Queen's hands and her breast and did embrace her and the Queen kissed her'.[5] Lettice was delighted by this, as was the Earl of Essex, who 'is in exceeding favour here'.[6] It was certainly an encouraging sign, and Lettice left court with good reason to hope that this was just the first step in rebuilding her relationship with Elizabeth. But could the tumultuous events of the past two decades really be forgiven and forgotten?

On the Queen's side, it appeared not. Unbeknown to Lettice, this was the last occasion on which she would ever see Elizabeth, who had no intention of allowing her kinswoman back into her favour or her court. Their meeting had been nothing but a superficial show – almost certainly for Essex's benefit – and within a matter of days the Queen was reported to be using 'some wonted unkind words' about her kinswoman.[7] She steadfastly refused to meet with her again, no matter what Essex might say. It was a devastating result, and all at once Lettice's hopes of a reconciliation and a possible return to court life had been dashed. Feeling downcast, she left London under a cloud and resigned herself to returning to her husband at Drayton Bassett.

AS TIME PASSED, Lettice's meeting with the Queen became more distant. She spent her days quietly at Drayton Bassett, perhaps disappointed and frustrated with the way in which events had transpired. Soon there were more worrying matters to contend with, for the relationship between the monarch and Lettice's son was also about to take a turn for the worst.

Following the Queen's meeting with his mother, like Lettice, Essex was hopeful that relations between the two women would improve. It was in his interests for them to get along, and Elizabeth's hatred of his mother was a source of great embarrassment for him. He was as frustrated as Lettice when the two women failed to build bridges. Though he had been the undoubted favourite for some time, there were many who snapped at his heels, waiting for an opportunity to take his place. Essex's old enemy Sir Walter Ralegh was among them, as was Lord Burghley's son, the hunchbacked Robert Cecil. Even though Essex and Cecil had spent part of their boyhoods together in Burghley's household, the two men loathed one another. This is particularly ironic given that, in his final letter to Burghley, Essex's father had relayed his hope that 'I would have his [Essex] love towards those which are descended from you spring up and increase with his years.'[8] Cecil had become a prominent figure at court following the death of Walsingham, and the Queen was coming to rely on him increasingly. He was a man of great ability, and when his father died in 1598 – much to the Queen's grief – he assumed the role of her Secretary of State.[9] This only swelled Essex's hostility to him, for his own influence with the Queen and in the political arena was beginning to wane – the Queen was distressed by rumours that Essex was conducting an affair with Lady Mary Howard, though he had convinced her that there was no truth in them. He was also vehemently opposed to the idea of a peace with Spain that was being mooted at this time, in response to the peace that had been made between France and Spain. Despite Cecil supporting the notion of peace, in his usual manner Essex did not refrain from speaking his mind. He wanted to launch an offensive to crush the might of the Spanish for good, but ultimately the Queen felt that to do so would prove too costly. Camden reported that Burghley had said that Essex 'breathed nothing but war, slaughter, and blood', and rather than letting the matter lie, Essex ordered the publication of a leaflet that set out all of his views, much to the Queen's fury.[10] She was fast becoming weary of his petulant outbursts. Evidence of just how far his relationship with Elizabeth had unravelled was about to be revealed in the most shocking of terms.

Following the death of Lettice's first husband, Walter, the problem of Ireland had remained a continual thorn in the Queen's side. News had recently arrived informing the Queen that her army had been crushed, and its leader killed by the Earl of Tyrone, leader of the native Irish forces. It was England's worst military defeat in years, and the situation needed to be resolved. In the summer, the Queen desperately sought to appoint a new Lord Deputy, and looked to Lettice's brother William. He was one of Essex's crucial supporters, and in need of all of the allies that he could get, Essex was eager for William to remain at court. Instead he suggested Sir George Carew, who was a member of Robert Cecil's faction. The Queen was not impressed with Carew's nomination, and Essex was angered by her cool response. So angered, that in a moment of pure frustration, on 1 July he committed the ultimate insult by turning his back on her. Elizabeth was furious at this blatant display of discourtesy, and in a rage she lashed out and hit him, giving him 'a box on the ear'.[11] She 'bid him be gone with a vengeance', but she had not counted on his shocking retort.[12] Equally outraged and forgetting all protocol in a moment of madness, Essex reached for his sword. Those around him were quick to react, and he was prevented from doing any more. The witnesses to this scene were appalled, but rather than repenting of his actions and begging for forgiveness, the Earl 'swore that he would not put up so great an indignity, nay that he could not, even at Henry VIII's hand', before storming from the room.[13] Once again his hot-headedness had got the better of him, but this time he had gone too far. Indeed, his actions were to have more significant consequences, and this incident marked the beginning of his end.

Though no action was taken against Essex following his altercation with the Queen, if Lettice had learned of it then she would have been wise to urge her son to show caution. Essex, however, seemed to think himself invincible, and continued to antagonize the Queen, offering no apology for his behaviour. The relationship between them had changed, and his behaviour towards her was strikingly different from that of his stepfather: he paid her very little deference, and rather than submitting to the Queen's outbursts in the way that Leicester had once done, Essex snapped back at her. There was only so much of this that Elizabeth was prepared to take. She was also greatly angered when he showed himself to be supportive of the relationship between his friend, the Earl of Southampton, and Elizabeth Vernon. Elizabeth was one of the Queen's maids, and was also Essex's cousin. She and Southampton were passionately in love, but though they sought the Queen's permission to marry, she expressly forbade it. This did not prevent the couple from continuing their relationship, and within a few months Elizabeth learned that she was pregnant. They now had no choice, and it was with Essex's support that Southampton and his mistress were secretly married at Essex House in August. Once again, the Queen was incensed when she discovered the truth, and even more so with Essex's deception. There was worse to come.

Despite her apparent forgiveness of all of Essex's appalling behaviour, the relationship between the Queen and her favourite was becoming increasingly fraught. To exacerbate matters, Essex was extremely vocal in his criticism of the Queen and Council's approach to the Irish problem. He rejected every candidate suggested for the role of Lord Deputy – even his friend, Penelope's lover Charles Blount, Lord Mountjoy, was deemed to be unsuitable by the Earl. The result was that he was left with no choice but to accept the position himself. So it was that Lettice's son began preparing to follow in the footsteps that his father had first taken more than two decades earlier. Even now, though, he did not learn from his mistakes, and he bickered with the Queen over the best way to approach the campaign. Whenever he did not get his own way he sulked, and waited for the Queen to give in to his demands. By now he knew that his influence with Elizabeth was starting to wane, and that her patience was wearing thin. His acceptance of the role in Ireland, then, was part of a desperate bid to repair his standing with the Queen and restore his dwindling finances. Only time would tell whether this roll of the dice would be successful.

In March 1599, the Earl of Essex sailed for Ireland with the largest army England had ever gathered, numbering 16,000.[14] Among the company were his stepfather, Sir Christopher Blount, who was by now a trusted member of Essex's circle, and the Earl of Southampton. The party was forced to endure a rough crossing in the Irish Sea. On 14 April, Essex arrived in Dublin, and from there his strategy was simple: he planned to crush the Earl of Tyrone's rebel force in Ulster in a short, sharp attack. It turned out that he had wildly underestimated his opponent.

WITH ESSEX IN Ireland, Lettice's daughter Penelope, daughter-in-law Frances, and the Countess of Southampton retired from London to Chartley. Lettice would also have seen this as an opportunity to spend some time with the ladies while they were there, and together they all waited anxiously for news from Ireland. There is no indication as to what Lettice's feelings at the departure of her husband and son on campaign may have been, but like those at court, she cannot have failed to recognize Essex's dwindling influence with the Queen. She would thus have been praying that his mission was a great success. When news came, though, it was not good.

Essex's power had gone to his head, and not for the first time he took it upon himself to ignore the Queen's commands. Prior to his departure, she had given orders that he was only to knight those who had shown exceptional valour in battle, but instead Essex created eighty-one new knights. He also made Southampton his Master of Horse, against the Queen's express command. Inevitably, the Queen discovered what he had done, and his flagrant disregard for her instructions only served to heighten her growing disillusionment.[15] More crucially, rather than marching to Ulster to destroy Tyrone, he lingered, instead quelling smaller pockets of rebellion elsewhere. The Queen was incensed, and wrote to him furiously, demanding that he proceed against Tyrone at once. By now Essex had squandered both time and money, and to make matters worse he had fallen ill with dysentery. This only increased his lethargy, and when he received the Queen's demands he knew that his forces no longer had the military strength to defeat Tyrone. The mighty army that he had brought with him had been diminished as a result of disease, famine, desertion or death in service: now only around four thousand men remained.

With him ever in her thoughts, Lettice wrote to her son while he was in Ireland. She took it upon herself to offer him advice, and in the circumstances he would have done well to heed her words:

My dear and most noble child,

In the midst of your infinite troubles, I must needs satisfy my own heart with sending you one farewell, with these caveats, that, as I would not, like myself or sex, persuade your invincible courage to cowardice, so yet, my sweet Robin, give me leave to put you in mind that the true valour in a great commander, thoroughly known, is as well shown, and to better purpose, in wise politic carriage and government, than it can possibly be in too much hazard and adventuring his own person. Wherefore, be wise as valiant, and think what a high price your country and friends hold you at, amongst the which I am not the least, that hold you dearest.[16]

She had also sent Essex and her husband a comforting message: 'The Lord of Heaven bless and keep you both, that with heart's joy I may see your faces again, with safe return.' She was eager to see her son, but the Queen forbade Essex to return home until he had fulfilled his promise to bring Tyrone to his knees. Her anger at his behaviour and conduct was palpable. This was only exacerbated by the fact that, during his absence, his enemies at court were provided with the perfect opportunity to speak against him – and he knew it. Matters were about to become a whole lot worse, for the final campaign to crush Tyrone went disastrously. Tyrone proposed a six-week renewable truce, and against the Queen's express command Essex agreed. With his forces so badly weakened, in his eyes there was no reasonable alternative. Like his father before him, Essex had failed to achieve success in Ireland, and had actually done rather worse.

When she learned of what he had done, the Queen was livid. Feeling that the only option was now to explain himself in person, Essex made a badly judged decision. Contrary to the Queen's orders, on 24 September, after less than six months in Ireland, he set sail for England 'in all haste', leaving the remainder of his army behind – without their leader. Once again his hot-headed impetuosity had got the better of him, but he felt confident that if he could explain his position to the Queen before his enemies were given the chance to move against him, then all would be well.[17] As soon as he landed he journeyed at breakneck speed to Nonsuch Palace, where the court was in residence. Arriving on the morning of 28 September, he was so desperate to see the Queen that he abandoned all protocol and completely forgot himself – again. Covered in mud and dust as a result of his speedy journey, Essex hurried to the Royal Apartments and burst into the Queen's bedchamber unannounced. The sight that greeted him was wholly unexpected: the Queen, usually presented as the icon of splendour and magnificence, was in a state of undress. Her wig and cosmetics were absent, and the extravagant jewels that usually adorned her person had not yet been placed. As her bedchamber was an exclusively female domain, Elizabeth was shocked by this unexpected intrusion, and more so when she saw that it was Essex, who had evidently disobeyed her commands to remain in Ireland until summoned home. Despite her humiliation, she managed to retain her composure. It was at this moment that Essex's mistake dawned on him, and in a rare display of humility he fell on his knees before her. He seemed to think that this would be enough for her to forgive his earlier discourtesy, and when he left the Queen's chamber it was with an assurance that all was well between them. Later that morning he was given a more formal audience, by which time the Queen was properly attired. Yet later that day, it became clear that all was not well after all, and that evening Essex was ordered to 'keep his chamber'.[18] At his request Penelope hastened to court, but there was little that she could do. She and Lettice, who had been informed of her son's arrival back at court, could only watch and wait as events unfolded.

The following day, the Privy Council presented Essex with a list of charges regarding the Irish campaign – chiefly his disobedience and inability to follow orders. Though he spiritedly defended his conduct, his answers were not good enough, and he was sent to York House on the Strand under house arrest. Here he was to remain for the next six months. In his melancholy he fell ill, and, still popular, this only increased public sympathy for him.

As the 1590s had progressed, Essex's behaviour towards the Queen had grown increasingly arrogant and disrespectful. Time and again Elizabeth had forgiven his petulant displays of sulking and his explosions of rage – behaviour that she had never had to endure from Leicester or any other of her male favourites. That she tolerated it for so long says much about her fondness for him. Eventually, though, such displays and such blatant disrespect for her and her commands had worn the Queen down, and she had become thoroughly tired of it. Cadiz had undoubtedly been the peak of Essex's career, but from there things had taken a drastic downward spiral. He had numerous enemies at court, chiefly Robert Cecil, but ultimately his undoing was all his own. His behaviour in Ireland had been the final straw – it was clear that he could not be trusted to obey orders, and his ambition was becoming dangerous. No longer would he enjoy the influence he had once wielded, and more crucially, never again would he see the Queen.

Essex's fall alarmed his family. Lettice was greatly agitated, but she knew that her own position with the Queen made it impossible for her to intercede on her son's behalf. Essex's wife, meanwhile, was reported to be 'a most sorrowful creature for her husband's captivity'.[19] The only member of the family with any influence left was Penelope, and she was prepared to do whatever it took to secure her beloved brother's freedom. In December, Rowland White observed that 'The two ladies Northumberland and Rich all in black were at court; they were humble suitors to have the Earl removed to a better air for he is somewhat straightly lodged.'[20] Dorothy had once again been received at court, but her blatant support for her disgraced brother could only spell trouble. In a clear demonstration of where her loyalties lay, Lettice's cousin Lady Philadelphia Scrope had donned the same colour.[21] Penelope worked tirelessly on Essex's behalf, sending the Queen several costly gifts and growing gradually more distressed by reports that her brother had fallen sick. The Queen was in no mood to listen, and White reported that while Penelope's 'letters are read, her presents received, but no leave granted'.[22] Her softer approach had achieved nothing, leaving Penelope with no choice but to resort to harsher tactics.

In a letter that is generally dated to early 1600, Penelope's inheritance of her mother's spirit shone through when she wrote a defence of her brother to the Queen. Her letter was not, however, the traditional plea for mercy, and did nothing but rile the Queen:

I early hoped this morning to have had my eyes blessed with your beauty, but seeing the same vanish to a cloud, and meeting with spirits that did presage by the wheels of your chariot some thunder in the air, I must express my fears to that divine oracle from whom I received a doubtful answer, unto whose power I must again sacrifice the tears and prayers of the afflicted, that must despair in time, if it be too soon to importune heaven when we feel the miseries of hell, or that words directed to your wisdom should out of season be delivered for my unfortunate brother, that all men have liberty to defame us.[23]

Her love for her brother was evident when she tried to justify his actions, and urged the Queen to show clemency:

If his offences were capital, is he so base a creature that his love and service to you and the State deserved no absolution, after so hard punishments, or so much as to answer in your presence, who would vouchsafe more justice than partial judges, or enemies combined to build his ruin, and glut themselves with revenge, and rise by his overthrow? Unless you check them, the last course will be his last breath, since their evil instruments have sufficient poison in their

hearts to infect the service; and when they are in their full strength,
they will, like the giants, make war against heaven.

Penelope's reference to Essex's enemies and her attempts to blame them for her brother's faults did not go down well. She ended her letter by entreating the Queen to let 'your power be no more eclipsed than your beauty, and imitate the highest in not destroying those that trust only in your mercy'.[24] This letter was probably the subject of a comment made by a contemporary on 8 February, that 'Lady Rich has written again to Her Majesty, but in other kind of language, and they say my Lord [Essex] relenteth much, but the resolution is taken what course he shall run'.[25] Either way, the letter was not well received, and the Queen remained unmoved. To further exacerbate the situation, Penelope's actions had landed her in trouble, too.

It is probable that Lettice was fully aware of Penelope's letter – she may even have read it, for unable to wait in the countryside any longer, by January 1600 she was in London where she waited anxiously for news. A portrait of her painted at around this time shows an attractive yet careworn face.[26] In an attempt to soften the Queen's heart, it was reported that 'The Lady Leicester sent the Queen a New Year's gift, which was very well taken.'[27] The nature of the gift is unknown, but if Lettice took this to be a good sign she was to be mistaken. On 2 February, Rowland White had been told that 'This day seven night my Ladies Leicester and Rich were at Mr Beck's house upon Richmond Green and were humble suitors to her Majesty to have access unto her; but they returned back again without comfort.'[28] Whether Lettice attempted to approach the Queen personally is unclear – if she did then no record of it has survived, but either way the Queen was not in a hurry to do her any favours.

Lettice was naturally distressed when she heard of the imprisonment of her 'Sweet Robin', and was determined to do everything she could to secure his release. She was also desperate to be near him, and by the middle of February she had moved closer to York House. She simply could not let matters lie, and though her behaviour was not deliberately antagonistic, the Queen was incensed. On 25 February, it was reported that 'Mislike is taken that his mother and friends have been in a house that looks into York Garden where he uses to walk and have saluted each other out of a window.'[29] Lettice's protective love for her son overcame all reason, and she was fearful lest Essex should become one of the Queen's victims.

Despite his imprisonment, Essex was still allowed access to pen and paper. Given the circumstances he could easily have been forgiven for forgetting to write to his mother, but Lettice evidently felt differently. It may have been around this time that she wrote to him, urging him to

Bestow some time a few idle lines on your mother who otherwise may grow jealous that you love her not so well as she deserves, which blot I know you will take away. And, as she hath made you the chief comfort of her life, so I doubt not of your noble nature but that you will be careful to maintain it with all childlike kindness.[30]

He was a thirty-four-year-old man with other matters on his mind, yet still Lettice suffocated him and treated him as if he were a small boy.

With Penelope's letter and her own movements having served only to inflame the Queen, Lettice tried another tactic in an attempt to soften her resolve towards her son. She knew how fond Elizabeth was of finery, and it was heard that, stretching her finances once more, she had 'in hand a gown she will send the queen which will cost her £100 [£12,500] at least'.[31] This 'most curious fine gown' was nothing more than an attempt to bribe the Queen into releasing her son, and one that Lettice hoped would pay off.[32] Due to their broken relationship, Lettice was unable to deliver her gift personally, so she sought an intermediary. On 2 March, the gown was presented to the Queen by Lady Mary Shelton, one of her favourite ladies, and it was reported that the Queen 'liked it well'.[33] It was an encouraging start, but Elizabeth was fully aware of the meaning behind it. She was in no hurry to do either Lettice or Essex any favours, and she refused to be bribed in such a way. She was too clever to accept such a gift, and she therefore 'did not accept or refuse it only answered that things standing as they did it was not fit for her to desire what she did'.[34] More worryingly, Lettice was also left in little doubt that her son had now well and truly fallen from grace. The costly gift had not worked – she did not dare to ask for it back, and Essex remained imprisoned.

Just days later, on 8 March, Rowland White was reporting that there had been 'an expectation that Lord Essex should have come to his own house'.[35] Once again, Lettice's overbearing nature put a stop to this, for White continued to relate that 'it is conjectured that Ladies Leicester, Southampton, Northumberland and Rich assembled themselves at Essex House to receive him, which hindered it'.[36] The disappointment of Lettice and her daughters can well be imagined, and more so when on 10 March, by 'Her Majesty's express command', Lettice was ordered to remove herself from Essex House.[37] She wasted no time in doing so, and the reason for her removal became apparent when, on 22 March, Essex was at last allowed to return to Essex House. The time for the revelries he had once enjoyed there had long since passed, for the Earl was still a prisoner. Nevertheless, there was better news when, four days after his arrival, Lettice was given the opportunity to visit her son. Sir Richard Berkeley, Essex's jailer at Essex House, was able to inform Sir Robert Cecil that 'The Countess of Leicester came hither by water this afternoon, attended on with a man and one gentlewoman, and stayed here with my Lord of Essex not two hours, and returned by water again.'[38] Permission for Lettice to visit may have been given in response to a petition she made to the Queen via Cecil. Given her antipathy towards Lettice and Essex's disgrace, it is surprising that Elizabeth agreed to such a meeting. Lettice's claim that she sought to see her son 'once before her departure' helped to convince the Queen that, if she conceded, Lettice would leave London and become less troublesome.[39] Lettice herself was aware that she needed to tread carefully, which was why, by her own admittance, she did not dare to 'crave any further grace at this time, how glad soever she would be of it'.[40] What passed between mother and son during their meeting is unknown – perhaps Lettice urged her son to show some contrition for his behaviour, and conform to whatever demands the Queen made of him. Whatever the truth, she realized that for the time being there was no more that she could do for him. She had no choice, and was forced to leave her beloved son behind as she left Essex House and London, and departed for Drayton Bassett once more.

THE QUEEN AND Council had been so concerned with the matter of Essex that they had not had much opportunity to dwell on Penelope's recent letter to her royal mistress. It had not been forgotten, though, and on 29 March the contemporary Dudley Carleton remarked that 'Lady Rich, once more summoned to answer about her letter, feigns sickness, and has stolen into the country. The Earl of Essex finds his own house further from court than the Lord Keeper's, having no longer the help of a friend at hand.'[41] She could not avoid the summons forever, however, and when Penelope did appear before the Council, she stood her ground. She resolutely maintained her loyalty to the Queen, but in a bold demonstration of courage, she also protested her devotion to her brother. Other than her impertinence she had not committed any crime, and Penelope was released unpunished. Notwithstanding this, the Queen never fully forgave her for meddling in matters that she felt did not concern her. Unfortunately, at the end of May her strongly worded letter to the Queen 'was lately printed, not from friendship or faction, but hope of gain; a few were sold, but it was soon suppressed. Lady Rich will have the worst of it, as she has been sent for to interpret her riddles, and is come.'[42] Never again would Penelope enjoy the same favour with Elizabeth. Now all of Lettice's faction had forfeited their former indulgence with the Tudor Queen.

FROM THE COUNTRYSIDE, Lettice learned that in June, Essex was once more returned to York House. Here he was interrogated by eighteen commissioners, the charges having been drawn up by Sir Edward Coke, the Attorney-General.[43] Among them were Lettice's brother, William, who doubtless found the situation uncomfortable as his loyalties to Queen and nephew were torn. The hearing lasted for thirteen hours, but no conclusions were drawn. Essex was therefore forced to endure an agonizing wait while the commissioners reported back to the Queen, who now had to decide upon his fate. At the end of August she made a decision: hoping that her former favourite had learned his lesson, Essex was granted his liberty. However, he was stripped of all of his public offices, meaning that his political career was now in shreds. Lettice greeted the news of Essex's freedom with a sense of immense relief, but both she and the Earl were disappointed when it quickly became clear that a restoration to royal favour was not on the cards. In spite of his freedom, Essex was still forbidden from attending court, and for the time being he chose to retreat quietly into the country.

Elizabeth made her feelings about Essex clearer still when, in September, she refused to renew his licence for sweet wine. This came as a great blow to him, for he had been hugely dependent on the income it yielded. He wrote to the Queen, desperate to try and regain her favour, but evidence of how far Elizabeth's attitude towards him had cooled was palpable when he received no reply. Completely ignorant of how fortunate he had been to avoid greater punishment thus far, for Essex this was the final straw: he was hell-bent on revenge, and his mind turned to rebellion.

CHAPTER 20

The Arch-Traitor Essex

As the year 1601 began, Lettice's relief at her son's release turned to anxiety once more. This was because Essex's initial distress at the loss of the Queen's favour moved from 'sorrow and repentance to rage and rebellion'. As Lettice's husband Blount later testified, it was shortly after 'the Earl had his liberty, he began to treat and consult with me again in Essex House', which before long had become a centre for all of those who were members of Essex's disaffected circle.[1] Essex had many supporters, for his popularity had not dwindled, and it was with these friends that he now began to plot. The Earl himself became progressively paranoid that his enemies at court – chiefly Robert Cecil – were planning to move against him. Determined to get there first, he planned a coup whereby he would gain control of the City, and crucially, the Tower. The Queen would not be harmed, but would be forced to impeach his 'potent adversaries' – chiefly Cecil and Ralegh.[2] He himself would then resume his rightful place by the Queen's side, when he would insist on being appointed Lord Protector. Lettice, who always made it her business to know what was going on in her son's life, was deeply worried by what she heard. If, though, she wrote to Essex during this time – as is likely – then her letters have not survived, and must have been destroyed. She was more concerned still when, as Blount later confessed, Essex 'sent for me out of the country not many days before this rebellion'.[3]

The Council were well aware of the goings-on at Essex House, and what was more, Essex and his friends knew it, too. With this in mind the Earl's friends tried to convince him to escape, but Essex would have none of it and was determined to press on with his coup. He was now severely paranoid, and convinced that plots were being hatched to take his life – rumours abounded that Ralegh and Lord Cobham were at the centre of one such attempt. On 3 February, Essex's good friend Southampton headed a meeting at Drury House in the City.[4] Essex himself was not present, but in his absence his friends discussed the best course of action for the Earl to take in order to avoid falling into the clutches of his enemies. They did not have long to consider, as on Saturday 7 February Essex was summoned to court to stand before the Council. Both he and his supporters panicked, and in his unstable state of mind he plotted a reckless, ill-thought-out scheme to seize control of the Queen and the government.

Lettice – wisely – was at Drayton Bassett at this time.[5] She was aware of her son's dissatisfaction at the Queen's treatment of him, and fully supported him in his indignation. But a rebellion against the monarch was another matter altogether. Such action was treasonous, and if it were not successful, her son risked the safety of his entire family. Whether she approved or not, Lettice had some knowledge of what was afoot, but her involvement went no further. The same could not be said of her husband, Sir Christopher Blount, and her eldest daughter Penelope, both of who were active conspirators.

Claiming illness, Essex failed to present himself at court on the appointed day, and instead remained at Essex House making plans. In his desperation, the Earl had become frantic, and could think only of regaining his former power. His plot, though, would demonstrate a reckless show of stupidity. It relied largely on the support of the people, whom Essex was confident would rise and follow him. On the afternoon of 7 February, while Essex was at home, some of his supporters had made a trip to the South Bank. There, at The Globe theatre, having paid forty shillings they gave orders for a performance of Shakespeare's *Richard II* to be staged.[6] The play was an attempt to rouse the citizens of London to show their support for Essex in what was to come, and included the banned abdication scene. In reality, Essex had no intention of removing the Queen from her throne, merely of removing her advisors – the Earl's enemies. Even so, the conspirators were playing a dangerous game.

ON THE MORNING of Sunday 8 February, the Earl of Worcester and three members of the Council arrived at Essex House. They had come to ascertain the reason for Essex's failure to present himself before them the previous day, and were horrified when the Earl gave orders for them to be locked in the house. Among them was Lettice's brother, William, but family loyalties, it seemed, counted for nothing. William, who was later awarded the post of Treasurer of the Household in return for his support in the proceedings against Essex, remembered that 'they contemptuously used us, not only with opprobrious speeches, but violent deeds, imprisoning us under lock and key'.[7] It was now time for Essex to put his plans into action. The contemporary chronicler John Stow recorded that 'about ten of the clock before noon, Robert Devereux, Earl of Essex, assisted by sundry noblemen, and gentlemen, in warlike manner entered the city of London at the Temple Bar, crying for the Queen'.[8] According to Essex's enemy Robert Cecil, before he left the Earl had been busy fortifying Essex House, which he had 'furnished with all manner of warlike provisions'.[9] His preparations complete, Essex had marched out of his London home accompanied by more than a hundred armed men, including his stepfather, Sir Christopher Blount. Over the past decade and more, Lettice's husband had shown himself to be a loyal ally to Essex, but on this occasion his participation would prove to be a fatal error.

Essex had always been uncommonly popular – 'the darling of London' – and as he and his armed party marched towards the City he called out to the citizens in an attempt to rally them to his cause.[10] However, the sight of the armed men did nothing to rouse them, and instead encouraged people to keep to their houses. This came as a great disappointment to the Earl, who had been confident that the support of the Londoners would win the day for him. Indeed, Camden reported that Essex believed that he 'was loved in the City, by most that were much addicted to his fame and fortune; which he believed absolutely to be true'.[11] He was totally deluded, for his popularity was as nothing compared with the people's loyalty to the Queen. They were astonished by Essex's taking up arms against her, and were eager to do all that they could in order to protect their monarch and distance themselves from his treason.

Meanwhile, when word reached the court of Essex's armed uprising, the Council were quick to act. There was 'great bustling to put themselves in defence, with such weapons as the place furnished; a barricade of coaches was made in the broad passage between that and Charing Cross, and people from Westminster and the adjoining hamlets flocked with such weapons as they had'.[12] A warrant was immediately issued:

Whereas the Earl of Essex and his confederates have taken arms against the Queen's Majesty, and have this day been proclaimed traitors, and thereby are to be prosecuted as traitors and rebels: These are, in her Majesty's name, straightly to charge and command you, upon your allegiance, forthwith to arm yourselves, as many as can with horse and armour, and the rest as foot with pike and shot, presently to repair hither and with us to march to the Court for the defence of her Majesty's person, or otherwise as you shall be commanded; and the shot to be furnished with bullet, powder and match convenient.[13]

The Queen was irate when she was informed of Essex's treason, and a contemporary reported that 'The Queen was so far from fear that she would have gone out in person to see what any rebel of them all durst do against her, had not her councillors with much ado stayed her.'[14] Her heart was now well and truly hardened; Essex had gone too far. It was clear that if the rebellion was successfully crushed, there was now no way back for him.

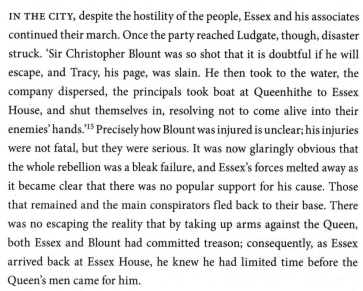

IN THE CITY, despite the hostility of the people, Essex and his associates continued their march. Once the party reached Ludgate, though, disaster struck. 'Sir Christopher Blount was so shot that it is doubtful if he will escape, and Tracy, his page, was slain. He then took to the water, the company dispersed, the principals took boat at Queenhithe to Essex House, and shut themselves in, resolving not to come alive into their enemies' hands.'[15] Precisely how Blount was injured is unclear; his injuries were not fatal, but they were serious. It was now glaringly obvious that the whole rebellion was a bleak failure, and Essex's forces melted away as it became clear that there was no popular support for his cause. Those that remained and the main conspirators fled back to their base. There was no escaping the reality that by taking up arms against the Queen, both Essex and Blount had committed treason; consequently, as Essex arrived back at Essex House, he knew he had limited time before the Queen's men came for him.

The Earl barricaded himself and his supporters into his home, and rapidly began burning incriminating papers. Were there letters from his mother among them? It was later reported that he had destroyed 'divers papers that were in a little casket, whereof one was, as he said, a history of his troubles'.[16] Soon, the Queen's forces had arrived at Essex House, headed by the Lord Admiral Charles Howard of Effingham – the husband of Lettice's cousin, Katherine Carey. Essex was determined not to give in without a fight, but he was not the only one who was intent on obtaining a result, for 'the Queen said she would not sleep till they were had out'.[17]

It was not only Essex and his band of followers who were trapped inside the house, but his wife and Penelope, too. While the rebellion had been underway, Penelope and the Countess of Essex had spent their time entertaining the Earl of Worcester and the Queen's envoys, who were still being held hostage. It was with the latter in mind that, finding Essex unwilling to surrender, Cecil reported that 'the Lord Admiral threatened to blow up the house, which he had forborne to do because my Ladies Essex and Rich were within it'.[18] Some action needed to be taken, and it was now that 'Sir Robert Sidney signified to the Earl, in the General's name, that they would give two hours respite for the ladies and gentlewomen to be removed.'[19] Essex accepted this, which encouraged Sidney to press further: 'And yourself, my Lord, what mean you to do? For the house is to be blown up with gunpowder unless you will yield.'[20] The Earl answered desperately that 'they should the sooner fly to heaven'.[21] However, 'upon remonstrance and persuasion that their grievance should be brought to the Queen, they seemed utterly to despair, Essex saying there was none near the Queen that would be suffered to make a true report of this action, or speak a good word for him'.[22]

He had by now realized that his cause was lost, and knowing that there was no alternative, at ten o'clock that evening Essex and his associates 'yielded to Her Majesty's mercy'.[23] From that moment, rather than showing remorse, Essex adopted his usual petulant attitude of pride, insisting that he had not committed treason. He was taken to Lambeth Palace for the night, but there was no question as to his ultimate destination. The following morning, he and his friend Southampton were conveyed by water to the Tower, there to await the Queen's decision as to their fate. It was not just Essex and his associates who were in dire peril, but Penelope, too. She had played no active role in her brother's rebellion, but she had still done her utmost to rally support for him. Her steadfast loyalty to her brother had led her into stormy waters, and she was placed in the custody of Henry Seckford, the Keeper of the Privy Purse.

Upon his arrival at the Tower, proud Essex was housed in the thirteenth-century Devil's Tower, which was later renamed the Devereux Tower after its notorious inmate.[24] For greater security, Sir Thomas Howard was appointed Constable of the Tower to oversee his care; so shocked were many of Essex's contemporaries by his actions that many believed he was 'more like a monster than a man'.[25] Robert Cecil, meanwhile, made his thoughts on the fallen Earl perfectly clear:

Being but a boy in years, and a child in experience, he has been graced with more than common dignities. Her Highness first made him master of the horse, then master of her ordnance, and first a member and then president of her Privy Council. Afterwards, besides many other private gifts of value, amounting not to less than £300,000 [£30,192,000], she advanced him to the dignity of Earl Marshal, and confirmed him Lord General of her forces in Ireland; where how traitorously he behaved himself I would his own soul might be judge.[26]

Sir Christopher Blount, in the time being, was in a weakened state due to his injuries. Even so, it was clear that he would live, though it was some days before he was well enough to be questioned properly. Having regained some strength, it became apparent that Blount's primary motive for supporting his stepson in his treason was religion. Despite his past double-dealings, at heart he was a true Catholic, and while they were at opposite ends of the religious spectrum, Essex was able to offer him some reassurance in this quarter: 'The Earl did give him comfort that if he came to authority there should be a toleration for religion. He was wont to say that he did not like that any man should be troubled for his religion.'[27] Blount had, it seems, resigned himself to the fact that he was unlikely to be granted mercy, and as such had signed papers to the effect that he 'Desires as a last request, that Her Majesty will assure herself that if he could in twelve years have seen her gracious eyes, there is no man living could have drawn him into any offensive action.'[28] This seems to suggest that from the time of his marriage to Lettice, which had taken place almost twelve years previously, like his wife, Blount had been denied royal favour, and it provides another reason for his decision to join his stepson's plot.

There is no record of how Lettice came to learn of the disastrous failure of her son's rebellion, and how deeply embroiled her daughter had also become. Given her intense love for her children, her reaction and anxiety can be easily imagined, and she must have been greatly fearful of what their fates might be. Realizing that no amount of fine dresses and begging could alter the situation, she remained at Drayton Bassett. Equally uncertain is how she came to learn of her husband's injuries, but it became immediately apparent where her true loyalties lay. There is no record of her attempting to see or communicate with her husband during this time, and she realized that to do so would be unwise – possibly even dangerous. Her children were her greatest concern, and even then she was fully aware that for Essex, the future looked bleak: those who had committed treason rarely went unpunished.

THE AWE-INSPIRING WESTMINSTER Hall, built by William II in 1097, had witnessed many notable events.[29] It had hosted the coronation banquets of monarchs, and it had been here that, in January 1559, Lettice had witnessed the joyous celebrations staged for the coronation of her royal kinswoman. The atmosphere on the morning of 19 February was, however, vastly different than it had been on that day. A 'raised platform, about two yards high and six yards square, was erected at the upper end of the hall', as it prepared to witness the trial of the Earls of Essex and Southampton.[30] Westminster Hall had been used to host many such trials, including those of Sir Thomas More, the Duke of Somerset and the Duke of Northumberland – the trial of Essex was no different. At nine o'clock that morning, Essex and Southampton were brought into the Hall and made to stand at the bar. A contemporary remembered that 'When he [Essex] first came to the bar, his countenance was unsettled; but once in, he showed the greatest resolution and contempt of death, real or assumed.'[31] Lettice's son chose to convey himself with his usual pride, and spoke in his own defence in a spirited manner. It was not the first time that Essex's arrogance had drawn comment. As the trial got underway, a further contemporary report related that

The charges were, Essex's attempt to surprise the court, his coming in arms to London to raise rebellion, and defending his house against the Queen's forces. To the two last he answered that he was driven for his life; to the first, that it was never resolved upon, and had it been, it was only to throw himself at the Queen's feet, and tell such things of his enemies as should make them odious and restore him to her favour. He spoke bravely, and his chief care evidently was, as he had ever lived popularly, to leave a good opinion in the people's minds now at parting. He loudly protested his faith and loyalty to the Queen and State.[32]

Although he was steadfast in his declaration of loyalty to the Queen, he had undeniably committed treason. The Queen was determined to let justice take its course; all of her former warm feelings towards Essex had now dissolved. She had told the French ambassador, just days earlier, that she had pandered to him for too long, and that his behaviour had been shameful. She now had no kind words for him, and on the day of the rebellion had been determined to face him 'in order to know which of the two of them ruled'.[33] The evidence was compelling, but the proceedings were exhausting for all involved, and dragged on until seven o'clock that evening. Given the severity of the charges, a guilty verdict was inevitable. Among the peers that sat in judgement against the two Earls was Lettice's unsavoury son-in-law, Lord Rich. He had no wish to be connected with his wife's treasonous family any longer, and was doing all that he could to disassociate himself. More poignantly, her brother William was also there, and was one of those who gave evidence against his nephew. Both Essex and Southampton were condemned as traitors: the sentence was the full-blown horror of a traitor's death: hanging, drawing and quartering.

The news of her son's condemnation can have come as no surprise to Lettice, but no matter how expected, the realization that he had been sentenced to a traitor's death still came as a great shock. She had already lost two sons in the first years of their lives, and another in violent circumstances abroad; her letters to Essex are testament to just how precious he was to her, but she was helpless to protect him.

Following their trial, Essex and Southampton were returned to the Tower. There, a contemporary related that 'I hear that he begins to relent, and acknowledges, among other faults, his arrogant behaviour at his trial.'[34] He was, however, about to make a far more shocking revelation. Two days after the trial, Essex made a private confession in which he incriminated Penelope, his beloved sister, and her lover, Charles Blount, Lord Mountjoy. Mountjoy was by now in Ireland, where he had been sent to replace Essex, and had played no part in Essex's rebellion. He had, however, agreed to earlier plans that aimed to release Essex from his house imprisonment by using the army. More dangerously, in his absence his house had been used as a rendezvous for the conspirators. Essex's claims against his sister are more difficult to comprehend, and seem to have been motivated by nothing more than a less than chivalrous desire to shift the blame. He denied all responsibility for his actions, instead claiming that Penelope 'did continually urge me on with telling me how all my friends and followers thought me a coward and that I had lost all my valour; and thus that she must be looked to, for she had a proud spirit'.[35] On a personal level, given the closeness of Lettice's family, Essex's claims against his sister came as a devastating betrayal. But his words had little effect, for despite her involvement Penelope was set at her liberty. Her brother's treachery left her heartbroken – feelings that Lettice shared – and she made her distress clear in a letter to the Lord Admiral. She bitterly declared that 'it is known that I have been more like a slave than a sister, which proceeded out of my exceeding love rather than his authority'.[36] The close relationship that the siblings had once shared was in ruins, and the lives of Lettice's family would never be the same again.

ESSEX'S ENEMY ROBERT Cecil claimed that the Earl of Southampton had been led astray, thanks to his loyalty to the Earl. Following his intercession, Southampton's sentence was commuted to life imprisonment: he would not face the axe after all. Moreover, the clemency of King James ensured that he was later released and reunited with Elizabeth Vernon, by whom he had several more children.[37] If Essex and his family were hopeful that the same mercy might be extended to him, they were cruelly mistaken; it was not long before the Earl realized that his days were numbered. Now all that he could do was prepare to meet his end.

For a man of Essex's pride, who had been raised with a profound sense of dignity and respect for his lineage, making a good death was of paramount importance. He wanted to die well, and to show the world that he left it a brave soldier. There were reports that he had begged the Queen for a private execution within the confines of the Tower, a request that was duly granted, and for which he wrote to the Queen giving thanks. This is unlikely to have been the true tale. More probable is the explanation provided by Bourchier Devereux, that the 'true reason was, that Essex was now as ever the darling of the people, who could not be made to believe that he had received a fair trial'.[38] Despite their failure to support his rebellion, Essex was still extremely popular with the citizens of London. Hence in order to avoid a public outcry at his death, the Queen and Council deemed a private execution wisest. The King of France believed – probably quite rightly – that this was in direct contrast to Essex's wishes, and that 'he desired nothing more than to die in public'.[39] Similarly, the Queen had commuted the sentence of hanging, drawing and quartering to beheading, as was customary in the case of noblemen.

Essex's preparation for death did not include making a will, and neither did he ask to see his wife or children; his youngest daughter, Dorothy, was just two months old.[40] With this in mind, it is also unsurprising that he did not ask to see his mother, knowing as he undoubtedly did that

Lettice was in a torment of anxiety over the imminent fate of her beloved son. There is no record of her attempting to intercede and save him, or beseeching others to do so on her behalf – she was politically astute enough to understand that to do so would be pointless. She herself held no influence, and now her whole family lay under the very dark cloud of the Queen's displeasure. She was forced to live with the knowledge that her final precious son would soon be dead.

WITHIN THE CONFINES of the Tower on the evening of 24 February, Essex was preparing to meet his end on the morrow. According to a contemporary report,

> On Tuesday night, between ten and twelve o'clock, he opened his window, and said to the guard, 'My good friends, pray for me, and tomorrow you shall see in me a strong God in a weak man; I have nothing to give you, for I have nothing left but that which I must pay to the Queen tomorrow in the morning.'[41]

At eight o'clock on the morning of Wednesday 25 February, the Lieutenant and sixteen Tower guards led Essex out from the Devil's Tower. He was dressed fully in black, in 'a gown of wrought velvet, a suit of satin, a felt hat, all in black, and a little ruff about his neck', and was accompanied by three clergymen: Dr Mountfort, Dr Barlow and Mr Ashton.[42] The journey was an exceedingly short one, for the scaffold had been erected on nearby Tower Green. There, 'where the church stands', was a scaffold 'three yards square and railed round'; from his rooms Essex would have been able to hear, and perhaps also see, as his final stage was erected.[43] Though only travelling a short distance,

> all the way from his chamber to the scaffold, he called to God to give him strength and patience to the end, and said 'O God, give me true

repentance, true patience, and true humility, and put all wordly thoughts out of my mind;' and he often entreated those that went with him to pray for him.[44]

As he arrived, he would have seen 'a form near unto the place whereon sat the Earls of Cumberland and Hertford, the Viscount Byndon, the Lord Thomas Howard, the Lord Darcy, the Lord Compton'.[45] These men had witnessed Essex's rise in the Queen's favour, watched as he fell, and would soon be able to report on his end.

Showing more humility in his final moments than he had demonstrated in the entirety of his life, Essex stood on the scaffold surveying the scene. He took off his hat and 'made reverence to the Lords', before repenting of his sins and asking for forgiveness:[46] 'My Lords and you, my Christian brethren, who are here to be witnesses of this my just punishment,' he began, 'I confess to the glory of God that I am a most wretched sinner, and that my sins are more in number than the hairs of my head.'[47] He continued to explain that

I have bestowed my youth in wantonness, lust and uncleanness, and that notwithstanding divers good motions from the spirit of God put into me, the good which I would, I have not done, and the evil which I would not, I have done. For all which I humbly beseech my Saviour Christ to be a mediator to the Eternal Majesty for my pardon; especially for this my last sin, wherein so many for love of me have been drawn to offend God, their sovereign and the world. I beseech God to forgive it us, and to forgive it me, the most wretched of all. And I beseech God to send her Majesty a prosperous reign and a long life, [if] it be His will! I beseech God give her a wise and an understanding heart. O Lord, bless her and the nobles and ministers of the State. And I beseech you and all the world to hold a charitable opinion of me for my intention to her wards, whose death, I protest, I never meant, nor violence to her person. And I desire all the world to forgive me even as I do freely and from my heart forgive all the world. I never was, I thank God, atheist not believing the Word and Scriptures, neither Papist trusting in my own merits, but hope for my salvation from God by the mercy and merits of my Saviour, Jesus. This faith I was brought up in, and here am now ready to die in, beseeching you all to join your souls with me in prayer, that my soul may be lifted up above all earthly things in my prayers. For now I will give myself to my private prayers, yet for that I beseech you to join with me, I will speak that you may hear.[48]

It was a moving speech, and having unburdened himself Essex removed his ruff and gown, making his way towards the block. One of his chaplains stepped forward, urging him not to fear death, to which he responded that 'having been divers times in places of danger, yet where death was never so present nor certain, he had felt the weakness of flesh, and, therefore, now in this greater conflict desired God to strengthen him'.[49] The Earl knelt before the block, and in the traditional manner the executioner asked for his forgiveness. 'I forgive thee, thou art a minister of justice,' he replied, before beginning his prayers.[50] When he had finished, he asked the executioner what sign was needed from him, and he spread his arms wide out,

his doublet taken off, in a scarlet waistcoat and bowing towards the block, he said, 'With humility and obedience to Thy commandments, in obedience to Thy ordinances to Thy good pleasure, O Lord, I prostrate myself to my deserved punishment.' So laying flat along on the board, his arms stretched out and laying down his head and setting it to the block with these last words in his mouth, 'Lord Jesus, receive my soul,' it was severed by the axe from his corpse at three blows, the first deadly and absolutely depriving sense and motion.[51]

It took three heavy blows of the axe to sever Essex's head from his body – but it was the first one that was fatal.[52] The executioner picked up the detached head, 'in which the eyes remained open and turned towards heaven, and the expression of the face unchanged, and holding it up, cried, "God save the Queen!"'[53] Her favourite was now dead.

One of those present may have relayed the manner in which Essex met his death to his mother, from which Lettice would have gleaned some comfort. She did not dare to ask for her son's body for burial, and following his execution Essex's broken remains were interred in the Chapel of St Peter ad Vincula within the Tower. He was laid to rest besides two others who had lost their lives as a result of imprisonment in the Tower: Philip Howard, Earl of Arundel, and the Duke of Norfolk, whose trial Essex's own father had once witnessed.[54]

Essex's death left his wife widowed for the second time, and his five children fatherless. His two younger sons would both die young, but his eldest, Robert, was forced to live with the knowledge of his father's treason. His grandmother, however, took a keen interest in his welfare, and he in turn was extremely fond of her.

LETTICE HAD LOST her adored son, but her husband Sir Christopher Blount still lived. Overcome, though, with grief over Essex's death, she had been scrupulously distancing herself from Blount. On 24 February, Richard Bancroft, Bishop of London, had written to Cecil, reporting that during Blount's last visit to London, he had brought with him Lettice's 'best jewels', including 'a clock or watch set with diamonds' reportedly worth more than £400 (£40,000).[55] Bancroft was acting on Lettice's behalf, and though he did not know what had become of the jewels, he advised Cecil that if one of her trusted servants were sent to Blount, 'to understand what he had done with them, they might so be got'.[56] Whether this took place or not is uncertain, but it seems improbable that Lettice ever saw her jewels again. Further to this, in what was an attempt to protect herself, in March she claimed that Blount had 'induced her to sell lands worth £5,700 (£574,000) and to part with others to the Earl of Essex, whose favour he courted, so that she has little but what came from her first husband, the Earl of Leicester'.[57] She went further still, asserting that 'These lands were extended for debts to the Queen, but Sir Christopher got a fresh lease and conveyed it away, and got others of her lands into his own hands.'[58] Lettice had not only disassociated herself from her husband, but she had also now abandoned him to his fate.

Blount 'was pressed with his own confessions, and the confession of the Earl of Essex himself, who had accused him as the inciter of him to this crime'.[59] He had yet to stand trial for his treason, and did not do so until 5 March. He was still so weak from his injuries that he had to be carried to Westminster Hall in a chair. He was tried alongside four others: Sir Charles Danvers, Sir John Davis, Sir Gilly Merrick and Henry Cuffe, all of whom had participated in the rebellion. Blount strongly denied that he had wished any harm upon the Queen, although he, Danvers and Davis all admitted that 'it was their design to come to the Queen with so strong a force, that they might not be resisted'.[60] Like his stepson before him, Blount and those he was tried with were all found guilty and sentenced to a traitor's death. However, he had resolved not to submit meekly to his fate, and at some time prior to 18 March he wrote to the Lord Admiral and Cecil:

> *If by the discovery of my former life you have found that the natural heart of this distressed carcass hath endeavoured out of his own motions to the preservation of my prince and country, and that whatsoever hath been rebellious in the same hath grown out of an extreme rot, with the happy taking away whereof all influence of disobedient humours are from my spirits removed, my confident hope is that your Honours will not only show the reports of my unspeakable sorrows, but will be yourselves affectionate petitioners to beg me out of the thralldom of Justice. I beg not the continuance of my life for my own benefit, but that her Majesty and you her noble Councillors will advise her how the same may, when her service requireth, be issued. I pray the Lord Admiral to beg me of the Queen's Majesty for one of*

his assured and trusty men of war, and you, hopeful Mr Secretary, for
a watchful and faithful falconer. Friends I have many, but desire not
other solicitors than yourselves.[61]

He was desperate to live, and his plea did not end there. Another letter
followed in a similar vein:

That I have lived thus long showeth the virtuous performance of your
noble promises, and this God hath wrought by your means that her
Majesty hath been pleased to turn the face of death from me, I beseech
you, even as you have begun, continue to move her to mercy, whereof
the more she bestoweth, the more in true glory and love of her people
she increaseth. What my former carriage hath been is sufficiently
made known to your nobleness; of what I might be is only in God's
hand and yours to assist her Majesty to conceive. But in this you
may be confident, that by taking my life her Majesty little increaseth
her coffers or addeth contentment to those that shall behold how
sorrowful I die for the offence I have made to her Highness in this my
last fault, that ever heretofore was so much hers, and ever hereafter
should have been.[62]

Perhaps he also begged his wife to intercede, but if he did then no trace of
it has survived, and she made no such attempt. Like Essex, Blount would
have to die.

Blount was not granted the luxury of a private execution in the same
manner as Essex. On the morning of 18 March, Blount and Sir Charles
Danvers were led out to Tower Hill, where three days earlier a scaffold had
been erected by torchlight.[63] As they were of noble descent, their sentence
had been commuted to beheading, but the three men condemned
alongside them had been executed as traitors at Tyburn five days earlier.[64]
Having watched his colleague die first, as Blount mounted the scaffold
he made a long speech in which he professed that he died a true Catholic,

and took the opportunity to address one of the charges brought against him by his stepson:

> *Although the time now require to lay all other matters aside, and to crave mercy of God for my sins: yet seeing I am accused to have incited the Earl of Essex to this great crime, I will speak the truth as I desire the salutation of my soul. Above three years agone it is that I first perceived the Earl's mind discontented, and inflamed with ambition.*[65]

If she heard of her husband's final speech, Lettice would doubtless have risen to her son's defence. Despite his words, Blount insisted that neither he nor Essex ever 'intended to do violence to her Majesty's person'.[66] Shockingly, he did admit that 'if fortune had not failed our enterprises, I know not whether the matter could have been accomplished without blood drawn from herself'.[67] He begged forgiveness of Sir Walter Ralegh, who was present 'for wrong done you, and for my particular ill intent towards you'.[68] Ralegh willingly gave it. He made no mention of his wife – perhaps he too had given up on their marriage – but he did refer to the Queen. Thanking her for the forgiveness he had been told she had granted him, he continued to beseech God to forgive him 'and forgive me my wicked thoughts, my licentious life, and this right arm of mine, which (I fear me) hath drawn blood in this last action'.[69] His final thoughts conveyed, Blount 'subjected his neck to the stroke of the executioner with a mind undaunted', dying 'very manfully and resolutely'.[70] Like Essex, Blount's remains were interred in the Chapel of St Peter ad Vincula.

The events of February 1601 had been disastrous for Lettice: she had lost her beloved son, her husband, and had also faced the prospect of losing her eldest daughter, Penelope. With the deaths of Essex and Blount 'was the rebellion pacified, and peace restored', but Lettice's family had been completely shattered.[71] Once again she was forced to pick up the broken pieces of her life, and for the first time, she would do so alone.

CHAPTER 21

Mildly Like a Lamb

A MOOD OF SOMBRE despair lingered around the corridors of Richmond Palace in March 1603. The Queen had fallen gravely ill, and it was obvious that she would not recover. At the beginning of the month it had been reported that 'All are in a dump at court; some fear present danger, others doubt she will not continue past the month of May, but generally all are of opinion that she cannot overpass another winter.'[1] Time was not on Elizabeth's side, and the forty-five-year reign of the Virgin Queen was drawing to a close: she was sixty-nine years old. The Queen herself, though, refused to give in to death. Rejecting all food and drink, she also refused to go to bed, knowing that once she was there she would never again leave it. Defiantly, she lay on the floor of her chamber on a pile of cushions, barely speaking to those who tried to rouse her. Lettice's cousin, Robert Carey, a constant presence at court, remembered that 'She remained upon her cushions four days and nights at the least. All about her could not persuade her either to take any sustenance or go to bed.'[2] Elizabeth had sunk into a deep depression, for the previous month her close friend the Countess of Nottingham – Lettice's cousin – had died.[3] Everyone knew that 'The Queen loved the Countess well, and hath much lamented her death, remaining ever since in a deep melancholy that she must die herself, and complaineth much of many infirmities wherewith she seemeth suddenly to be overtaken.'[4] She also knew all too well that all eyes were now turned towards her successor.

As early as 1598, Lettice's son Essex had been writing to the man that most believed would take Elizabeth's place: James VI of Scotland, the only son of Mary, Queen of Scots. He was not alone, and others at court had also been cultivating the Scottish King's favour. Following the disaster that had engulfed Lettice and her kin following Essex's rebellion, the family had been left without a male figurehead and protector – a role that neither of Lettice's sons-in-law, Lord Rich and the Earl of Northumberland, were prepared to assume. As such, Lettice and her daughters – Penelope, who had forfeited the Queen's favour, and Dorothy – had prudently adopted quiet lives. It was left to other members of the family, chiefly Lettice's Carey cousins, to ingratiate and align themselves with the new dynasty that it was believed would soon be in power.

Everyone at court, however, was neglecting one crucial point: Elizabeth had not officially named him as her successor. For many years she had steadfastly refused to confer this honour upon anyone, and even now in her final illness she would not be moved, fearing lest those around her should abandon her. Neither was James VI the only candidate for the English throne, for Arbella Stuart, granddaughter of Bess of Hardwick, also had a claim. It was, nevertheless, James's that was generally believed to be the strongest, and most people were of the opinion that he would succeed smoothly.

Having finally been coerced into bed, as her closing hours drew in on 23 March, the Queen at last gave an indication of her heir. Robert Carey recalled that 'by putting her hand to her head, when the King of Scots was named to succeed her, they all knew he was the man she desired should reign after her'.[5] She was failing fast, and between two and three o'clock the following morning, Elizabeth I died 'mildly like a lamb, easily like a ripe apple from a tree'. She had remained unmarried and childless until the end, with the result that her death signalled the demise of the Tudor dynasty: Henry VIII's legitimate direct line was now extinct.

Not only did Elizabeth's death mark the end of a significant era in English history, but with her also died more than two decades of rivalry with Lettice. Elizabeth had been in Lettice's life since the very beginning, and had always had some hand in how the events of her life were played out. Until the end, the two kinswomen had never been reconciled; their former closeness had disappeared following Lettice's wedding, and the damage had proved irreparable. It seems unlikely that Elizabeth felt any remorse about this as her end approached, and Lettice's own feelings at her passing can only have been of relief and hope for the future. Theirs was a rivalry that Lettice, rather than Elizabeth, had survived. For both herself and her family the Queen's death signified the lifting of the dark cloud that had hung over them all in recent years. It was now the beginning of a brand new and exciting chapter: it was one that Lettice was eager to begin.

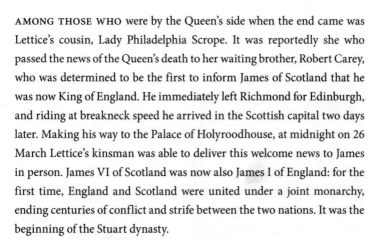

AMONG THOSE WHO were by the Queen's side when the end came was Lettice's cousin, Lady Philadelphia Scrope. It was reportedly she who passed the news of the Queen's death to her waiting brother, Robert Carey, who was determined to be the first to inform James of Scotland that he was now King of England. He immediately left Richmond for Edinburgh, and riding at breakneck speed he arrived in the Scottish capital two days later. Making his way to the Palace of Holyroodhouse, at midnight on 26 March Lettice's kinsman was able to deliver this welcome news to James in person. James VI of Scotland was now also James I of England: for the first time, England and Scotland were united under a joint monarchy, ending centuries of conflict and strife between the two nations. It was the beginning of the Stuart dynasty.

For James, as the son of another of Elizabeth's rivals, Mary, Queen of Scots, his succession was not just a personal triumph but one also for former supporters of his mother. When the King received the news he turned to Carey, saying, 'I know you have lost a near kinsman and a loving mistress but take my hand, I will be as good a master to you.'[6] He was true to his word, and not just to Carey.

ON 28 APRIL, Elizabeth I was given an elaborate state funeral at Westminster Abbey. The role of chief mourner that was often assigned to a family member was instead given to the Marchioness of Northampton, rather than to Lettice or any of her kin.[7] The Queen was laid to rest in the same tomb as her half-sister, Mary, which was also close to the grave of Lettice's mother. A magnificent monument, commissioned on the orders of Elizabeth's successor, was erected and still survives as a lasting testament to this celebrated Tudor queen.

Meanwhile, the new King of England and his family were making their way towards London. James I was a mature man of almost thirty-seven years, who had become King of Scotland just a year after his birth following the forced abdication of his mother. Though his mother had been unashamedly Catholic, to the disappointment of her supporters James was a devoted Protestant. He therefore had no intention of restoring the Catholicism that his mother would have instilled had she succeeded to the English throne, and instead was intent upon continuing with Elizabeth's religious policies. He was a highly intelligent man, but both his appearance and his habits drew comment from his contemporaries. He was of medium height, but in childhood he had suffered from rickets that made his steps uneven. It was also noted that he slobbered when he drank, and that he rarely washed. Even so, James's popularity was bolstered by the fact that he had already done two things that Elizabeth had failed to achieve: he was married, his wife being Anne of Denmark, and the couple had three surviving children.[8] More crucially, two of these children were boys: the affable and charming Prince Henry, and the awkward and gawky Prince Charles, who suffered from several physical deformities, but had survived against all odds. He was a weak child whose development was slow; he suffered from rickets and speech problems, and was three years old before he could walk. His problems with speech would continue for the rest of his life, and he spoke with a stammer.

Though Lettice herself remained at Drayton Bassett, her family were heavily involved in James's smooth succession. Many of her siblings were still alive, and less than two months after his accession, her brother William was created Baron Knollys of Greys as a token of thanks for his support. The following August the King and Queen would do him the great honour of visiting him at Lettice's childhood home of Greys Court, where they stayed for a night before travelling to Windsor.[9] For Penelope, meanwhile, the arrival of a new monarch signalled a period of rehabilitation, and the new King favoured her. This became immediately apparent when she was sent north, there to accompany Queen Anne south from the Scottish border. The new Queen took an instant liking to Penelope, whom she appointed a member of her household, and she quickly became a favourite. With the onset of James's reign, Penelope once more became the court darling, and regularly participated in the masques and entertainments that so delighted Queen Anne. Notable among them was Ben Jonson's *Masque of Blackness*, performed at court on Twelfth Night in 1605, in which Penelope played the part of Ocyte. Her disgrace with Queen Elizabeth was all but forgotten. Her lover Lord Mountjoy, who had been in Ireland since the fall of the Earl of Essex, was also held in high esteem. Returning to England soon after James's accession, he was reunited with Penelope and their children. On 21 July, Mountjoy was created Earl of Devonshire as a reward for his services.[10] Queen Anne was also fond of Lettice's daughter Dorothy, who was honoured when she was asked to stand as godmother to the King and Queen's daughter, Princess Mary, following her birth on 8 April 1605.[11] The Devereux family were very much back in the game.

James's court was vastly different from Elizabeth's. While the latter had been full of merriment presided over by a queen who loved to be seen and adored, James shied away from such attention. Never fond of showiness or display, he instead preferred outdoor pursuits, and was particularly enthusiastic about hunting. It was therefore his consort, Anne, and his heir, the popular and cultured Prince Henry, who largely embraced the visual aspects of court life and entertainment in James's stead. Aside from a host of favourites, it was Essex's former enemy, Robert Cecil, who established himself firmly by James's side in politics. The King was heavily reliant on him, and it was Cecil who would dominate the political arena until his death in 1612.[12]

LETTICE WAS DELIGHTED by the change in her family's fortune that James I's accession brought, and she was grateful that his magnanimity also extended to her. James bore her none of the ill will so frequently demonstrated by his predecessor, and in a gracious move, he generously cancelled out all of the debts that had been owed to the Crown since Leicester's death in 1588. Suddenly, all of the financial worries that had burdened Lettice for the last fifteen years vanished in an instant. It appeared that life was about to become prosperous, but it was not long before, once again, all that Lettice had striven for came under threat.

IN 1603, FIFTEEN years had passed since Leicester's death. Although Lettice had nothing to do with her husband's illegitimate son, Robin Sheffield, he still lingered in the background. Upon the accession of King James he decided that the time had now come to move into the foreground. Back in 1588, on the same day that the Earl of Leicester died, Lady Douglas Sheffield and her husband returned from the French court, where Sir Edward Stafford had been serving as ambassador. She once again resumed her post at court, and began to build a relationship with her son, Robin Sheffield. Leicester's 'base son' was fourteen at the time of his father's death, and as he grew, he too began to spend time at court. He was an intelligent man, and like his father had a keen interest in navigation. As such, he completed both a voyage to the West Indies and a disastrous circumnavigation – only one man returned alive, and all of the ships were lost.[13] He had not forgotten whose son he was, and he was eager that those around him ought to remember it, too. In his will Leicester had left him well provided for – something that grated on Lettice, who had particularly resented Robin's ownership of Kenilworth. Robin in turn was no fonder of Lettice, and shortly after Queen Elizabeth's death he decided to prove that his parents had in fact been married, thus rendering him Leicester's only legitimate male heir. His assertion was an attempt to lay claim to all of the titles and lands of his late father; if he were successful it would prove that Lettice's second husband had been a bigamist, rendering her marriage null and void.

Little wonder, then, that when word reached Lettice of Robin Sheffield's actions, she was quick to respond. Though she was by now sixty years old, she was determined to fight her corner with all the spirit she had possessed in her youth – unsurprisingly, for there was much at stake. On 10 February 1604, Lettice filed a bill in the Star Chamber against her second husband's 'base son', confidently asserting that his claim to be legitimate was false. It had been many years since she had been at court, but Lettice still had powerful allies in the King's Chief Minster Robert Cecil and Sir Robert Sidney. More significantly, she also produced fifty-six witnesses who testified that her husband had never considered Robin Sheffield to be his legitimate son.

In what became known as 'the great cause', Robin Sheffield was fixed upon proving her wrong. It was at this time that his mother, Douglas, emerged from the shadows. Initially, she had been reluctant, but now she was determined to support her son, and testified that she and Leicester had indeed been married. This is highly unlikely to have been true, and nobody believed either Douglas or Robin Sheffield's claims. Robin would claim that Lettice had removed crucial papers from the 'evidence house' at Kenilworth that proved the truth of his legitimacy – certainly if such papers had existed, it would have been in Lettice's interests to have done so, but there is equally no evidence that she did. The testimony of his mother was the best that Robin had to offer, but it was not enough to secure a verdict in his favour. The case dragged on for more than a year, but it ultimately fell apart. When delivering judgement in her favour on 4 May 1605, Cecil described Lettice in glowing terms; he praised her for standing by Leicester, though 'she was long disgraced with the Queen'. In reality Lettice had had no choice, for if Robin Sheffield had been successful she stood to lose everything. That was something that she was simply not prepared to let happen.

Robin Sheffield was devastated by the result, and left England for good. In so doing he abandoned his wife and their children, and instead took his mistress Elizabeth Southwell (not the same Elizabeth that bore Essex's illegitimate son) with him. His mother tried to maintain contact with him, but Douglas died in December 1608, and was buried beside her husband Edward Stafford in St Margaret's Church, Westminster. Robin, meanwhile, lived out his days largely in Florence, where he died on 6 September 1649.[14] He never came into what he believed to be his rightful inheritance, and though for Lettice the legal dispute was at an end and she had achieved a favourable result, she was not given time to enjoy her retirement.

IN THE YEARS following the execution of her son, Lettice's energies were largely devoted to her grandchildren. She had always cherished a particular soft spot for Essex's son and namesake, Robert, who stirred fond memories in her of her own son. Theirs was an endearing relationship, and not only did the pair write regular letters, but Robert also visited his grandmother at Drayton Bassett most winters. She was therefore delighted when he too became a recipient of the new King's favour. At James's accession, twelve-year-old Robert carried the King's sword before him when he made his ceremonial entry into London in April, and he was appointed to serve in the household of Prince Henry. Even more gratifying was the fact that James also restored his hereditary title of the earldom of Essex that his father had forfeited following his condemnation. There was now a new Robert Devereux, Earl of Essex.

Young Robert was not Lettice's only grandchild, and in total she came to have nineteen surviving grandchildren, as well as great-grandchildren that were born during her lifetime. She was fond of all of them, and Penelope and her children frequently visited her at Drayton Bassett. Their presence was clearly good for her, and in September 1606 Penelope would write to Robert Cecil that 'My mother, I think, will grow young with their company.'[15] By 1604, Dorothy's marriage to the Earl of Northumberland had also produced four surviving young children – Dorothy, Lucy, Algernon and Henry – and they too spent time with their grandmother during their youths. In 1604, Dorothy's husband was also granted Syon House in fee simple, meaning that he now had permanent tenure of the property. Owning the house that the family had called home for many years gave Northumberland the encouragement he needed to begin making extensive improvements to it, and the royal couple were regular visitors.[16] Sadly, it was all about to go horribly wrong.

JAMES I WAS a Protestant monarch, yet English Catholics had rejoiced at his accession. They were hopeful that his reign would bring the toleration to practise their religion freely that they had been denied during the latter years of the Elizabethan regime. Following the Papal Bull of 1570 that saw Pope Pius V excommunicate the Queen, English Catholics had been treated with increasing severity, and many were heavily fined and imprisoned for their faith. They were therefore disappointed to discover that James's policy was no different, and it was this that led a group of men to conspire to blow up the King and the royal family when Parliament met in 1605. Many of the conspirators, including the leader Robert Catesby, had also once participated in the Essex Rebellion, while Francis Tresham was a distant relation of Lettice's.[17] Through Queen Elizabeth's good graces these men had been pardoned, but now they plotted infinitely worse. In November 1605, the plot was discovered, causing a huge stir with the King and the government. The conspirators were ruthlessly sought out, and after a standoff at Holbeach House in the Midlands, many were killed or injured.[18] For those that survived there was to be no mercy, and in

January 1606 eight men, including Guido Fawkes, were hung, drawn and quartered in London.[19] The Gunpowder Plot would also have disastrous consequences for members of Lettice's own family.

One of the key plotters was Thomas Percy, a relative of Lettice's son-in-law, and Dorothy's husband, Henry Percy, Earl of Northumberland.[20] When it came to light that Thomas had dined with the Earl on the evening of 4 November – the day before the conspirators had planned to blow up Parliament – Northumberland fell under a cloud of suspicion. He strenuously denied any involvement, but despite his protestations he was arrested and sent to the Tower for questioning. To make matters worse, Thomas had been shot during the skirmish at Holbeach.[21] When Northumberland heard of this, he wrote to the Council on 10 November begging them desperately to send a good surgeon to tend to him, 'for none but he can show me clear as the day or dark as the night'.[22]Thomas's injuries were fatal, and to Northumberland's despair his death meant that his kinsman was unable to clear him of conspiracy.

Northumberland's arrest had a great impact on Dorothy and her children, and Lettice would have done her best to support her daughter and grandchildren. Northumberland's separation from his young family was difficult. Although he and Dorothy had had their differences in the past, Dorothy now followed in the footsteps of her mother and her sister and adopted the role of intercessor. She had inherited much of her mother's temperament, and so persistent was she in her petitions to Robert Cecil for her husband's release that he eventually refused to see her. Dorothy had, it seems, gone too far, for Cecil explained to her husband that he 'forebore to return any one harsh word to the contumelious language she used'.[23] Needless to say, Dorothy's appeals were unsuccessful, but fortunately for Northumberland, her behaviour did not affect the conditions in which he was kept. He was housed in the Martin Tower, where his lodgings were comfortable, and his family were allowed to visit him regularly. On 26 June 1606, his case was heard in the Star Chamber, and, unconvinced that he was completely innocent as he claimed, he was deprived of all of his honours. Additionally, he was fined the crippling sum of £30,000 (£3,019,000) and sentenced to life imprisonment in the Tower.[24] It could have been worse, for he had avoided a sentence of death, and the fine was later reduced to £11,000 (£1,107,000): by 1613 the balance had been cleared. His imprisonment, though, was destined to continue, and before long his family had actually moved into the Tower with him.

MATTERS WERE DIFFICULT not only for Lettice's younger daughter, but for her eldest, too. Lettice herself felt helpless, for there was little that she could do to aid them. In the same year that the Gunpowder Plot came to light, after fourteen years of marriage and many years of playing the cuckold, Lord Rich decided that he could tolerate forty-two-year-old Penelope's infidelity no longer. Her brother was dead, and all of the powerful influence he had once been able to wield to Rich's advantage had gone with him. As a consequence, Rich deemed her family to be of no further use to him. He began proceedings to divorce Penelope, and on 14 November their marriage came to an end on the grounds of adultery. Nevertheless, both parties were legally forbidden from remarrying while the other lived – terms to which Penelope paid little heed. She and her lover Charles Blount were still passionately in love, and had resolved to be together. It was a situation with which Lettice could wholeheartedly sympathize.

Ignoring the legal terms of her separation from Lord Rich, on 26 December Penelope and Charles were finally married. The wedding took place at Lettice's former home of Wanstead, where the couple now resided, and was performed by Charles's chaplain, William Laud.[25] It is most probable that Lettice knew of her daughter's nuptials, and she may also have visited them at Wanstead. If she did then the house would have been full of memories for her, not all of them pleasant, for it was here that her son 'the Noble Imp' had died. History appeared to be repeating itself, for the King was maddened when he learned that Penelope and Charles had married. He was set on making divorce laws tighter in an attempt to enforce stricter rules on morality, and told Blount to his face that he had got a 'fair woman with a black soul'.[26] There was little time to dwell further on the matter, however, for just months later tragedy struck. At nine o'clock on the evening of 3 April 1606, Charles died of a respiratory infection at Savoy House on the Strand.[27] On 7 May, he was buried in St Paul's Chapel in Westminster Abbey, although no monument for him was ever erected. The love that he and Penelope had shared had endured many obstacles, and they had fought hard to be together. She was left crushed by his loss, and was forced to contend with a further blow when it became clear that because their marriage was not legally recognized, their children were deemed to be illegitimate. Fiercely protective of her children in the same way that Lettice was, there was no question of Penelope letting the matter lie. Despite her grief, she was forced to undergo a lawsuit that dragged on, and of which she would not live to reap the benefits.

<hr />

FOR AS MUCH as the reign of James I had promised Lettice and her family prosperity, it had also brought her two daughters great heartache. Following the death of her short-lived second husband, Penelope and her children retreated to the familiar countryside that Drayton Bassett provided. Here Lettice was able to spend time with her daughter and her grandchildren, condoling and sharing in their grief. The comforting presence of her mother was just the kind of balm that Penelope needed, and Lettice in turn was more protective of her vulnerable daughter than usual. As the summer months drew to a close and Penelope returned home to Wanstead, neither she nor her mother could have realized that that summer would be the last that they would spend together.

As Lettice continued with her quiet retirement in the countryside, she was kept abreast of affairs by letters from her daughters and grandchildren. She may have been told that, during the following summer of 1607,

Penelope had travelled to London from Wanstead. Soon after her arrival she fell ill, and it quickly became clear that her malady was serious. Reports about her final illness are fragmentary, and there may not even have been time to get a message to Lettice. It came as a heart-breaking shock when she received the news that forty-four-year-old Penelope had died on 7 July at Westminster.[28] The bond shared by mother and daughter ran deeper than most, due in part to the fact that Penelope was also Lettice's first-born child. In the space of just over a year Penelope and Charles's five children had become orphans, and her four surviving children by Lord Rich were now motherless.

Even by contemporary standards, when mortality was much higher than today, the loss that Lettice had been forced to bear was extreme. She had been widowed three times over, and of the six children that she had born – most of whom she had watched grow to maturity, only to have them taken from her just as they entered their prime – just one, Dorothy, now survived. As she mourned the loss of her dearly beloved daughter, Lettice was forced to accept that the world as she had known it was rapidly coming to an end. Time was passing, and so too were those she loved.

CHAPTER 22

The Wars with Thunder, and the Court with Stars

FOLLOWING THE EXECUTION of her third husband, Sir Christopher Blount, Lettice had chosen not to remarry, instead turning her attention to her grandchildren. In her later years she was active in arranging marriages for them, and was eager that they ought to make advantageous matches. She cannot have been pleased, then, when the marriage of her favourite grandson, Robert, third Earl of Essex, culminated in disaster.

On 5 January 1606, just days before his fifteenth birthday, Robert had been married to the beautiful Frances Howard, the daughter of the Earl of Suffolk.[1] Although Lettice was not there to witness her grandson's wedding, she heartily approved of it, for it was a good match for Robert: as a member of the prestigious Howard family, Frances was distantly related to both Lettice and Robert.[2] The impetus for the marriage had little to do with Lettice, for some sources say that it was the bride's mother, the Countess of Suffolk, who was the driving force.[3] Frances herself was only eight months older than her groom, and as such the couple were judged to be too young to live together at this time. It was not until the beginning of 1609, when young Robert returned from a tour of Europe, that the couple began to cohabit. Unfortunately, it was a notoriously unhappy marriage. Although Robert loved his wife and took her to visit his grandmother at Drayton Bassett, his feelings were not reciprocated. Frances later began an affair with Robert Carr, one of the King's favourites, and in 1613 her marriage to Robert was annulled on the grounds that he was impotent. Lettice was naturally sympathetic to her grandson, and it was to her that Robert turned when his marriage culminated in failure. He retreated from court to Lettice's former home of Chartley, now his main Staffordshire residence. From here he made regular visits to his grandmother's house at nearby Drayton Bassett, and the two became close companions. As fate would have it, Robert had had a lucky escape: having remarried to Robert Carr, with whom she had been conducting an affair while married to Robert, Frances later caused a sensation when she admitted to poisoning Carr's friend, Sir Thomas Overbury. Overbury had been greatly opposed to the marriage of his friend to Frances, primarily because it would bring Carr into alliance with the Howards. This caused an estrangement between the two friends, and Carr supported Overbury's imprisonment in the Tower in 1613 for contempt. But Frances greatly resented Overbury's interference in the matter, and sought to destroy him. With the connivance of her friend, Anne Turner, Frances began to send Overbury 'poisoned food and medicine' in the form of tarts and jellies in his Tower quarters. As a result, five months after his imprisonment he died a slow and agonizing death. It was two months later that Frances and Carr were married. It seemed like the perfect crime, but it was one that would return to haunt her.

Soon after Overbury's death, rumours began to circulate that the unfortunate man had been poisoned. The gossip persisted, and subsequent investigations swiftly confirmed that poisoned items had indeed been sent to him while he was in the Tower. All of the evidence pointed in the direction of Frances and her husband, and in 1615, two years after Overbury's death, a state trial was held to determine the truth of the matter.

The trial was sensational, and when the judge asked Frances 'art though guilty of this felony and murder, or not guilty?' she astounded everyone by pleading guilty. All of those involved were found guilty and sentenced to death, including Frances and her husband, the latter of whom was almost certainly guiltless. Frances and Carr were sent to the Tower but, despite admitting her guilt, Frances was spared the death penalty. Her accomplice, Anne Turner, was not so fortunate, and was taken to Tyburn, where she was hanged. Although she survived, Frances was imprisoned in the Tower, where she remained until 1622.[4] Finally, the King pardoned her, and with her husband Carr she retired into a life of obscurity. The Devereux family never had anything more to do with her.

ROBERT HAD INHERITED much of his father's hot-headedness, and in 1611 an argument with Prince Henry drew blood when Robert hit the Prince with a tennis racquet, after the Prince had called him the son of a traitor. His father's treachery was a sore point, but he nevertheless resolved matters with the Prince. After 1614, Robert frequently brought his friend Arthur Wilson to visit his grandmother, who recorded many of the details of their visits. These show that the three often spent their time in recreational pursuits, including hunting, in which Lettice still took great pleasure despite her advancing years. She was nevertheless delighted when Robert eventually married again in 1630, taking as his second wife Elizabeth Paulet. Apart from occasional visits elsewhere, Lettice was now spending her time almost exclusively at Drayton Bassett, where she was living in luxury.

An inventory of Lettice's goods compiled after her death reveals that, despite Blount's plundering of her jewel collection, she still owned a substantial number of pieces. These included two clocks, one of crystal and one in a gilt case, 'seven diamond rings', a 'unicorn's horn in gold' and a 'pomander and pearl chain'.[5] Her wardrobe was also impressive, and she owned at least nine gowns – mostly expensive black – including 'one black plush gown'.[6] There were numerous undergarments and accompaniments, such as the 'furred petticoat, with hares fur', and the 'three kirtles embroidered with gold'.[7] She had always had expensive tastes.

Lettice's bedchamber was furnished with a great tester bed with scarlet curtains, while numerous chairs and a folding table were scattered elsewhere in the room. She would sit under a square canopy, next to which lay a trunk containing an assortment of objects that tell us about her everyday life and interests. There was a brush, an 'hour glass of ebony', two embroidered copies of the New Testament, 'three purses of velvet, and about forty pairs of gloves'.[8] She clearly still spent much of her time engaged in needlework, for there were also 'divers laces, little bodkins, blue pins, silver pins, and a box of divers sorts of ribbons', as well as an assortment of needles, scissors, silk and thread.[9]

When she was at home and without visitors, Lettice did not lack for company. Her sister Katherine still resided with her at Drayton although it is unclear precisely when Katherine took up permanent residence; it was probably some time after the death of her second husband, Sir Philip Boteler, in 1592. The sisters had always been close to one another, and, like Lettice, Katherine had chosen not to remarry when she was widowed for the second time.

ON 3 MARCH 1617, at Drayton Bassett, Lettice hosted the wedding of her granddaughter, Essex's daughter, Frances Devereux, to Sir William Seymour. She may also have had a hand in organizing the match, for the Seymours were a reputable family – although William had already endured a turbulent history. The grandson of Lady Katherine Grey and her husband the Earl of Hertford, on 22 June 1610 William had been clandestinely married to King James's cousin – and potential rival to the throne – Arbella Stuart.[10] Arbella was the lady who in childhood Lettice and Leicester had once considered as a bride for their short-lived son, Lord Denbigh. When the King had discovered Arbella's marriage he had displayed similar fury to that shown by Queen Elizabeth on so many occasions, and the couple had been thrown into separate imprisonment. William had managed to escape and fled into exile abroad, but Arbella was

not so fortunate. She died a prisoner in the Tower in 1615, having never been reconciled with the King.[11] Following her death William was able to return to England, where he was gradually restored to royal favour. He was particularly friendly with Lettice's grandson and his bride's brother, Robert, Earl of Essex, who had played a significant role in arranging the marriage.

Before long Lettice also had the welfare of other of her grandchildren to consider, for in August 1619 she lost her only surviving child, Dorothy. Dorothy's final illness was sudden, falling ill of a fever at Syon. Her husband Northumberland was still imprisoned in the Tower, becoming known as the Wizard Earl due to the scientific experiments in alchemy and astrology he conducted while there, but her younger daughter Lucy was by her side when the end came. Lettice was left heartbroken by the loss of her last surviving child, as were Dorothy's family. Despite his imprisonment, Northumberland greatly mourned his wife and planned an impressive funeral for her. Lettice was not present as Dorothy's body was floated down river on a barge from Syon to Petworth, where she was interred with great pomp in the Percy crypt.[12] It would be another two years before her husband was eventually set at liberty, and during that time much had changed.

BY THE TIME of Dorothy's death, both of her daughters were married and assured of promising futures. Her eldest daughter, Dorothy, was married to Robert Sidney, the great-nephew of Lettice's husband Leicester.[13] This must have been greatly pleasing to Lettice, for Dorothy's husband would later inherit the title of Earl of Leicester, ensuring that she became known as Countess of Leicester in the same manner as her grandmother.[14] Lucy, the younger of Lettice's granddaughters, had been married to James Hay, a widower with two children who was created Earl of Carlisle in 1622. Lucy's father was greatly opposed to this marriage, but his imprisonment in the Tower at the time it took place – 6 November 1617 – prevented him from doing more than voicing his objections.[15]

IN 1622, LETTICE was nearly eighty years old. She had now outlived three husbands and all of her children, much to her great sorrow. At this time it is little wonder that her thoughts had turned to making provisions for the future, and on 15 October she made her will. Despite her age she described herself as being 'in perfect health and memory', although in her letters during this period she often referred to her 'shaky hand'.[16] The will was drawn up in the presence of three people, all of whom were members of her household: Richard Chamberlain, Humphrey Coles and Grace Kettle, and began with a heartfelt declaration: 'first I bequeath my soul to God my Creator assuredly hoping that through the death and passion of Christ Jesus my only Saviour, Redeemer and Intercessor in whom I steadfastly believe that through his bloodshedding all my sins are remitted and washed away.'[17]

At this time her will served no further purpose, for death had yet to claim her. Its next victim was in fact the King, James I, who died at Theobalds – the same house to which Lettice and Leicester had once retreated following the death of Lord Denbigh – on 27 March 1625. James's cultivated son Prince Henry had died unexpectedly from typhoid in 1612, and it was his unlikely son, Charles, who now succeeded him.

During his childhood his charismatic brother, Henry, had overshadowed Charles and, as such, nobody had ever expected him to succeed. He was a great contrast to some of the more imposing monarchs under which Lettice had lived, and his reign would not be a success. Shortly after his father's death, Charles I married the French Catholic Princess, Henrietta Maria, a greatly unpopular match. It seems improbable that Lettice ever became acquainted with the new King and Queen, for there was certainly no longer any place for her at court. Nevertheless, she would doubtless have heard about them from her grandchildren, many of whom were active

329

there. Her granddaughter Lucy, Countess of Carlisle, was particularly favoured, and was a great friend of the Queen's. Lettice described Lucy as her 'noble daughter', but the events of the court no longer concerned her; they were now nothing more than a mere matter of gossip.[18]

She was still in remarkably good health in spite of her advancing years, and was well respected by the local community at Drayton Bassett. Elizabeth Jenkins refers to her becoming 'an active and highly thought-of old lady, good to the poor and a brisk and benevolent grandmother'.[19] This was certainly the way in which she wanted to be remembered, and her epitaph made reference to her charitable dealings, and in her will she left £100 (£9,000) to 'the poor at Warwick'.[20]

THE WORLD AS Lettice had known it was rapidly changing: many of her nineteen grandchildren were now parents themselves, something that can only have served to heighten her awareness of her age. As the 1620s turned to the 1630s, death became a growing consideration, for most of Lettice's friends and acquaintances were now gone. Yet in 1632 the contemporary John Pory had reported that she was still able to walk a mile a day, a testament to her general wellbeing. That same year, however, on 25 May, her brother William, ennobled as Earl of Banbury by Charles I, died. He was taken home to Rotherfield Greys, and buried in the church beneath the monument that he had built in honour of their parents. More tragedy came later that year when her beloved sister Katherine also died and she was closely followed by her sister Anne the following year. Both her brother and her sisters had been younger than Lettice, and it was not long before she too began to feel her age.

TWO YEARS AFTER the death of her brother, Lettice's health had begun to fail fast. In November 1634, she reached the extraordinary age of ninety-one, but it quickly became apparent that it would be the last year she would celebrate. The precise nature of her final illness is unknown, but it was 'upon Christmas Day in the morning', that Lettice closed her eyes on the world for the final time at Drayton Bassett. Bourchier Devereux claimed that several of her family members were by her side at the end, and this is certainly possible. A contemporary recalled that her death 'instantly put a great part of this court and town into mourning', the only recorded remark her death drew.[21] What is undeniable is that she had lived a full life, endured heartache and tragedy of the deepest kind, and experienced highs and lows on an extraordinary scale. Bourchier Devereux summarized in terms that are remarkably accurate: 'Whatever were her faults, she was a warm and affectionate mother and friend; and possessed a courage no danger could daunt, a spirit no misfortune could cast down.'[22] She had outlived all of her siblings save one, Francis, to who she left the sum of £100 (£9,000) in her will.[23] More poignantly perhaps, she was the last of the great Elizabethan survivors: of all of those who had played a role at court, who had shone and made their mark on the pages of English history, it was Lettice who had outlived them all.

Several weeks after Lettice's death, on 17 January 1635, her will was proven. Not only had she considered her family while making her final bequests, but she had also made provision for her servants, giving orders that following her death her household was to be maintained for one month, in order that 'my servants in that time may the better provide for themselves'.[24] Even though she claimed to own very little, her wealth at the time of her death was substantial, totalling more than £6,000 (£535,000).

An inventory of her goods compiled soon afterwards reveals the extent of the luxury that Lettice had become accustomed to living in throughout the course of her long life. Many of her belongings had been in her possession since the time of her marriage to Leicester, and perhaps even prior to it. She had not lived on quite the same scale as Queen Elizabeth once had, but she still had plenty in terms of material wealth. As such, the bequests that she made to 'some few of my friends and special regard to my servants', served to provide more than 'some little memory'.[25] Her first bequest was a touching one for her 'dear Grandchild' and executor, Robert. To him she left 'my great diamond that I usually wear of my thumb, as my best jewel to my worthiest child hoping he will accept of what else I may leave him'.[26] Robert was one of the few to receive a personal bequest, for Lettice continued to relate that 'For the rest of my grandchildren I have nothing worthy to give them, but do heartily pray to God to bless them all and theirs.'[27]

'My body I commit to decent and Christian burial without pomp at the discretion of my executors and to be laid at Warwick by my dear Lord and husband the Earl of Leicester with whom I desire to be entombed.'[28] These were the instructions Lettice had left in her will for the manner of her burial, and two months after her death, in February 1635, her request was granted. The magnificent double tomb shared by the couple still survives, made of alabaster and marble, and mounted with the effigies that show them both resplendent in their coronets.[29] Close by is the tomb of 'the Noble Imp', while Lettice's brother-in-law Ambrose, Earl of Warwick, lies parallel.

Next to Lettice's double tomb the epitaph written by Gervase Clifton, husband of her granddaughter Penelope Rich, can still be seen.[30] This offers the best summary of her life, from one who knew her well. The most poignant lines relate

> *There you may see that face, that hand,*
> *Which once was the fairest in the land.*
> *She that in her younger years,*
> *Matched with two great English peers;*
> *She that did supply the wars*
> *With thunder, and the court with stars.*
> *She that in her youth had been,*
> *Darling to the maiden Queen;*
> *Till she was content to quit*
> *Her favour, for her favourite.*

The last two lines accurately convey the strength of Lettice's feelings for both Elizabeth and Leicester, and the double tomb – still as impressive now as it was at the time of its construction – serves as a tangible reminder of the reason Lettice became Elizabeth's rival. It shows a couple who once outraged the Queen of England – perhaps even broke her heart. As such, there is much truth in the statement that 'Queen Elizabeth hated Lettice Devereux bitterly, and it was all because of Robert Dudley, Earl of Leicester.'[31] It is therefore both poignant and significant that the female figures that adorn either side of the double tomb are said to represent War and Peace.

In Lettice's veins almost certainly ran the royal blood of the Tudors, and she is likely to have been the illegitimate granddaughter of Henry VIII. As such, the woman who feared her as a rival was not only her cousin, but also her aunt. During her lifetime, though, Lettice had loved Leicester dearly, and it is fair to say that he was the true love of her life. So much so that she was prepared to risk losing the Queen's favour in order to join her life with his, but in return he had never been fully hers. She had always been forced to share him. To all outward appearances she predominantly accepted this without complaint, and did not let it affect her marital relationship. There is no doubt that Leicester had loved her in return, but his allegiance to – and love for – Elizabeth inevitably divided his loyalties. As a result, he was always forced to put the Queen's needs before those of his wife. Death had ultimately separated Elizabeth and Leicester, but Lettice was determined that her union would live on in memory. It is therefore she who triumphantly shares both his tomb and his association in death: she, Lettice Knollys, the woman who had won Leicester's heart – the very same that had once belonged to Elizabeth.

EPILOGUE

AT THE TIME of Lettice's death the world as she had known it had long since disappeared. England had evolved into a country that was barely recognizable from the one into which she was born, made all the more apparent by the fact that the succession of James I had united both Scotland and England under one monarchy. Although James had called himself Rex Pacificus (King of Peace), by 1634 England was embroiled in yet another war: the Thirty Years' War which pitted Protestant nations against Catholic. Tastes were becoming more sophisticated, noticeable in the fashions and architecture of the country: both James I and Charles I employed the talented Inigo Jones, who built the Queen's House at Greenwich in the Italian style of Palladio, and the Banqueting House which attached itself to Elizabeth's former Palace of Whitehall. Both James I and Charles I relied heavily on favourites – more so than Elizabeth had ever done. This proved to be disastrous, and Charles's favourite, the Duke of Buckingham (who had also been a favourite of James I's), had been murdered as a result of the influence he wielded over the King.

Although her children and many of her grandchildren had made their mark on the world, few of them made the same impact as Lettice. She had lived through the reigns and witnessed the stories of seven monarchs (including Lady Jane Grey), and though she was now gone, the world continued to turn. Her family and the later generations remained heavily involved in the events of the court and the country, and would continue to be so long after her death.

The personal rule of Charles I descended into chaos, and in 1642 the country broke out in Civil War as King and Parliament vied for control.

Lettice's grandchildren and family found themselves embroiled in the tangled web that was about to ensue. It was a war that did not take family loyalties into consideration, and – in this instance – cousins found themselves on opposing sides.

With the exception of her younger brother Francis, Lettice had outlived all of her siblings. Francis died in 1648, leaving behind him many children that included a daughter, Lettice, who married the prominent Parliamentarian John Hampden in 1640. Lettice's beloved grandson, Robert Devereux, third Earl of Essex, became Captain-General of the Parliamentarian forces, but did not succeed in achieving military glory. Neither did he live to see the end of the war; on 10 September 1646 he died at Essex House after suffering from a stroke. It was later reported that his funeral hearse and effigy had been 'most shamefully handled' and despoiled, probably at the hands of some 'notorious cavaliers'.[1] Despite a second marriage to Elizabeth Paulet, Robert died childless, and his title of Earl of Essex passed to Walter Devereux, a cousin of Robert's grandfather and Lettice's first husband.[2]

Penelope's eldest son, Robert Rich, inherited the title of Earl of Warwick when his father – who had purchased the earldom for £10,000 (£979,000) – died in 1619. He was an adventurer, who travelled to the West Indies before returning to England in time for the Civil War. Like his cousin, Warwick supported Parliament and was on good terms with Oliver Cromwell. Such good terms that his grandson and namesake, Robert Rich, was later married to Cromwell's daughter, Frances. He died on 19 April 1658, the same year as Cromwell.

Warwick's younger brother, Henry, followed in the footsteps of other members of his family by becoming a royal favourite of Charles I. He was created first Earl of Holland, but later became dangerously embroiled in the Civil War and was accused of changing sides. At the beginning of spring 1649 – just a few weeks after the execution of Charles I – Holland was condemned for high treason and sentenced to death. His brother Warwick petitioned for his life, but to no avail. He was executed at New Palace Yard, Westminster, on 9 March.

Like his elder half-brothers, Mountjoy Blount was also successfully raised to the peerage. In 1627 he was created Earl of Newport, and he too fought in the Civil War. Unlike either of his half-brothers or his cousin Essex, Newport was a staunch Royalist, and loyally served Charles I until he was taken prisoner at the beginning of 1646. He survived to witness both the end of the Civil War and the Restoration of the monarchy in 1660, dying on 12 February 1666 in Oxford. He was buried in Christ Church Cathedral in the city.

Of Lettice's two granddaughters by her daughter Dorothy, Lucy was destined to have an interesting career. A great favourite of Queen Henrietta Maria, at the outbreak of the Civil War Lucy tried to associate herself with her male relatives as far as she could. Following the execution of Charles I, though, she became involved in plans that looked to restore the monarchy. The result was that she was briefly imprisoned in the Tower, and although she survived the experience, she died on 5 November 1660, shortly after Charles II's restoration. She was buried at Petworth. Her brother Algernon fought for Parliament during the Civil War, but nevertheless managed to ingratiate himself with Charles II. His final years were spent at Petworth in quiet retirement. It was there that he died on 13 October 1668, and there that he was buried with his two sisters.

THROUGH HER NUMEROUS grandchildren and relatives, Lettice's bloodline continues to this day. Thus her inheritance has proved to be enduring. Her story provides a unique example of a woman who witnessed the highs and lows of the Tudor and early Stuart court, who was once loved and then loathed by Queen Elizabeth, and whose family were involved in some of the most monumental events of the day. They would continue to be so long after Lettice had left the stage, ensuring that though she was no longer present, her posterity and her spirit lived on.

APPENDIX 1

Epitaph to Lettice,
Countess of Leicester

Gervase Clifton's epitaph next to Lettice's tomb in St Mary's Church, Warwick:

Upon the death of the excellent and pious Lady Lettice, Countess of Leicester, who died upon Christmas Day in the morning, 1634

> *Look into this vault and search it well,*
> *Much treasure in it lately fell;*
> *We all are robbed, and all do say*
> *Our wealth was carried this away.*
> *And that the theft might near be found*
> *Tis buried closely under ground:*
> *Yet if you gently stir the mould,*
> *There all our loss you may behold:*
> *There you may see that face, that hand,*
> *Which once was the fairest in the land.*
> *She that in her younger years,*
> *Matched with two great English peers.*
> *She that did supply the wars*
> *With thunder, and the court with stars.*
> *She that in her youth had been,*
> *Darling to the maiden Queen;*
> *Till she was content to quit*
> *Her favour, for her favourite.*

Whose gold thread, when she saw spun,
And the death of her brave son,
Thought it safest to retire
From all care and vain desire,
To a private country cell
Where she spent her days so well,
That to her the better sort
Came as to an Holy Court.
And the poor that lived near
Death nor famine could not fear.
Whilst she lived, she lived thus,
Till that God, displeased with us,
Suffered her at last to fall,
Not from him, but from us all.
And because she took delight
Christ's poor members to invite,
He fully now requites her love,
And sends his angels from above,
That did to Heaven her soul convey
To solemnise his own birth day.

Following in Lettice's Footsteps – Places to Visit

MANY OF THE places that Lettice once knew have long since vanished, including most of the sumptuous royal palaces of Tudor England. Both Leicester House and Wanstead, her main homes during the time of her marriage to the Earl of Leicester, are no longer extant. The buildings that do survive, however, were the scenes of some of the most poignant and significant moments of Lettice's life.

Greys Court, Oxfordshire

It was at Greys Court that Lettice's life began, and where she passed the majority of her childhood. The interior of the house has largely altered since Lettice's day, but she would have recognized much of the exterior and outer fabric. Similarly, the church of St Nicholas in the heart of the nearby village of Rotherfield Greys is now primarily the work of a later era. The most significant reminder of Lettice and her family, though, is the magnificent tomb effigy of her parents, flanked by fifteen of their children. Lettice is clearly distinguishable among them, although whether she ever saw this splendid memorial to her parents is unknown.

Chartley, Staffordshire

The manor house at Chartley where Lettice spent much of her marriage to Walter Devereux no longer survives, but the ruins of the crumbling castle of Chartley can be seen nearby. The church at Stowe, which may have been where at least one of her children were christened, also contains the tomb effigy of Walter Devereux, the grandfather of her first husband.

Kenilworth Castle, Warwickshire

Although the mighty castle of Kenilworth now lies in ruins, enough survives to convey the former glory that would have greeted Lettice and her contemporaries as they enjoyed their hunting parties and summer holidays. More significantly, it is still possible to get a flavour of the grandeur that would have been experienced by Queen Elizabeth and her court as they arrived for the Princely Pleasures in 1575. With this in mind, the spectacular Elizabethan Garden at Kenilworth has since been recreated, while Leicester's Gatehouse can also still be visited. Built in the 1570s, it was intended to provide a grand entrance to the castle before being turned into a private house in the following century. The elaborate alabaster fireplace, proudly displaying Leicester's initials, is housed inside, and once stood in the rooms used by Elizabeth I.

St Mary's Church, Warwick

Lettice's final resting place in the town of Warwick is fittingly marked. In the Beauchamp Chapel within St Mary's can be seen the splendid tomb that she shares with the Earl of Leicester. It is surrounded with eighteenth-century ironwork by Nicholas Paris. Next to it is the flattering epitaph, composed by Gervase Clifton following her death. Also within the beautiful chapel is the poignant monument to Lettice and Leicester's young son, 'the Noble Imp', as well as that of Leicester's brother, Ambrose, Earl of Warwick.

NOTES AND REFERENCES

The following abbreviations are used in the Notes and References:

CSPD   Calendar of State Papers, Domestic Series
CSPF   Calendar of State Papers, Foreign Series
CSPS   Calendar of State Papers, Spanish
CSPV   Calendar of State Papers, Venetian
HMC   Historical Manuscripts Commission
L & P   Letters and Papers of Henry VIII
SP   State Papers
TNA   The National Archives
WCRO   Warwickshire County Records Office

Introduction

1. G.L. Craik, *The Romance of the Peerage, or Curiosities of Family History*, Vol. I (London, 1849), p. 5.
2. R. Lacey, *Robert, Earl of Essex: An Elizabethan Icarus* (London, 1971), p. 15.
3. G.E. Cokayne (ed.), *The Complete Peerage of England, Scotland, Ireland, Great Britain and the United Kingdom*, 12 vols (London, 1910–59), p. 140.
4. L. Johnson, *The Tain of Hamlet* (Cambridge, 2013), pp. 264–5.
5. Charlotte Boyle, the Queen's ancestress, was the wife of William Cavendish, fourth Duke of Devonshire. Charlotte was descended three times from Lettice.

Chapter 1: Hiding Royal Blood

1. The church dates from Norman times, but little of the original structure now remains and the surviving fabric is mostly the work of the Victorian era.
2. According to a note in St Nicholas's Church, there is a suggestion that the final lady may be Dorothy, the first wife of William Knollys. However, it is more likely that it represents one of the Knollys's daughters who died young or was stillborn, and whose name has not survived. Dorothy can, though, be seen on the top of the tomb canopy, next to the kneeling effigy of William. Lettice is represented at the head of her sisters, although her sister Mary was older. This can be explained by the fact that Lettice was married. Mary's life is obscure to us, and she is not known to have married. Francis Knollys's badge was

the elephant – a creature considered to be faithful, wise and pleasing to God. His wife's was the cygnet, believed to be dignified and good company.

3. S. Varlow, 'Sir Francis Knollys's Latin Dictionary: New Evidence for Katherine Carey', *Bulletin of the Institute of Historical Research* (2006), p. 2. Lettice's date of birth is sometimes given as 8 November, but her father's entry makes it clear that her birth took place on the Tuesday after All Hallow's Day, which was 6 November.

4. The dictionary dates from 1551. It is now in a private collection.

5. Varlow, 'Sir Francis Knollys's Latin Dictionary', p. 1.

6. Ibid., p. 2.

7. In later years the name Lettice became more common: Lettice had four nieces, a granddaughter, and a sister-in-law who all shared her name.

8. John Malpas dates Francis's birth to 1515, which is among several dates that have been suggested. See F.J. Malpas, 'Sir Francis Knollys and Family' (Reading Library, 1993) p. 7; Rookes was part of the confiscated property of Sir Richard Empson, who was executed by Henry VIII in 1510.

9. Malpas, 'Sir Francis Knollys', p. 7.

10. The name Peniston is variously spelt, and also appears as Penistone and Pennyston. I have opted to use the spelling that appears most frequently.

11. O. Garnett, *Greys Court* (Rotherham, 2010), p. 25.

12. See Malpas, 'Sir Francis Knollys', p. 7.

13. Nothing more is known of Mary's life, but Jane, the youngest sister, was married to Sir Richard Wingfield in around 1537 or 1538. The Wingfield family resided at Kimbolton Castle in Cambridgeshire. It was at Kimbolton that Katherine of Aragon, Henry VIII's first wife, died on 7 January 1536. Jane and her husband had one son, Thomas.

14. See Malpas, 'Sir Francis Knollys', p. 9.

15. Robert was buried in St Helen's Church, Bishopsgate. His monument was destroyed during the Great Fire of London.

16. The couple would have a son and three daughters.

17. The question of which of the two Boleyn sisters was the elder has been hotly debated. There is, though, good reason to believe that it was Mary who was the eldest.

18. Lacey, *Robert, Earl of Essex*, p. 15.

19. A. Weir, *Mary Boleyn: 'The Great and Infamous Whore'* (London, 2011), p. 92.

20. Weir suggests that this may have been the case, and that Mary may have first caught the King's eye in 1522.

21. Carey continued to receive grants until May 1526. It is highly unlikely, however, that the affair was still going on at this time.

22. Fitzroy died at the age of seventeen on 23 July 1536, and was buried in St Michael's Church, Framlingham.

23. In 1522, long after her affair with the King had come to an end, Bessie was married to Gilbert Tailboys, by who she had three children. She later married Edward Clinton, first Earl of Lincoln, and the couple had three daughters.

24. Anthony Hoskins argues that Henry Carey, as well as Katherine, was the King's child, based on several factors, including the fact that Henry was referred to as 'the King's son' in a 1535 source. See A. Hoskins, 'Mary Boleyn's Carey Children: Offspring of King Henry VIII?' *Genealogists' Magazine*, 25:9 (1997).

25. L & P, XII, Part II (952).

26. Cited in S. Freedman, *Poor Penelope: Lady Penelope Rich, an Elizabethan Woman* (London, 1983), p. 207.

27. Ibid.

28. Ibid.

29. L & P, VI (1111). Anne Boleyn's mother was also called Elizabeth, so the choice of name served as a compliment to both grandmothers.

30. L & P, VI (1112).

31. Stafford was the second son of Sir Humphrey Stafford and Margaret Fogge. His family was distantly related to the Stafford dukes of Buckingham.

32. L & P, VII (1655).

33. Ibid.

34. Ibid.

35. Weir, *Mary Boleyn*, p. 220.

36. Weir offers this theory as a possibility. See *Mary Boleyn*, p. 214.

37. Thomas Newton came from a family of Cheshire origin. He studied at both Oxford and Cambridge.

38. T. Newton, 'An epitaph upon the worthy and honourable lady, the Lady Knowles' (1569).

39. L & P, VIII (609).

40. Katherine died on 7 January 1536 at Kimbolton Castle. Her funeral was conducted on 29 January at Peterborough Abbey.

41. L & P, XII, Part II (889).

42. L & P, XII, Part II (890); L & P, XII, Part II (911).

43. L & P, XIV, Part II (572).

44. W. Knollys, *Papers relating to Mary Queen of Scots* (London, 1872–6), p. 14.

45. J.A. Lawson (ed.), *The Elizabethan New Year's Gift Exchanges 1559–1603* (Oxford, 2013), p. 89.

46. There is some suggestion that Dudley was named after Robert's elder brother, Ambrose, but he is more likely to have been named after Robert, who was high in the Queen's favour.

47. Malpas speculates that the unnamed girl was born at some time in 1557. This is possible, but she could equally have been born in the gaps between other children, chiefly in 1544, 1547, 1551, 1560 or 1561.

48. CSP Scotland, 1547–63, I (811).

49. HMC Ancaster (1893), p. 461. At New Year 1562, the Duchess made Katherine Knollys a gift of 'a pair of sleeves'.

50. Weir, *Mary Boleyn*, p. 148.

51. P. Croft and K. Hearn, '"Only matrimony maketh children to be certain …": Two Elizabethan Pregnancy Portraits', *British Art Journal*, 3:3 (2002), pp. 19–24.

52. This also coincides with a birth date of either March or April 1524.

53. Her final resting place is unknown, but she may have been buried in St Andrew's Church close to Rochford Hall.

54. The Tresham family later gained notoriety during the reign of Elizabeth I for their Catholicism. Sir Thomas's grandson, also called Thomas, built Rushton Triangular Lodge and Lyveden New Bield, two buildings in his native Northamptonshire laden with Catholic symbolism. It was the eldest son of the second Thomas, Francis, who was one of the conspirators in the Gunpowder Plot of 1605.

55. It is unclear exactly how many children Lettice Peniston had with Sir Robert Lee. Malpas says that the couple had a son and three daughters, while other sources suggest that there may have been two sons and two daughters.

56. CSP Scotland, 1547–63, I (811).

57. Newton, 'An epitaph'.

58. Garnett, *Greys Court*, p. 2.

59. Ibid., p. 25. Sir Francis Lovell was a supporter of Richard III. Following the latter's death at Bosworth in 1485, all of his estates were confiscated by Henry VII and redistributed to his supporters.
60. J. Chandler (ed.), *John Leland's Itinerary: Travels in Tudor England* (Dover, 1993), p. 372.
61. Ibid.
62. Greys Court has significantly altered since Lettice's day, and is now largely the work of later centuries. It remained in the Knollys family until 1686, and is now owned by the National Trust, which acquired it in 1969.

Chapter 2: Darling to the Maiden Queen

1. Malpas, 'Sir Francis Knollys', p. 14.
2. W. Camden, *The Historie of the Most Renowned and Victorious Princesse Elizabeth, Late Queene of England* (London, 1630), p. 11.
3. C. Garrett, *The Marian Exiles* (London, 1966), p. 211.
4. Mary's father, James V, had died just six days after her birth. Mary was his only surviving legitimate heir, and her mother, Mary de Guise, assumed her care.
5. Malpas, 'Sir Francis Knollys', p. 16. Ewelme had almshouses and a school that had been established in the fifteenth century by William de la Pole, Duke of Suffolk, and his wife Alice. Alice was the granddaughter of the celebrated poet Geoffrey Chaucer, and her splendid tomb can still be seen in the church at Ewelme today.
6. Elisabeth was the French King's eldest daughter by his wife Catherine de Medici. She would later marry Philip II of Spain and become Queen Consort.
7. During the 1540s, Henry seems to have travelled widely in Europe, and Elizabeth I later employed him on several diplomatic missions.
8. J. Foxe, *Acts and Monuments*, ed. Rev. S. Reed, VI (London, 1838), p. 348.
9. All four boys left Eton in 1563.
10. See the dedication of B. Young, *Diana of de Montemayor* (London, 1598).
11. Add MS 18985.
12. See S. Adams (ed.), *Household Accounts and Disbursement Books of Robert Dudley, Earl of Leicester* (London, 1995), for numerous examples.
13. CSP Scotland, 1563–69, II (811).
14. W.J. Thoms (ed.), *Anecdotes and Traditions, Illustrative of Early English History and Literature*, Camden Society (London, 1839), pp. 70–1.
15. Lawson (ed.), *Gift Exchanges*, pp. 59, 78.
16. On 25 May, Jane and Guildford were married in a splendid ceremony at Durham Place, Northumberland's London residence on the Strand.
17. J.G. Nichols (ed.), *Chronicle of the Grey Friars of London* (London, 1851), p. 80.
18. In an attempt to save his life, Northumberland had converted to Catholicism before his execution. It was to no avail, and he was beheaded on Tower Hill.
19. All three of these men were later burned at the stake: Latimer and Ridley died in Oxford on 16 October 1555, while Cranmer was forced to watch. He himself was also burned in Oxford on 21 March 1556.
20. C. Wriothesley, *A Chronicle of England during the Reigns of the Tudors, from AD 1485 to 1559*, ed. W.D. Hamilton, Camden Society, II (London, 1877), p. 119.
21. Nichols (ed.), *Chronicle of the Grey Friars*, p. 91.
22. CSPV, Mary 1555–1558, VI (884).
23. CSPS, Elizabeth 1568–1579, II, p. 370.

24. Garrett, *The Marian Exiles*, p. 211.
25. Pierre Viret was born into a Catholic family in Switzerland. After attending university in Paris, Viret converted to Protestantism. He later began preaching, in the course of which he travelled to Geneva where he met John Calvin.
26. Garrett, *The Marian Exiles*, p. 211.
27. D. Constable (ed.), *Letters of John Calvin compiled from the original manuscripts and edited with historical notes by Dr Jules Bonnet*, II (Edinburgh, 1857), pp. 421–2.
28. Ibid.
29. J.R. Dasent (ed.), *Acts of the Privy Council of England*, New Series (London, 1890), p. 145.
30. This was the burning of John Rogers, who died at Smithfield.
31. Wriothesley, *Chronicle*, II, p. 133; Nichols (ed.), *Chronicle of the Grey Friars*, p. 97.
32. Camden, *The Historie*, p. 20.
33. As Weir highlights, Stafford had waited nine years following the death of Mary Boleyn before remarrying. Dorothy Stafford was a distant relative of his, and the couple would have three sons and two daughters together. See Weir, *Mary Boleyn*, p. 233.
34. Foxe, *Acts and Monuments*, p. 348.
35. Garrett, *The Marian Exiles*, p. 212.
36. Ibid.
37. Camden, *The Historie*, p. 175.
38. Garrett believes that the eldest son, Henry, is also unlikely to have been one of the five children in exile. See Garrett, *The Marian Exiles*, p. 213.
39. Katherine was married first to Sir Edward Burgh, and then to John Neville, Baron Latimer.
40. CSPV, Mary 1555–1558, VI (884).
41. Ibid.
42. Grindal was a protégé of Ascham's, and died of the plague in 1548. Ascham succeeded him in the role of Elizabeth's tutor, and he already had an excellent reputation for his scholarly abilities.
43. Cited in F. von Raumer, *The Political History of England, During the 16th, 17th and 18th Centuries*, I (London, 1837), p. 141.
44. Cited in A.F. Pollard, *Tudor Tracts 1532–1588* (New York, 1964), p. 334.
45. The beautifully embroidered book still survives, and is now in the Bodleian Library, Oxford.
46. Camden, *The Historie*, p. 6.
47. The precise date of Katherine Parr and Thomas Seymour's marriage is unknown, but it is likely to have been in May 1547.
48. Wriothesley, *Chronicle*, II, p. 103.
49. CSPS, Mary 1553, XI, p. 440.
50. Guildford and the Duke of Suffolk were both executed on Tower Hill, while Jane was beheaded within the relative privacy of the confines of the Tower of London. All three were laid to rest in the Chapel of St Peter ad Vincula within the Tower.
51. Wriothesley, *Chronicle*, II, p. 113.
52. Foxe, *Acts and Monuments*, p. 428.
53. These same rooms had been lavishly redecorated for Anne Boleyn's coronation in 1533, which was the first time she occupied them.
54. CSPS, Mary 1554, XII, p. 13.
55. Wriothesley, *Chronicle*, II, p. 116.
56. Ibid. Woodstock had originally been a royal hunting lodge, but under Henry II it was

transformed into a magnificent royal palace. By the reign of Mary I, however, the palace had fallen into disrepair. Today a single stone marks the site on which it once stood, and can be found in the grounds of Blenheim Palace.

57. Bedingfield had wholeheartedly supported Mary during the 1553 summer coup, and was well rewarded for his loyalty. He was made a Privy Councillor and granted an annual pension of £100 (£20,000). His family home was Oxburgh Hall in Norfolk, where his descendants have lived ever since.

58. CSPV, Mary 1555–1558, VI (884).

59. Ibid.

60. Children were often given the same name as their godparents, and Elizabeth Knollys would later become a favourite of Elizabeth's. She was also the godmother of Henry Carey's eldest son, John.

61. Cited in M.A.E. Wood, *Letters of Royal and Illustrious Ladies*, III (London, 1846), p. 280. Wood incorrectly dates this letter to 1553. Given that Katherine probably did not leave England until early in 1557, this cannot have been the case.

62. Most people were sceptical that the Queen really was pregnant, but Mary convinced herself that it was true.

63. Camden, *The Historie*, p. 8.

Chapter 3: Captive to the Charms of Lettice Knollys

1. CSPV, Mary 1555–1558, VI (884).

2. Camden, *The Historie*, p. 6.

3. J. Nichols, *The Progresses and Public Processions of Queen Elizabeth*, I (London, 1823), p. 36.

4. The occasion was often marked with jousts and tournaments, at which the Queen distributed prizes to the participants.

5. CSPV, Mary 1555–1558, VI (1549).

6. J. Harington, *Nugae Antiquae: Being a Miscellaneous Collection of Original Papers in Prose and Verse: Written in the Reigns of Henry VIII, Queen Mary, Elizabeth, King James, etc*, II (London, 1779), p. 312.

7. J. Strype, *Ecclesiastical Memorials, Relating Chiefly to Religion, and the Reformation of it ... Under King Henry VIII, King Edward VI and Queen Mary I* (Oxford, 1822), p. 10.

8. Camden, *The Historie*, p. 10.

9. CSPV, Mary 1555–1558, VI (884).

10. Ibid.

11. Foxe's work served as an important piece of propaganda for the Elizabethan regime, and one on which they were able to capitalize.

12. E. Duffy, *Fires of Faith: Catholic England under Mary Tudor* (Yales, 2009), p. 82.

13. Garrett, *The Marian Exiles*, p. 212.

14. In a later letter to his wife, Francis asked Katherine to deliver his good wishes to Lady Stafford, who was a favourite at court.

15. This is the date on which Sir Francis Knollys was sworn into the Privy Council.

16. Anthony Hoskins suggests that the title of Hunsdon that Henry Carey was granted by Elizabeth I was significant. He suggests that this title may have referred to the royal residence of Hunsdon that was used as a palace for Henry VIII's children, and that may have been where the Carey children were sent. Although this is a possibility, it is one that is not supported by any contemporary evidence.

17. G.B. Harrison (ed.), *The Letters of Queen Elizabeth* (London, 1935), pp. 82–3.
18. TNA LC 2/4/3, f. 53v.
19. Howard was Anne Boleyn's cousin, and would later marry Henry Carey's daughter, another Katherine Carey.
20. TNA LC 2/4/3, f. 53v.
21. Kate had joined Elizabeth's household by October 1536, possibly through the auspices of Thomas Cromwell. By 1547 she had become Elizabeth's governess, and was incredibly close to her charge.
22. Lawson (ed.), *Gift Exchanges*, p. 108.
23. Ibid., p. 115.
24. Anne was the daughter of Sir Thomas Morgan and Elizabeth Whitney. Her marriage to Henry Carey was a happy one that produced twelve children, but Henry was not a faithful husband. His lovers included a Venetian lady, Emilia Lanier. He also had illegitimate children.
25. Lansdowne MS 3, f. 191v-192.
26. T. Borman, *Elizabeth's Women: The Hidden Story of the Virgin Queen* (London, 2009), p. 197.
27. Mary was certainly alive in 1566, but after that there is no trace of her in contemporary sources.
28. Borman, *Elizabeth's Women*, p. 196.
29. Ibid., p. 191.
30. K. Bundesen, '"No other faction but my own": Dynastic Politics and Elizabeth I's Carey Cousins', unpublished PhD thesis (University of Nottingham, 2008), p. 26.
31. CSPS, Elizabeth 1558–1567, I, p. 21.
32. The couple had two daughters, Lettice and Frances.
33. Lansdowne MS 62, f. 123.
34. E. Jenkins, *Elizabeth and Leicester* (London, 1961), p. 124.
35. Harington, *Nugae Antiquae*, p. 124.
36. See Borman, *Elizabeth's Women*, p. 219.
37. Syon was granted to the Knollyses in May 1560 on the basis of a thirty-one-year lease, while Francis was also appointed Keeper of Syon for life.
38. Knollys, *Papers relating to Mary Queen of Scots*, pp. 65–6.
39. Ibid., p. 67.
40. Ibid., p. 63.
41. Wriothesley, *Chronicle*, II, p. 143; Camden, *The Historie*, p. 57.
42. Camden, *The Historie*, p. 17.
43. Nichols, *Progresses*, I, p. 43.
44. TNA PRO, E 101/429/3, f. 121.
45. Nichols, *Progresses*, I, p. 38.
46. Pollard, *Tudor Tracts 1532–1588* (New York, 1964), p. 367.
47. CSPS, Elizabeth 1558–1567, I, p. 108.
48. Ferdinand and Charles were the sons of the Holy Roman Emperor, Ferdinand I. Eric of Sweden was later deposed in 1568, due to insanity.
49. Camden, *The Historie*, p. 29.
50. C. Haigh (ed.), *Elizabeth I* (London and New York, 1988), p. 20.
51. CSPS, Elizabeth 1558–1567, I, p. 45.
52. CSPV, Elizabeth 1558–1580, VII (659).
53. CSPV, Elizabeth 1558–1580, VII (26).
54. Hastings hailed from Ashby-de-la-Zouch in Leicestershire, and was married to Anne

Stafford. Anne was the daughter of Henry Stafford, Duke of Buckingham, and Katherine Wydeville, the sister of Edward IV's queen. The couple had eight children.

55. W. Bourchier Devereux, *Lives and Letters of the Devereux Earls of Essex*, I (London, 1853), p. 3.

56. Walter's grandfather fought for Henry VIII at the Battle of Flodden in 1513, attended the Field of the Cloth of Gold in 1520, journeyed to Gravelines to meet the Emperor Charles V the same year, and sat in judgement on the Duke of Buckingham at his trial for treason the following year. In such high favour with the King was he that when Henry's daughter, Mary, was sent to Ludlow Castle at the beginning of 1525 to establish her own household, Walter's grandfather was appointed her Steward. Later that year, on 22 August, he was honoured further when he was appointed Chief Justice of South Wales. He was married to Mary Grey, a daughter of Thomas Grey, first Marquess of Dorset (great-grandfather of Lady Jane Grey), and the couple had three sons and a daughter. Mary died on 22 February 1538, and the following year Walter remarried, taking as his second wife the daughter of Robert Garnish, Margaret. Margaret gave birth to a son and a daughter, providing further security for the Devereux line: Edward Devereux would marry Catherine Arden; the couple are ancestors of the present Viscount Hereford. Katherine Devereux married Sir James Baskerville.

57. B.A. Harrison, *The Tower of London Prisoner Book: A Complete Chronology of the persons known to have been detained at their majesties' pleasure, 1100–1941* (Leeds, 2004), p. 180.

58. Bourchier Devereux, *Lives and Letters*, I, p. 7. Richard was the second but eldest surviving son of Walter Devereux by Mary Grey.

59. The evidence for the place of Walter's birth comes in the form of funeral charges that were laid out at the time of his death. It was here stated that his body was returned to 'the castle of Carmarthen, where he was born'. See Devereux Papers, V, f. 22.

60. Cokayne, *Complete Peerage*, V, p. 329.

61. Edmund Tudor died of plague just three months before the birth of his son.

62. Elizabeth later married Sir John Vernon, and their daughter, Elizabeth, later became one of the Queen's ladies. Anne married Sir Henry Clifford.

63. Cokayne says 13 October 1547. See *Complete Peerage*, V, p. 140.

64. The inscription on the tomb reads 'Here lyeth the body of ye right honourable Sir Walter Devereux, of ye King's most noble order of ye garter knight, Viscount Hereford, Lord Ferrers of Chartley, who deceased … and ye body of Lady Mary, his wife, daughter of ye Lord Thomas Marquess Dorset, who deceased ye xxii day of February, A.D. MLXXXVII. Here lyeth also ye body of Lady Margaret, his second wife, daughter of Robert Garnish of Kenton …' Following Walter's death his widow married William Willoughby of Parham. She was buried in Stowe church at her own request on 21 July 1599, so must have died shortly before.

65. Camden, *The Historie*, p. 80.

66. Devereux Papers, III (14).

67. Bourchier Devereux, *Lives and Letters*, I, p. 11.

68. In 1601, long after Walter's death, his portrait was recorded in an inventory of Lettice's household possessions, and prior to that it had been displayed at another of her homes. TNA LR 1/137, f. 80r.

69. Bourchier Devereux dates the marriage to either 1561 or 1562. See *Lives and Letters*, I, p. 8.

70. It is possible, too, that Walter's mother, Dorothy, may have travelled from Lamphey to attend; at New Year 1562, Lady Devereux presented the Queen with 'six handkerchiefs edged with gold', and while this does not provide any clearer information about the date

of Lettice's wedding, it is indicative that her mother-in-law may have been in London in order to participate.

Chapter 4: The Goodliest Male Personage in England

1. Cited in S. Gristwood, *Elizabeth and Leicester* (London, 2007), p. 71.
2. In a letter to Burghley in 1587, Robert mentioned that his birthday was 24 June. It has been suggested that he was born in 1533, but 1532 is a more likely date.
3. Derek Wilson suggests that he may have been born at Halden in Kent. See D. Wilson, *Sweet Robin: A Biography of Robert Dudley, Earl of Leicester 1533–1588* (London, 1981), p. 10.
4. Warwick Castle had undergone a string of owners, including Richard III.
5. Chandler (ed.), *John Leland's Itinerary*, p. 461.
6. One of the ships that accompanied Frobisher's third voyage in 1578 was called the *Bear of Leycester*, in honour of Robert.
7. E. Fenton (ed.), *The Diaries of John Dee* (Charlbury, 1998), p. 335.
8. S. Watkins, *Elizabeth I and her World: In Public and in Private* (London, 1998), p. 168; E. Goldring, *Robert Dudley, Earl of Leicester, and the World of Elizabethan Art: Painting and Patronage at the Court of Elizabeth I* (London, 2014), p. 3.
9. R. Strong, 'Faces of a Favourite: Robert Devereux, 2nd Earl of Essex, and the Uses of Portraiture', *British Art Journal*, 5:2 (2004), pp. 80–90; Goldring, *Robert Dudley, Earl of Leicester*, p. 6.
10. Examples can be found in the National Portrait Gallery, the Victoria and Albert Museum, Parham House and the Wallace Collection, to name but a few.
11. This name was reportedly used in the last words of Thomas Radcliffe, Earl of Sussex, who was Robert Dudley's enemy. Recorded by Robert Naunton, as Sussex was on his deathbed in 1583, he supposedly warned his friends to 'beware of the Gypsy' for 'he will be too hard for you all, you know not the beast so well as I do'. See R. Naunton, *Fragmenta Regalia* (London, 1641), p. 19.
12. Camden, *The Historie*, p. 44.
13. Dudley Papers, XIII, f. 25; Adams (ed.), *Household Accounts*, p. 140.
14. Adams (ed.), *Household Accounts*, p. 85.
15. J. North (ed.), *England's Boy King: The Diary of Edward VI 1547–1553* (Welwyn Garden City, 2005), p. 128.
16. The rebellion was named after its leader, Robert Kett.
17. In 1552, Anne gave birth to a daughter who died. She herself died the same year, and despite two further marriages, Ambrose would never have children.
18. Cited in Goldring, *Robert Dudley, Earl of Leicester*, p. 43.
19. The couple had no children, and following John's death Anne would remarry, taking Sir Edward Unton as her second husband. However, she was later declared to be a lunatic, and was given over to the care of her son, Henry. She died in 1588.
20. For details of the wedding see North (ed.), *England's Boy King*, p. 56.
21. Ibid.
22. Sir Francis Knollys's stepfather, Sir Thomas Tresham, had been among those who the Duke of Northumberland had tried to rally to Jane's cause. As a staunch Catholic, though, Sir Thomas had instead proclaimed Mary queen at Northampton.
23. Robert's eldest brother, John, had already been tried alongside his father on 18 August.
24. J.G. Nichols (ed.), *The Chronicle of Queen Jane and Two Years of Queen Mary*, Camden Society 48 (London, 1850), p. 33.

25. Ibid., p. 35.
26. Ibid.
27. Wriothesley, *Chronicle*, II, pp. 106–7.
28. CSPS, Mary 1553, XI, p. 280.
29. The carving features the bear and ragged staff that the Dudleys adopted as their symbol, surrounded with a floral border that displays acorns for Robert, roses for Ambrose, gillyflowers for Guildford, and honeysuckle for Harry.
30. He was probably buried in the Church of St John the Baptist, Penshurst.
31. Jane Dudley died at Chelsea, either on 15 January (the date of her inquisition post-mortem), or 22 January (the date on her tomb). She is buried at Chelsea Old Church, where her tomb still survives, although badly damaged.
32. Philip's father, the Emperor Charles V, abdicated in favour of his son in January 1556.
33. Robert later recollected witnessing this sad incident. Harry's date of birth is unknown; he was the youngest of the Dudley brothers, and I have estimated that he was probably born in around 1537 judging by the approximate dates of birth of his siblings.
34. It had in fact been a triple wedding, for besides Jane and Guildford and Katherine and Henry, Jane's younger sister Katherine Grey had also been married. Her husband was Henry Herbert, heir of the Earl of Pembroke. However, following the accession of Mary I the marriage was annulled on the grounds of non-consummation.
35. Ascham became Elizabeth's tutor in 1548 following the death of her former tutor, William Grindal. Prior to this he had taught Robert.
36. CSP Foreign, Elizabeth 1562, V (439).
37. Camden, *The Historie*, p. 32.
38. Ibid., p. 20.
39. See Adams (ed.), *Household Accounts*, for numerous examples of this.
40. See the Dudley Papers for examples.
41. See Adams (ed.), *Household Accounts*, for examples.
42. CSPS, Elizabeth 1558–1567, I, p. lx.
43. CSPD, Elizabeth, Addenda, p. 73.
44. This tale emerged in 1587, when a young man appeared at the Spanish court claiming to be the couple's son. His identity has never been established, and he vanished from the records. That there was any truth to his tale is highly unlikely.
45. Lawson (ed.), *Gift Exchanges*, pp. 38, 48.
46. CSPS, Elizabeth 1558–1567, I, p. 38.
47. Ibid., I, p. 133.
48. Ibid., I, p. 112.
49. Ibid., I, p. 117.
50. Cited in Freedman, *Poor Penelope*, p. 12.
51. CSPS, Elizabeth 1558–1567, I, pp. 57–8.
52. Adams (ed.), *Household Accounts*, p. 65.
53. CSPS, Elizabeth 1558–1567, I, p. 140.
54. Ibid., I, p. 175.
55. Cumnor Place was demolished in 1810.
56. CSPS, Elizabeth 1558–1567, I, p. 175.
57. See C. Skidmore, *Death and the Virgin: Elizabeth, Dudley and the Mysterious Fate of Amy Robsart* (London, 2010).
58. Wilson, *Sweet Robin*, p. 126.
59. The origins of the bear and the ragged staff are unclear, but initially they seem to have been used by the Beauchamp family independently. The first Earl of Warwick to use the

two together regularly was Richard Neville, 'the Kingmaker', who was married to Anne Beauchamp.

60. A. Francis Steuart (ed.), *Sir James Melville: Memoirs of His Own Life, 1549–93* (London, 1929), p. 91.

61. Margaret Lennox was the daughter of Henry VIII's elder sister, Margaret, Queen of Scots, and her second husband, Archibald Douglas. She was married to Matthew Stuart, Earl of Lennox, and the couple had two surviving sons, of which Henry was the eldest.

Chapter 5: Flirting with the Viscountess

1. Lansdowne MS 3, 88.

2. Bourchier Devereux, *Lives and Letters*, I, p. 12.

3. The ruins of Chartley Castle are now a Scheduled Monument.

4. J. Leland as cited in T. Harwood, *Erdeswick's Survey of Staffordshire* (London, 1844), p. 56.

5. Chartley Manor House no longer survives, having been accidentally destroyed by fire in 1781. Dr Robert Plot commissioned the engraving for his book, *Natural History of Staffordshire*.

6. Harwood, *Erdeswick's Survey of Staffordshire*, p. 56.

7. This is all that remains of Chartley Manor House, and the structure of the house has entirely vanished.

8. Bourchier Devereux, *Lives and Letters*, I, p. 12.

9. Lawson (ed.), *Gift Exchanges*, p. 93.

10. The part of the gift roll that lists what the Queen gave in return is sadly missing.

11. Bourchier Devereux, *Lives and Letters*, I, p. 59.

12. Ibid., p. 77.

13. Lawson (ed.) *Gift Exchanges*, p. 90.

14. Ibid.

15. Freedman, *Poor Penelope*, p. iv.

16. Bourchier Devereux states that Dorothy's birth took place in 1565, but this cannot have been the case, as Lettice's son was born late that year.

17. CSPS, Elizabeth 1558–1567, I, p. 451.

18. Their eldest daughter, Elizabeth, was born in around 1579, and Lettice was born in approximately 1583. According to Malpas, the family resided at a house in Blackfriars, known as Lygon's Lodging, which was on lease from William More of Loseley. See Malpas, 'Sir Francis Knollys', p. 37.

19. CSPS, Elizabeth 1558–1567, I, p. 465.

20. Charles was also the cousin of Philip II of Spain.

21. Cited in S. Adams, 'The Earl of Leicester and his affinity', in S. Adams, *Leicester and the Court: Essays on Elizabethan Politics* (Manchester, 2002), p. 140.

22. Ibid.

23. Ibid.

24. Ibid.

25. Sir Nicholas Throckmorton had been suspected of complicity in the Wyatt Rebellion, and was sent to the Tower. He was eventually released but fled abroad. He later became Queen Elizabeth's ambassador in France.

26. CSPS, Elizabeth 1558–1567, I, p. 472.

27. Ibid.

28. Ibid.

29. Jenkins, *Elizabeth and Leicester*, p. 125.
30. CSPS, Elizabeth 1558–1567, I, p. 472.
31. Ibid.
32. Jenkins, *Elizabeth and Leicester*, p. 125.
33. Bourchier Devereux, *Lives and Letters*, I, p. 8; Cokayne, *The Complete Peerage*, V, p. 141.
34. Walter's grandfather had been appointed Keeper of Netherwood Park on 27 January 1513.
35. Lacey, *Robert, Earl of Essex*, p. 6.
36. Lacey, however, states that his name was chosen in honour of the first Robert Devereux, who accompanied William of Normandy to England in 1066. See Lacey, *Robert, Earl of Essex*, p. 6.
37. See HMC Bath, V, p. 150.
38. Lacey, *Robert, Earl of Essex*, p. 9.
39. Women who suckled their own babies were thought to be unfashionable.
40. WCRO, MI 229.
41. Sir Philip Sidney was the son of Leicester's sister, Mary, and her husband Sir Henry Sidney.
42. Cecil was created Baron Burghley on 25 February 1571; Bourchier Devereux, *Lives and Letters*, I, p. 166.
43. Lacey, *Robert, Earl of Essex*, p. 20.
44. Ibid., p. 15.
45. Lansdowne MS 24, f. 208.
46. Ibid.
47. See Young's dedication of his translation of *Diana of de Montemayor*, 1598. Young also remembered seeing Penelope 'in a public show at the Middle Temple, where your honourable presence with many noble lords and fair ladies graced and beautified those sports'.
48. HMC Salisbury, III (435).
49. R. Edwards, *A Boke of Very Godly Psalmes and Prayers. Dedicated to the Lady Letice Viscountesse of Hereford* (London, 1570).
50. Ibid.
51. Ibid.
52. Ibid.

Chapter 6: Death with his Dart hath us Bereft

1. The supper room is part of the visitor route at the Palace of Holyroodhouse, and as such can still be visited.
2. To this day mystery surrounds the events of Kirk o'Field, but it is accepted that Darnley and his servant survived the explosion and were killed after.
3. Bothwell was imprisoned in Dragsholm in Zeeland, and died there having gone insane on 14 April 1578. His mummified corpse was on display in Faarevejle church for centuries.
4. George Douglas, the brother of the castle's owner, Sir William Douglas, aided her escape. It was not her first attempt.
5. Knollys, *Papers relating to Mary Queen of Scots*, p. 64.
6. CSP Scotland, 1547–63, I (792).
7. CSP Scotland, 1547–63, I (798).
8. Sir Richard le Scrope, Lord Chancellor of Richard II, had built Bolton. The castle

underwent significant damage during the reign of Henry VIII when the King gave orders for it to be defaced. This was in retribution for Bolton's owner, Baron Scrope, participating in the Pilgrimage of Grace against the King in 1536.

9. Knollys, *Papers relating to Mary Queen of Scots*, p. 14.
10. Ibid.
11. Ibid.
12. Ibid.
13. Ibid., p. 15.
14. Ibid.
15. CSP Scotland, 1547–63, I (772).
16. CSP Scotland, 1547–63, I (786).
17. Knollys, *Papers relating to Mary Queen of Scots*, p. 15.
18. Ibid., p. 17.
19. Ibid., p. 19.
20. Ibid., p. 21.
21. Ibid., pp. 60–1.
22. Ibid., p. 61.
23. Lawson (ed.), *Gift Exchanges*, p. 118.
24. Knollys, *Papers relating to Mary Queen of Scots*, pp. 66–7.
25. CSP Scotland, 1563–69, II (953).
26. CSP Scotland, 1563–69, II (954).
27. Knollys, *Papers relating to Mary Queen of Scots*, p. 64.
28. T. Wright (ed.), *Queen Elizabeth and her Times: A Series of Original Letters, Selected from the Inedited Private Correspondence of the Lord Treasurer Burghley, the Earl of Leicester, the Secretaries Walsingham and Smith, Sir Christopher Hatton, etc*, I (London, 1838), p. 308.
29. Ibid.
30. Ibid., pp. 308–9.
31. CSP Scotland, 1563–69, II (958).
32. Tutbury Castle is now a ruin.
33. CSP Scotland, 1563–69, II (958).
34. CSP Scotland, 1563–69, II (963).
35. CSP Scotland, 1563–69, II (978).
36. HMC Salisbury, I (1314).
37. As would be expected, however, the epitaph stated that Katherine was the daughter of Mary Boleyn and William Carey.
38. Hoskins, 'Mary Boleyn's Carey Children'.
39. Newton, 'An epitaph'.
40. Ibid.
41. Eight casket letters were produced, supposedly written from Mary to the Earl of Bothwell. Moray claimed that they provided proof that the couple had colluded together to murder Darnley. The English accepted them to be genuine.
42. The Percys were a renowned Catholic family; Thomas's father had been executed for his role in the Pilgrimage of Grace, and though he himself had been restored to royal favour, his interests remained intrinsically Catholic. Charles Neville, meanwhile, had always been opposed to Elizabeth's Protestant policies.
43. Thomas Howard, fourth Duke of Norfolk, was Queen Elizabeth's second cousin, and he was also related to Lettice. He was the son of Henry Howard, Earl of Surrey, a first cousin to both Mary and Anne Boleyn.

44. Henry Hastings was the son of Walter's maternal uncle, Francis Hastings, second Earl of Huntingdon.

45. HMC Salisbury, I (1343).

46. Ibid.

47. Leslie, a staunch Catholic, was one of Mary's most steadfast supporters. He worked tirelessly on Mary's behalf, even enduring prison and exile for her cause. He died in Brussels in 1596.

48. S. Haynes (ed.), *Collection of State Papers Relating to Affairs in the Reigns of King Henry VIII, King Edward VI, Queen Mary and Queen Elizabeth, From the Year 1542 to 1570 ... Left by William Cecil, Lord Burghley ... at Hatfield House* (London, 1740), p. 532.

49. There is no evidence that this was in fact the case, but it was a claim that was made by Henry Wotton, a diplomat who later joined Essex's service. However, this was not until 1594, and his account was not published until 1641 so should be treated with caution. See H. Wotton, *A parallel betweene Robert late Earle of Essex, and George late Duke of Buckingham written by Sir Henry Wotton* (London, 1641).

50. Bourchier Devereux refers to him in *Lives and Letters*, I, p. 8.

51. She was reputedly detained in St Mary's Guildhall while in the city.

52. Bourchier Devereux, *Lives and Letters*, I, p. 14.

53. Ibid.

54. Ibid., p. 15.

55. Ibid.

56. Ibid.

57. Ibid.

58. Cokayne (ed.), *The Complete Peerage*, p. 140.

59. Ibid., p. 16.

60. Harrison (ed.), *Letters of Queen Elizabeth*, p. 62.

61. Despite a number of unsuccessful attempts to return to England, Westmorland remained in foreign exile. He died in Flanders in 1601.

62. CSPS, Elizabeth 1568–1579, II, p. 394.

Chapter 7: Faithful, Faultless, Yet Someway Unfortunate, Yet Must Suffer

1. Edward III founded the Order of the Garter in 1348. It is still the highest order of chivalry in the realm.

2. A likeness of Walter wearing his Garter robes can be found in the Heinz Archive at the National Portrait Gallery.

3. Anne was the only child of Henry Bourchier, second Earl of Essex. When her father died, she was unable to inherit the viscounty of Bourchier and the earldom of Essex, and thus both became extinct in the male line. Anne had been married to William Parr, the younger brother of Queen Katherine. It was a notoriously unhappy marriage, and Anne later eloped with her lover, causing a great scandal. Her marriage to Parr was later annulled, and at the end of her life Anne was living at Benington, her estate in Hertfordshire. It was here that she died.

4. Henry Bourchier, second Earl of Essex, was the son of William Bourchier by Anne Wydeville. Anne was the sister of Edward IV's queen, Elizabeth Wydeville. He married twice, but his daughter was the product of his first marriage to Mary Saye. He died on 13 March 1540.

5. Edward Clinton had been married to Henry VIII's former mistress, and mother of his illegitimate son, Bessie Blount. The couple had three daughters, and Clinton subsequently married twice more. He served Queen Elizabeth as ambassador to France, and died on 16 January 1585.

6. SP 86, f. 163–4.

7. Several other portraits of Walter also survive, notably in Ipswich Museum. Interestingly, a photograph of a wood-carving that supposedly represents Walter and Lettice can be found in the Heinz Archive at the National Portrait Gallery, but the location of the original is unknown. A Flemish, seventeenth-century double portrait from the collection of the Viscount Hereford supposedly also shows Walter and Lettice. It does not bear any resemblance to their known portraits, and appears to be a romantic representation – if they are indeed the sitters.

8. Camden, *The Historie*, p. 64.

9. Sir William Fitzwilliam was married to Henry Sidney's sister, Anne.

10. Camden, *The Historie*, p. 64.

11. Ibid.

12. Freedman, *Poor Penelope*, p. 32.

13. Most of the Palace of Whitehall was destroyed by fire in 1698. In its time, though, it was the largest palace in Europe. Fragments of the Palace still survive, notably Inigo Jones's seventeenth-century Banqueting House, Henry VIII's tennis courts and a Tudor undercroft.

14. Bourchier Devereux, *Lives and Letters*, I, p. 30.

15. Ibid.

16. Ibid.

17. Ibid., pp. 30–1.

18. Ibid., p. 31.

19. Ibid.

20. Ibid., p. 31.

21. This was Robert Rich, second Baron Rich.

22. Bourchier Devereux, *Lives and Letters*, I, p. 34.

23. Ibid., p. 34.

24. Ibid.

25. Ibid., p. 37.

26. Ibid., p. 39.

27. Ibid., p. 43.

28. Ibid., pp. 43–4.

29. Ibid., p. 44.

30. Ibid., p. 47.

31. Camden, *The Historie*, p. 65.

32. Ibid., p. 64.

33. Bourchier Devereux, *Lives and Letters*, I, p. 51.

34. Ibid., p. 77.

35. Ibid.

36. Ibid., p. 78.

37. J. Jones, 'The benefit of the auncient bathes of Buckstones vvhich cureth most greeuous sicknesses, neuer before published' (London, 1572).

38. HMC Bath, V, p. 139. Lady Grace Mildmay is of particular interest. Married to Sir Anthony Mildmay in 1567, Grace became known for dispensing medicines free of charge. She saw it as her charitable duty to tend to the sick poor, and also provided remedies for friends. It was Lady Gresham's husband, Thomas, who founded the Royal Exchange in 1565.

39. In 1495, Henry VII granted the manor of Coleshill to Simon Digby, who was the deputy Constable of the Tower of London. Coleshill had been in the hands of the Digby family ever since. George Digby married Abigail Henningham, and together they had several children. Their eldest son, George, died in 1586, making the couple's younger son, Robert, his father's heir.

40. George was the son of John Digby, and became the ward of Sir Francis Knollys in March 1560.

41. Gerald FitzGerald was the son of the Earl of Kildare, and was of Irish origin.

42. There were seven sons and three daughters. During the Civil War, Parliamentarian forces at Geashill Castle besieged Lettice. She was rescued, and retired to Coleshill where she died on 1 December 1658.

43. The Old Hall is now a hotel, and is one of the oldest buildings in Buxton. It was largely rebuilt in 1670.

44. Cited in Malpas, 'Sir Francis Knollys', p. 68. I have been unable to corroborate this story, and neither does Malpas cite his source. It is certainly true, however, that others left their marks, so it is therefore possible that Lettice did the same.

Chapter 8: His Paramour, or his Wife

1. J. Foster (ed.), 'Disbrowe-Dyve', in *Alumni Oxonienses 1500–1714* (Oxford, 1891), p. 429.

2. P. Collinson (ed.), *Letters of Thomas Wood, Puritan, 1566–1577* (London, 1960), p. 14. The affair probably started in around 1571.

3. E. Lodge (ed.), *Illustrations of British History*, III (London, 1838), pp. 17–18.

4. Douglas was born in either 1542 or 1543.

5. William Howard was the half-brother of Elizabeth's maternal grandmother, Elizabeth Boleyn. They were both the children of Thomas Howard, second Duke of Norfolk; Elizabeth, though, was a product of the Duke's first marriage, while William was born of his second marriage.

6. The wedding took place on an unknown date in the autumn.

7. John was the only son and heir of Edmund Sheffield and his wife, Anne.

8. Jenkins, *Elizabeth and Leicester*, p. 186.

9. D.C. Peck (ed.), *Leicester's Commonwealth: The Copy of a Letter Written by a Master of Art of Cambridge (1584) and Related Documents* (London, 1985), p. 82.

10. Ibid., p. 86.

11. Foster (ed.), 'Disbrowe-Dyve', in *Alumni Oxonienses 1500–1714*, p. 429.

12. Camden, *The Historie*, p. 80.

13. Ibid., p. 373.

14. HMC Bath, V, pp. 142–7.

15. S. Adams (ed.), 'The Armada Correspondence in Cotton MSS Otho E VII and E IX', *The Naval Miscellany*, ed. M. Duffy (London, 2003), p. 77.

16. If it were Douglas, as is most likely, then it could have been written at any point after the death of her husband in 1568 and before Leicester's marriage to Lettice in 1578. If it were Lettice, then it must have been written between 1576 and 1578.

17. C. Read, 'A Letter from Robert, Earl of Leicester, to a Lady', *Huntingdon Library Bulletin*, 9 (1936), pp. 15–26.

18. Ibid.

19. A full discussion of the letter can be found in Read, 'A Letter', pp. 15–26.

20. Ibid.

21. Dudley Papers, III, pp. 142–7.
22. Ibid.
23. Ibid.
24. Read, 'A Letter', pp. 15–26.
25. T. Rogers, *Leicester's Ghost*, ed. F.B. Williams (Chicago, 1972), p. 30.
26. PROB 1/1.
27. Camden, *The Historie*, p. 80.
28. J. Rickman, *Love, Lust, and License in Early Modern England: Illicit Sex and the Nobility* (Aldershot, 2008), p. 52.
29. A. Somerset, *Ladies in Waiting: From the Tudors to the Present Day* (London, 1984), p. 85.
30. Bourchier Devereux, *Lives and Letters*, I, p. 56.
31. Ibid., p. 82.
32. Ibid., p. 83.
33. Ibid., p. 88.
34. Ibid., p. 80.
35. Ibid., p. 97.
36. J.S. Brewer and W. Bullen (eds), *Calendar of the Carew Manuscripts preserved in the Archiepiscopal Library at Lambeth, 1515–1603*, II (London, 1867–70), p. 8.
37. Bourchier Devereux, *Lives and Letters*, I, p. 99.
38. Lawson (ed.), *Gift Exchanges*, pp. 172, 178.
39. Ibid., p. 170.
40. Kent History and Library Centre, U1475 E93.
41. See R.M. Warnicke, *Wicked Women of Tudor England: Queens, Aristocrats, Commoners* (New York, 2010), pp. 114–15.
42. Three days of jousts were ordered at the Palace of Whitehall in order to celebrate the couple's nuptials, in which Lettice's brother Henry participated. Her youngest sister Katherine, meanwhile, carried the bride's train.
43. Elizabeth's saddle is still on display at Warwick Castle; Laneham, as cited in Nichols, *Progresses*, I, p. 3.
44. Elizabeth had first visited Leicester at Kenilworth in 1566. She also visited in 1568 and 1572.
45. Kenilworth was the magnificent stronghold of John of Gaunt, who spent lavishly on it in the fourteenth century. Under him Kenilworth became an important residence, and when his son became Henry IV in 1399 the castle became royal property.
46. E. Goldring, 'Portraits of Queen Elizabeth I and the Earl of Leicester for Kenilworth Castle', *Burlington Magazine*, 147:1231 (2005), p. 654.
47. Kenilworth Castle is now a ruin, administered by English Heritage. In the nineteenth century it became the setting for Sir Walter Scott's novel, *Kenilworth*, a romantic interpretation of the story of Leicester, Elizabeth and Amy Robsart. See W. Scott, *Kenilworth, a Romance* (Edinburgh, 1821).
48. Henri would later succeed as Henri III following the death of his brother, Charles IX. He was also later elected as King of Poland and Grand Duke of Lithuania.
49. Anjou was scarred by smallpox when he was eight. He never married.
50. R. Langham, *A Letter*, ed. R.J.P. Kuin (Leiden, 1983), p. 40.
51. E. Goldring, *Robert Dudley, Earl of Leicester*, p. 261.
52. HMC De L'Isle, p. 291.
53. Ibid., pp. 278–98.
54. Ibid., p. 287.
55. Langham, 'A Letter', p. 43.

56. According to Malpas, this was not the first occasion on which the Queen had stayed with Lettice. He relates that in September 1571 Elizabeth visited Lettice and her husband at Marks Hall in Latton, a property that Essex had inherited upon the death of Anne Bourchier. I have been unable to corroborate this claim. See Malpas, 'Sir Francis Knollys', p. 62.

57. Brewer and Bullen (eds), *Calendar of the Carew Manuscripts*, p. 21.

58. Ibid.

59. Harrison (ed.), *The Letters of Queen Elizabeth*, p. 125.

60. John Norris's grandfather had been executed for adultery with Anne Boleyn. John became one of the most famous English soldiers. Francis Drake was knighted in 1581, and gained notoriety during the Spanish Armada.

61. Bourchier Devereux, *Lives and Letters*, I, p. 116.

62. Ibid., p. 120.

63. Ibid., p. 121.

Chapter 9: Great Enmity

1. Camden, *The Historie*, p. 80.

2. Brewer and Bullen (eds), *Calendar of the Carew Manuscripts*, p. 476.

3. Cited in Bourchier Devereux, *Lives and Letters*, I, p. 123.

4. Ibid.

5. Ibid., p. 127.

6. Lawson (ed.), *Gift Exchanges*, pp. 184–5.

7. Cited in Bourchier Devereux, *Lives and Letters*, I, p. 125.

8. Ibid., p. 126.

9. Ibid.

10. Ibid.

11. Ibid., pp. 127–8.

12. Ibid., p. 129.

13. Ibid., p. 130.

14. Ibid.

15. Ibid.

16. HMC De L'Isle, p. 36.

17. CSPS, Elizabeth 1568–1579, II, p. 511.

18. Peck (ed.), *Leicester's Commonwealth*, p. 82.

19. Dorothy was born Dorothy Bray, and was the daughter of Sir Edmund Bray and Jane Halliwell. She had served three of Henry VIII's queens, and had conducted an affair with Katherine Parr's brother. She had been married to Edmund Brydges, second Baron Chandos, by whom she had five children. Edmund died in 1573, and the following year Elizabeth I visited her at her marital home, Sudeley Castle. On an unknown date some time after the death of her first husband, Dorothy was married to William Knollys. She was approximately twenty years his senior.

20. CSPS, Elizabeth 1568–1579, II, p. 511.

21. Ibid.

22. Camden, *The Historie*, p. 80.

23. Ibid.

24. Bourchier Devereux, *Lives and Letters*, I, p. 135.

25. Ibid.

26. Ibid., p. 136.

27. Ibid., p. 137.
28. Ibid.
29. Camden, *The Historie*, p. 80.
30. Kent History and Library Centre, U1475 E93.
31. Ibid.
32. Cited in Bourchier Devereux, *Lives and Letters*, I, p. 138.
33. Ibid.
34. Ibid.
35. Ibid.
36. Devereux Papers, V, f. 20b.
37. Ibid.
38. Ibid.
39. Ibid.
40. HMC Salisbury, II (421).
41. W. Murdin (ed.), *A Collection of State Papers relating to Affairs in the Reign of Queen Elizabeth from the Year 1571 to 1576* (London, 1759), p. 301.
42. Ibid.
43. Ibid.
44. HMC Salisbury, II (421).
45. HMC Salisbury, II (422).
46. Ibid.
47. Cited in Bourchier Devereux, *Lives and Letters*, I, p. 145.
48. Peck (ed.), *Leicester's Commonwealth*, p. 82; Camden, *The Historie*, p. 80.
49. Peck (ed.), *Leicester's Commonwealth*, p. 82.
50. Ibid.
51. Camden, *The Historie*, p. 80.
52. A. Collins (ed.), *Letters and Memorials of State, in the reigns of Queen Mary, Queen Elizabeth, etc … Written and collected by Sir Henry Sidney, etc* (London, 1746), p. 141.
53. Ibid.
54. Ibid., p. 140.
55. Collins (ed.), *Letters and Memorials of State*, p. 140.
56. Camden, *The Historie*, p. 80.
57. Ibid.
58. Collins (ed.), *Letters and Memorials of State*, p. 142.
59. Cited in Goldring, *Robert Dudley, Earl of Leicester*, p. 304.
60. Ibid.
61. Bourchier Devereux, *Lives and Letters*, I, p. 165.
62. Ibid.
63. Ibid., p. 166.
64. Information about George Devereux is patchy, but he certainly came to spend some time with his nephew, by whom he was knighted in Cadiz. He was also later implicated in the Essex Rebellion.
65. See E.J. Jones, 'The death and burial of Walter Devereux, earl of Essex, 1576', *The Carmarthen Antiquary*, I (1941), pp. 186–8.
66. PROB 11/58/438.
67. Lacey, *Robert, Earl of Essex*, p. 13.
68. H.A. Lloyd, 'The Essex Inheritance', *Welsh History Review/Cylchgrawn Hanes Cymru*, 7 (1974–5), p. 31; Devereux Papers, V, 3.
69. PROB 11/58/438, f. 248.

70. Ibid.
71. Ibid.

Chapter 10: Up and Down the Country

1. Collins (ed.), *Letters and Memorials of State*, p. 147.
2. Bourchier Devereux, *Lives and Letters*, I, p. 166.
3. Cecil House was located on the Strand, and had become Burghley's London residence in 1560. It underwent great change over the centuries, and was eventually demolished in 1829. Burghley purchased Theobalds in 1563, and he immediately began a programme of rebuilding. James I was later so fond of the house that he persuaded Burghley's son to exchange it with the Palace of Hatfield. Aside from a few small ruins, nothing now remains of Theobalds.
4. The exact date of Robert Cecil's birth is unknown, but the year may have been 1563.
5. Lady Mildred Cecil was the eldest daughter of Sir Anthony Cooke, who invested heavily in the education of his children. The renowned scholar Roger Ascham later claimed that Mildred's academic abilities were on a par with those of Lady Jane Grey.
6. Lansdowne MS 24, f. 28.
7. Lawson (ed.), *Gift Exchanges*, p. 207.
8. Devereux Papers, V (9).
9. Devereux Papers, V (24).
10. Lansdowne MS 24, f. 26.
11. Ibid.
12. Ibid.
13. Ibid.
14. Ibid.
15. Ibid.
16. Ibid.
17. Malone Society, 'Dramatic Records in the Declared Accounts of the Treasurer of the Chamber 1558–1642', *Collections*, VI (Oxford 1962), p. 13.
18. Ibid., p. 14.
19. Interestingly, Leicester's Men were the first group of players to be awarded a royal patent.
20. Lansdowne MS 24, f. 28.
21. Ibid.
22. Devereux Papers, V (24).
23. PROB 11/58/438.
24. In total the Digbys had three sons and a daughter, but their dates of birth are unclear. At least one of the sons, John, was not born until 1580.
25. Lansdowne MS 24, f. 28.
26. Varlow, *The Lady Penelope*, p. 53.
27. Camden, *The Historie*, p. 80; Peck (ed.), *Leicester's Commonwealth*, p. 76.
28. See SP 12/148, f. 83.
29. Warnicke, *Wicked Women*, p. 118.
30. Peck (ed.), *Leicester's Commonwealth*, p. 76.
31. Some writers have asserted that this marriage took place a year after the execution of Frances's first husband, but an Inquisition Post Mortem makes it clear that this was not the case. The couple were happily married until the time of Frances's death in 1559.

32. Peck (ed.), *Leicester's Commonwealth*, p. 76.

33. Bourchier Devereux, *Lives and Letters*, I, p. 167.

34. John Whitgift was appointed Archbishop of Canterbury in August 1583, in place of Edmund Grindal. He also later became a member of Elizabeth's Privy Council.

35. Bourchier Devereux, *Lives and Letters*, I, p. 168.

36. Devereux Papers, V, f. 34b.

37. In 1551, the two young sons of Katherine Willoughby, Duchess of Suffolk, had contracted the sweating sickness while studying at Cambridge. They fled to Buckden, but tragically both died within an hour of one another.

38. S. Varlow, *The Lady Penelope: The Lost Tale of Love and Politics in the Court of Elizabeth I* (London, 2007), p. 54.

39. *Leicester's Commonwealth* actually implicated that Leicester had caused Lady Lennox to be poisoned. See Peck (ed.), *Leicester's Commonwealth*, p. 86.

40. Like Lettice's family, Bridget had spent time on the Continent during the reign of Mary I. Her marriage to Francis Russell, second Earl of Bedford, was her third, but she did not get along well with her stepchildren. She would later be chief mourner at the funeral of Mary, Queen of Scots.

41. Lawson (ed.), *Gift Exchanges*, p. 227.

42. HMC Rutland, I, p. 26.

43. CSPS, Elizabeth 1558–1567, I, p. 175.

44. King's Manor is now part of the University of York.

45. Devereux Papers, V (55).

46. Sidney was abroad from 1572 to 1575, and spent much of his time in Italy.

47. Peck (ed.), *Leicester's Commonwealth*, p. 105.

48. Bundesen, '"No other faction but my own"', p. 117. Following their marriage, Elizabeth and her husband divided their time between the court, where Elizabeth continued in her service to the Queen, and Guernsey, where Thomas was Governor. Theirs would prove to be a happy marriage that produced three children, Thomas, Anne and Elizabeth. Anne married John St John of Lydiard Tregoze in Wiltshire. She died in 1638 having given birth to thirteen children, and her tomb effigy can still be seen in St Mary's Church, Lydiard Tregoze.

Chapter 11: A Marriage in Secret

1. S.B. MacLean, 'The Politics of Patronage: Dramatic Records in Robert Dudley's Household Books', *Shakespeare Quarterly*, 44:2 (1993), p. 180.

2. Hertford was the son of the fallen Lord Protector, Edward Seymour, and his wife, Anne Stanhope.

3. Following her death, Katherine's husband was eventually restored to favour. It is her eldest son, Edward, that the present Dukes of Somerset are descended from.

4. Mary Grey married the Queen's Serjeant Porter, Thomas Keyes. He was a widower with children, and when the Queen discovered their marriage the couple never saw one another again. She and her husband were both imprisoned, and though Keyes was later released, his health was broken by the conditions of his imprisonment. He died on 3 September 1571. Mary was later rehabilitated, but died aged thirty-three on 20 April 1578.

5. HMC Rutland, I, p. 26.

6. Borman, *Elizabeth's Women*, p. 217.

7. Hatton was a seasoned courtier, and in 1572 he had been made a Gentleman of the Privy Chamber and Captain of the Guard.
8. The Kenilworth Game Book does reveal that Lettice hunted at Kenilworth at some time in 1578, when she killed a buck. Her daughter Penelope and Lady Derby were also present, but the date in 1578 is unrecorded.
9. T. Birch, *Memoirs of the Reign of Queen Elizabeth from the year 1581 till her Death*, I (London, 1754), pp. 2–3.
10. Camden, *The Historie*, p. 80; Peck (ed.), *Leicester's Commonwealth*, p. 76.
11. Camden, *The Historie*, pp. 80–1.
12. Goldring, *Robert Dudley, Earl of Leicester*, pp. 265–6.
13. Adams (ed.), *Household Accounts*, p. 178.
14. Dudley Papers, III (61).
15. Ibid.
16. Ibid.
17. Ibid.
18. Ibid
19. At the time of their marriage, Pembroke had been thirty-nine, and Mary fifteen. Their marriage was his third, his first wife having been Lady Katherine Grey, the younger sister of Lady Jane Grey. That marriage was annulled, and Pembroke then married Lady Katherine Talbot. His marriage to Mary Sidney produced four children, two sons and two daughters. Their sons succeeded their father as the third and fourth Earls of Pembroke.
20. Dudley Papers, III (61).
21. Rickman, *Love, Lust, and License in Early Modern England*, p. 55.
22. Dudley Papers, III (61).
23. Ibid., p. 81.

Chapter 12: One Queen in England

1. Lawson (ed.), *Gift Exchanges*, p. 201.
2. Ibid.
3. Camden, *The Historie*, p. 127.
4. It was almost certainly Simier's proximity to the Duc that allowed him to emerge unscathed from his crime.
5. Sir Francis Walsingham had barely escaped with his life, while it is estimated that around 70,000 Huguenots were killed in the whole of France.
6. CSPS, XI (681).
7. CSPS, Elizabeth 1580–1586, III, p. 2.
8. The bargeman survived the ordeal. The assassin, Thomas Appletree, was caught and sentenced to death. However, he was pardoned on the scaffold through the Queen's good graces.
9. It is certainly plausible that Leicester was responsible; rumours abounded that he had also attempted to poison Simier. There is no conclusive proof, though, that this was the case.
10. Camden, *The Historie*, p. 129.
11. A decade later, the couple's fortune would become even more apparent when Sir Walter Ralegh dared to make a clandestine match with another of the Queen's ladies, Bess Throckmorton. It was a marriage that, as with Katherine Grey and her husband before them, saw the newlyweds cast into the Tower. Bess and Ralegh were both eventually released. However, Ralegh would later find himself returned to the Tower, and was finally executed during the reign of James I.

12. Peck (ed.), *Leicester's Commonwealth*, p. 26.
13. Ibid.
14. This line appears in the epitaph composed by Gervase Clifton, who was married to Lettice's granddaughter, Lady Penelope Rich. It can now be seen next to her tomb in St Mary's Church, Warwick.
15. Ibid.
16. Peck (ed.), *Leicester's Commonwealth*, p. 26.
17. Ibid., p. 128.
18. Harleian MS 6992, f. 57.
19. SP 12/148, ff. 75–85.

Chapter 13: A She-Wolf

1. Jenkins, *Elizabeth and Leicester*, pp. 244–5.
2. Read, 'A Letter', pp. 15–26.
3. Elizabeth visited in 1573, 1576, twice in 1577, 1578, 1579 and 1585. See S. Adams, *Leicester and the Court: Essays on Elizabethan Politics* (Manchester, 2002), p. 327.
4. Sadly, Leicester House no longer survives, for the majority of it was demolished in the late seventeenth century. Later renamed Essex House, Devereux Court now marks the area where it once stood. Similarly, most of the St Clement Danes that Lettice would have been familiar with was destroyed during the Great Fire of London. The current building is the work of Sir Christopher Wren, and dates from 1682.
5. Jenkins, *Elizabeth and Leicester*, p. 204.
6. Nichols, *Progresses*, II, p. 42.
7. Dudley Papers, V, f. 16.
8. Ibid.
9. Ibid.
10. Goldring, *Robert Dudley, Earl of Leicester*, p. 121.
11. In his 1582 will, Leicester made bequests to both of these women.
12. The Queen had granted the lordship and castle of Denbigh, North Wales, to Leicester in 1563. The castle is now in ruins, having been slighted during the Civil War by the Parliamentarian forces. In 1578, Leicester also began building a church in Denbigh, but it was abandoned in 1584 when the project ran out of money. The ruins of St David's Church can still be seen in the town today.
13. Jenkins, *Elizabeth and Leicester*, p. 252.
14. Devereux Papers, V, f. 63b.
15. See A. Feuillerat (ed.), *Complete Works of Sir Philip Sidney* (London, 1912–26).
16. His mother was Elizabeth Baldry.
17. Leez Priory is now a plush wedding location.
18. Rich later became Lord Chancellor under Edward VI, and was a wholly unpleasant character. He also participated in the torture of Anne Askew, who was burned for heresy in 1546. He died in 1567.
19. Lansdowne MS 31, f. 105.
20. Lansdowne MS 885, f. 86.
21. TNA PRO 31, 3/28/417.
22. Dudley Papers, V, 44.
23. Cited in Freedman, *Poor Penelope*, pp. 57–8.
24. Ibid., p. 58.

25. CSPS, Elizabeth 1580–1586, III, p. 451.
26. CSPS, Elizabeth 1580–1586, III, p. 477.
27. Ibid.
28. CSPD, Elizabeth 1581–1590, 161, p. 114.
29. Ibid.
30. Bourchier Devereux, *Lives and Letters*, I, p. 156.
31. Ibid.
32. Perrot had served as Lord Deputy of Ireland, and it was in relation to this that he was arrested and condemned for treason. He was accused of having knowledge and involvement in the O'Rourke rebellion while in Ireland, and of making treasonous remarks about the Queen. Perrot defended himself, but the court that tried him was full of his enemies. Despite the intervention of the Earl of Essex, Perrot remained in the Tower with a death sentence looming over him. It was there that he died in September 1592. Before his death he had begged the Queen to be good to his son and especially to his daughter-in-law.
33. The portrait dates to around 1600, and for some time was thought to represent Lettice. The presence of the parrot, however, clearly identifies the sitter as being Dorothy.
34. Cited in R. Turvey, *The Treason and Trial of Sir John Perrot* (Cardiff, 2005), p. 180.
35. The Fleet Prison was built in 1197, and over the centuries housed some notorious inmates, including the seventeenth-century poet John Donne. Ironically, he was also imprisoned for marital reasons. The Fleet was rebuilt several times, but was finally demolished in 1846.
36. Lansdowne MS 39, f. 171.
37. Carew Castle still survives, although now in ruins. In 1558, it had been granted to Dorothy's father-in-law, Sir John Perrot, who began a programme of modernizing his home.

Chapter 14: My Sorrowful Wife

1. See Adams (ed.), *Household Accounts*.
2. Additionally, the earlier years of 1558–61 also survive.
3. Adams (ed.), *Household Accounts*, p. 2.
4. Ibid., pp. 245, 268.
5. Ibid., p. 313.
6. Baynard's Castle once stood in Blackfriars, but was destroyed during the Great Fire of London. It was at Baynard's that Richard III assumed the title of king in 1483.
7. Adams (ed.), *Household Accounts*, p. 239.
8. Ibid., p. 294. Dampard seems to have been employed to run small errands for Leicester on occasion, and there are several entries in his accounts for rewards paid to him. She would also have had the services of a whole host of servants besides, and at some time a former servant of her father's, Martin Johnson, entered her household, although his occupation is unknown. Johnson is referred to in Sir Francis Knollys's will, when the latter bequeathed him some money. See PROB 11/88/135, f. 122.
9. Dudley Papers, V, f. 16.
10. Ibid.
11. Dudley Papers, V, f. 16.
12. This is a copy of Aristotle's *Works*. The cover features Leicester's initials, and the bear and ragged staff.

13. Goldring, *Robert Dudley, Earl of Leicester*, p. 3.
14. Dudley Papers, V, f. 16.
15. Dudley Papers, IX, f. 33.
16. Add MS 18985.
17. Dudley Papers, VI, f. 35.
18. When The Theatre was dismantled, parts of it were used in the building of William's theatre, The Globe, in Southwark.
19. Spenser is best known for *The Faerie Queene*, which celebrates the Tudor dynasty, and more significantly, Elizabeth I.
20. Spenser dedicated this work to Leicester's nephew, Sir Philip Sidney.
21. Dudley Papers, XI, f. 38.
22. Adams (ed.), *Household Accounts*, pp. 197, 255.
23. Cited in Jenkins, *Elizabeth and Leicester*, p. 281.
24. Dudley Papers, VII, f. 56.
25. M. Margetts, 'Lady Penelope Rich: Hilliard's Lost Miniatures and a Surviving Portrait', *Burlington Magazine*, 130:1027 (1988), p. 759. It is not known exactly when the portrait came to be at Longleat.
26. Dudley Papers, IV (52).
27. Ibid.
28. Dudley Papers, X, f. 41.
29. Elizabeth Knollys's portrait is now in the collection of the National Portrait Gallery.
30. Gower may have gained his introduction to court through the auspices of Sir Thomas Kytson. Gower had painted a pair of portraits of Kytson and his wife in 1573, and following his royal appointment proceeded to paint many members of Elizabeth's court.
31. Hilliard produced several miniatures of Elizabeth, and he also produced her second Great Seal, as well as a design for a third. He was the dominant figure in his field until the arrival of Isaac Oliver in the 1590s, and would continue as Court Limner to James I. See G. Reynolds, *The Sixteenth- and Seventeenth-Century Miniatures in the Collection of Her Majesty the Queen* (London, 1999), p. 65.
32. Margetts, 'Lady Penelope Rich', p. 758.
33. Strong, 'Faces of a Favourite', p. 90.
34. Goldring, *Robert Dudley, Earl of Leicester*, p. 275.
35. HMC Bath, V, p. 222.
36. CSPS, Elizabeth 1580–1586, III, p. 452.
37. The two met while Leicester was at Buxton, taking the medicinal waters for his health. Mary spent many of her years of imprisonment in Derbyshire, under the custodianship of the Earl of Shrewsbury, Bess of Hardwick's fourth husband.
38. Cited in Wilson, *Sweet Robin*, p. 246.
39. Peck (ed.), *Leicester's Commonwealth*, p. 131.
40. Jenkins, *Elizabeth and Leicester*, p. 287.
41. Peck (ed.), *Leicester's Commonwealth*, p. 89.
42. Cited in A. Kendall, *Robert Dudley: Earl of Leicester* (London, 1980), p. 199.
43. H. Nicholas (ed.), *Memoirs of the Life and Times of Sir Christopher Hatton* (London, 1847), p. 381.
44. Ibid., p. 382.
45. Ibid., p. 383.
46. CSPD, Elizabeth 1581–1590, 172, p. 192.
47. Ibid.
48. CSP Scotland, 1584–85, VII, p. 248.

49. Adams (ed.), *Household Accounts*, p. 197. The sex of the child is unknown. Little is known of Richard and Joan's marriage, including the date that they were married. She was the daughter of John Heigham, a Puritan Suffolk gentleman. The couple had six children between 1586 and 1595.

50. A. Chéruel, *Marie Stuart et Catherine de Médicis* (Paris, 1858), p. 341.

51. Wotton, *A parallel*, p. 1.

52. Add MS 32092, f. 48.

53. Ibid.

54. Egerton MS 3052.

55. Birch, *Memoirs*, II, p. 282.

56. Peck (ed.), *Leicester's Commonwealth*, p. 80.

57. F.A. Youngs, *The Proclamations of the Tudor Queens* (Cambridge, 1976), p. 24.

58. Peck (ed.), *Leicester's Commonwealth*, p. 257.

Chapter 15: Our Mistress's Extreme Rage

1. Adams (ed.), *Household Accounts*, pp. 211–12.

2. Ibid., p. 226.

3. Charles V was the nephew of Katherine of Aragon.

4. It is uncertain precisely when or why William acquired his nickname, 'the Silent'. There are several explanations, the most common of which is that during a conversation with the French king, the monarch unwittingly revealed information that William had not known. He responded with silence, not revealing that he had been unaware of what the French king had shared with him.

5. Parma was the son of Ottavio Farnese and Margaret, who was an illegitimate daughter of the Emperor Charles V. She herself had served as Governor of the Netherlands twice, from 1559 to 1567, and again in 1578 to 1582.

6. Adams (ed.), *Household Accounts*, pp. 234, 236.

7. Ibid., p. 245.

8. Ibid., p. 259.

9. Ibid. The Earl of Derby was Henry Stanley, who was married to Lady Margaret Clifford, the cousin of Lady Jane Grey.

10. Adams (ed.), *Household Accounts*, p. 290.

11. HMC De L'Isle, p. 290.

12. Ibid.

13. Ibid., p. 291.

14. Goldring, *Robert Dudley, Earl of Leicester*, p. 258.

15. HMC Salisbury, III (192).

16. Sir Thomas Leigh was the son and namesake of his father, who had been Lord Mayor of London from 1558 to 1559. The former abbey of Stoneleigh had been acquired by him in 1558, and remained the home of the Leigh family until 1590. Interestingly, the Leigh family were related to the novelist Jane Austen, who visited the house in 1806. It made such an impact on her that she used details of the house in several of her novels.

17. CSP Foreign, Elizabeth September 1585–May 1586, p. 8.

18. J. Bruce (ed.), *The Correspondence of Robert Dudley, Earl of Leycester, During his Government of the Low Countries, in the Years 1585 and 1586*, Camden Society, XXVII (London, 1844), p. 5.

19. Ibid., p. 6. Some of Leicester's armour can still be seen in the Royal Armouries.

20. Lacey, *Robert, Earl of Essex*, p. 35.

21. Bourchier Devereux, *Lives and Letters*, I, p. 179.

22. Ibid., p. 173.

23. Bruce (ed.), *Correspondence of Robert Dudley*, p. 9.

24. Ibid.

25. Bourchier Devereux, *Lives and Letters*, I, p. 173.

26. Cited in Freedman, *Poor Penelope*, p. 68.

27. Dudley Papers, VI, p. 42.

28. Bruce (ed.), *Correspondence of Robert Dudley*, p. 12.

29. Camden, *The Historie*, p. 63.

30. The brothers-in-law were Thomas West and Philip Boteler, the husbands of Lettice's sisters Anne and Katherine.

31. Camden, *The Historie*, p. 63.

32. Ibid., p. 64.

33. Bruce (ed.), *Correspondence of Robert Dudley*, pp. 31–2.

34. Cotton MS Galba C IX, f. 128.

35. Bruce (ed.), *Correspondence of Robert Dudley*, pp. 95–6.

36. Ibid., p. 96.

37. Ibid.

38. Ibid., p. 98.

39. Ibid., p. 102.

40. Harrison (ed.), *Letters of Queen Elizabeth*, p. 174.

41. Ibid., pp. 174–5.

42. Ibid.

43. Thomas Dudley later seems to have worked for Leicester's brother, Ambrose. He died in 1593; Bruce (ed.), *Correspondence of Robert Dudley*, p. 112.

44. J. Stow, *The Annales of England* (London, 1592), p. 112.

45. Ibid.

46. Bruce (ed.), *Correspondence of Robert Dudley*, p. 112.

47. Ibid.

48. Ibid.

49. Ibid.

50. Ibid.

51. Harleian MS 287 1.

52. Cotton MS Galba C VIII, f. 46.

53. Ibid.

54. Bruce (ed.), *Correspondence of Robert Dudley*, p. 144.

55. Ibid., p. 151.

56. Ibid.

57. Cotton MS Galba C IX, f. 179.

58. Harrison (ed.), *Letters of Queen Elizabeth*, pp. 178–9.

59. B.L. Beer (ed.), *A Summarie of the Chronicles of England, Diligently Collected, Abridged, And Continued unto this Present Year of Christ, 1604, by John Stow* (Lewiston, 2007), p. 403.

60. Camden, *The Historie*, p. 64.

61. Bruce (ed.), *Correspondence of Robert Dudley*, p. 429.

62. Ibid., p. 417.

63. Cited in Kendall, *Robert Dudley*, p. 217.

64. Ibid.

65. Anthony Babington had been a page in the household of Mary's former custodian, the Earl of Shrewsbury. In time, while travelling abroad he met and came under the influence of many who were eager to effect Mary's release.

66. This was done with the complicity of both the local brewer and a double agent, Gilbert Gifford. Gifford arranged for letters to and from Mary to be smuggled in and out of Chartley in a beer barrel, but unbeknown to Mary and her supporters, the letters were intercepted by Walsingham and his colleagues.

67. Beer (ed.), *A Summarie*, p. 403. The conspirators were executed in two groups, but such was the public outcry at the bloodthirsty and barbaric manner in which the first group were killed, that the Queen gave orders that the second group were to be killed more mercifully. They were to be hanged until they were dead, before the second part of their sentence was carried out.

68. It was at Fotheringhay that the future Richard III had been born in 1452. A single block of stonework is now all that remains of the once-mighty castle.

69. Bruce (ed.), *Correspondence of Robert Dudley*, p. 431.

70. Harrison (ed.), *The Letters of Queen Elizabeth*, p. 181.

Chapter 16: A Continual Fever

1. When the executioner picked up her head it fell to the ground, and he was left holding her wig.

2. Mares (ed.), *The Memoirs of Robert Carey*, p. 7.

3. Beer (ed.), *A Summarie*, p. 403.

4. A monument marking the spot where he fell at Zutphen still survives.

5. CSPD, Elizabeth 1581–90, 188, p. 402.

6. Bourchier Devereux, *Lives and Letters*, I, p. 186.

7. Cited in Fenton (ed.) *The Diaries of John Dee*, p. 342.

8. Bourchier Devereux, *Lives and Letters*, I, p. 187.

9. Ibid.

10. Ibid.

11. Ibid.

12. Ibid.

13. Ibid., p. 188.

14. Ibid.

15. Ibid., p. 189.

16. One example of these rare medals can be seen in the National Portrait Gallery.

17. CSPS, Elizabeth 1587–1603, IV, p. 173.

18. CSPD, Elizabeth 1581–1590, 213, p. 514.

19. Ibid.

20. Ibid.

21. Mare (ed.), *The Memoirs of Robert Carey*, p. 9.

22. Ibid., p. 11.

23. Harley 6798, f. 87.

24. CSPS, Elizabeth 1587–1603, IV, p. 418.

25. Sir Henry Norris had been Henry VIII's Groom of the Stool, and his marriage to Mary Fiennes had produced three surviving children. He had also been an ally of Anne Boleyn, which easily explains why he was a target – almost certainly falsely – in the plot to topple her.

26. Marjory never held an official position at court, but she had known the Queen since the reign of Mary I, and the two had become good friends.

27. CSPD, Elizabeth 1581–1590, 215, p. 538.

28. Ibid. The letter is now in the National Archives. Elizabeth saved many of Leicester's private letters, and about twenty of these now survive. Most of her letters to him were probably destroyed.

29. Dudley Papers, II, 265.

30. Ibid., 273.

31. Ibid.

32. Cornbury Park is now a private estate, but the room in which Leicester is thought to have died still survives.

33. Camden, *The Historie*, p. 145.

34. CSPS, Elizabeth 1587–1603, IV, p. 420.

35. Ibid., pp. 420–1.

36. Ibid., p. 431.

37. Ibid.

38. Ibid.

39. M. Gray, *Hamlet's Secrets Revealed: The Real Shakespeare* (Bloomington, 2001), p. 546.

40. Cited in V.J. Watney, *Cornbury and the Forest of Wychwood* (London, 1910), p. 88.

41. PROB 1/1.

42. Ibid.

43. The Chapel is still largely original aside from the Dudley tombs and some seventeenth-century damage.

44. PROB 1/1.

45. Ibid.

46. Ibid.

47. A. Weir, *Elizabeth the Queen* (London, 1998), p. 398.

48. PROB 1/1.

49. Ibid.

50. Ibid.

51. Chandler (ed.), *John Leland's Itinerary*, p. 462.

52. Warnicke, *Wicked Women*, p. 125.

53. Beer (ed.), *A Summarie*, p. 412.

54. Cited in Watney, *Cornbury and the Forest*, p. 90.

Chapter 17: My Best Friend

1. PROB 1/1.

2. Dudley Papers, IV, 94.

3. Ibid., 33.

4. HMC Salisbury, III (761).

5. Ibid., IV (2).

6. The precise date is uncertain, but the fact that the wedding took place in July is referred to in CSPD, Elizabeth Addenda 1547–1565, p. 23.

7. His mother was a registered recusant in 1577.

8. Many examples of these can still be seen. Baddesley Clinton, Oxburgh Hall and Harvington Hall contain numerous priest holes.

9. William Allen hailed from Lancashire, and was educated at Oxford. He was publicly

opposed to Elizabeth I's Protestant regime, leaving him with no choice but to travel abroad. He took up residence at Louvain in the 1560s.

10. See WCRO, MI 229 collection.

11. While imprisoned in the Bastille in 1585. Morgan's association with Blount is noteworthy, for he was a Catholic gentleman who had been involved in many of the plots to supplant Elizabeth with Mary, Queen of Scots.

12. Freedman, *Poor Penelope*, p. 74.

13. Katherine Willoughby's second marriage was to Richard Bertie, by whom she had two children.

14. Lansdowne MS 62, f. 78r.

15. Craik, *Romance of the Peerage*, p. 149.

16. WCRO, MI 229.

17. Ibid.

18. See WCRO, MI 229 collection for numerous examples.

19. HMC Salisbury, IV (309).

20. Ibid., III (965).

21. Ibid.

22. WCRO, MI 229.

23. Ibid.

24. Ibid.

25. Craik, *Romance of the Peerage*, p. 151.

26. Ibid.

27. In the nineteenth century the Prime Minister Robert Peel owned Drayton. He demolished the old manor house and instead built a brand new house on the site, where Queen Victoria and Prince Albert visited him in 1843. It was later demolished when it ceased to be the home of the Peel family.

28. Penelope also continued to visit Chartley, her childhood home.

29. Add MS 18985.

30. Ibid.

31. Warnicke, *Wicked Women*, p. 127.

32. Cited in Watney, *Cornbury and the Forest*, p. 90.

33. Ibid.

34. Ibid.

35. CSPD, Elizabeth Addenda 1547–1565, p. 23.

36. CSPD, Elizabeth 1591–1594, 246, p. 386.

37. Watney, *Cornbury and the Forest*, p. 90.

38. Ibid.

39. C. Cross, *The Puritan Earl: The Life of Henry Hastings, Third Earl of Huntingdon* (London, 1966), p. 56.

40. Ibid.

41. Camden, *The Historie*, p. 37.

42. PROB 11/75/493.

43. See Jenkins, *Elizabeth and Leicester*, p. 367.

44. His great-grandfather was William Blount. Catherine Leigh was the daughter of Sir Thomas Leigh of St Oswald's, Yorkshire.

45. He also had a brother, William, and a sister, Anne.

46. F.M. Jones, *Mountjoy 1563–1606: The Last Elizabethan Deputy* (Dublin, 1958), p. 21.

47. In total the couple had had five children, one of whom died in infancy.

48. Penelope was baptized on 30 March at St Clement Danes.

49. WCRO, MI 229.
50. Sir Francis Walsingham was buried in Old St Paul's Cathedral, but his monument was sadly destroyed during the Great Fire of London.
51. HMC Salisbury, IV (20).
52. Birch, *Memoirs*, II, p. 75.
53. Her mother was Ursula St Barbe. Walsingham House no longer survives.
54. Dr Lancelot Andrew performed this service.
55. HMC Salisbury, IV (31).
56. Elizabeth was the daughter of Sir Thomas Southwell by his third wife, Nazaret Newton. She had arrived at court in either 1588 or 1589, and later married Sir Barrington Molyns.
57. Thomas's sister, Anne, also courted scandal by becoming embroiled in an affair with Edward de Vere, Earl of Oxford. The relationship provoked both anger and violence, and Thomas himself challenged the Earl to a duel.
58. CSPD, Elizabeth 1595–1597, 253, p. 74.
59. PROB 11/167/42. Walter Devereux became very close to his half-brother, Robert, third Earl of Essex. Lettice attempted to make arrangements for Walter's marriage, but there is no evidence that this ever took place. He died on 26 July 1641 at Essex House, and was buried at St Clement Danes.
60. Rickman, *Love, Lust, and License*, p. 53.
61. Mares (ed.), *The Memoirs of Robert Carey*, p. 14.
62. Bourchier Devereux, *Lives and Letters*, I, p. 233.
63. Murdin (ed.), *State Papers*, p. 646.
64. Maulette went on to become the tutor of James I's daughter, Elizabeth of Bohemia.
65. G. Maulette, *Deuoreux Vertues teares for the losse of the most christian King Henry, third of that name, King of Fraunce; and the vntimely death, of the most noble & heroicall gentleman, VValter Deuoreux, who was slaine before Roan in Fraunce. First written in French, by the most excellent and learned gentlewoman, Madam Geneuuefue, Petau Maulette*, trans. G. Markham (London, 1597).
66. Tragically, the baby died the month after his birth.
67. When Sidney died, Margaret married for a third time, taking Thomas Hoby as her third husband.
68. Margaret died on 4 September 1633, and is buried in the church at Hackness, near Scarborough.
69. WCRO, MI 229.
70. Ibid.
71. WCRO, MI 229.

Chapter 18: Disgraced Persons

1. CSPD, Elizabeth 1591–1594, 246, p. 326.
2. The circumstances of his death are certainly mysterious, and poison does seem to have been a serious possibility.
3. Freedman, *Poor Penelope*, p. 94.
4. The couple had four children together. Penelope would later marry Sir Robert Naunton, by whom she had a daughter named Penelope. Meanwhile, Thomas's wife later remarried the renowned astronomer Sir William Lower.
5. Though the verdict of suicide was upheld, many believed that the Earl had been murdered.

Some suspected Sir Christopher Hatton, and Walter Ralegh later referred to his guilt as though it were well known.

6. Petworth House is now largely the work of the seventeenth century, and is administered by the National Trust. The Percy vault still survives in nearby St Mary's Church. During their ownership, Syon became known as the White House.

7. HMC Bath, V, p. 261.

8. L.R. Betcherman, *Court Lady and Country Wife: Royal Privilege and Civil War, Two Noble Sisters in Seventeenth-Century England* (Chichester, 2005), p. 4.

9. HMC Salisbury, X (179).

10. He had been born on 6 October 1573 at Cowdray House in Sussex. He was the son of Henry Wriothesley, second Earl of Southampton, and Mary Browne.

11. Freedman, *Poor Penelope*, p. 101.

12. Craik, *Romance of the Peerage*, p. 149. This was dated 10 September 1595.

13. See WCRO, MI 229 collection.

14. Ibid.

15. HMC De L'Isle, p. 163.

16. Ibid.

17. Ibid.

18. Ibid.

19. WCRO, MI 229.

20. Ibid.

21. CSPV, Elizabeth 1592–1603, IX (463).

22. Ibid., IX (488).

23. PROB 11/88/135.

24. Ibid.

25. Ibid.

26. He died at Somerset House on the Strand. As his end approached, the Queen offered to create him Earl of Wiltshire. However, he declined, quipping, 'Madam, as you did not count me worthy of this honour in life, then I shall account myself not worthy of it in death.'

27. Camden, *The Historie*, p. 175.

28. Malpas, 'Sir Francis Knollys', p. 123.

29. HMC Salisbury, VI (42).

30. WCRO, MI 229.

31. HMC Salisbury, VII (55).

32. HMC De L'Isle, p. 268.

33. WCRO, MI 229.

34. Ibid.

35. Ibid.

36. Cited in Craik, *Romance of the Peerage*, p. 167.

37. Penelope died in 1599 at the age of around five or six. Henry died when he was approximately one year old.

38. HMC De L'Isle, p. 322.

Chapter 19: Some Wonted Unkind Words

1. Collins (ed.), *Letters and Memorials of State*, II, pp. 92–3.

2. Ibid.

3. Ibid.

4. Ibid., p. 92.
5. Ibid., pp. 92–3.
6. Ibid.
7. Ibid., p. 95.
8. Murdin (ed.), *State Papers*, p. 302.
9. Burghley died on 4 August 1598, and is buried in St Martin's Church, Stamford.
10. Camden, *The Historie*, p. 126.
11. Ibid., p. 219.
12. Ibid.
13. Ibid.
14. Jones, *Mountjoy 1563–1606*, p. 46.
15. L. Hopkins, *Elizabeth I and her Court* (New York, 1990), p. 101.
16. WCRO, MI 229.
17. Camden, *The Historie*, p. 244.
18. Collins (ed.), *Letters and Memorials of State*, II, pp. 127–9.
19. Bourchier Devereux, *Lives and Letters*, II, p. 88.
20. Collins (ed.), *Letters and Memorials of State*, II, 149.
21. Philadelphia Scrope was married to Thomas, Lord Scrope, by whom she had one child, a son named Emmanuel. The magnificent tomb effigy she shares with her husband still survives in St Andrew's Church in Langar, Nottinghamshire.
22. Collins (ed.), *Letters and Memorials of State*, II, 159.
23. CSPD, Elizabeth 1580–1625, Addenda, 34, p. 398.
24. Ibid.
25. CSPD, Elizabeth 1598–1601, 274, p. 392. Traditionally this letter has been dated to 1 January 1600, but there is some debate over whether it may have been written later.
26. The location of this portrait, of English origin, is now, sadly, unknown. It was sold at Sotheby's in 1974.
27. Craik, *Romance of the Peerage*, p. 181.
28. HMC De L'Isle, p. 435.
29. Collins (ed.), *Letters and Memorials of State*, II, p. 171.
30. WCRO, MI 229.
31. Collins (ed.), *Letters and Memorials of State*, II, p. 171. Elizabeth is believed to have owned approximately two thousand dresses at the time of her death.
32. Collins (ed.), *Letters and Memorials of State*, II, p. 174.
33. Ibid.
34. Ibid.
35. Ibid.
36. Ibid.
37. Bourchier Devereux, *Lives and Letters*, II, p. 95.
38. HMC Salisbury, X (72).
39. Ibid., XIV (140).
40. Ibid.
41. CSPD, Elizabeth 1598–1601, 274, p. 414.
42. Ibid., p. 439.
43. Like Essex, Coke was a former pupil at Trinity College, and became a renowned barrister and judge. Among the numerous noteworthy cases for which he led the prosecution were those of the Gunpowder Plot conspirators.

Chapter 20: The Arch-Traitor Essex

1. Camden, *The Historie*, p. 195.
2. Ibid., p. 301
3. Ibid., p. 195.
4. Drury House no longer exists, but was once the home of Sir Robert Drury. Drury Lane was named after him.
5. Lacey, *Robert, Earl of Essex*, p. 15.
6. The cheapest seats available at The Globe were those in the open-air courtyard, for which the price was a penny.
7. CSPD, Elizabeth 1598–1601, 278, p. 556.
8. Beer (ed.), *A Summarie*, p. 457.
9. CSPD, Elizabeth 1598–1601, 278, p. 547.
10. Lacey, *Robert, Earl of Essex*, p. 71.
11. Camden, *The Historie*, p 302.
12. CSPD, Elizabeth 1598–1601, 278, p. 550.
13. HMC Salisbury, XI (41).
14. CSPD, Elizabeth 1598–1601, 278, pp. 553–4.
15. Ibid., p. 550.
16. Ibid., p. 552.
17. Ibid., p. 550.
18. Ibid., p. 547.
19. Ibid., p. 550.
20. Ibid.
21. Ibid.
22. Ibid.
23. CSPD, Elizabeth 1598–1601, 278, p. 547.
24. Much of the Devereux Tower was rebuilt in the mid-eighteenth century; it once contained secret passages that connected it to the Tower Chapel of St Peter ad Vincula.
25. CSPD, Elizabeth 1598–1601, 278, p. 556.
26. Ibid.
27. CSPD, Elizabeth 1598–1601, 278, p. 579.
28. Ibid.
29. Westminster Hall was part of the Palace of Westminster. In its time it was the largest hall in England, and probably also in Europe.
30. Bourchier Devereux, *Lives and Letters*, II, p. 149.
31. CSPD, Elizabeth 1598–1601, 278, p. 590.
32. Ibid.
33. Cited in Weir, *Elizabeth the Queen*, p. 463.
34. CSPD, Elizabeth 1598–1601, 278, p. 590.
35. Cited in Freedman, *Poor Penelope*, pp. 145–6.
36. Ibid., p. 147.
37. The couple had two sons and two daughters, one of whom was named Penelope, probably in honour of Lettice's daughter. Southampton died in Holland in 1624, and Elizabeth, still alive, never remarried. She died in 1655.
38. Bourchier Devereux, *Lives and Letters*, II, p. 185.
39. Cited in R. Winwood, *Memorials of Affairs of State*, I (London, 1725), p. 309.
40. According to Bourchier Devereux, Dorothy was born on 20 December 1600.
41. CSPD, Elizabeth 1598–1601, 278, p. 592.

42. HMC Salisbury, XI (180).

43. CSPD, Elizabeth 1598–1601, 278, p. 595.

44. Ibid, p. 592.

45. HMC Salisbury, XI (180).

46. Ibid.

47. Ibid.

48. Ibid.

49. Ibid.

50. Ibid.

51. Ibid.

52. R. Cavendish, 'The Execution of the Earl of Essex', *History Today*, 51:2 (2001), p. 111.

53. Bourchier Devereux, *Lives and Letters*, II, p. 190. John Stow reported that when the executioner left the Tower, many people recognized him, and loving Essex as they did, proceeded to beat him. Stow believed that they were intent on murder, but fortunately the executioner was rescued.

54. Philip Howard, Earl of Arundel, had been a former favourite of the Queen's. The Duke of Norfolk was his father, who had been executed in 1572. Arundel converted to Catholicism and became a recusant, who was arrested and confined in the Tower in 1585. An inscription he carved during his imprisonment still survives in the Beauchamp Tower, and he was comforted by the presence of his faithful dog. He died of dysentery while still a prisoner in 1595, and was buried in the Tower. However, during the reign of James I, at the petition of his wife and son, his remains were removed from the Tower, and interred in the Fitzalan Chapel at Arundel Castle. Some of them are also in Arundel Cathedral.

55. HMC Salisbury, XI (75).

56. Ibid.

57. CSPD, Elizabeth 1598–1601, 279, p. 23.

58. Ibid.

59. Camden, *The Historie*, p. 190.

60. W. Cobbett (ed.), *A Complete Collection of State Trials and Proceedings for High Treason and Other Crimes and Misdemeanours from the Earliest Period to the Present Time* (London, 1809), p. 1410.

61. HMC Salisbury, XI (119).

62. Ibid.

63. Beer (ed.), *A Summarie*, p. 459.

64. Cobbett (ed.), *State Trials*, p. 1413.

65. Camden, *The Historie*, p. 194.

66. Ibid.

67. Ibid.

68. Cobbett (ed.), *State Trials*, p. 1414.

69. Ibid., p. 1416.

70. Camden, *The Historie*, p. 194; Cobbett (ed.), *State Trials*, p. 1416.

71. Camden, *The Historie*, p. 194.

Chapter 21: Mildly Like a Lamb

1. CSPD, Elizabeth 1601–1603, 287, pp. 295–309.

2. Mares (ed.), *The Memoirs of Robert Carey*, p. 58.

3. The Countess of Nottingham died on 25 February at Arundel House on the edge of the Strand. She was buried in Chelsea Old Church.

4. CSPD, Elizabeth 1601–1603, 287, pp. 295–309.

5. Mares (ed.), *The Memoirs of Robert Carey*, p. 59.

6. Ibid, p. 129.

7. Helena Snakenborg was the Swedish third wife of William Parr, Marquess of Northampton. She had arrived in England in 1564 in the entourage of Princess Cecilia of Sweden, who was visiting Queen Elizabeth. It was here that she met and fell in love with her future husband, and she later became one of Elizabeth's maids of honour. Following the death of her husband in 1571, Helena remarried Thomas Gorges, by whom she had eight children. She died in 1635 and is buried in Salisbury Cathedral.

8. James and Anne had been married in Oslo on 23 November 1589. Anne's journey to Scotland had been marred by repeated bad weather, and thus James decided to set out to collect his bride-to-be personally. They finally met in Oslo.

9. Nichols, *The Progresses and Public Processions of Queen Elizabeth*, III, p. 5. The royal couple had travelled to Greys from Oxford.

10. He was also included in the Somerset House Conference portrait of 1604, which now hangs in the National Portrait Gallery.

11. Princess Mary was born at Greenwich Palace, where her elaborate christening was staged on 5 May. Tragically, the little princess died of pneumonia on 16 September 1607. Her tomb can still be seen in Westminster Abbey.

12. Robert Cecil died of cancer at Marlborough. He was laid to rest in the church at Hatfield, where his tomb still survives.

13. See G.F. Warner (ed.), *The Voyage of Robert Dudley, afterwards styled Earl of Warwick and Leicester and Duke of Northumberland, to the West Indies, 1594–1595* (London, 1899).

14. The fate of his corpse is unknown; in 1674 it is known to have been in the monastery at Boldrone, but from there its final resting place is uncertain.

15. HMC Salisbury, CXCIII (15).

16. In the year of his accession alone, James visited Syon twice, and Queen Anne also visited by herself on several occasions.

17. Francis Tresham was the grandson of Thomas Tresham by his first wife, Mary Parr. Thomas's second wife was Lettice's paternal grandmother, Lettice Peniston.

18. Robert Catesby, John and Christopher Wright were all killed at Holbeach, and others, including Thomas Percy, were injured.

19. On 30 January 1606, Sir Everard Digby, Robert Wintour, John Grant and Thomas Bates were all hung, drawn and quartered at St Paul's Churchyard. The following day the same fate was meted out to Guido Fawkes, Thomas Wintour, Ambrose Rookwood and Robert Keyes in Old Palace Yard, Westminster. Fawkes managed to jump from the gallows and break his neck, ensuring that he was dead before the latter part of his sentence could be carried out.

20. Thomas Percy's great-grandfather was the fourth Earl of Northumberland, thus making him a distant cousin of Henry Percy, the ninth Earl.

21. Percy and Robert Catesby had reportedly been hit by the same bullet, which killed Catesby and injured Percy – fatally, as would soon become clear.

22. CSPD, James I 1603–1610, XVI, p. 250.

23. Cited in Freedman, *Poor Penelope*, p. 157.

24. Betcherman, *Court Lady and Country Wife*, p. 9.

25. During the reign of Charles I, Laud became Archbishop of Canterbury. In 1640, though, he was accused of treason and imprisoned in the Tower. He was beheaded on 10 January 1645 on Tower Hill.

26. Cited in Jones, *Mountjoy 1563–1606*, p. 180.
27. He was a heavy tobacco smoker, which worsened his condition. The use of tobacco had been popularized at court by Sir Walter Ralegh.
28. Penelope's biographer Sylvia Freedman believes that Penelope is buried in All Hallows, Barking-by-the-Tower, where three of her brother Robert's children are also buried. Freedman found a record dating to 7 October 1607 that states that 'A Lady Devereux' was buried in the church that day. See Freedman, *Poor Penelope*, p. 195.

Chapter 22: The Wars with Thunder, and the Court with Stars

1. Thomas Howard, first Earl of Suffolk, was married to Katherine Knyvet. James I favoured him, and he began remodelling Audley End House in Saffron Walden.
2. France's father was a son of the fourth Duke of Norfolk, whose father was the Earl of Surrey. In turn, Surrey was a cousin of Lettice's maternal grandmother, Mary Boleyn.
3. P.E.J., Hammer, *The Polarisation of Elizabethan Politics: The Political Career of Robert Devereux, 2nd Earl of Essex, 1585–1597* (Cambridge, 1999), p. 28.
4. Frances and Carr had a daughter together, Anne, who became Countess of Bedford. Frances died on 23 August 1632.
5. Add MS 18985.
6. Ibid. Black was a colour that was favoured by the nobility, not only because it was a demonstration of wealth, but also because it hid any dirt.
7. Ibid.
8. Ibid.
9. Ibid.
10. Arbella and Seymour had been married on 22 June 1610 at Greenwich Palace. News of their secret marriage leaked out almost immediately.
11. There are reports that she died insane, and it is clear that she was in great distress at the time of her death. She refused all food, subsequently falling ill and dying on 25 September 1615. She was laid to rest in Westminster Abbey.
12. Unfortunately there is no monument to mark the site of her grave.
13. Sidney was the son of Robert Sidney and his wife, Barbara Gamage. His grandmother was Leicester's sister, Mary.
14. By the time of her mother's death, Dorothy and Robert already had two small children – Lettice's great-grandchildren Dorothy and Philip – and the family resided at the Sidney family home of Penshurst Place in Kent. Dorothy Sidney's portrait still hangs in the Long Gallery at Penshurst Place.
15. Northumberland offered Lucy a dowry of £20,000 (£1,958,000) if she let him choose her husband. It was an offer she refused. Though neither of her parents were there to witness her wedding, the King, the Prince of Wales and the Duke of Buckingham were in attendance, with the King giving away the bride.
16. PROB 11/167/42.
17. Ibid.
18. CSPD, Charles I 1629–1631, p. 139.
19. Jenkins, *Elizabeth and Leicester*, p. 368.
20. PROB 11/167/42.
21. W. Knowler (ed.), *The Earl of Strafford's Letters and Despatches*, 2 vols. (London, 1739), p. 359.
22. Bourchier Devereux, *Lives and Letters*, I, p. 162.

23. PROB 11/167/42.
24. Ibid.
25. Ibid.
26. Ibid.
27. Ibid.
28. Ibid.
29. Nicholas Johnson, who had his workshop in Southwark, may have made it.
30. In Lettice's will, Gervase Clifton was to be the recipient of 'my best great pearl to hang at his ear, and the hatband, and a diamond ring with God's blessing'. PROB 11/167/42.
31. Lacey, *Robert, Earl of Essex*, p. 15.

Epilogue

1. Harwood, *Erdeswick's Survey of Staffordshire*, p. 59.
2. Like Lettice's first husband, the Walter Devereux who now inherited was the grandson of Walter Devereux, Viscount Hereford.

BIBLIOGRAPHY

Manuscript Sources

British Library

Add MS 22583, Add MS 32092, Add MS 64081, Add MS 18985, Cotton MS Galba C, Cotton Otho C X, Egerton MS 3052, Harleian MS 287, Harleian MS 6992, Harley 6798, Lansdowne MS 3, Landsowne MS 24, Lansdowne MS 31, Lansdowne MS 39, Lansdowne MS 62, Lansdowne MS 76, Lansdowne MS 885, RP 6340

Institute of Historical Research

Dudley and Devereux Papers, available via Microfilm

Kent History and Library Centre

U1475 E93

National Archives

E 178/1446, E 367/1313, LC 2/4/3, LR 1/137, PRO 31, 3/28/417, PRO E 101/429/3, PRO E 351/1795, PROB 1/1, PROB 11/58/438, PROB 11/88/135, PROB 11/167/42, SP 9/93, SP 12/148, WARD 7/18/39

Warwickshire County Records Office

MI 229

Printed Primary Sources

Adams, S. (ed.), *Household Accounts and Disbursement Books of Robert Dudley, Earl of Leicester* (London, 1995).

Ascham, R., *The Whole Works of Roger Ascham*, ed. J.A. Giles (London, 1864–5).

Ascham, R., *The Schoolmaster*, ed. L.V. Ryan (New York, 1967).

Bagot, W., *Memorials of the Bagot Family* (London, 1824).

Bain, J., Mackie, J.D., *et al.* (eds), *Calendar of the State Papers Relating to Scotland and Mary, Queen of Scots, 1547–1603*, Vols I–XIII, part ii (Edinburgh, 1898–1969).

Baker, J.H. (ed.), *Reports from the Lost Notebooks of Sir James Dyer*, Vol. I (London, 1994).

Batho, G.R. (ed.), *The Household Papers of Henry Percy, Ninth Earl of Northumberland* (London, 1962).

Beer, B.L. (ed.), *A Summarie of the Chronicles of England, Diligently Collected, Abridged, And Continued unto this Present Year of Christ, 1604, by John Stow* (Lewiston, 2007).

Bell, D.C., *Notices of the Historic Persons Buried in the Chapel of St Peter ad Vincula* (London, 1877).

Bindoff, S. (ed.), *The House of Commons, 1509–1558* (London, 1982).

Birch, T., *Memoirs of the Reign of Queen Elizabeth from the Year 1581 till her Death*, 2 vols (London, 1754).

Bourchier Devereux, W., *Lives and Letters of the Devereux Earls of Essex*, 2 vols (London, 1853).

Boyle, J. (ed.), *Memoirs of the Life of Robert Carey … Written by Himself* (London, 1759).

Brewer, J.S. and Bullen, W. (eds), *Calendar of the Carew Manuscripts preserved in the Archiepiscopal Library at Lambeth, 1515–1603*, 4 vols (London, 1867–70).

Brewer, J.S., Gairdner, J. and Brodie, R.H. (eds), *Letters and Papers, Foreign and Domestic, of the Reign of Henry VIII, 1509–47*, 21 vols and addenda (London, 1862–1932).

Brown, H.F. (ed.), *Calendar of State Papers Relating to English Affairs in the Archives of Venice, Volume 9, 1592–1603* (London, 1897).

Brown, R. (ed.), *Calendar of State Papers Relating to English Affairs in the Archives of Venice, Volume 6, 1555–1558* (London, 1877).

Bruce, J. (ed.), *The Correspondence of Robert Dudley, Earl of Leycester, During his Government of the Low Countries, in the Years 1585 and 1586*, Camden Society, XXVII (London, 1844).

Bruce, J. (ed.), *Calendar of State Papers Domestic: Charles I, 1629–31* (London, 1860).

Burnet, G., *The History of the Reformation of the Church of England* (London, 1880).

Byrne, M. St C. (ed.), *The Lisle Letters* (Chicago, 1980).

Camden, W., *The Historie of the Most Renowned and Victorious Princesse Elizabeth, Late Queene of England* (London, 1630).

Chandler, J. (ed.), *John Leland's Itinerary: Travels in Tudor England* (Dover, 1993).

Chéruel, A., *Marie Stuart et Catherine de Médicis* (Paris, 1858).

Clifford, D.J.H. (ed.), *The Diaries of Lady Anne Clifford* (Stroud, 1992).

Cobbett, W. (ed.), *A Complete Collection of State Trials and Proceedings for High Treason and Other Crimes and Misdemeanours from the Earliest Period to the Present Time* (London, 1809).

Collins, A. (ed.), *Letters and Memorials of State, in the reigns of Queen Mary, Queen Elizabeth, etc … Written and collected by Sir Henry Sidney, etc*, 2 vols (London, 1746).

Collins, A.J. (ed.), *Jewels and Plate of Queen Elizabeth I: The Inventory of 1574* (London, 1955).

Collinson, P. (ed.), *Letters of Thomas Wood, Puritan, 1566–1577* (London, 1960).

Constable, D. (ed.), *Letters of John Calvin compiled from the original manuscripts and edited with historical notes by Dr Jules Bonnet*, II (Edinburgh, 1857).

Craik, G.L., *The Romance of the Peerage, or Curiosities of Family History*, Vols I–IV (London, 1849).

Crawford, A. (ed.), *Letters of the Queens of England* (Stroud, 2002).

Dasent, J.R. (ed.), *Acts of the Privy Council of England*, New Series (London, 1890).

Dickens, A.G. (ed.), *Clifford Letters of the Sixteenth Century* (London, 1962).

Edwards, R., *A Boke of very Godly Psalmes and Prayers, dedicated to the Lady Letice Vicountesse of Hereforde* (London, 1570).

Ellis, H. (ed.), *Original Letters Illustrative of English History, Including Numerous Royal Letters*, 3rd series, Vols II–IV (London, 1846).

Fenton, E. (ed.), *The Diaries of John Dee* (Charlbury, 1998).

Feuillerat, A. (ed.), *Complete Works of Sir Philip Sidney*, 4 vols (London, 1912–26).

Feuillerat, A. (ed.), *Documents Relating to the Revels at Court in the Time of King Edward VI and Queen Mary* (Louvain, 1914).

Foster, J. (ed.), 'Disbrowe-Dyve', in *Alumni Oxonienses 1500–1714* (Oxford, 1891).

Foxe, J., *Acts and Monuments*, ed. Rev. S. Reed, VI (London, 1838).

Francis Steuart, A. (ed.), *Sir James Melville: Memoirs of His Own Life, 1549–93* (London, 1929).

Godwin, F., *Annales of England* (London, 1630).

Grafton, R., *An Abridgement of the Chronicles of England* (London, 1564).

Green, M.A.E., *Letters of Royal and Illustrious Ladies of Great Britain*, 3 vols (London, 1846).

Green, M.A.E. (ed.), *Calendar of State Papers Domestic: James I, 1603–1610* (London, 1857).

Green, M.A.E. (ed.), *Calendar of State Papers Domestic: Elizabeth, 1591–94* (London, 1867).

Green, M.A.E. (ed.), *Calendar of State Papers Domestic: Elizabeth, 1595–97* (London, 1869).

Green, M.A.E. (ed.), *Calendar of State Papers Domestic: Elizabeth, 1598–1601* (London, 1869).

Green, M.A.E. (ed.), *Calendar of State Papers Domestic: Elizabeth, 1601–3 With Addenda 1547–65* (London, 1870).

Hall, E., *Chronicle*, ed. C. Whibley (London, 1904).

Halliwell, J. (ed.), *Ancient Inventories Illustrative of Domestic Manners of the English in the Sixteenth and Seventeenth Centuries* (London, 1854).

Harington, J., *Nuguae Antiquae: Being a Miscellaneous Collection of Original Papers in Prose and Verse: Written in the Reigns of Henry VIII, Queen Mary, Elizabeth, King James, etc* (London, 1779).

Harrison, G.B. (ed.), *The Letters of Queen Elizabeth* (London, 1935).

Haynes, S., *Collection of State Papers Relating to Affairs in the Reigns of King Henry VIII, King Edward VI, Queen Mary and Queen Elizabeth, From the Year 1542 to 1570 … Left by William Cecil, Lord Burghley … at Hatfield House* (London, 1740).

Hayward, M. (ed.), *The 1542 Inventory of Whitehall* (London, 2004).

Historical Manuscripts Commission, *Calendar of the Manuscripts of the Most Honourable the Marquess of Salisbury*, I (London, 1883).

Historical Manuscripts Commission, *The Manuscripts of His Grace the Duke of Rutland, preserved at Belvoir Castle*, Vol. I (London, 1888).

Historical Manuscripts Commission, *The Manuscripts of Lord Middleton*, ed. W.S. Stevenson (London, 1911).

Historical Manuscripts Commission, *Report on the Manuscripts of Lord De L'Isle and Dudley, preserved at Penshurst Place*, Vols I and II (London, 1925).

Historical Manuscripts Commission, *Calendar of the Manuscripts of the Most Honourable the Marquess of Bath, preserved at Longleat, Wiltshire, 1533–1659*, Vol. V (London, 1980).

Holinshed, R., *Holinshed's Chronicles of England, Scotland and Ireland*, 6 vols (London, 1807).

Hughes, P.L. and Larkin, J.F. (eds), *Tudor Royal Proclamations* (London, 1964).

Hume, M.A.S (ed.), *Chronicle of King Henry VIII of England* (London, 1889).

Hume, M.A.S. (ed.), *Calendar of Letters and State Papers relating to English Affairs, preserved principally in the Archives of Simancas, Elizabeth I*, 4 vols (London, 1892–9).

Hume, M.A.S., Tyller, R., *et al.* (eds), *Calendar of Letters, Despatches, and State Papers, relating to the Negotiations between England and Spain, preserved in the Archives at Simancas and Elsewhere, 1547–1558* (London, 1912–54).

Jones, J., 'The benefit of the auncient bathes of Buckstones vvhich cureth most greeuous sicknesses, neuer before published' (London, 1572).

Jordan, W.K. (ed.), *The Chronicle and Political Papers of King Edward VI* (London, 1966).

Knollys, W., *Papers relating to Mary Queen of Scots* (London, 1872–6).

Knowler, W. (ed.), *The Earl of Strafford's Letters and Despatches*, 2 vols (London, 1739).

Knox, T.F. *et al.* (eds), *The First and Second Diaries of the English College, Douay* (London, 1878).

Langham, R., *A Letter*, ed. R.J.P. Kuin (Leiden, 1983).

Lawson, J. (ed.), *The Elizabethan New Year's Gift Exchanges 1559–1603* (Oxford, 2013).

Lemon, R. (ed.), *Calendar of State Papers Domestic: Edward VI, Mary and Elizabeth, 1547–1580* (London, 1856).

Lemon, R. (ed.), *Calendar of State Papers Domestic: Elizabeth, 1581–90* (London, 1865).

Lodge, E. (ed.), *Illustrations of British History*, III (London, 1838).

Luders, A. *et al.* (eds), *Statutes of the Realm*, 11 vols (London, 1810–28).

Malone Society, 'Dramatic Records in the Declared Accounts of the Treasurer of the Chamber 1558–1642', *Collections*, VI (Oxford 1962).

Mares, F.H. (ed.), *The Memoirs of Robert Carey* (Oxford, 1972).

Maulette, G., *Deuoreux Vertues teares for the losse of the most christian King Henry, third of that name, King of Fraunce; and the vntimely death, of the most noble & heroicall gentleman, VValter Deuoreux, who was slaine before Roan in Fraunce. First written in French, by the most excellent and learned gentlewoman, Madam Geneuuefue, Petau Maulette*, trans. G. Markham (London, 1597).

McClure, N.E., *The Letters and Epigrams of Sir John Harington* (London, 1930).

Murdin, W. (ed.), *A Collection of State Papers relating to Affairs in the Reign of Queen Elizabeth from the Year 1571 to 1576* (London, 1759).

Newton, T., 'An epitaph upon the worthy and honourable lady, the Lady Knowles' (1569).

Nicholas, H. (ed.), *Memoirs of the Life and Times of Sir Christopher Hatton* (London, 1847).

Nichols, J., *The Progresses and Public Processions of Queen Elizabeth*, 3 vols (London, 1823).

Nichols, J.G. (ed.), *The Diary of Henry Machyn: Citizen and Merchant-Taylor of London, from AD 1550 to AD 1563* (London, 1848).

Nichols, J.G. (ed.), *The Chronicle of Queen Jane and of Two Years of Queen Mary*, Camden Society 48 (London, 1850).

Nichols, J.G. (ed.), *Chronicle of the Grey Friars of London* (London, 1851).

North, J. (ed.), *England's Boy King: The Diary of Edward VI 1547–1553* (Welwyn Garden City, 2005).

Orchard Halliwell, J. (ed.), *The Private Diary of John Dee*, Camden Society XIX (London, 1842).

Orchard Halliwell, J. (ed.), *Letters of the Kings of England* (London, 1846).

Peck, D.C. (ed.), *Leicester's Commonwealth: The Copy of a Letter Written by a Master of Art of Cambridge (1584) and Related Documents* (London, 1985).

Plot, R., *The Natural History of Staffordshire* (Oxford, 1686).

Pollard, A.F., *Tudor Tracts 1532–1588* (New York, 1964).

Robinson, H. (ed.), *Original Letters Relative to the English Reformation*, I (Cambridge, 1846–7).

Rogers, T., *Leicester's Ghost*, ed. F.B. Williams (Chicago, 1972).

Starkey, D. (ed.), *The Inventory of King Henry VIII*, trans. P. Ward (London, 1998).

Stevenson, J. *et al.* (eds), *Calendar of State Papers, Foreign Series, of the Reign of Elizabeth I, 1558–1591* (London, 1863–1969).

Stow, J., *A Summarie of Englyshe Chronicles* (London, 1565).

Stow, J., *The Annales of England* (London, 1592).

Stow, J., *A Survey of London*, ed. C.L. Kingsford, 2 vols (Oxford, 1908).

Stow, J., *Two London Chronicles*, ed. C.L. Kingsford, Camden Miscellany (London, 1910).

Strype, J., *Ecclesiastical Memorials, Relating Chiefly to Religion, and the Reformation of it ... under King Henry VIII, King Edward VI and Queen Mary I*, 3 vols (Oxford, 1822).

Thoms, W.J. (ed.), *Anecdotes and Traditions, Illustrative of Early English History and Literature*, Camden Society (London, 1850).

Tytler, P.F., *England under the Reigns of Edward VI and Mary, Illustrated in a Series of Original Letters*, 2 vols (London, 1839).

Warner, G.F. (ed.), *The Voyage of Robert Dudley, afterwards styled Earl of Warwick and Leicester and Duke of Northumberland, to the West Indies, 1594–1595* (London, 1899).

Winwood, R., *Memorials of Affairs of State*, Vol. I (London, 1725).

Wood, M.A.E., *Letters of Royal and Illustrious Ladies of Great Britain*, 3 vols (London, 1846).

Wotton, H., *A parallel betweene Robert late Earle of Essex, and George late Duke of Buckingham written by Sir Henry Wotton* (London, 1641).

Wright, T. (ed.), *Queen Elizabeth and her Times: A Series of Original Letters, Selected from the Inedited Private Correspondence of the Lord Treasurer Burghley, the Earl of Leicester, the Secretaries Walsingham and Smith, Sir Christopher Hatton, etc*, 2 vols (London, 1838).

Wriothesley, C., *A Chronicle of England during the Reigns of the Tudors, from AD 1485 to 1559*, ed. W.D. Hamilton, Camden Society (London, 1875, 1877).

Young, B., *Diana of de Montemayor* (London, 1598).

Secondary Sources

Adams, S., 'A Godly Peer? Leicester and the Puritans', *History Today*, 40:1 (1990), pp. 14–19.

Adams, S., 'The Dudley Clientele', in G.W. Bernard (ed.), *The Tudor Nobility* (Manchester, 1992).

Adams, S., 'The Papers of Robert Dudley, Earl of Leicester, III: The Countess of Leicester's Collection', *Archives*, 22:94 (1996), pp. 1–26.

Adams, S., *Leicester and the Court: Essays on Elizabethan Politics* (Manchester, 2002).

Adams, S. (ed.), 'The Armada Correspondence in Cotton MSS Otho E VII and E IX', *The Naval Miscellany*, ed. M. Duffy (London, 2003).

Alford, S., *Kingship and Politics in the Reign of Edward VI* (Cambridge, 2002).

Alford, S., *Burghley: William Cecil at the Court of Elizabeth I* (New Haven and London, 2008).

Amin, N., *Tudor Wales* (Stroud, 2014).

Anglo, S., *Spectacle, Pageantry and Early Tudor Policy* (Oxford, 1969).

Archer, J.E., Goldring, E. and Knight, S. (eds), *The Progresses, Pageants, and Entertainments of Queen Elizabeth I* (Oxford, 2007).

Arnold, J., *Queen Elizabeth's Wardrobe Unlock'd* (London, 1988).

Ashdown, D.M., *Ladies-in-Waiting* (London, 1976).

Ashdown, D.M., *Tudor Cousins: Rivals for the Throne* (Sutton, 2000).

Auerbach, E., *Tudor Artists* (London, 1954).

Auerbach, E., *Nicholas Hilliard* (Boston, 1961).

Axton, M., *The Queen's Two Bodies: Drama and the Elizabethan Succession* (Cambridge, 1978).

Bald, R.C., 'Leicester's Men in the Low Countries', *Review of English Studies*, 19 (1943), pp. 395–7.

Batho, G.R., 'The Finances of an Elizabethan Nobleman: Henry Percy, Ninth Earl of Northumberland (1564–1632)', *Economic History Review*, 9:3 (1957), pp. 433–50.

Becker, L.M., *Death and the Early Modern Englishwoman* (Aldershot, 2003).

Beer, A., *Bess: The Life of Lady Ralegh, Wife to Sir Walter* (London, 2005).

Betcherman, L.R., *Court Lady and Country Wife: Royal Privilege and Civil War, Two Noble Sisters in Seventeenth-Century England* (Chichester, 2005).

Blakiston, N., 'Nicholas Hilliard at Court', *Burlington Magazine*, 96:610 (1954), pp. 17–18.

Borman, T., *Elizabeth's Women: The Hidden Story of the Virgin Queen* (London, 2009).

Bradford, C.A., *Blanche Parry, Queen Elizabeth's Gentlewoman* (London, 1935).

Bradford, G., *Elizabethan Women* (New York, 1969).

Brady, C., *The Chief Governors: The Rise and Fall of Reform Government in Tudor Ireland 1536–1588* (Cambridge, 1994).

Brindley, D., *The Collegiate Church of St Mary Warwick: The Beauchamp Chapel* (Much Wenlock, 1997).

Bundesen, K., '"No other faction but my own": Dynastic Politics and Elizabeth's Carey Cousins', unpublished PhD thesis (University of Nottingham, 2008).

Butler, L., 'Leicester's Church, Denbigh: An Experiment in Puritan Worship', *Journal of the British Archaeological Association*, 37 (1974), pp. 40–62.

Buxton, J., *Sir Philip Sidney and the English Renaissance* (London, 1964).

Canny, N.P., *The Elizabethan Conquest of Ireland: A Pattern Established, 1565–76* (London, 1976).

Castor, H., *She-Wolves: The Women Who Ruled England before Elizabeth* (London, 2010).

Cavendish, R., 'The Execution of the Earl of Essex', *History Today*, 51:2 (2001).

Christy, M., 'The Progresses of Queen Elizabeth through Essex and the Houses in which She Stayed', *Essex Review*, 26 (1917), pp. 115–29.

Clark, J., 'The Buildings and Art Collections of Robert Dudley Earl of Leicester (With Notes on his Portraits)', unpublished MA thesis (Courtauld Institute, London, 1981).

Clark, J., 'A Set of Tapestries for Leicester House in The Strand: 1585', *Burlington Magazine*, 125:962 (1983), pp. 280–1, 283–4.

Cokayne, G.E. (ed.), *The Complete Peerage of England, Scotland, Ireland, Great Britain and the United Kingdom*, 12 vols (London, 1910–59).

Collins, A.J., 'The Death-Warrant of Robert Earl of Essex', *British Museum Quarterly*, 16:2 (1951), pp. 37–8.

Cooper, T., *A Guide to Tudor and Jacobean Portraits* (London, 2008).

Cressy, D., 'Kinship and Kin Interaction in Early Modern England', *Past and Present*, 113 (1986), pp. 38–69.

Croft, P. (ed.), *Patronage, Culture and Power: The Early Cecils* (London, 2002).

Croft, P. and Hearn, K., '"Only matrimony maketh children to be certain …": Two Elizabethan Pregnancy Portraits', *British Art Journal*, 3:3 (2002), pp. 19–24.

Cross, C., *The Puritan Earl: The Life of Henry Hastings, Third Earl of Huntingdon* (London, 1966).

Duffy, E., *Fires of Faith: Catholic England under Mary Tudor* (New Haven and London, 2009).

Dunlop, I., *Palaces and Progresses of Elizabeth I* (London, 1962).

Dunn, J., *Elizabeth and Mary: Cousins, Rivals, Queens* (New York, 2004).

Ellis, S.G., *Ireland in the Age of the Tudors* (London, 1998).

Elton, G.R., *England under the Tudors* (London, 1955).

Foister, S., *Holbein and England* (New Haven and London, 2004).

Foyster, E., *Manhood in Early Modern England: Honour, Sex, and Marriage* (London, 1999).

Fraser, A., *Mary Queen of Scots* (London, 1969).

Fraser, A., *King James* (London, 1974).

Fraser, A., *The Weaker Vessel: Woman's Lot in Seventeenth-Century England* (London, 1984).

Fraser, A., *The Six Wives of Henry VIII* (London, 1992).

Freedman, S., *Poor Penelope: Lady Penelope Rich, an Elizabethan Woman* (London, 1983).

Gairdner, J., 'Mary and Anne Boleyn', *English Historical Review*, 8:29 (1893), pp. 53–60.

Garnett, O., *Greys Court* (Rotherham, 2010).

Garrett, C., *The Marian Exiles* (London, 1966).

Gittings, C., *Death, Burial and the Individual in Early Modern England* (London, 1984).

Goldring, E., 'Portraits of Queen Elizabeth I and the Earl of Leicester for Kenilworth Castle', *Burlington Magazine*, 147:1231 (2005), pp. 654–60.

Goldring, E., *Robert Dudley, Earl of Leicester, and the World of Elizabethan Art: Painting and Patronage at the Court of Elizabeth I* (London, 2014).

Gordon, A., '"A Fortune of Paper Walls": The Letters of Francis Bacon and the Earl of Essex', *English Literary Renaissance*, 37:3 (2007), pp. 319–36.

Gray, M., *Hamlet's Secrets Revealed: The Real Shakespeare* (Bloomington, 2001).

Grey, J. and Gunn, S.J., 'A Letter of Jane, Duchess of Northumberland, in 1553', *English Historical Review*, CXIV (1999), pp. 1267–71.

Gristwood, S., *Elizabeth and Leicester* (London, 2007).

Guy, J., *Tudor England* (Oxford, 1990).

Haigh, C. (ed.), *Elizabeth I* (London and New York, 1988).

Hammer, P.E.J., *The Polarisation of Elizabethan Politics: The Political Career of Robert Devereux, 2nd Earl of Essex, 1585–1597* (Cambridge, 1999).

Harris, B.J., *English Aristocratic Women 1450–1550* (Oxford, 2002).

Harrison, B.A., *Tower of London Prisoner Book: A Complete Chronology of the Persons Known to have been Detained at Their Majesties' Pleasure, 1100–1941* (Leeds, 2004).

Hart-Davis, A., *What The Tudors and Stuarts Did For Us* (London, 1996).

Hart, K., *The Mistresses of Henry VIII* (Stroud, 2009).

Harwood, T., *Erdeswick's Survey of Staffordshire* (London, 1844).

Hasler, P.W. (ed.), 'Appendix XI: The Role of the Marian Exiles', *The History of Parliament: The House of Commons 1558–1603* (1981).

Hayward, M. (ed.), *Dress at the Court of King Henry VIII* (Leeds, 2007).

Henry, L.W., 'The Earl of Essex as Strategist and Military Organizer (1596–7)', *English Historical Review*, 68:268 (1953), pp. 363–93.

Hibbert, C., *Elizabeth I: A Personal History of the Virgin Queen* (London, 1992).

Hilton, L., *Elizabeth: Renaissance Prince* (London, 2014).

Hopkins, L., *Elizabeth I and her Court* (New York, 1990).

Hoskins, A., 'Mary Boleyn's Carey Children: Offspring of King Henry VIII?' *Genealogists' Magazine*, 25:9 (1997).

Howey, C.L., 'Dressing a Virgin Queen: Court Women, Dress, and Fashioning the Image of England's Queen Elizabeth I', *Early Modern Women*, 4 (2009), pp. 201–8.

Hudson, H.H., 'Penelope Devereux as Sidney's Stella', *Huntingdon Library Bulletin*, 7 (1935), pp. 89–129.

Hume, M., *The Courtships of Queen Elizabeth: A History of the Various Negotiations for her Marriage* (London, 1904).

Hurstfield, J., *The Queen's Wards: Wardship and Marriage under Elizabeth I* (London, 1958).

Irish, B.J., 'The Sidneys and Foreign Affairs, 1575–1578: An Unpublished Letter of Sir Henry Sidney', *English Literary Renaissance*, 45:1 (2015), pp. 90–119.

Ives, E., *The Life and Death of Anne Boleyn* (Oxford, 2004).

James, S., *Women's Voices in Tudor Wills, 1485–1603: Authority, Influence and Material Culture* (Farnham, 2015).

Jenkins, E., *Elizabeth and Leicester* (London, 1961).

John, L.C., 'The Date of the Marriage of Penelope Devereux', *PMLA*, 49:3 (1934), pp. 961–2.

Johnson, L., *The Tain of Hamlet* (Cambridge, 2013).

Jones, E.J., 'The Death and Burial of Walter Devereux, Earl of Essex, 1576', *The Carmarthen Antiquary*, I (1941), pp. 186–8.

Jones, F.M., *Mountjoy 1563–1606: The Last Elizabethan Deputy* (Dublin, 1958).

Kendall, A., *Robert Dudley: Earl of Leicester* (London, 1980).

Kent, W., *The Lost Treasures of London* (London, 1947).

Kingsford, C.L., 'Essex House, Formerly Leicester House and Exeter Inn', *Archaeologia or Miscellaneous Tracts Relating to Antiquity*, 73 (1923), pp. 1–52.

Kingsley, N. (ed.), *Warwickshire Country Houses* (Guildford, 1994).

Lacey, R., *Robert, Earl of Essex: An Elizabethan Icarus* (London, 1971).

Lacey, R., *The Life and Times of Henry VIII* (London, 1972).

Langston, B., 'Essex and the Art of Dying', *Huntingdon Library Quarterly*, 13:2 (1950), pp. 109–29.

Lawson, J.A. (ed.), *The Elizabethan New Year's Gift Exchanges 1559–1603* (Oxford University Press, 2013).

Lawson, S. (ed.), *Kenilworth Castle* (London, 2006).

Leiman, M. and Parker, G., 'Treason and Plot in Elizabethan Diplomacy: The "Fame of Sir Edward Stafford" Reconsidered', *English Historical Review*, 111:444 (1996), pp. 1134–58.

Levine, M., *The Early Elizabethan Succession Question* (California, 1966).

Levine, M., *Tudor Dynastic Problems* (London, 1973).

Lloyd, H.A., 'The Essex Inheritance', *Welsh History Review/Cylchgrawn Hanes Cymru*, 7 (1974–5), pp. 13–39.

Loades, D., *The Tudor Court* (Oxford, 2003).

Lovell, M.S., *Bess of Hardwick: First Lady of Chatsworth, 1527–1608* (London, 2005).

MacLean, S.B., 'The Politics of Patronage: Dramatic Records in Robert Dudley's Household Books', *Shakespeare Quarterly*, 44:2 (1993), pp. 175–82.

Malpas, F.J., 'Sir Francis Knollys and Family', unpublished manuscript (Reading Library, 1993).

Margetts, M., 'Lady Penelope Rich: Hilliard's Lost Miniatures and a Surviving Portrait', *Burlington Magazine*, 130:1027 (1988), pp. 758–61.

McCoy, R., 'From the Tower to the Tiltyard: Robert Dudley's Return to Glory', *Historical Journal*, 27:2 (1984), pp. 425–35.

Mears, N., 'Courts, Courtiers, and Culture in Tudor England', *Historical Journal*, 46:3 (2003), pp. 703–22.

Merton, C., 'The Women who Served Queen Mary and Queen Elizabeth: Ladies, Gentlewomen and Maids of the Privy Chamber, 1553–1603', unpublished PhD thesis (Trinity College Cambridge, 1992).

Moody, J. (ed.), *The Private Life of an Elizabethan Lady: The Diary of Lady Margaret Hoby 1599–1605* (Stroud, 1998).

Morton, R.C., 'The Enterprise of Ulster', *History Today*, 17 (1967), pp. 114–21.

Mounts, C.E., 'Spenser and the Countess of Leicester', *ELH*, 19:3 (1952), pp. 191–202.

Peck, G.T., 'John Hales and the Puritans during the Marian Exile', *Church History*, 10:2 (1941), pp. 159–77.

Perry, M., *The Word of a Prince: A Life of Elizabeth I* (Woodbridge, 1990).

Porter, L., *Mary Tudor: The First Queen* (London, 2007).

Purcell, J.M., 'A Cup for My Lady Penelope', *Modern Language Notes*, 45:5 (1930), p. 310.

Raumer, F. von, *The Political History of England, During the 16th, 17th and 18th Centuries*, I (London, 1837).

Read, C., 'A Letter from Robert, Earl of Leicester, to a Lady', *Huntingdon Library Bulletin*, 9 (1936), pp. 15–26.

Reynolds, A., *In Fine Style: The Art of Tudor and Stuart Fashion* (London, 2013).

Reynolds, G., *The Sixteenth- and Seventeenth-Century Miniatures in the Collection of Her Majesty the Queen* (London, 1999).

Rickman, J., *Love, Lust, and License in Early Modern England: Illicit Sex and the Nobility* (Aldershot, 2008).

Ridley, J., *Bloody Mary's Martyrs* (New York, 2001).

Robertson, J., 'Sir Philip Sidney and Lady Penelope Rich', *Review of English Studies*, 15:59 (1964), pp. 296–7.

Ross, J., *The Men Who Would Be King: Suitors to Queen Elizabeth I* (London, 1975).

Rowell, C., *Petworth: The People and the Place* (Swindon, 2012).

Scarisbrick, D., *Jewellery in Britain 1066–1837* (Norwich, 1994).

Scarisbrick, D., *Tudor and Jacobean Jewellery* (London, 1995).

Scott, W., *Kenilworth* (London, 1821).

Sims, A., *Pleasures and Pastimes in Tudor England* (Stroud, 1999).

Skidmore, C., *Edward VI: The Lost King of England* (London, 2007).

Skidmore, C., *Death and the Virgin: Elizabeth, Dudley and the Mysterious Fate of Amy Robsart* (London, 2010).

Snow, V.F., *Essex the Rebel: The Life of Robert Devereux, the Third Earl of Essex 1591–1646* (Lincoln, 1970).

Somerset, A., *Ladies-in-Waiting: From the Tudors to the Present Day* (London, 1984).

Somerset, A., *Elizabeth I* (London, 1991).

Starkey, D., *Elizabeth: Apprenticeship* (London, 2001).

Starkey, D., *Monarchy: England and her Rulers from the Tudors to the Windsors* (London, 2006).

Stopes, C.C., *Henry, 3rd Earl of Southampton* (London, 1922).

Strong, R., *Portraits of Queen Elizabeth I* (Oxford, 1963).

Strong, R., *Tudor and Jacobean Portraits* (London, 1969).

Strong, R., *The Cult of Elizabeth: Elizabethan Portraiture and Pageantry* (London, 1977).

Strong, R., 'The Leicester House Miniatures: Robert Sidney, 1st Earl of Leicester and His Circle', *Burlington Magazine*, 127:991 (1985), pp. 694, 696–701, 703.

Strong, R., 'Faces of a Favourite: Robert Devereux, 2nd Earl of Essex, and the Uses of Portraiture', *British Art Journal*, 5:2 (2004), pp. 80–90.

Stump, D. and Felch, S.M. (eds), *Elizabeth I and her Age* (New York, 2009).

Tallis, N., *Crown of Blood: The Deadly Inheritance of Lady Jane Grey* (London, 2016).

Thurley, S., *Royal Palaces of Tudor England* (London, 1993).

Thurley, S., *Hampton Court: A Social and Architectural History* (New Haven and London, 2003).

Thurley, S., *Whitehall Palace: The Official Illustrated History* (London, 2008).

Turvey, R., *The Treason and Trial of Sir John Perrot* (Cardiff, 2005).

Varlow, S., 'Sir Francis Knollys's Latin Dictionary: New Evidence for Katherine Carey', *Bulletin of the Institute of Historical Research* (2006).

Varlow, S., *The Lady Penelope: The Lost Tale of Love and Politics in the Court of Elizabeth I* (London, 2007).

Vickers, M., 'The Medal of Robert Dudley, Earl of Leicester in the Bibliothèque Nationale', *Numismatic Chronicle*, 141 (1981), pp. 117–19.

Wagner, J.A., *Historical Dictionary of the Elizabethan World: Britain, Ireland, Europe, and America* (Chicago and London, 1999).

Warnicke, R.M., 'Anne Boleyn's Childhood and Adolescence', *Historical Journal*, 28:4 (1985), pp. 939–52.

Warnicke, R.M., *The Rise and Fall of Anne Boleyn* (Cambridge, 1989).

Warnicke, R.M., *Wicked Women of Tudor England: Queens, Aristocrats, Commoners* (Basingstoke, 2012).

Watkin, J.R., *Lord Leicester's Warwickshire: The Life and Legacy of Robert Dudley* (Warwick, 2011).

Watkins, S., *Elizabeth I and her World: In Public and in Private* (London, 1998).

Watkins, S., *Mary Queen of Scots* (London, 2001).

Watkins, S.B., *Lady Katherine Knollys: The Unacknowledged Daughter of King Henry VIII* (Winchester, 2014).

Watney, V.J., *Cornbury and the Forest of Wychwood* (London, 1910).

Weir, A., *Children of England: The Heirs of King Henry VIII, 1547–1558* (London, 1996).

Weir, A., *Elizabeth the Queen* (London, 1999).

Weir, A., *Mary Boleyn: 'The Great and Infamous Whore'* (London, 2011).

Whitelock, A., *Mary Tudor: England's First Queen* (London, 2010).

Whitelock, A., *Elizabeth's Bedfellows: An Intimate History of the Queen's Court* (London, 2014).

Wilson, D., *Sweet Robin: A Biography of Robert Dudley, Earl of Leicester 1533–1588* (London, 1981).

Wilson, D., *The Uncrowned Kings of England: The Black Legend of the Dudleys* (London, 2005).

Wilson, J., *Entertainments for Elizabeth I* (Woodbridge, 1980).

Wilson, J., 'The Noble Imp: The Upper-Class Child in English Renaissance Art and Literature', *Antiquaries Journal*, 70 (1990), pp. 360–79.

Woodhouse, E., 'Propaganda in Paradise: The Symbolic Garden Created by the Earl of Leicester at Kenilworth, Warwickshire', *Garden History*, 36:1 (2008), pp. 94–113.

Young, A., *Tudor and Jacobean Tournaments* (London, 1987).

Youngs, F.A., *The Proclamations of the Tudor Queens* (Cambridge, 1976).

ACKNOWLEDGEMENTS

IT HAS BEEN my greatest pleasure to continue working with Michael O'Mara Books, and I am extremely grateful for the enthusiasm and support that I have received from the whole team. Once again, my simply amazing editor Fiona Slater has to take a great deal of the credit: her insights and dedication have been invaluable, and she has always been unwaveringly supportive. I would also like to thank Becky McCarthy and Alara Delfosse for all of their hard work.

Thanks are also due to my agent, Andrew Lownie. The staff at the British Library, National Archives, Kent History and Library Centre, and the Institute of Historical Research have all been wonderful and exceedingly helpful. Especial thanks go to Viscount De L'Isle, for allowing me to access the Kenilworth Game Book and include my research in the book. I would also like to thank the guides at Longleat and St Mary's Church, Warwick, who were extremely helpful and patient when answering my endless questions. Similarly, I am very grateful to the staff and volunteers at Greys Court, and my most particular thanks go to Lynn Holmes and Gill Ovey. Lynn generously gave up her time to share her meticulous research on the Knollys family with me, while Gill kindly arranged for me to access the Knollys Chapel in St Nicholas's Church, Rotherfield Greys.

Thanks are due to Elizabeth Norton for her insights into the Blount family, and Estelle Paranque, who thoughtfully took the time to read the unedited manuscript and make helpful suggestions. I am also very grateful to my PhD supervisors, Ellie Woodacre and James Ross, for allowing me to take time out from my thesis to finish the book on time. A huge thank you has to go to Tracy Borman, whose work has been so inspiring to me, and who read the manuscript at such short notice. I am indebted to Alison Weir for all of her support, and whose research into the parentage of Katherine Carey has been invaluable and formed the basis of my own conclusions on the subject. I am also grateful for the continued support of Sarah Gristwood and Chris Warwick.

Writing this book has meant months of hibernation, and throughout this time I am extremely fortunate to have had the understanding and encouragement of my friends and family. Thank you so much to Sian Cossins, Ed Gulliford, Kate, Chris, Chloe and Paige Bundy, Chloe Paxton, Hollie Markham, Kerrie Britten, Keita Weston, Gwenda and Colin Peters.

I would also like to say a special thank you to two little stars, Charlie and Olivia, who have brought so much happiness into my life. Thank you for patiently putting up with me when I've been unable to play, and for all of your love and enthusiasm. If I could offer you one piece of advice it would be to follow your dreams and never give up, and I will always encourage you both to do so.

As always, my parents have been marvellously supportive. Thanks to my dad, for reading parts of the book for me and restoring my faith in my writing ability. My mum, Sylvia, has constantly boosted my confidence and refused to allow me to give up when I've felt like I couldn't do it. She has been my inspiration, and there could not be a more worthy dedicatee for the book.

Lastly but by no means least, I would like to say a heartfelt thank you to my wonderful partner, Matthew Peters, who has stuck by me – and Lettice – unswervingly. Thank you for everything, but particularly for all of your very wise words of encouragement, without which I don't think I'd have been able to put pen to paper. Thank you for believing in me, and most of all, thank you for being you: you are simply the best.

INDEX

LK indicates Lettice Knollys, Countess of Leicester.

Act of Supremacy (1559) 40–1
Act of Uniformity:
 (1549) 23
 (1559) 40–1
Allen, Cardinal William 248
Anglo–Spanish war (1585–1604) 252, 269
Anne, Queen of England xiii, 314, 315
Anne of Cleves, Queen of England xiii, 4, 10, 13, 30, 33
Armada Portrait 243–4
Arthur, Prince of Wales 2
Ascham, Roger 31, 66
Ashley, Kate 42, 43, 49, 68
Ashton, Thomas 88

Babington, Anthony 226
Babington Plot (1587) 226, 248
Bancroft, Richard, Bishop of London 307
Barrett, Lettice xi, xviii, 189
Baynard's Castle 201
Beauchamp Chapel, St Mary's, Warwick x, 209–10, 243, 245, 256, 340
Bedford, Bridget Russell, Countess of 162
Bedford House 162, 255
Bedingfield, Sir Henry 35
Benington 151, 158, 163, 183–4, 252–3
Berkeley, Sir Richard 290
Bess of Hardwick 206, 207, 312
Bestney, Robert 95
Blount, Charles, Lord Mountjoy xi, xii, xiv, xv, 256–8, 274, 276, 282, 302, 321–2
Blount, Sir Christopher xi, xiv, xx, xxiii,
  xxix, 230, 247–51, 252–4, 256, 265, 268, 269, 270, 273, 276, 282, 293, 294, 295, 297, 299, 307–10, 324, 326
Blount, Elizabeth 'Bessie' 6
Blount, Isabella xii, 258
Blount, James 256
Blount, Mountjoy xii, 257–8, 336
Blount, Penelope xii, 257
Blount, Scipio xii, 274
Blount, St John xii, 258
Blount, Sir Thomas 73, 74, 247
Blount, William, Lord Mountjoy 257–8
Blundeville, Ranulph, Earl of Chester 78
Boleyn, Anne, Queen of England xiii, 7–8, 9, 10, 11–12, 13, 15, 30–1, 32, 238
Boleyn, George 12
Boleyn, Mary xix, 4–8, 9, 10, 12, 16–17
Boleyn, Sir Thomas 4
Bolton Castle 94, 97, 98
Bonner, Bishop Edmund 27
Borman, Tracy 167
Boteler, Sir Philip xi, xix, 226, 327
Boulogne, siege of (1544) 20, 58
Bourchier, Anne 107, 151
Bourchier Devereux, Walter 53, 55, 78, 79, 87, 303, 331
Bowes, Robert 196
Broughton, Richard 145, 150, 161, 162
Broxbourne 198
Brydges, Eleanor 166–7
Buckingham, Duke of 334
Burbage, James 202–3

Burghley, Lady Mildred 154, 203
Buxton xxii, 116–17, 128, 139, 159, 234, 237, 239

Cadiz, raid on (1596) 269–71, 273, 274
Calvin, John 26, 27, 28
Camden, William xxvi–xxvii, 27, 29, 31–2, 37, 38, 39, 50, 55, 60, 66, 108, 109, 114, 122, 124, 142, 143, 144, 147, 149, 159, 168, 171, 178, 213, 219, 239, 255, 271, 280, 296
Carew Castle 199
Carew, Sir George 281
Carew, Sir Peter 127–8
Carey, Henry 6–7, 10, 11, 42, 44, 271–2
Carey, Katherine (mother of LK) see Knollys, Katherine
Carey, Katherine (cousin of LK) 44, 46, 48, 297
Carey, Philadelphia see Scrope, Lady Philadelphia
Carey, Robert 229, 233, 235, 236, 261, 311, 312, 313
Carey, Sir William 4, 5, 6, 7, 10
Carleton, Dudley 291
Carlisle Castle 92, 93, 94
Carmarthen Castle 54
Carr, Robert 324–6
casket letters 101
Castelnau, Michel de 173
Catesby, Robert 319
Catholic Church xiv, xix, xxvi, 3, 9, 17, 19, 23, 24, 25–8, 33, 35, 40, 41, 60, 93, 94, 101, 103, 132, 175, 196, 213, 214–15, 226, 234, 248, 261, 270, 299, 309–10, 314, 319, 329, 334
Catholic League 261
Cave, Sir Ambrose xix, 82–3
Cave, Margaret xi, xix, 82–3
Cecil House 153–4
Cecil, Sir Robert 153, 251, 272, 273, 279–80, 281, 286, 290, 293, 295, 298, 299, 303, 307, 308–9, 315–16, 317–18, 319, 320
Cecil, William, Lord Burghley xiv–xv,

xxvi, xxix, 15, 20, 26, 40, 61, 70, 72, 73, 74, 84, 86, 88, 89, 93, 94, 95, 96, 97, 98, 102, 104, 110, 111, 112, 113, 114, 127, 137–8, 140, 146–7, 150, 151, 153, 154, 155–6, 157–8, 161, 175, 182, 186, 199, 209, 216, 229, 230, 247, 263, 268, 272, 279, 280
Chamberlain, Richard 329
Chandos, Lady Dorothy 142, 159, 277
Chapuys, Eustace 9
Charles I, King of England xxiii, 314, 329, 330, 334, 335, 336
Charles II, King of England 336
Charles V, Holy Roman Emperor 9, 26, 33, 214
Charles of Styria, Archduke 84
Chartley Manor xv, 53, 54, 78–80, 81, 82, 83, 91, 94, 96, 97, 98, 101, 103, 104, 105, 106, 110, 111–12, 134–5, 137, 138, 141, 143, 144, 145, 150, 151, 153, 154, 218–19, 226, 253, 283, 325, 339–40
Cheyne, Anne 197
Church of England 3, 9
Civil War, English (1642–51) 334–5, 336
Clifford, Lady Anne 231
Clifton, Gervase 332–3, 337–8, 340
Cobham, Lord 294
Coke, Sir Edward 292
Coles, Humphrey 329
Coleshill 117, 158, 160
Cornbury Park xvii, xxiii, 216, 238–9, 242
Council of the North 163
Cranmer, Thomas, Archbishop of Canterbury 9, 23, 26, 27
Cromwell, Oliver 335
Cromwell, Thomas 8, 10, 12
Cuffe, Henry 308
Cumnor Place 73, 74, 242, 249

Dakins, Margaret xi, xii, xvi, 254–5, 262
Dampard (footman) 201
Danvers, Sir Charles 308, 309
Davies, Bishop Richard 150
Davis, Sir John 308

Davison, William 210, 217, 220, 221, 223, 228, 229

Dee, John 47–8, 59

Denbigh, Robert, Lord ('the Noble Imp') xi, xxii, 189, 190, 193, 206–12, 243, 247, 321, 332, 340

Devereux Family: family tree xii

Devereux, Dorothy (daughter of Robert, Earl of Essex) (granddaughter of LK) xii, 303

Devereux, Dorothy (daughter of LK) xii, xv, xxi, xxii, xxiii, 82, 88, 89, 100, 111, 134, 137, 158, 161, 162, 163, 188, 195–9, 204, 206, 214, 231–2, 252, 254, 263, 266–7, 268, 278, 286, 312, 315, 319, 320, 323, 328, 336

Devereux, Dorothy (daughter of Dorothy Devereux) (granddaughter of LK) xii, 319, 328, 336

Devereux, Frances (granddaughter of LK) xii, 327–8

Devereux, Francis xii, 103, 188, 208

Devereux, George 150

Devereux, Lucy, Countess of Carlisle 319, 328–9, 336

Devereux, Penelope (daughter of LK) xii, xiv, xv, xxi, xxii, xxiii, 8, 78, 80–1, 82, 88, 89–90, 100, 111,134, 137, 150–1, 158, 159, 161, 162, 163, 191–4, 195, 197–8, 205, 225, 249, 253, 256, 257–9, 263, 264, 265, 268–9, 270, 273, 274, 276, 282, 283, 285, 286–9, 291, 294, 29708, 302, 310, 312, 315, 319, 321–2, 323, 332, 335

Devereux, Penelope (niece of LK) 234

Devereux, Penelope (granddaughter of LK) xii, 276

Devereux, Sir Richard 19, 53–4, 210

Devereux, Robert, second Earl of Essex xii, xv–xvi, xx, xxiii, xxvii, xxix, 5, 87–9, 111, 112, 113, 134, 137, 146–7, 150, 151, 152, 153–4, 156, 161, 163, 190–1, 194, 205, 210, 211–12, 215, 217, 218, 220, 225, 229, 230–1, 232–3, 237, 238, 239, 241, 244, 247, 250, 251, 252, 253, 254, 255, 256, 257, 258–62, 263, 264, 265–76, 277–92, 293–310, 311–12, 315, 318

Devereux, Robert, third Earl of Essex 259–60, 276, 324, 332

Devereux, Walter (son of LK) xii, xvi, xxii, xxiii, 103, 137, 158, 192, 252, 254–5, 261–2

Devereux, Walter (grandson of LK) xii, 276

Devereux, Walter (illegitimate son of Robert, Earl of Essex) xii, 260, 276

Devereux, Walter, first Earl of Essex (first husband of LK) xii, xvi, xx, xxii, 53–6, 78, 79–80, 81, 82, 83, 87, 88, 89, 90, 96, 100, 101–6, 107, 108, 109–12, 113–16, 117, 120, 125–30, 134–6, 137–51, 153, 154, 155, 156, 157, 158, 159–60, 163,168, 171, 184, 191, 193, 242, 260, 280, 339, 340

Digby, Abigail 117

Digby, Sir George 117

Digby, Robert 117

Drake, Sir Francis xviii, 59, 135, 202, 230, 235, 252

Drayton Bassett xxix, 253, 260, 263, 268–9, 275, 279, 291, 294, 300, 314, 318, 319, 322, 324, 325, 326, 327, 330, 331

Drury House 294

Dublin Castle 126, 147

Dudley Castle 58, 121

Dudley, Ambrose, Earl of Warwick xvi, 59, 60, 61, 62, 63, 64–5, 67, 75, 76, 104–5, 130, 159, 169, 189, 210, 224, 231, 247, 255–6, 332, 340

Dudley, Arthur 68

Dudley, Edmund 57

Dudley, Guildford xiii, xxii, xxviii, 25, 33, 61, 62, 63, 64, 65, 82

Dudley, Harry 62, 63, 64–5

Dudley, John (brother of Robert Dudley) 59, 61, 62, 63, 64, 75

Dudley, John, Duke of Northumberland xvi, 24, 25, 57–8, 59, 61–2, 66

Dudley, Robert, Earl of Leicester xii, xiv, xvi–xvii, xviii, xx, xxi, xxii, xxiii, xxv, xxvi, xxviii, xxxi, 8, 15, 56, 57, 58–77, 79, 83, 84, 85–90, 92, 95, 98, 102, 103, 104, 111, 112, 113, 115–16, 117–25, 127, 128–34, 136, 137, 141–8, 149, 150, 151–2, 153–4, 156, 158–64, 165–72, 173, 174–85, 196–9, 190, 191, 194–8, 200–13, 214–27, 228–45, 246, 247–50, 252, 253, 254, 255, 256, 257, 258, 264, 265, 268, 272, 281, 286, 308, 316–18, 327, 328, 329, 331, 332, 333, 339, 340

Dudley, Thomas 222

Durham Place 82, 106, 110, 111, 128, 139, 140

Edward VI, King of England xiii, xxii, 12, 19, 20, 21, 23, 24–6, 27, 31, 32, 53–4, 60, 61, 62, 65, 66, 67, 153

Edwardes, Roger 90

Elizabeth I, Queen of England xiii, xiv, xv, xvi, xvii, xviii, xix, xx, xxi, xxii, xxv–xxviii, xx, xxx, xxxi–xxxii
  Armada Portrait 243–4
  Babington Plot (1587) and 226, 248
  birth xxii, 9–10, 11
  Chartley visit 134–5
  childhood 11, 12, 13, 14, 16, 18, 23, 24, 25, 27, 30–7
  coronation 47–8
  court 51–2
  death xxiii, xxx, 311–14, 315, 317, 319
  Essex (Robert Devereux, second Earl of Essex) and 212, 230, 231, 247, 258, 259, 260, 261, 262, 263, 264, 268, 270, 273, 274, 275, 276, 277, 278, 279, 280, 281–92
  Essex Rebellion (1601) and 293, 294, 295, 296–7, 298, 303, 304, 305, 307, 308, 309–10
  household, LK as part of 37, 39, 43–7, 48, 51–3, 67, 68, 73
  Katherine Knollys and 6, 9–10, 11, 13, 16, 36–7, 41, 42–3, 45, 46, 47, 93–8, 100, 101
  Kenilworth visit 130–4, 171–2

Leicester (Robert Dudley, Earl of Leicester) and 57, 59, 64, 65–75, 76–7, 79, 84, 85, 86–7, 119, 120, 122–3, 125, 127, 128, 129, 130–4, 152, 160, 167, 171–2, 174, 175–85, 186, 188, 189, 194–5, 196–7, 208, 209, 210, 215, 216, 217, 220–4, 233, 234, 238, 239, 240–1, 243, 246, 247, 254, 264, 268, 293, 294, 295, 296–7, 298, 303, 304, 305, 307, 308, 309–10, 333

LK's secret marriage to Leicester, informed of xxii, xxxi–xxxii, 172, 173–4, 175–85

marriage, question of 48–53, 83, 84, 85, 91, 131–2, 174–7, 188, 191, 196

Mary, Queen of Scots and 75–7, 92, 93, 101, 102, 103, 106, 204, 218, 226–7, 228, 229

Northern Rebellion (1569) and 101, 103–6

Ridolfi Plot (1571) 105

rivalry with LK xxv–xxvi, xxvii, xxviii, xxxi–xxxii, 86–7, 171, 173–85, 186, 189, 191, 194, 197, 209, 212, 221–4, 228, 232–3, 237, 243, 246, 247, 250, 252, 254, 255–6, 271, 274–6, 277–9, 280–1, 286, 312–13, 333

Spanish Armada and 234–7

succession 38–48, 55

Throckmorton Plot (1583) and 248

Wanstead portrait/Peace portrait 171

Ely Place 58

Eric of Sweden, Prince 49

Essex House 89, 265, 266–7, 269, 274, 276, 282, 290, 291, 293, 294, 295, 297, 335

Essex Rebellion (1601) xiv, xxiii, 292, 293–307, 319

Eton College 21

Ewelme 20

Farnese, Alessandro, Duke of Parma 215, 229, 230, 233, 237

Fawkes, Guido 320

Ferdinand, Archduke 49

Ferdinand I, Holy Roman Emperor 84
Feria, Count de 50, 68, 70, 71
Fettiplace, Bridget 189
Fitzgerald, Gerald, Lord Offaly xi, xix, 117, 204
Fitzgerald, Lettice 204
Fitzroy, Henry 6
Fitzwilliam, Sir William 109, 114, 135
Fleet Prison 198
Fotheringhay Castle 226, 228, 229
Foxe, John 21, 28, 31, 40, 48, 202
François I, King of France 5
François II, King of France xiii, 75
François, Duc d'Anjou 132, 167, 174–6, 177, 188, 191
Freedman, Sylvia 249–50
Frobisher, Sir Martin 59
Fryer, Francis 95

Gammage, Margaret 120
Garrett, Christina 26
Gascoigne, George 131
Gawdy (servant) 268
Gheeraerts, Marcus 171
Gilbert, Sir Humphrey xix
Globe theatre 294–5
Goldring, Elizabeth 132, 188
Gower, George xviii, 181, 205, 243
Grafton, Richard 59
Great Fire of London (1666) 229
Greenwich Palace xxii, 5, 25, 107, 176
Greves, Thomas 116–17
Grey, Lady Jane xxii, 24, 25, 32, 33, 42, 50, 53, 61–2, 64, 65, 66, 82, 166, 334
Grey, Lady Katherine 50, 166, 178, 327
Grey, Mary 166–7
Greys Court, Rotherfield Greys xviii, 1, 2, 3, 14, 18, 20, 21, 22, 23, 42, 47, 49, 54, 81, 82, 154, 155, 157, 158, 183, 184, 186, 190–1, 210–11, 214, 271, 272, 315, 330, 339
Grindal, William 31
Guildford, Sir Henry 58
Guildford, Jane 57, 58
Gunpowder Plot (1605) 319–21

Hale, John 11
Hampden, John 335
Hampden, Lettice 335
Hampton Court 35, 97, 139, 154, 157
Harington, Sir John 46
Hastings, Dorothy 53, 54
Hastings, George, Earl of Huntingdon 53
Hastings, Henry, third Earl of Huntingdon 65, 101, 102, 103, 104, 107, 158, 161, 162–3, 190, 191, 192, 193, 195, 198, 244, 254–5, 262
Hatfield house 10, 30, 32, 35, 39, 66
Hatton, Sir Christopher 167, 176, 208, 209, 241, 261
Hay, James 328–9
Heigham, Joan xi, xx, 210
Heneage, Sir Thomas 221
Henri II, King of France 21
Henri III, King of France 132, 203, 261, 262
Henri IV, King of France 261
Henrietta Maria, Queen of England 329, 336
Henry, Prince of England 314, 326, 329
Henry VI, King of England 21
Henry VII, King of England xiii, 2, 54, 57
Henry VIII, King of England xiii, xix, xxii, xxvii, xxx, 2, 3, 4, 5–8, 9, 10, 11–12, 13, 15, 16, 19, 20, 24, 25, 30–1, 32, 34, 53, 57–8, 193, 206, 281, 312, 333
Hepburn, James, Earl of Bothwell xiii, 92
Hertford, Earl of 166, 305, 327
Hever Castle, Kent 4
Hewes, William 147
Hilliard, Nicholas 205
Holbeach House 319–20
Holland, Dr 272
Holland, Earl of 335
Holmes, Mathias 89
Howard, Charles 122
Howard, Lord Admiral Charles, second Baron Howard of Effingham 42, 46, 65, 235, 236, 297, 302, 308
Howard, Lady Elizabeth xi, 4
Howard, Frances 324–6

Howard, Katherine xiii, 13, 30, 65
Howard, Lady Mary 280
Howard, Philip, Earl of Arundel 307
Howard, Sir Thomas 298, 305
Howard, William, first Baron Howard of
    Effingham 120
Huguenots 175, 261

Ireland xvi, xxii, 80, 93, 108–11, 112–16,
    125–8, 129, 135–6, 137, 138, 139,
    141, 142, 143–4, 146, 150, 193, 197,
    236, 280–1, 282–5, 286, 299, 302, 315
Islands Voyage 274

James I, King of England (King James
    VI of Scotland) xiv, xxi, xxiii, 89, 92,
    196, 206, 303, 311–12, 313, 314–16,
    318, 319, 322, 327, 329–30, 334
Jenkins, Elizabeth 86, 186, 330
Jones, Inigo 334
Jones, John 116
Jonson, Ben 242, 245, 315

Katherine of Aragon, Queen of England
    xiii, 3, 5, 6, 7, 8, 9, 11, 24, 32
Kempe, William 202
Kenilworth Castle xxii, xxvi, 76, 129,
    130–1, 132–4, 137, 144–5, 158–9,
    160, 161, 167, 171, 190, 216, 217, 237,
    253, 256, 317, 340
Kenilworth Game Book 129, 144
Kett's Rebellion (1549) 60
Kettle, Grace 329
Killigrew, Sir Henry 208
King's Manor, York 163, 254
Knell, Thomas 149
Knollys Family: family tree xi
Knollys, Anne xi, xvii, 14, 28, 29, 100,
    182, 330
Knollys, Dudley xi, 14, 15, 46
Knollys, Edward xi, xvii, 14, 15, 95
Knollys, Elizabeth xi, xviii, xxi, 14, 43, 44,
    48, 94, 96, 97, 128, 164, 232, 263
Knollys, Sir Francis (father of LK) xi,
    xviii, xix, xx, xxi, xxii, xxiii, 1–4, 10,

13–14, 16, 17, 19–21, 22–3, 24–5,
    26–7, 28–30, 40, 41, 42, 45, 47, 50,
    52, 60, 88, 92–8, 99, 100, 129, 167–8,
    184, 189, 190–1, 204, 218, 222, 238–
    9, 250, 259, 271, 272
Knollys, Sir Francis (brother of LK) xi,
    xviii, 14, 26, 67, 166, 186, 189, 219,
    234, 244, 271, 331, 335
Knollys, Henry (uncle of LK) xviii–xix, 3,
    21, 29, 98, 100
Knollys, Henry (brother of LK) xi, xix,
    2, 26, 27, 28, 29, 52, 82–3, 105, 110,
    113–14
Knollys, Katherine (mother of LK) xi,
    xviii, xix, xx, xxii, 1, 4, 5–7, 9–10, 11,
    12, 13–14, 15–16, 17–18, 19–20, 22,
    27, 28, 29–30, 36–7, 41–5, 46–7, 78,
    93, 94–5, 96, 97–100, 180, 272
Knollys, Katherine (sister of LK) xi, xix,
    46, 100, 117, 204, 225–6, 253, 327,
    330
Knollys, Lettice, Countess of Leicester xx
    Ambrose Dudley death and 255–6
    birth xxii, 1–2
    bloodline 336
    Blount marriage xxiii, 247–54, 268,
        307–10
    childhood 9, 18, 19, 21–3, 29–30, 32
    children *see under individual child
        name*
    death xxiii, 331–3, 334
    Devereux family tree and xii
    education 21–2
    Elizabeth I coronation and 48
    Elizabeth I household, part of 37, 39,
        43–7, 48, 51–3, 67, 68, 73
    Elizabeth I informed of secret marriage
        to Leicester xxii, xxxi–xxxii, 172,
        173–4, 175–85
    Elizabeth I rivalry with xxv–xxvi,
        175–85, 189, 191, 194, 197, 209, 212,
        221–4, 228, 232–3, 237, 246, 255–6,
        274–6, 277–9, 286, 312–13
    Elizabeth I visit to Chartley and 134–5
    epitaph to 337–8

Essex death and 304–5, 307

Essex fall from grace and 286, 288–92, 293

Essex Rebellion and 293–300

Essex trial and 300–2

Francis Knollys death and 271–2

Henry VIII's granddaughter 9

James I and 314–15, 316

Knollys family tree and xi

Leicester death and 237–45, 246–7

Leicester funeral and 242–3, 244–5

Leicester marriage xxii, xxi–xxxii, 164, 165–72, 186–99, 200–13, 214, 215, 216, 217–18, 219–20, 221–4, 225–6, 227, 229–31, 237–41

Leicester, relationship with before marriage 77, 85–7, 90, 109, 115, 116, 117–18, 120, 122, 123, 124–5, 128–30, 131, 132–4, 141–5, 148, 149, 151–2, 158–64

Leicester's Commonwealth and *see Leicester's Commonwealth*

longevity xxvii, 329, 330–1, 335

Lord Denbigh death and 206–12

mother's death and 94, 95, 96, 97, 98, 100

Robin Sheffield, files case against xxiii, 256, 316–18

son, Walter, killed in Rouen xxiii, 261–2

Tudor character traits 9

Walter Devereux death and 145, 146, 147, 148, 149, 150, 151, 152, 153, 154–6, 157–8

Walter Devereux marriage xxii, 55–6, 78–84, 87–90, 91, 101, 103, 104, 105, 106, 107, 108, 110, 111–12, 113, 116–18, 125, 126, 127, 128, 134, 135, 137, 138, 139, 140, 141, 145, 146, 147, 148, 149, 150, 151, 152, 153, 154–6, 157–8

Knollys, Mary xi, 15, 43, 52

Knollys, Maud xi, 14, 15

Knollys, Odelia xi, xx, 233–4

Knollys, Richard xi, xx, 14, 170, 184, 210, 271

Knollys, Robert (grandfather of LK) 2, 3

Knollys, Robert (brother of LK) xi, xx, 14, 45, 182, 335

Knollys, Thomas xx, 219, 233–4, 271

Knollys, Sir William, Earl of Banbury xi, xx–xxi, 1, 14, 95, 105, 117, 159, 219, 233, 244, 271, 272–3, 281, 292, 295, 301, 315, 330

Lacey, Robert xxvii, 5, 89

Lambeth Palace Library 202

Lamphey Palace 54, 81–2, 137, 146, 191, 211

Laneham, Robert 131

Langside, Battle of (1568) 92

Lea, Rowland 63

Lee, Sir Robert 3

Leicester House xx, xxii, 149, 175, 187, 188, 189, 190, 194, 195, 200, 201, 202, 203, 204, 206, 214, 215, 217, 219, 222, 247, 253, 265, 339

Leicester's Commonwealth xxvi–xxvii, 121, 124, 128, 141–2, 147–8, 159–60, 164, 168, 181, 182, 207, 212–13

Leicester's Ghost (poem) (Rogers) 124

Leicester's Men 157, 165, 201, 202–3

Leigh, Catherine 256

Leigh, Sir Thomas 216

Leighs Priory 192

Leighton, Thomas xi, xviii, xxi, xxx, 164

Leland, John 18, 58–9, 79

Lennox, Lady Margaret 76, 91, 162, 168

Leslie, John, Bishop of Ross 102, 103

Lincoln, Edward Clinton, Earl of 107

Longleat House 181, 204, 205

Lord Leycester's Hospital 245

Louis XII, King of France xiii, 4–5

MacPhelim, Sir Brian 108, 112, 126–7

Mary, Queen of Scots xiii, xxiii, xxv, 20, 74, 75–7, 85, 91–2, 93, 94, 95, 96, 97–8, 100–2, 103, 105, 116, 162, 173, 196, 204, 206–7, 213, 216, 218–19, 226–7, 228–9, 234, 235, 248, 266, 312, 313

Mary I, Queen of England xxii, 24, 25, 26, 27, 30, 32–3, 34–6, 37, 38–9, 40, 41, 49, 62, 63, 64, 65, 66, 202, 214
Maulette, Madame de 262
Mauvissière, French Ambassador 186, 194, 203–4, 210
Medici, Catherine de 132
Mendoza, Bernardino de 196, 206
Merrick, Sir Gilly 308
Meulan, Steven van der 15
Moray, Earl of 101
More, Sir Thomas 193, 300
Morgan, Anne 43
Morgan, Thomas 249
Musselburgh, battle of (1547) 20

Needwood Forest 79
Netherlands 214–15, 216–17, 219–25, 228, 229–30, 231, 233–4, 245, 249, 257, 272
Newport, Thomas 218
Newton, Thomas 11, 18, 99
Nonsuch Palace 207, 285
Norris, Sir Henry 237–8
Norris, John 135
Norris, Marjory 238
North, Roger, Lord 169, 182
Northaw 231–2
Northern Rebellion (1569) 101, 103–6

O'Neill, Turlough Luineach 108, 112, 114, 125, 126
Overbury, Sir Thomas 325

Paget Place 187
Paget, Lord 187
Palace of Whitehall xxii, 110, 180, 334
Palmer, Julius 21, 28
Parham House, Sussex 195
Parliament 3, 20, 23, 24, 25, 27, 41, 50, 51, 65, 253, 266, 319, 320, 334–5, 336
Parma, Duchess of 72–3
Parr, Katherine xiii, 30–1, 32
Parry, Blanche 45
Paulet, Sir Amyas 218

Paulet, Elizabeth 326, 335
Pembroke, Henry Herbert, second earl of 169–70
Peniston, Lettice 2, 3, 16–17
Percy, Algernon xii, 267, 319, 336
Percy, Henry, ninth Earl of Northumberland xi, xii, xv, xxi, 266, 267, 320
Percy, Thomas 320
Percy, Thomas, seventh Earl of Northumberland 101
Perrot, Sir John 197, 198, 266
Perrot, Penelope 266
Perrot, Sir Thomas xi, xii, xv, 197–9, 219, 231–2, 266
Petworth xxi, 266, 328, 336
Philip II, King of Spain 26, 33, 39, 49, 65, 214, 216, 229, 230, 234, 236, 241, 248, 252, 269, 270–1, 274
Pinkie Cleugh, Battle of (1547) 20
Pius V, Pope 319
Pole, Cardinal Reginald 27
Poley, Margaret 247
Pory, John 330
Princely Pleasures (1575) xxii, 133, 158, 340
Protestant Church xxii, xxvi, 3, 17, 19–20, 21, 22, 23, 24, 25–7, 28, 32, 33, 40–1, 55, 60, 88, 94, 101, 162, 166, 175, 202, 213, 214, 215, 248, 250, 314, 319, 334
Puritans xviii, 89, 93, 193, 218

Quadra, Bishop de 48, 69, 70, 72–3, 162

Radcliffe, Thomas, Earl of Sussex 147, 173, 178
Ralegh, Sir Walter 203, 212, 215, 230, 232, 233, 274, 279, 293, 294, 310
Rathlin Island 135–6
Renard, Simon 35
Rich, Henry xii, 256
Rich, Lettice xii, 225
Rich, Richard, first Baron Rich 168–9, 193, 269, 270

Rich, Robert, second Baron Rich 111, 113, 192, 335

Rich, Robert, third Baron Rich xi, xii, xv, xxi, 191, 192–4, 195, 225, 244, 256, 257, 258, 266, 269, 270, 301, 312, 321, 323

Richard III, King of England 226

Richmond Palace xxiii, 35, 311

Ridolfi Plot (1571) 105

Rizzio, David 91–2

Robsart, Amy xxvi, 60–1, 70, 71, 72–5, 119, 165, 184

Robsart, Sir John 60

Rogers, Thomas 124

Rotherfield Church 14, 15, 22

Russell, Anne 231, 255

Rutland, Earl of 167

Rycote 237–8

Savoy House 322

Scrope, Lady Philadelphia 44, 286–7, 313

Scrope, Lord 93, 94

Scrope, William 93

Seymour, Anne 61

Seymour, Edward 19, 20, 24, 53, 58, 61

Seymour, Jane xiii, 12–13, 19, 30–1

Seymour, Sir Thomas 31, 32

Seymour, Sir William 327–8

Shakespeare, William:
  A Midsummer's Night's Dream xxix
  Hamlet xxix
  Love's Labour's Lost 267–8
  Richard II 294–5

Sheffield, Lady Douglas 119–24, 129, 130, 142, 144, 163–4, 168, 187, 188, 210

Sheffield, John, second Baron Sheffield 120

Sheffield, Robin xxiii, 121, 124, 256, 316–18

Shelton, Lady Mary 166–7, 289

Sherley, Sir Thomas 220

Sidney, Sir Henry 65, 109, 110–11, 135, 136, 143–4, 148, 149, 153

Sidney, Lady Mary 71, 170, 181–2, 195, 213

Sidney, Sir Philip xv, 8, 88, 137, 151, 163, 191–2, 195, 196, 217–18, 219, 223, 225, 228, 229, 256, 258

Sidney, Sir Robert 269, 277, 298, 317, 328

Sidney, Thomas 262

Silva, Guzmán de 83, 85, 86

Simier, Jean de 174–7

Sixtus V, Pope 235

Somerset, Anne 124–5

Southwell, Elizabeth xii, 260, 318

Spanish Armada (1588) xxiii, 235–7, 240, 248, 252

Spenser, Edmund 126, 203

St Clement Danes, church of 187, 189

St James's Palace 38

St Mary's Church, Warwick xvi, xxviii, 30, 74, 209, 244, 245, 256, 337–8, 340

St Paul's Cathedral 229

St Quentin, Battle of (1557) 65

Stafford Castle 135

Stafford, Dorothy 28, 29, 41

Stafford, Sir Edward 124, 316, 318

Stafford, William 10, 13, 28, 29, 41

Star Chamber xxiii, 251, 317, 320–1

Stokes, Adrian 160

Stow, John 59, 295

Stuart family: family tree xiii

Stuart, Lady Arabella 206, 207, 312, 327–8

Stuart, Charles 206

Stuart, Lord Darnley, Henry xiii, 76–7, 91, 92, 101, 162, 206

Suffolk, Frances Brandon, Duchess of 160, 250

Sutton, Elizabeth 246–7

Syon House xv, xx, 11, 46–7, 82, 198, 266, 319, 328

Talbot, Gilbert 119

The Theatre, Shoreditch 203

Theobalds 153, 209, 232, 329

Thirty Years' War (1618–48) 334

Throckmorton Plot (1583) 248

Throckmorton, Sir George 8

Throckmorton, Sir Nicholas 85

Tower of London xix, 12, 25, 33, 34, 35, 53, 62, 63, 64, 65, 166, 178, 198, 229, 266, 293, 298–9, 302, 303, 304, 305, 307, 320–1, 325, 326, 328–9, 336
Tresham, Francis 319
Tresham, Sir Thomas 16–17
Tudor family 2, 4, 9, 18, 31, 34, 45, 177, 179, 187, 312, 333, 336, 339; family tree xiii
Tudor, Edmund 54
Turner, Anne 325, 326
Tutbury Castle 98, 100, 101–2, 103
Tyndall, Humphrey 169, 170
Tyrone, Earl of 280, 283, 284

Vaughan, Katherine xi, 45
Vavasour, Sir Thomas 260
Vernon, Elizabeth 281–2, 303

Wallingford Castle 20
Walsingham House 259
Walsingham, Frances xi, xii, 195, 229, 258–9, 283
Walsingham, Sir Francis xiv, 132, 137–8, 141, 143, 145, 150, 193, 195, 196, 203, 206, 217, 218, 221, 225, 226, 229, 241, 248, 280
Wanstead House xvii, xxii, xxxi, 163, 168–9, 171, 173, 175, 176, 177, 178, 180, 182, 194, 198, 200, 201, 207, 208, 209, 210, 215, 228, 239, 243, 253, 265, 321, 322, 323, 339
Wanstead portrait/Peace portrait 171
Warwick Castle 58–9, 75, 76, 130, 207

Warwick, Richard Beauchamp, Earl of 243
Waterhouse, Edward 88, 145, 146, 149, 150, 153
Weller, Thomas 29
West, Thomas xi, xvii
Westminster Abbey xix, 14, 19, 47–8, 98, 99, 272, 314, 322
Westminster Hall 48, 106, 300, 308
White, Nicholas 97
White, Rowland 269, 277, 278, 286, 287, 288, 290
Whitgift, Dr John 161
Whorwood, Anne 61
Whorwood, Sir William 61
William II, King of England 300
William, Prince of Orange 215
Willoughby, Katherine, Duchess of Suffolk 15, 28, 41, 250
Wilson, Arthur 326
Winchester Cathedral 26
Wood, Anthony 59
Woodstock Palace 35, 216
Wotton, Sir Henry 211
Wright, Robert 161
Wriothesley, Henry, third Earl of Southampton 267–8, 281, 282, 283, 290, 294, 298, 300, 301, 302, 303
Wyatt Rebellion (1554) 33–5, 63
Wyatt, Sir Thomas 33, 34

York House 286, 288, 291
Young, Bartholomew 89